ENGLISH 3200

A Programed Course
in Grammar and Usage

By JOSEPH C. BLUMENTHAL

HARCOURT, BRACE & WORLD, INC.

New York   Chicago   Atlanta   Dallas   Burlingame

THE SERIES

ENGLISH 2600 (A Clothbound Edition and a Paperbound Edition)
ENGLISH 3200 (A Clothbound Edition and a Paperbound Edition)
TEST BOOKLET and TEACHER'S MANUAL for Each Book

ABOUT THE AUTHOR

Joseph C. Blumenthal received his A.B. and A.M. degrees from the University of Michigan. He also did graduate work at the University of Chicago and at Columbia University. From 1938 to 1959 he was Head of the English Department at Mackenzie High School in Detroit. He is now devoting his full time to textbook writing. Among his writings are the *Common Sense English* series, the *English Workshop* series (with John E. Warriner and others), and *The English Language* series (with Louis Zahner and others).

THE TEST BOOKLET

A 64-page test booklet accompanies each purchased copy of ENGLISH 3200. Included in the removable tests are a Pre-Test, two Mastery Tests—Form A and Form B—for each of the twelve units in the text, two Halfway Tests, and a Final Test. The test booklets may also be purchased separately.

PREFACE

ENGLISH 3200 is a programed course in grammar, sentence-building, usage, and punctuation designed for the advanced grades of high school English. For college freshmen, it will provide a quick recapitulation of the elements of language that high school graduates are expected to have mastered.

This new programed text reviews, though at a faster pace, the units presented in **ENGLISH 2600**. Moreover, each of these units is augmented by problems not included in the more elementary program. In addition, a very substantial part of **ENGLISH 3200** deals with more advanced devices of sentence construction and more sophisticated types of subordination. The book also has lessons on the placing of modifiers, dangling construction, parallelism, the reference of pronouns, and other grammatical concepts.

If this should be your first experience with a programed textbook, you will be interested in knowing why some educators consider programed instruction the greatest advance in education since the invention of movable type. Programed texts are making rapid headway as a teaching method in the armed services, in business, and in many of the great industries of this country for the following reasons:

1. When a course is programed, it is broken down into very minute and carefully arranged steps—approximately 3200 in the case of the present book—through which you reason your way, one small step at a time. There is no separation, as in conventional textbooks, between explanation and exercises; the two are woven tightly together. Every step—or frame—calls for a written response, which requires both *thinking* and *concentration*. Thinking your way, step by step, through a program is like following a very gradual path up a steep mountain. Without becoming winded or losing your footing, you suddenly discover that you have reached the top!

2. Programs are constructed on the principle of "errorless learning." The steps are so small and their order is so logical that, with reasonable concentration, you are not likely to make many mistakes. Should you, now and then, write the wrong answer, you are corrected immediately—before the error can become established. It is as though a watchful teacher were constantly looking over your shoulder—ready to put you back on the track the moment you wander off. Using a programed textbook is the nearest approach to having a private tutor.

3. With the usual language textbook, you first study the explanation, which you may or may not understand thoroughly. Next, you apply what you have studied to the exercises in the text—often with a feeling of uncertainty. Usually, it is not until the next day that you discover whether or not you did the exercises correctly.

With **ENGLISH 3200,** however, as soon as you turn the page, you find out whether your reasoning was right. At this point something very important happens. The instant you find out that your answer is right, all doubt disappears and the idea "takes root," so to speak, in your brain.

The psychologists who developed programing call this *reinforcement,* and it is a most important factor in learning. The more often reinforcement takes place and the more quickly it follows the writing of your answer, the better you learn!

4. With programed instruction, you can progress at your own best rate. Many students have completed entire courses in a fraction of the time required by the traditional textbook method and have demonstrated a better mastery of the subject matter. With programed instruction, your mind is constantly in high gear. You lose no time waiting for other students to recite, correcting other students' papers, or listening to a discussion of other students' mistakes. In the rapidly developing world of today, education is becoming a longer and longer road. The time you save by this new scientific method can be used to advance yourself in literature, composition skills, discussion, and creative activities.

How to Use **ENGLISH 3200**

Each step (or frame) requires that you perform some operation. For example, in many of the frames, you will do one of two things:

    1. If there is a blank line, write in the missing word or letter.

      Example: Jones is the name of a _*person*_ .

    2. If there are two or more words or letters in parentheses, underline the correct answer.

      Example: Jones is the name of a (*person, place*).

(*Note:* Your teacher will tell you whether to write your answers in the book or to write them in a separate notebook or on separate sheets of paper.)

The first work frame is Frame 2 (on page 3). After you complete Frame 2, turn to Frame 3 *in the same position* on the next *right-hand* page (page 5). In the column to the left of Frame 3, you will find the correct answer to Frame 2. If your answer is not correct, turn back and correct it before doing Frame 3. You will always find the answer to a frame in the column to the left of the frame that you are to do next. Thus, you find the answer to Frame 3 to the left of Frame 4, the answer to Frame 4 to the left of Frame 5, and so on.

Go completely through the book, taking only the top gray frame on each right-hand page (3, 5, 7, 9, 11, etc.) until you reach the end. When you reach the end of the book, turn back to page 1 and follow the second band —a white one—through the book, still working only on the *right-hand* pages. Then proceed to the third horizontal band, which is gray, going through all the *right-hand* pages. Continue in this way through the fourth, fifth, and sixth bands. When you come to the last white band on the last *right-hand* page (Frame 1608), turn back to page 2 and start reading the gray bands at the top of the *left-hand* pages. Continue following each horizontal band through the *left-hand* pages. The last frame is 3208 on page 530.

The alternating bands of white and gray will make it easy for you to stay on the same horizontal band as you advance through the book. Since both frame and answer are numbered (each in the lower right corner), you will always know where you are and where to go next.

Getting the Most from **ENGLISH 3200**

1. Whenever you are puzzled for the correct answer to a frame, read the frame very carefully again. Many of the frames contain clues that guide you to the right answer, although the clues gradually diminish as the lesson advances. You are not likely to make a mistake very often. When you do, look back a few frames and try to straighten out your thinking. When you can't help yourself, consult your teacher. With an ordinary textbook, it is difficult for your teacher to discover where your thinking jumped the track. With a programed text, your teacher can help you immediately at the precise point where you need assistance.

2. Take as much time as you need in figuring out your answer. But once you write your answer, *lose no time* in turning to the next frame to check its correctness. Scientific experiment has proved that the quicker you check your answer, the better you learn. *Even the lapse of a few seconds makes a big difference.*

3. ENGLISH 3200 is designed for students mature enough to want to improve their minds by thinking things through for themselves—the most effective way of learning and remembering. No student has paid a greater compliment to this book than the one who said, "It makes me think too much." Exercising your brain, like exercising your muscles, is sometimes a bit strenuous. But it is this effort that will develop your power to think systematically and to reason logically.

If you will use **ENGLISH 3200** in a mature way, you may discover, as did those students who have used **ENGLISH 2600,** that you have acquired a better knowledge of grammar and usage—and in a fraction of the usual time. You may find, too, that you have developed your ability to think and to concentrate in a way that will be useful to you in all your studies—both in high school and in college. You will have profited by the latest and most exciting discoveries of science about how people learn!

JOSEPH C. BLUMENTHAL

CONTENTS

Lesson 1 The Subject and Verb in the Simple Sentence

[Frames 2–40]

(a) adverb (b) adjective 268	The invention (a) of the automobile has changed American life (b) in many ways. (a) _____ *phrase;* (b) _____ *phrase* 269
different from 536	a. **while, when, as if, because, unless, although,** etc. b. **who (whose, whom), which, that** In which group are the clause signals that are used to start adjective clauses? _____ 537
he 804	If you lose a noun when making a participial phrase, put this noun back at the *beginning* of your main statement. *Aunt Mae lives alone.* **She is often lonesome for company.** Fill in the blank space: *Living alone,* _____ **is often lonesome for company.** 805
b 1072	**Frank certainly was a hero.** The noun **hero** follows the linking verb **was** and is therefore a (*subject complement, direct object*). 1073
spy, the 1340	**The telephone operator wears a headset leaving her hands free to operate the switchboard.** 1341

a. willingly, 1608	The squaws spent their time a. **tanning hides,** _____ b. **meat was cured, and** _____ c. **sewing moccasins.** _____ 1609
c the companions with whom he associates. *or* ... whom he associates with. 1875	a. dangling word group b. nonparallel construction c. faulty comparison **We trust that you will find him one of the best, if not the best, camper at Michiwaki.** **We trust that you will find him one of the best** _____ _____. 1876
cards 2142	**The dishes** *were laid* **on the sink.** What *were laid* on the sink? _____ 2143
a linking 2409	The use of **badly,** instead of **bad,** after the linking verb **feel** is widespread in informal usage, even though it violates our general rule. **I feel** (*bad, badly*) **about it.** Since **feel** is used as a linking verb in this sentence, the adjective (*bad, badly*) is correct in formal writing or speaking. 2410
they 2676	**Every applicant is asked whether** (*they have, he has*) **had any experience.** 2677
a. ; *or* — b. — *or* ; 2943	The frames that complete this lesson provide good oppor- tunities for using semicolons, colons, and dashes effectively. In several sentences, either one of two marks would be considered correct. Do not add any commas. **Before twenty-one, a girl tries to look old after twenty-one, she tries to look young.** 2944

A sentence is a group of words that gives us a sense of completeness.

> a. **The barking dog**
> b. **The dog is barking.**

Which group of words is a sentence—*a* or *b?* _____

2

(a) adjective
(b) adverb

269

(a) For many years, Mr. Hobbs has slept (b) during the sermon.

(a) _____ *phrase;* (b) _____ *phrase*

270

---

b

537

I have a friend *who raises tropical fish.*

The adjective clause *who raises tropical fish* modifies the noun _____.

538

Aunt Mae

805

Which of two sentences you subordinate depends on which idea you prefer to put in the background of the sentence.

> a. *Reaching for the sugar,* **I knocked over a glass.**
> b. **I reached for the sugar,** *knocking over a glass.*

Which of the two sentences emphasizes the accident that occurred? _____

806

---

subject complement

1073

> a. **A hero Frank certainly was.**
> b. **Frank certainly was a hero.**

Which sentence gives greater emphasis to the subject complement **hero?** _____

1074

---

headset, leaving

1341

The textile mill closing   hundreds of employees were thrown out of work.

_____

1342

b. curing meat, 1609	The Owens want a house a. **with a fireplace,** _____ b. **having a garage, and** _____ c. **with a screened porch.** _____ 1610
c campers at Michiwaki, if not the best. 1876	UNIT **8**: MAKING SUBJECT AND VERB AGREE Lesson **53** Keeping Your Mind on the Subje [Frames 1878–1917]
dishes 2143	PRESENT PAST PAST PARTICIPLE **lie** (to rest) **lay** **(have) lain** **lay** (to put) **laid** **(have) laid** **Laid** is never a form of **lie.** Would you ever use **laid** when you mean **rest?** (*Yes, No*) 2144
bad 2410	**We feel** *unhappy* **about losing the game.** **We feel** *bad* **about losing the game.** In both sentences the verb **feel** is followed by an adjective. Are both sentences correct? (*Yes, No*) 2411
he has 2677	**Everybody was happy, and I didn't want to spoil** (*their, his*) **fun.** 2678
old; 2944	**Their lemon chiffon pie** well, I just can't find words to **describe it.** 2945

<table>
<tr>
<td>

b

2

</td>
<td>

The dog is barking.

This group of words is a sentence because it gives us a sense of (*completeness, incompleteness*).

3

</td>
</tr>
<tr>
<td>

(a) adverb
(b) adverb

270

</td>
<td>

The smoke (a) from the forest fire could be seen (b) in several states.

(a) _____ *phrase;* (b) _____ *phrase*

271

</td>
</tr>
<tr>
<td>

friend

538

</td>
<td>

I have a friend *who raises tropical fish.*

An adjective clause signal is always a *pronoun.* This pronoun stands for the noun that the entire clause modifies.

In the above sentence, the pronoun *who* stands for the noun _____ .

539

</td>
</tr>
<tr>
<td>

a

806

</td>
<td>

a. *Reaching for the sugar,* **I knocked over a glass.**
b. **I reached for the sugar,** *knocking over a glass.*

Which sentence emphasizes the action that led to the accident? _____

807

</td>
</tr>
<tr>
<td>

a

1074

</td>
<td>

His *strong, calloused* **hands were no strangers to work.**

The most common position of adjectives is (*before, after*) the nouns they modify.

1075

</td>
</tr>
<tr>
<td>

closing, hundreds

1342

</td>
<td>

The water level was dropping   all danger of a flood was past.

_____

1343

</td>
</tr>
</table>

b. with a garage, and 1610	We shall need a board a. **six feet in length,** _____ b. **two feet wide, and** _____ c. **one inch thick.** _____ 1611
	A singular subject requires a singular verb; a plural subject requires a plural verb. This is what we mean when we say that the subject and verb must agree in number. **We Washes Cars** This sign, seen on a garage, looks absurd because the sub-ject **We** is plural, but the verb **Washes** is _____. 1878
No 2144	Underline the correct word: **My missing wallet** (_lay, laid_) **in the snow all winter.** 2145
Yes 2411	_GOOD_ and _WELL_ Always use the adverb **well**—never the adjective **good**—to describe an action. A person eats _well_, plays _well_, or works _well_. a. **This pen writes** _well_. b. **This pen writes** _good_. Which sentence is correct? _____ 2412
their 2678	From here on, write in the pronoun that is appropriate for formal usage: **Nobody was ever more confused about** _____ **rela-tives than I.** 2679
pie— 2945	**Campers are expected to supply the following items sheets, blankets, pillowcases, and towels.** 2946

completeness 3	**The dog is barking.** This group of words gives us a sense of completeness because it (1) *names* what we are talking about, and (2) *tells* something about it. Which two words belong to the *naming part* of the sentence? _____ _____ <div align="right">4</div>
(a) adjective (b) adverb 271	Some words can be used as either <u>prepositions</u> or <u>adverbs</u>. These words, such as *before, behind, after, past, through, down,* and *around,* generally refer to direction. To decide how such a word is used, look for an *object.* If you find an object, the word in question is a (*preposition, adverb*). <div align="right">272</div>
friend 539	**I have a friend** *who raises tropical fish.* The noun that the adjective clause modifies and the noun that the pronoun *who* stands for are (*the same word, different words*). <div align="right">540</div>

b
 	
807
	Put a comma after any participial phrase that comes at the beginning of a sentence.
	    a. *Thinking the paint was dry* **I sat on the bench.**
	    b. **We removed the tree** *shading the flower beds.*
	Which sentence requires a comma? _____
	<div align="right">808</div>

before 1075	a. **His** *strong, calloused* **hands were no strangers to work.** b. **His hands,** *strong* **and** *calloused,* **were no strangers to work.** In which sentence are the italicized adjectives given more emphasis? _____ <div align="right">1076</div>
dropping. All *or* dropping; all 1343	**Ellen gets angry over trifles but forgives and forgets quickly.** _____ <div align="right">1344</div>

a. six feet long, 1611	**A real friend is** a. **considerate,** _____ b. **helpful, and** _____ c. **sympathizes with you.** _____ 1612
singular 1878	If all agreement errors sounded as bad as **"We Washes Cars,"** we would have no problem. However, we cannot always trust our ears in selecting a verb to match the subject. Without stopping to think, underline the verb which sounds right to your ear. (Don't score your answer right or wrong.) **One of you** (*is, are*) **always teasing the other.** 1879
lay 2145	Fill in the missing forms: PRESENT PAST PAST PARTICIPLE **lay** (to put) _____ **(have)** _____ 2146
a 2412	WRONG: **This pen writes** *good.* This sentence is wrong because the adjective *good* cannot modify the verb _____. 2413
his (her) 2679	**Almost anyone can increase** _____ **reading rate considerably.** 2680
items: 2946	**The Student Council makes suggestions in regard to such matters as lockers, the lunchroom, and homework and Mr. Shepard, the principal, discusses these suggestions with the faculty.** 2947

The dog 4	**The dog is barking.** Which two words *tell* something about **the dog** and therefore belong to the *telling part* of the sentence? _____ _____ 5
preposition 272	a. **The dog trotted** *behind.* b. **The dog trotted** *behind* **the car.** In which sentence is *behind* a preposition because it is followed by an object? _____ 273
the same word 540	**I have a friend** *who raises tropical fish.* The pronouns that start adjective clauses are called **relative pronouns** because they *relate* (or *connect*) the adjective clause to the sentence. The clause signal *who* in the above sentence is called a _____ *pronoun.* 541
a 808	Put a comma before a participial phrase at the end of a sentence only if it modifies the subject at the beginning of the sentence. a. **We found Mr. Jenkins** *hoeing his garden.* b. **Mr. Jenkins was in the backyard** *hoeing his garden.* Which sentence requires a comma? _____ 809
b 1076	a. **His** *strong, calloused* **hands were no strangers to work.** b. **His hands,** *strong* **and** *calloused,* **were no strangers to work.** The italicized adjectives in sentence *b* are given more emphasis because they (*are, are not*) in their usual position. 1077
trifles but 1344	**Cheap paper is made from wood pulp high-grade paper is made from rags.** _____ 1345

c. sympathetic.

1612

If *are* (wrong) sounded right, you will see why you can't always trust your ear.

1879

a. **One is stuck.**
b. **One (of the wheels) is stuck.**

Sentence *a* doesn't indicate whether **One** means a key, a window, a seat, or a wheel. We therefore add the prepositional phrase **of the wheels** to make our meaning clear.

The subject in both *a* and *b* is the pronoun _____.

1880

---

laid, (have) laid

2146

In this and the following frames, underline the correct forms of **lie** and **lay**:

(*Lay, Lie*) **your books aside and** (*lay, lie*) **down to rest for a while.**

2147

---

writes

2413

Underline the correct word:

Brush your clothes (*good, well*) **before putting them away.**

2414

---

his (her)

2680

Both women made the welfare of children _____ **chief concern in life.**

2681

---

homework;

2947

Somebody   maybe it was Lenore   had let the cat out of the bag.

2948

is barking 5	a. **The argument was useless.** b. **A useless argument.** Which group of words is a sentence because it gives us a sense of completeness—*a* or *b?* _____ 6
b 273	a. **Ralph fell** *down* **the stairs.** b. **Ralph fell** *down.* In which sentence is *down* a preposition? _____ 274
relative 541	**I have a friend** *who raises tropical fish.* The relative pronoun *who* starts the adjective clause. It also stands for the noun _____, which the clause modifies. 542
b 809	In this and the following frames, combine each pair of sentences by changing the italicized sentence to a participial phrase. Insert a comma wherever needed. **I read the list of winners.** *I hoped to see my name.* _____ _____ 810
are not 1077	a. **The team,** *tired* **and** *discouraged,* **trudged back to the locker room.** b. **The** *tired* **and** *discouraged* **team trudged back to the locker room.** In which sentence are the italicized adjectives given more emphasis? _____ 1078
pulp. High-grade *or* pulp; high-grade 1345	**It was a wonderful party the best I have ever attended.** _____ 1346

page 11

Parallel construction is a way of streamlining your writing—of giving your sentences smooth, clean lines. It is based on a very simple idea: Say similar things in a (*different, similar*) way.

1614

One

1880

One of the wheels <u>is</u> stuck.

The noun **wheels** is not the subject of the above sentence.

It is the object of the preposition _____.

1881

Lay, lie

2147

PRESENT	PAST	PAST PARTICIPLE
lie (to rest)	**lay**	**(have) lain**
lay (to put)	**laid**	**(have) laid**

I (*laid, lay*) awake, trying to recall where I had (*lain, laid*) my receipt.

2148

---

well

2414

Although **good** should not be used as an adverb, **well** may be used as an adjective to mean *in good health, of good appearance,* or *satisfactory.*

    a. **Stir the paint** *well* **before using it.**
    b. **Our dog is now** *well* **again.**

Well is used as an adjective in sentence (*a, b*).

2415

---

their

2681

Everyone has _____ own ideas about what constitutes success in life.

2682

Somebody—
Lenore—

2948

Murray is allergic to several foods   for example, eggs and chocolate.

2949

a. **Helping his friend.**
b. **With the help of his friend.**
c. **Joe helped his friend.**

Which group of words is a sentence because it gives us a sense of completeness—*a, b,* or *c?* _____

a

6

7

---

a. **Ralph fell** *down* **the stairs.**
b. **Ralph fell** *down.*

In sentence *a, down* is a preposition because it is followed by the object **stairs.**

In sentence *b, down* is an adverb that modifies the verb

a

274

_____.

275

I have a friend *who raises tropical fish.*

In the above sentence the relative pronoun *who* is the subject of the verb _____.

friend

542

543

Continue to follow the directions for the previous frame:

I read the list of winners. **I hoped to see my name.**

_____

_____

I read the
list of winners,
hoping to see
my name.

810

811

Underline the word or phrase which is emphasized by a change from its normal position:

For fifty years Grandmother attended the same church.

a

1078

1079

There were Mother's best dishes   scattered all over the yard and filled with mud.

_____

party, the

1346

1347

similar 1614	Try to apply parallel construction whenever you use the co-ordinating conjunctions **and, but,** and **or,** which generally connect words or word groups of the same type. **Edison paid little attention to** *what he ate* **or** *his clothes.* In this sentence, does the conjunction **or** connect parallel word groups? (*Yes, No*) <div style="text-align:right">1615</div>
of 1881	<div style="text-align:center">**One of these steaks . . . enough for a meal.**</div> The verb has been omitted from this sentence. The verb we choose should agree in number with the word (*One, steaks*). <div style="text-align:right">1882</div>
lay, laid 2148	Underline the correct words: **Your books will** (*lay, lie*) **there until you** (*lay, lie*) **them somewhere else.** <div style="text-align:right">2149</div>
b 2415	Underline the correct words: **When the pressure is** (*good, well*), **the sprinkler works** (*good, well*). <div style="text-align:right">2416</div>
his (her) 2682	**If a housewife thinks of all the hungry people in the world, _____ will not waste food.** <div style="text-align:right">2683</div>
foods; *or* foods— 2949	**Your letter of application should state these facts your age, education, and experience.** <div style="text-align:right">2950</div>

c 7	The *naming part* of a sentence is called the **complete subject.** A **complete subject** is usually built around a noun (or pronoun) that is known as the **simple subject.** The **complete subject** is likely to be (*longer, shorter*) than the **simple subject**—or **subject,** as we usually call it. 8

fell
 	
275
	a. **The farmers stood** *around* **and chatted.**
	    b. **The farmers stood** *around* **the courthouse.**
	
	In which sentence is *around* a preposition? _____
	
	         276

raises
 	
543
	Let's take another look at the adjective clause signals.
	RELATIVE PRONOUNS: **who (whose, whom), which, that**
	       The student . . . *essay wins* **receives a scholarship.**
	Which relative pronoun would be appropriate in this sentence? _____
	
	         544

Reading the list of winners, I hoped to see my name. 811	*Mrs. Kern held on to the purse-snatcher.* **She shouted for help.** _____ _____ 812

For fifty years
 	
1079
	Underline the word or phrase which is emphasized by a change from its normal position:
	
	       Resign he will not.
	
	         1080

dishes (,) scattered 1347	**The return on a stock is called a dividend the return on a bond is called interest.** _____ 1348

No 1615	a. **Edison paid little attention to** *what he ate* **or** *his clothes.* b. **Edison paid little attention to** *what he ate* **or** *what he wore.* In which sentence does the conjunction **or** connect parallel word groups? _____ <div align="right">1616</div>
One 1882	Underline the correct verb: **One of these steaks** (*is, are*) **enough for a meal.** <div align="right">1883</div>
lie, lay 2149	Underline the correct words: **Mother** (*laid, lay*) **her glasses where she had usually** (*laid, lain*) **them.** <div align="right">2150</div>
good, well 2416	Underline the correct words: **You can't study** (*good, well*) **unless the light is** (*good, well*). <div align="right">2417</div>
she 2683	**Ask anybody where the Eiffel Tower is and** _____ **can tell you.** <div align="right">2684</div>
facts: 2950	**All the accommodations hotels, motor courts, and tourist homes were jammed with vacationists.** <div align="right">2951</div>

longer 8	**The old black dog** wagged its shaggy tail. The **complete subject** of this sentence consists of four words—**The old black dog.** The **simple subject,** or **subject,** is the one word _____. 9
b 276	a. **The bus went** *by* **without stopping.** b. **The bus went** *by* **the corner without stopping.** In which sentence is *by* a preposition? _____ 277
whose 544	**The lady whose car we bumped was very angry.** The adjective clause starts with the relative pronoun *whose* and ends with the word _____. 545
Holding on to the purse-snatcher, Mrs. Kern shouted for help. 812	**Mr. Day sued my father.** *He claimed that the accident was his fault.* _____ _____ 813
Resign 1080	Underline the word or phrase which is emphasized by a change from its normal position: **Of all the cakes I have ever eaten, this was the most delicious.** 1081
dividend. The *or* dividend; the 1348	**Ships are like people each having its own personality.** _____ 1349

b 1616	**Ray's trouble is not** *that he doesn't earn enough money* **but** *spending it foolishly.* Does the conjunction **but** connect parallel word groups? (*Yes, No*) 1617
is 1883	Once you state your subject, keep your mind on it until you select your verb. Don't let a noun in a prepositional phrase run away with your verb. **Our supply of scientific books** (*was, were*) **inadequate.** The noun **supply** is singular; the noun **books** is plural. We choose the verb _____ to agree with the subject _____. 1884
laid, laid 2150	Underline the correct words: **My pen has** (*lain, laid*) **on the desk ever since I** (*lay, laid*) **it there.** 2151
well, good 2417	How do you decide whether to use **good** or **well** after a "sense" verb? If the "sense" verb means an action, use **well** to describe this action. Underline the correct word: **I felt the cloth** (*good, well*) **before buying the coat.** 2418
he 2684	**Any person making a telephone call should give** _____ **name at once.** 2685
accommodations— **homes—** 2951	**The lighter seeds are scattered by the wind the heavier ones are distributed by squirrels.** 2952

The old black dog **wagged its shaggy tail.**

The *telling part* of a sentence is called the **complete predicate.**

The **complete predicate** of this sentence consists of _____ words. (How many?)

dog

9

10

UNIT 2: THE PROCESS OF COMPOUNDING

Lesson **8** Compound Parts and Compound Sentences

[Frames 279–321]

b

277

The lady whose car we bumped was very angry.
The lady   was very angry.

When we omit the adjective clause, do we have a complete sentence remaining? (*Yes, No*)

bumped

545

546

Mr. Day sued my father, claiming that the accident was his fault.

Fred stood at the window. **He saw the lightning strike.**

_____

_____

813

814

---

a. **The Turners had little ready money although they owned a lot of land.**
b. **Although they owned a lot of land, the Turners had little ready money.**

If you had written many sentences with the subject first, which sentence would break the monotony? _____

Of all the cakes I have ever eaten,

1081

1082

Red trudged to the sideline   wiping the mud from his face.

_____

people, each

1349

1350

page 19

No 1617	a. **Ray's trouble is not** *that he doesn't earn enough money* **but** *that he spends it foolishly.* b. **Ray's trouble is not** *that he doesn't earn enough money* **but** *spending it foolishly.* In which sentence does the conjunction **but** connect parallel word groups? _____ 1618
(verb) was **(subject) supply** 1884	**Several pieces of the puzzle** (*was, were*) **missing.** The noun **pieces** is plural, but the noun **puzzle** is singular. We choose the verb _____ to agree with the subject _____. 1885
lain, laid 2151	**To sit** means "to take a sitting position" or "to be in place." **To set** means "to place something." You always set *something.* You *set* a pan on the stove, a glass on the table, a box on the floor. **She** *set* **the pie on the windowsill to cool.** What was *set* on the windowsill? _____ 2152
well 2418	If the "sense" verb is used as a linking verb, as it more often is, follow it with the adjective **good** to modify the subject. **A warm coat** *feels* (= *is*) **good on a chilly day.** The adjective **good** modifies the subject _____. 2419
his 2685	# Lesson 75 Review: Pronoun Problems [Frames 2687–2718]
wind; 2952	**The water was close to the top of the levee and it was rapidly rising.** (Punctuate so as to make the second idea very forceful.) 2953

four 10	The complete predicate is built around the simple predicate, which we shall hereafter refer to as the **verb**. A **verb** makes—or helps to make—a statement about the subject. **The old black dog wagged its shaggy tail.** The **simple predicate**, or **verb**, around which the complete predicate is built is the one word _____. <div align="right">11</div>
	Mr. Smith | owns a garage. This sentence—like all complete sentences—can be divided into two major parts: the *complete subject* and the *complete* _____. <div align="right">279</div>
Yes 546	**A boy who had never fished before caught the most fish.** In this sentence the adjective clause starts with the relative pronoun _____ and ends with the word _____. <div align="right">547</div>
Standing at the window, Fred saw the lightning strike. 814	Eliminate the **and** by changing the italicized statement to a participial phrase: *The company expected a strike* **and bought a large amount of steel.** <div align="right">815</div>
b 1082	a. **When it was first delivered, the Gettysburg Address made little impression.** b. **The Gettysburg Address made little impression when it was first delivered.** If you had written many sentences with the subject first, which sentence would break the monotony? _____ <div align="right">1083</div>
sideline, wiping 1350	**Lesson 37 When Does a Sentence End?** [Frames 1352–1382] *page 21*

Parallel construction is also needed when you use the words **than, as,** and **as well as** to make comparisons.

Writing **is faster than** *to print.*

Are the italicized words parallel? (*Yes, No*)

People frequently make errors in subject-verb agreement because they have the mistaken idea that adding an *s* to a verb in the present tense makes it plural.

My shoe hurts.

The subject **shoe** is singular, and the verb **hurts** is singular. The word that ends in *s* is the (*subject, verb*).

After you *set* something, it *sits* there until you *set* it some-where else.

Fill in the missing words:

I _____ a chair on the porch so that Dad could _____

in the sun.

The popcorn smelled so *good* that we couldn't resist it.

We use the adjective *good* because the word **smelled** is used as (*an action, a linking*) verb in this sentence.

In this and the following frames, underline the correct pro-noun. Do not go "by ear," but think of a reason for each choice you make.

Between you and (*I, me*), Mrs. Colby doesn't like the gift.

We had only one objection to the house   its distance from school.

wagged 11	The *subject* and the *verb* are the most important words in any sentence because they carry most of the meaning. **Two small boys | rang our doorbell.** The *subject* of this sentence is the noun _____. The *verb* is the word _____. 12
predicate 279	**Mr. Smith and his son | own a garage.** The part of this sentence that now has two parts is the complete (*subject, predicate*). 280
who . . . before 547	**A boy who had never fished before caught the most fish.** **A boy caught the most fish.** When we omit the adjective clause, do we have a complete sentence remaining? (*Yes, No*) 548
Expecting a strike, the company bought a large amount of steel. 815	**We walked along the shore and** *looked for a place to swim.* _____ _____ 816
a 1083	For the sake of variety, move the adverb clause to the beginning of the sentence and set it off with a comma: **Dad would bring me a pennant whenever he returned from a trip.** _____ _____ 1084
	Many sentence fragments come about in this way. You start out, for example, by writing— **Walter plays golf.** Is this a complete sentence? (*Yes, No*) 1352

No 1619	a. *Writing* **is faster than** *printing*. b. *Writing* **is faster than** *to print*. c. *To write* **is faster than** *to print*. Which is the one sentence in which the construction is not parallel? _____ 1620
verb 1886	**My <u>shoes</u> <u>hurt</u>.** Now the subject **shoes** is plural, and the verb **hurt** is plural. The word that ends in *s* is the (*subject, verb*). 1887
set, sit 2153	PRESENT PAST PAST PARTICIPLE **sit** **sat** **(have) sat** **set** (to place) **set** **(have) set** The verb whose three forms are all alike is _____. 2154

a linking
 	
2420
	Underline the correct word in each sentence:
	
	    a. **Cheap perfume doesn't smell** (*good, well*).
	    b. **A person with a cold can't smell** (*good, well*).
	
	2421

me 2687	**Unless someone actually asks for your advice, don't offer** (*him, them*) **any.** 2688
house: *or* house— 2954	**Our cat likes only the most expensive foods for example, liver, salmon, and tuna fish.** 2955

(subject) boys (verb) rang 12	Throughout this book, we shall underscore the subject with one line and the verb with two lines. **Two small <u>boys</u> | <u>rang</u> our doorbell.** Indicate the *subject* and *verb* in the following sentence by underscoring: **A handsome blue car | stopped in front of our house.**　13
subject 280	**<u>Mr. Smith</u> | <u>owns</u> and <u>operates</u> a garage.** The part of this sentence that now has two parts is the complete (*subject, predicate*). 　　281
Yes 548	If a complete sentence does not remain after we omit the adjective clause, we have not selected the clause correctly. 　a. **The rope (which controls the curtain broke).** 　b. **The rope (which controls the curtain) broke.** The clause is correctly selected in sentence (*a, b*). 　　549
We walked along the shore, looking for a place to swim. 816	*Judy worked until midnight* **and finally completed her theme.** _____ _____ 　　817
Whenever he returned from a trip, Dad would bring me a pennant. 1084	For the sake of variety, move the adverb clause to the beginning of the sentence and set it off with a comma: **Sandy makes new friends wherever he goes.** _____ _____ 　　1085
Yes 1352	**Walter plays golf.** Because you recognize this as a complete sentence with a subject and a verb, you close it with a _____. (What punctuation mark?) 　　1353

b 1620	a. **To read a foreign language is easier than to speak it.** b. **Reading a foreign language is easier than speaking it.** c. **To read a foreign language is easier than speaking it.** Which is the one sentence in which the construction is not parallel? _____ 1621
subject 1887	SINGULAR: **My shoe hurts.** PLURAL: **My shoes hurt.** In either the singular or plural sentence, is there a final *s* on both the subject and the verb? (*Yes, No*). 1888
set 2154	PRESENT PAST PAST PARTICIPLE sit sat (have) sat set (to place) set (have) set Fill in the missing words: **Don't** _____ **the package where someone might** _____ **on it.** 2155
a. good b. well 2421	In this and the following frames, underline the correct modifier after you have decided whether the verb is used as an *action* or a *linking* verb: **Mr. Collins felt quite** (*angry, angrily*) **about the bill.** 2422
him 2688	(*We, Us*) **fellows can finish the job in a few hours.** 2689
foods; *or* foods— 2955	Lesson **83** How to Use Quotation Marks [Frames 2957–2994]

	A handsome blue car | stopped in front of our house. Are there any other two words in this sentence that tell as much of the "story" of this sentence as the subject and the verb? (*Yes, No*)
<u>car</u> <u><u>stopped</u></u> 13	14
	Compound means "having more than one part." When a structural part of a sentence consists of two or more parts, that part is said to be **compound**. **Mr. Smith and his <u>son</u> | <u><u>own</u></u> and <u><u>operate</u></u> a garage.** Both parts of this sentence are _____.
predicate 281	282
	a. **The blood (which flows from a wound) washes away the germs.** b. **The blood (which flows from) a wound washes away the germs.** The clause is correctly selected in sentence (*a, b*).
b 549	550
	A milk truck overturned and *caused a traffic jam for several miles.* _____ _____
Working until midnight, Judy finally completed her theme. 817	818
	For the sake of variety, move the adverb clause to the beginning of the sentence and set it off with a comma: **A host should not eat until every guest has been served.** _____ _____
Wherever he goes, Sandy makes new friends. 1085	1086
	Then as you continue thinking, you decide to qualify your statement by adding an adverb clause. **Walter plays golf.** *Although he prefers tennis.* Because you have already closed your sentence with a period, the clause becomes a sentence _____.
period 1353	1354

c 1621	Parallel construction does not mean having a word-for-word match between the parallel word groups. So long as the basic pattern is the same, minor differences do not matter. **Is he really** *calling the police* **or just** *pretending to call them?* In spite of their difference, the italicized word groups are parallel because *calling* is matched by _____. <div align="right">1622</div>
No 1888	**The window opens.** When you change this sentence to the plural, the final *s* on the verb **opens** (*remains, disappears*). <div align="right">1889</div>
set, sit 2155	Underline the correct words: **Tommy** (*set, sat*) **down where Mrs. Gibb had** (*set, sat*) **the biggest piece of cake.** <div align="right">2156</div>
angry 2422	**Your voice sounds** (*differently, different*) **on the tape.** <div align="right">2423</div>
We 2689	**Students should be encouraged to think for** (*themselves, theirselves*). <div align="right">2690</div>

	A **direct quotation** repeats a person's remark directly in his own words. An **indirect quotation** reports a person's remarks indirectly in someone else's words.
	
	    a. **Bob said, "I'll be home by ten."**
	    b. **Bob said that he would be home by ten.**
	
	The direct quotation is in sentence (*a, b*).
	<div align="right">2957</div>

No 14	Verbs have a special characteristic that helps us to identify them. Verbs are the only words that can show by a change in their spelling whether they mean *present* or *past* time; for example, **cook—cooked, see—saw, speak—spoke.** What is the *past* form of the verb **jump?** _____ <div align="right">15</div>
compound 282	**Mr. Smith and his son** | **own and operate a garage.** Although both the subject and the predicate of this sentence are compound, the sentence can still be divided into two major parts. These two major parts are the *complete subject* and the *complete* _____ . <div align="right">283</div>
a 550	The clause signal **where** can start either an adverb clause or an adjective clause. If the clause modifies a verb, it is considered an adverb clause. If the clause modifies a noun or pronoun, it is considered an _____ clause. <div align="right">551</div>
A milk truck overturned, causing a traffic jam for several miles. 818	*Several planes circled the airport* **and waited their turn to land.** _____ _____ <div align="right">819</div>
Until every guest has been served, a host should not eat. 1086	In this and the following frames, emphasize the italicized words by moving them from their normal position to another position in the sentence: **He never could understand** *geometry.* _____ <div align="right">1087</div>
fragment 1354	**Walter plays golf** *although he prefers tennis.* Although the sentence could have ended after **golf,** does it end at this point? (*Yes, No*) <div align="right">1355</div>

pretending 1622	*To face your problems squarely* **is more healthful than** *to run away from them.* In spite of their difference, the italicized word groups are parallel because the infinitive *To face* is matched by the infinitive _____ . 1623
disappears 1889	In the present tense, a verb without a final *s* may be either singular or plural (*I think, We think*), but with a final *s* (*he thinks, she thinks*), the verb is *always* singular. .?. **thinks.** Could this verb possibly have a plural subject? (*Yes, No*) 1890
sat, set 2156	Underline the correct words: **Why would anyone want to** (*sit, set*) **where George** (*set, sat*)? 2157
different 2423	**We looked through every drawer very** (*thorough, thoroughly*). 2424
themselves 2690	**Let's you and** (*me, I*) **try out for track.** 2691
a 2957	The word **that** is frequently used in changing a direct to an indirect quotation. Rewrite the following sentence to make the quotation indirect (and use no quotation marks). **Mother said, "I am ready."** **Mother said** _____ . 2958

jumped 15	PRESENT: **I never eat oysters.** PAST: **I never ate oysters.** In the changing of this sentence from *present* to *past* time, the only word that changed was the verb _____. <div align="right">16</div>
predicate 283	Any sentence that can be divided into two parts—a subject and a predicate—is a **simple sentence.** **Mr. Smith and his <u>son</u>	<u>own</u> and <u>operate</u> a garage.** Is this a simple sentence? (*Yes, No*) <div align="right">284</div>
adjective 551	a. **I eat at the store** *where I work.* b. **I eat** *where I work.* In one sentence the clause is an adverb clause because it modifies a verb; in the other, it is an adjective clause because it modifies a noun. The adjective clause is in sentence (*a, b*). <div align="right">552</div>
Circling the airport, several planes waited their turn to land. 819	A present participle always ends with the letters _____. <div align="right">820</div>
Geometry he never could understand. 1087	**I have never eaten** *such food.* _____ <div align="right">1088</div>
No 1355	**Walter plays golf** *although he prefers tennis.* This sentence does not end after **golf** because the adverb clause modifies the verb _____ in the main statement. <div align="right">1356</div>

to run 1623	**Miss Ross gets acquainted with her students by** *talking to* *them* **and** *discovering what their interests are.* Although the italicized word groups are quite different, they are parallel because the gerund *talking* is matched by the gerund _____. 1624
No 1890	We add an *s* to a verb in the present tense whenever we talk about any singular noun or about any singular pronoun in the third person (*he, she, it, one*). Underline the two subjects that would require a verb ending in *s*: **Planes The road They It** 1891
sit, sat 2157	Underline the correct words: **The box was still** (*sitting, setting*) **where I had** (*set, sat*) **it.** 2158
thoroughly 2424	**Barbara feels** (*bad, badly*) **about losing her bracelet.** 2425
me 2691	**I don't like mine as well as** (*yours, your's*). 2692

(that) she was ready.
 	
2958
	Use quotation marks ("quotes" for short) to enclose only a *direct* quotation—one that repeats a person's exact words.
	
	  a. **Dad said You can use the car, Jim.**
	  b. **Dad said that Jim could use the car.**
	
	Which sentence requires quotes because it is a direct quotation? ____
	
	2959

eat 16	PRESENT: **Some of the boys ride to school.** PAST: **Some of the boys rode to school.** Because **ride** is the only word that changed, we can be sure that it is a _____. 17
Yes 284	**The wind | was blowing.** **The water | was rough.** Each of these sentences can be divided into a subject and a predicate. Therefore each of these sentences is a _____ *sentence.* 285
a 552	**I eat at the store** *where I work.* The clause *where I work* is an adjective clause because it modifies the noun _____. 553
ing 820	A participle is considered a verbal because it has the char- acteristics of both a verb and an _____. 821
Such food I have never eaten. 1088	**I never expect to be** *a millionaire.* _____ 1089
plays 1356	Does the fact that a sentence could end at a certain point mean that it does end at this point? (*Yes, No*) 1357

discovering 1624	To avoid monotony, you may omit repeated words without destroying the parallelism. **Fractions** *can be changed to decimals,* **and** *decimals can be changed to fractions.* The three words that can be omitted from the word group after **and** are _____. 1625
The road, It 1891	**The ability of these children astonishes everyone.** The verb **astonishes** agrees with the subject, which is (*ability, children*). 1892
sitting, set 2158	**To rise** means "to go up" or "to get up." **To raise** means "to make something rise" or "to lift something." We always raise *something*—a cover, a window, or a cloud of dust. As a result of our action, the cover, the window, or the cloud of dust (*raises, rises*). 2159
bad 2425	**Rayna looked** (*beautiful, beautifully*) **in her new spring outfit.** 2426
yours 2692	**Mr. Crandall showed** (*we, us*) **boys his collection of old firearms.** 2693

a
 	
2959
	Always capitalize the first word of a direct quotation because it is the beginning of someone's sentence.
	
	    a. **Dad said, "you can use the car, Jim."**
	    b. **Dad said, "You can use the car, Jim."**
	
	Which sentence is correct? _____
	
	2960

verb
 	
17
	A small number of verbs have the same form for both present and past time; for example, *hit, cut, let, put, hurt, cost.*
	
	    a. **We** *hit* **the ball back and forth.**
	    b. **We** *bat* **the ball back and forth.**
	
	In which sentence could the verb mean either present or past time? _____ 18

simple 285	Now let's combine our two simple sentences into one sentence by using the conjunction **and.** **The wind was blowing, and the water was rough.** Can we divide this sentence so that it will have just a subject on one side and just a predicate on the other? (*Yes, No*) 286
store 553	a. **We camped** *where there were few trees.* b. **We camped on a field** *where there were few trees.* The adjective clause is in sentence (*a, b*). 554
adjective 821	A participial phrase can come either before or after the noun it modifies. (*True, False*) 822
A millionaire I never expect to be. 1089	**He would** *go* **in spite of everyone's advice.** _____ _____ 1090
No 1357	**We built a cottage | on a hill | overlooking a lake | which was surrounded by pine trees.** At how many points could this sentence have been ended before the final period? _____ 1358

can be changed 1625	**I feared** *that he would change his mind* **or** *that he would raise the price.* The three words that can be omitted from the word group after **or** are _____. 1626
ability 1892	**The ability of these children astonishes everyone.** The noun **children** is not the subject of the sentence but the object of the preposition _____. 1893
rises 2159	PRESENT PAST PAST PARTICIPLE **rise** (to get up) **rose** **(have) risen** **raise** (to lift) **raised** **(have) raised** Fill in the correct words: **Be sure to** _____ **when I** _____ **my hand.** 2160
beautiful 2426	**You can hear very** (*good, well*) **in the balcony.** 2427
us 2693	**I repeated the directions until I was sure that he understood** (*it, them*). 2694
b 2960	Underline the correct word: **Eleanor said to Sandy, "**(*that, That*) **is your third piece of pie."** 2961

a 18	Underscore the subject with one line and the verb with two lines: **Players from both teams scrambled over the field.** <div align="right">19</div>
No 286	**The <u>wind</u> <u>was</u> <u>blowing</u>, and the <u>water</u> <u>was</u> rough.** When we divide this sentence at the conjunction, we have a complete sentence—not just a subject or a predicate—on each side of the conjunction. This is not a simple sentence because we cannot divide it into two parts: a *subject* and a _____. <div align="right">287</div>

b
 	
554
	Although the clause signal **when** generally starts adverb clauses, it can also start an adjective clause.
	
	  a. **My friend telephoned** *when I was very busy.*
	  b. **My friend telephoned at a time** *when I was very busy.*
	
	The adjective clause is in sentence (*a, b*).
	<div align="right">555</div>

True 822	**Lesson 22 Subordination by Past Participles** <div align="right">[Frames 824–863]</div>
Go he would, in spite of everyone's advice. 1090	**Fran's** *original and imaginative paintings* **won the interest of a famous artist.** _____ _____ <div align="right">1091</div>
three 1358	**We built a cottage | on a hill | overlooking a lake | which was surrounded by pine trees.** This sentence could have been ended at each point marked by a vertical line. It does not end, however, until the final period because each phrase or clause modifies a word in the (*preceding, following*) phrase or clause. <div align="right">1359</div>

that he would 1626	Put parentheses ( ) around the three words that can be omitted without destroying the parallelism: **The bookkeeper keeps track of how much is coming in and how much is going out.** 1627
of 1893	a. **The ability of these children astonishes everyone.** b. **The ability of these children astonish everyone.** In which sentence is the verb correct? _____ 1894
rise, raise 2160	PRESENT PAST PAST PARTICIPLE **rise** (to go up) **rose** **(have) risen** **raise** (to lift) **raised** **(have) raised** Underline the correct word: **Food prices had (*risen, rose*) because of the severe drought.** 2161
well 2427	**I didn't sleep (*good, well*) because of the noise.** 2428
them 2694	(*Those, Them*) **are the finest cattle in the state.** 2695
That 2961	**Dad said, "You can use the car, Jim."** What punctuation mark separates the direct quotation from the words that introduce it? _____ 2962

ayers scrambled

19

Underscore the subject with one line and the verb with two lines:

A huge, spreading maple stands in front of the church.

20

---

predicate

287

A sentence made by joining two (or more) simple sentences with the conjunction **and, but,** or **or** is called a **compound sentence.**

a. **The wind was blowing, and the water was rough.**
b. **Mr. Smith and his son own and operate a garage.**

Which can be split into two separate sentences? _____

288

---

b

555

A man that looked like a reporter asked me several questions.

The adjective clause starts with the word _____

and ends with the word _____.

556

---

the *cracking* ice   a *falling* rock   a *steaming* potato

All the italicized words are used like adjectives because they

modify _____. (What class of words?)

824

Fran's paintings, original and imaginative, won ... *or* Original and imaginative, Fran's ...

1091

You can give a word or word group its greatest emphasis by leaving it in its normal position. (*True, False*)

1092

---

preceding

1359

A sentence is something like a train. A train might have only five cars. However, we cannot point to the fifth car and say, "There's the end of the train" until we look to make sure no more cars are coming.

A sentence also ends only when the (*first, last*) *grammatically connected* idea has been expressed.

1360

(how much is) 1627	Put parentheses ( ) around the two words that can be omitted without destroying the parallelism: **I showed Jimmie how to set the camera and how to take pictures.** 1628
a 1894	a. **The abilities of this child astonishes everyone.** b. **The abilities of this child astonish everyone.** In which sentence is the verb correct? _____ 1895
risen 2161	Underline the correct word: **As the water flows into the lock, the ship (*raises, rises*).** 2162
well 2428	**Taste the soup (*well, good*) before you add more salt.** 2429
Those 2695	**Are you going to ride with (*they, them*) or (*we, us*)?** 2696
a comma 2962	**Dad said, "You can use the car, Jim."** Both the comma and the period come (*before, after*) the quotation marks with which they are used. 2963

maple stands
<u>maple</u> <u>stands</u>

20

Underscore the subject with one line and the verb with two lines:

A large black cat with yellow patches emerged from the bushes.

21

---

a

288

a. **The <u>wind</u> <u>was blowing</u>, and the <u>water</u> <u>was</u> rough.**
b. **<u>Mr. Smith</u> and his <u>son</u> <u>own</u> and <u>operate</u> a garage.**

Which sentence is compound? _____

289

---

that . . . reporter

556

A man that looked like a reporter asked me several questions.

Write the sentence that remains after you remove the clause.

_____

_____

557

---

nouns

824

the *cracking* **ice**   **a** *falling* **rock**   **a** *steaming* **potato**

The italicized words, which resemble both adjectives and verbs, are participles.

They are *present* participles because they end in _____.

825

False

1092

Putting an adverb or an adverbial word group ahead of the subject should not be done too often because it is the exception rather than the rule. (*True, False*)

1093

---

last

1360

If you close a sentence with a period before you have included a *grammatically connected* word group, you produce a

sentence _____.

1361

(how to) 1628	Put parentheses ( ) around the two words that can be omitted without destroying the parallelism: **A tree can stand a strong wind because it is flexible and because it has deep roots.** 1629
b 1895	**The operation of this machine requires much skill.** The subject of this sentence is (*operation, machine*). 1896
rises 2162	Underline the correct words: **This (*raised, rose*) a problem that had never (*arose, arisen*) before.** 2163
well 2429	**This engine won't run (*good, well*) on ordinary gasoline.** 2430
them, us 2696	**(*Ours, Our's*) steers more easily than (*theirs, their's*).** 2697
before 2963	Now let's turn our sentence around: **"You can use the car, Jim," said Dad.** A comma still separates the quotation from the rest of the sentence. Does the comma still come before the quotes? (*Yes, No*) 2964

cat emerged 21	Continue to follow the directions for the previous frame: **An expensive silver pin disappeared from the counter.** 22
a 289	**The wind was blowing, and the water was rough.** This is a compound sentence because there is a complete sentence with a subject and verb both before and after the conjunction _____. 290
A man asked me several questions. 557	**A pessimist is a person who always expects the worst to happen.** The adjective clause starts with the word _____ and ends with the word _____. 558
ing 825	a. **the** _cracking_ **ice** a _falling_ **rock** a _steaming_ **potato** b. **the** _cracked_ **ice** a _fallen_ **rock** a _steamed_ **potato** The italicized words after letter _b_ are also used as adjectives. Were they also formed from verbs? (_Yes, No_) 826
True 1093	**Lesson 29 Some Useful Adverb Clause Devices** [Frames 1095–1133]
fragment 1361	Remember, too, that the length of a word group has nothing to do with its being a sentence or not. Two words may form a sentence provided they are a subject and verb and make sense by themselves. a. **Neighbors objected.** b. **The neighbors.** Which is a complete sentence? _____ 1362

and (because it) 1629	In this and the following frames, rewrite the word group in parentheses, making it parallel with the italicized phrase: *An old book* **is not necessarily better than** _____ _____. (one that is new) 1630
operation 1896	**The operation of this machine requires much skill.** If we changed **this machine** to **these machines,** would you need to change the verb? (*Yes, No*) 1897
raised, arisen 2163	Underline the correct words: **Although prices** (*rose, raised*), **my salary didn't** (*raise, rise*). 2164
well 2430	## Lesson 68 Review: Adjective and Adverb Problems [Frames 2432–2450]
Ours, theirs 2697	**People should try to see** (*theirselves, themselves*) **as others see them.** 2698
Yes 2964	**Dad said, "You can use the car, Jim."** **"You can use the car, Jim," said Dad.** When a comma and quotes or a period and quotes come together, always put the comma or period first. Punctuate this sentence completely: **This is going to be hard to explain sighed Jerry** 2965

pin <u>disappeared</u> 22	The pond across the road seldom freezes before December. 23
and 290	a. **The fall and winter are cold.** b. **The winters are cold, and the summers are hot.** Which is a simple sentence with a compound subject? _____ 291
who . . . happen 558	**The statistics which the speaker quoted were out-of-date.** The adjective clause starts with the word _____ and ends with the word _____. 559
Yes 826	a. **the** *cracking* **ice** **a** *falling* **rock** **a** *steaming* **potato** b. **the** *cracked* **ice** **a** *fallen* **rock** **a** *steamed* **potato** The italicized words after *b* are also participles because they were formed from verbs and are used as adjectives. However, they are not *present* participles because they do not end in _____. 827
	You are familiar with adverb clauses that begin with **if** and answer the question, "On what condition?" *If I had taken more time,* **I could have done better.** The verb in the clause consists of the two words _____ _____. 1095
a 1362	**The neighbors** These two words do not form a sentence because there is no _____ to make a statement about the subject **neighbors**. 1363

page 45

a new one. 1630	**The doctor advised Uncle John** *to get a pole* **and** _____ _____. (that he should go fishing) 1631
No 1897	**The opportunity for advancement seems very good.** If we changed **opportunity** to **opportunities,** would you need to change the verb? (*Yes, No*) 1898
rose, rise 2164	Two forms of **lie-lay, sit-set,** or **rise-raise** (of which only the first letters are printed) are needed in each sentence. Complete each word, remembering not to use any form of **lay, set,** or **raise** unless the sentence tells to *what* the action is done. **L_____ down and I'll l_____ a cold cloth on your forehead.** 2165
	In this and the following frames, underline the correct modifier or, in some cases, the word appropriate for formal usage: **You will** (*sure, surely*) **sleep** (*soundly, sound*) **after so much strenuous exercise.** 2432
themselves 2698	(*He, Him*) **and** (*I, me*) **were the only ones who knew.** 2699
"This is going to be hard to explain," sighed Jerry. 2965	a. **"You can't take it with you", said Mrs. Murphy.** b. **"You can't take it with you," said Mrs. Murphy.** Which sentence is correct? _____ 2966

<u>pond</u> <u><u>freezes</u></u> 23	**My only key to the house fell through a crack in the steps.** 24
a 291	a. **The fall and winter are cold.** b. **The winters are cold, and the summers are hot.** Which is a compound sentence? _____ 292
which . . . quoted 559	**This soap is for people whose skin is sensitive to ordinary soap.** The adjective clause starts with the word _____ and ends with the word _____. 560
ing 827	a. **the** *cracking* **ice**　　**a** *falling* **rock**　　**a** *steaming* **potato** b. **the** *cracked* **ice**　　**a** *fallen* **rock**　　**a** *steamed* **potato** The participles after *b* are **past participles.** The participles that do not end in -*ing* are the (*present, past*) participles. 828
◆ had taken 1095	The "if" idea can also be expressed without using the clause signal **if** at all. 　　<u>*Had* I *taken*</u> *more time,* **I could have done better.** We recognize this as a clause only because of its unusual word order. The subject *I,* instead of coming first, comes between the two parts of the _____. 1096
verb (*or* predicate) 1363	**The neighbors,** *who were annoyed by Harold's practicing his trombone at all hours of the day and night,* Now the subject **neighbors** is followed by a long adjective clause that modifies it. As yet, does the subject **neighbors** have a verb to tell what the annoyed neighbors *did?* (*Yes, No*) 1364

(to) go fishing.	**Peggy had the habit** *of turning on the radio* **and** _____ _____. (to forget to turn it off)
1631	1632
Yes	a. **The purpose of these laws . . .** b. **The purposes of this law . . .** Which subject would require a singular verb—*a* or *b?* _____
1898	1899
Lie, lay	Continue to follow the directions for the previous frame: **Uncle Mac I**_____ **some newspapers on the grass and** **I**_____ **down for a nap.**
2165	2166
surely, soundly	**He can't do the work** (*satisfactory, satisfactorily*) **in such a short time.**
2432	2433
He, I	**The amount of the bill surprised Dad more than** (*I, me*).
2699	2700
b	For variety, we sometimes split a quoted sentence and put the *he said,* or a similar expression, between its two parts. **"A blowout at high speed,"** *he said,* **"may prove fatal."** We must use two sets of quotes in order to exclude the words _____ from the quotation.
2966	2967

<u>key</u> <u>fell</u> 24	In this and the following frames, write *S* if the word group is just a subject; *P* if it is just a predicate; *SP* if it has both a subject and predicate which form a complete sentence: **my most difficult subject** _____ 25
b 292	a. **I paid my check and waited for my change.** b. **I paid my check, and the waiter brought me my change.** Which is a simple sentence with a compound predicate? 293
whose . . . soap 560	**The car which won the first automobile race traveled at five miles per hour.** The adjective clause starts with the word _____ and ends with the word _____. 561
past 828	Most past participles end in *-ed* (entertain*ed*), *-d* (tol*d*), *-en* (brok*en*), *-n* (tor*n*), and *-t* (ben*t*). The past participle of a verb is the form you would use after *have;* for example, *have* **opened,** *have* **broken,** *have* **torn.** The past participle of **see** is _____. 829
verb 1096	a. *I <u>had</u> <u>taken</u> more time* b. *<u>Had</u> <u>I</u> <u>taken</u> more time* Do both word groups contain exactly the same words? (*Yes, No*) 1097
No 1364	**The neighbors,** *who were annoyed by Harold's practicing his trombone at all hours of the day and night,* In spite of its eighteen words, this word group is still *not* a sentence but only a subject modified by a clause. It cannot become a sentence until we supply a verb to make a statement about the subject _____. 1365

(of) forgetting to turn it off. 1632	**Ruth's friends and relatives like her** *because she is generous* **and** _____. (her unselfishness) (*Note:* Do not repeat words unnecessarily.) 1633
a 1899	**One of you** (*is, are*) **always teasing the other.** Suppose that the prepositional phrase **of you** were omitted. Which verb would you choose to agree with the subject **One?** _____ 1900
laid, lay 2166	**Judy's coat has l**_____ **on that chair ever since she** **l**_____ **it there.** 2167
satisfactorily 2433	**Don's excuse seemed very** (*reasonable, reasonably*) **to his employer.** 2434
me 2700	**Dad was more surprised about the bill than** (*I, me*). 2701
he said 2967	**"A blowout at high speed,"** *he said,* **"may prove fatal."** If we omit the words *he said* from the above sentence, we have (*one sentence, two sentences*) remaining. 2968

S	*S, P,* or *SP?*
	paid all my expenses to the convention _____
25	26
a	a. **I paid my check and waited for my change.**
	b. **I paid my check, and the waiter brought me my change.**
	Which is a compound sentence? _____
293	294

which . . . race	Lesson **15** Variations of the Adjective Clause
	[Frames 563–591]
561	

seen	The past participle of **teach** is _____.
829	830

Yes	a. *I had taken more time*
	b. *Had I taken more time*
	Which word group by its unusual word order tells you that
	it is not a sentence but a clause? _____
1097	1098

neighbors	**The neighbors,** *who were annoyed by Harold's practicing his trombone at all hours of the day and night,* **complained.**
	Now we have a completed sentence because we have added
	the verb _____, which makes a statement
	about the subject **neighbors.**
1365	1366

unselfish. 1633	*Watching the game on television* **was almost as good as** _____. (if you were there) 1634
is 1900	a. **One of you is always teasing the other.** b. **One of you are always teasing the other.** In which sentence is the verb correct? _____ 1901
lain, laid 2167	**Why would anyone I**_____ **a glass where Wanda has** **I**_____ **it?** 2168
reasonable 2434	**You can** (*sure, surely*) **get a job** (*easily, easy*) **right before** **Christmas.** 2435
I 2701	(*It's, Its*) **all** (*your's, yours*) **for the asking.** 2702
one sentence 2968	**"A blowout at high speed,"** *he said,* **"may prove fatal."** Because the second part of the quotation is a continuation of the same sentence that was interrupted by *he said,* it begins with a (*small, capital*) letter. 2969

P 26	S, P, or SP? **the music stopped** _____ 27
b 294	**Fred's teammates shook his hand and patted him on the back.** Are there a subject and verb both before and after the conjunction **and?** (*Yes, No*) 295
	RELATIVE PRONOUNS: **who (whose, whom), which, that** These are the relative pronouns that serve as clause signals for _____ clauses. 563
taught 830	The past participle of **wear** is _____. 831
b 1098	a. *If I had taken more time,* **I could have done better.** b. *Had I taken more time,* **I could have done better.** The word order of the clause in sentence *b*—just like the clause signal _____ in sentence *a*—tells us that the word group is a clause. 1099
complained 1366	Could a word group consist of fifty or sixty words and still not be a sentence? (*Yes, No*) 1367

being there. 1634	**Frank had the choice** *of making up his back payments* **or** _____. (he would lose the car) 1635

a
 	
1901
	Here is another rule of subject-verb agreement:
	A verb should agree in number with its subject, not with a subject complement that may follow it.
	    a. **My favorite <u>fruit</u> is apples.**
	    b. **<u>Apples</u> are my favorite fruit.**
	Which sentence contains a plural subject? _____
	
	1902

lay, laid 2168	**Mother I_____ awake, wondering where she had I_____ her diamond ring.** 2169
surely, easily 2435	**The fan will run more** (*quiet, quietly*) **if you oil it** (*good, well*). 2436
It's, yours 2702	**Two girls, Irene and** (*she, her*), **did most of the art work.** 2703
small 2969	Underline the correct word: **"Everything here," complained Mrs. Jones, "(***Seems, seems***) to be out of order."** 2970

SP 27	S, P, or SP? **supplies electric power to several states** _____ 28
No 295	**Fred's teammates shook his hand and patted him on the back.** Is this a compound sentence? (*Yes, No*) 296
adjective 563	We sometimes use a preposition before the relative pronoun; for example, **with which, for which, to whom.** In such cases the preposition belongs to the adjective clause. **The pen** *with which he wrote* **was scratchy.** The first word of the adjective clause is (*with, which*). 564
worn 831	Past participles—like present participles—also form useful phrases that modify nouns and pronouns. **The woman,** *annoyed by the smoke,* **changed her seat.** The past participial phrase in this sentence modifies the noun _____. 832
If 1099	a. *If I had taken more time,* **I could have done better.** b. *Had I taken more time,* **I could have done better.** The adverb clause in sentence *b* is not better or worse than the adverb clause in sentence *a*. It enables you, however, to add greater (*clearness, variety*) to your sentences. 1100
Yes 1367	Each of the following news stories consists of several word groups. Where necessary, insert a period and a capital letter to show where one sentence ends and the next begins. **Roy dropped his penny into the slot and picked up the card which was supposed to tell his fortune his friends laughed because the card was blank.** 1368

(of) losing the car. 1635	**Our biggest problem is** *to plan programs* **and** _____ _____. (keeping up the members' interest) 1636
b 1902	**Tires ... my biggest expense.** The missing verb should agree in number with the subject (*Tires, expense*). 1903
lay, laid 2169	**Aunt Lou s**_____ **the biggest piece of pie at the place where Ronnie would s**_____. 2170
quietly, well 2436	**The company is usually quite** (*prompt, promptly*) **in giving service.** 2437
she 2703	**I like to play chess because it makes** (*you, me*) **think.** 2704
seems 2970	**"Everything here," complained Mrs. Jones, "seems to be out of order."** We set off **complained Mrs. Jones** with commas because it interrupts the quoted sentence. Both commas, as well as the period, come (*before, after*) the quotes. 2971

P 28	*S, P, or SP?* **my dad has a good sense of humor** _____ 29
No 296	**Fred's teammates shook his hand and patted him on the back.** Although this is not a compound sentence, one of its parts is compound. This sentence has a compound (*subject, predicate*). 297
with 564	**The pen with (which he wrote) was scratchy.** **The pen (with which he wrote) was scratchy.** Read each sentence, omitting the words in parentheses. If the remaining words are a sentence, the clause was correctly selected. The preposition **with** (*is, is not*) part of the clause. 565
woman 832	A past participial phrase can often be shifted about. *Annoyed by the smoke,* **the woman changed her seat.** **The woman,** *annoyed by the smoke,* **changed her seat.** **The woman changed her seat,** *annoyed by the smoke.* Can a past participial phrase be some distance away from the noun it modifies? (*Yes, No*) 833
variety 1100	*If you should hear of a job,* **let me know.** Eliminate the *If* in this clause by putting the subject between the two parts of the verb *should hear.* _____, let me **know.** 1101
fortune. His 1368	Continue to follow the directions for the previous frame. Be careful not to produce any sentence fragments. **To attract a deer a hunter attached a pair of antlers to his head mistaking him for a deer another hunter shot him he was not injured seriously.** 1369

(to) keep up the members' interest. 1636	The Potters were *the first to arrive* and _____ _____. (they left last) 1637
Tires 1903	a. **Tires . . . my biggest expense.** b. **My biggest expense . . . tires.** In which sentence would you use the singular verb **was**— *a* or *b?* _____ 1904
set, sit 2170	Our guest s_____ down before we had even s_____ the table. 2171
prompt 2437	**If you can think** (*clearly, clear*), **you should be able to write** (*good, well*). 2438
me 2704	**Let's you and** (*I, me*) **circulate a petition.** 2705
before 2971	Punctuate this sentence: **The only thing we have to fear said President Franklin D. Roosevelt is fear itself** 2972

SP 29	S, P, or SP? **a bottle of red ink** _____ 30

predicate
 	
297
	The most common conjunctions that connect the two parts of a compound sentence are **and, but,** and **or.**
	  a. **The movie bored the adults but pleased the children.**
	  b. **The movie bored the adults, but the children liked it.**
	In which sentence does the conjunction **but** connect the two parts of a compound sentence? _____
	
	298

is 565	**The doctor for whom Alice worked urged her to become a nurse.** The first word of the adjective clause is (*whom, for*). 566
Yes 833	**Ed threw himself on the grass,** *exhausted from the race.* The participial phrase is separated by several words from the word it modifies, the noun _____. 834
should you hear of a job, 1101	*If I were in your place,* **I should do the same thing.** The verb in the adverb clause is _____. 1102
ead. Mistaking him. He 1369	**Mr. McGeorge put up a scarecrow to keep the robins away from his strawberry patch later he saw a robin perching right on the scarecrow's head.** 1370

the last to leave. 1637	**Babe Ruth showed his self-confidence** *by pointing to a spot* **and** _____ _____. (he would hit a home run there) 1638
b 1904	**Young drivers are our main traffic problem.** Now let's turn this sentence around and supply the correct verb: **Our main traffic problem _____ young drivers.** 1905
sat, set 2171	**I s_____ my chair under a tree to avoid s_____ in the hot sun.** 2172
clearly, well 2438	**The legislature was** (*kind of, rather*) **indifferent to the passage of this bill.** 2439
me 2705	In this and the following frames, underline the pronoun that is appropriate for careful speech and formal writing: (*Who, Whom*) **will the American people elect to the Presidency next November?** 2706
"The only . . . fear," said President . . . Roosevelt, "is fear itself." 2972	Punctuate this sentence: **Whenever I play said Ruth Ann the dog jumps up on the piano** 2973

S 30	*S, P, or SP?* **the linoleum on our kitchen floor** _____ 31
b 298	a. **The movie bored the adults but pleased the children.** b. **The movie bored the adults, but the children liked it.** In which sentence is a comma used before the conjunction **but?** _____ 299
for 566	**The doctor for whom Alice worked urged her to become a nurse.** The adjective clause begins with the preposition **for** and ends with the word _____. 567
Ed 834	PRESENT PARTICIPLE: *Neglecting his friends,* **Carl read the newspaper.** PAST PARTICIPLE: *Neglected by his friends,* **Carl read the newspaper.** The phrase with the (*present, past*) participle represents Carl as *doing something.* 835
were 1102	a. *If I were in your place,...* b. *Were I in your place,...* The verb in clause *a* consists of one word—*were.* To eliminate the *If* in clause *b*, put the verb (*before, after*) the subject *I.* 1103
patch. Later 1370	A father advised his young son who was interested in collecting moths to go to the library and get a book on moths the boy came back with a book entitled *A Handbook for Young Mothers.* 1371

(by) hitting a home run there. 1638	*Being a good listener* **is just as important as** _____ _____. (the ability to talk well) 1639
is 1905	**The main attraction of the town is the fine shops.** Now let's turn this sentence around and supply the correct verb: **The fine shops** _____ **the main attraction of the town.** 1906
set, sitting 2172	**Although our costs have r**_____ **considerably, we have not r**_____ **our prices.** 2173
rather 2439	**The jury was** (*somewhat, sort of*) **surprised that the judge's sentence was not more** (*severe, severely*). 2440
Whom 2706	**It should have been** (*they, them*) **who were penalized.** 2707
"Whenever I play," said Ruth Ann, "the dog jumps up on the piano." 2973	Another way to obtain variety is to put the *he said* (or whatever expression you use) between two separate sentences. **"I can't believe it,"** *said Tom.* **"You must be joking."** If we omit the words *said Tom* from the above sentence, we have (*one sentence, two sentences*) remaining. 2974

S, P, or SP?

some parts of the world get mail only once or twice a year

_____

31

32

---

a. **I can call for you or meet you at school.**
b. **I can call for you, or we can meet at school.**

In which sentence does the conjunction **or** connect the two

parts of a compound sentence? _____

299

300

---

worked

The bottle *in* which the lotion comes costs more than the lotion.

Is the preposition *in* part of the adjective clause? (*Yes, No*)

567

568

---

present

PRESENT PARTICIPLE: *Neglecting his friends,* **Carl read the newspaper.**
PAST PARTICIPLE: *Neglected by his friends,* **Carl read the newspaper.**

The phrase with the (*present, past*) participle represents
Carl as *having had something done to* him.

835

836

---

before

a. *If I were in your place,* **I should do the same thing.**
b. *Were I in your place,* **I should do the same thing.**

The unusual word order of the clause in sentence *b* serves

the same purpose as the clause signal _____ in sentence

a in telling us that the word group is a clause.

1103

1104

---

moths. The
(boy)

**Annoyed by crows   a New Brunswick farmer set a box trap
for them   going to his trap the next day   he saw an unusual sight   a silver fox   and a litter of five little ones.**

1372

being a good talker. 1639	**Our purpose should be** *to discover the truth* **rather than** _____. (proving ourselves right) 1640
are 1906	In this and the following frames, underline the verb that agrees in number with its subject. Don't be fooled by the object of a preposition that might come between the subject and the verb or by a subject complement that might follow the verb. **The decision of the judges** (*is, are*) **final.** 1907
risen, raised 2173	Gloria r_____ the cover to see if the dough had r_____. 2174
somewhat, severe 2440	**Mrs. Rosen treats the kindergarten tots** (*lovely, in a lovely manner*). 2441
they 2707	**I cannot see how anybody in** (*their, his*) **right mind can believe such nonsense.** 2708
two sentences 2974	**"I can't believe it,"** *said Tom.* **"You must be joking."** To show that the second part of the quotation is a new sentence, we put a period after *Tom* and follow it with a (*small, capital*) letter. 2975

S, P, or SP?

moves through the water by a kind of jet propulsion _____

33

---

b

300

a. **I can call for you or meet you at school.**
b. **I can call for you, or we can meet at school.**

In which sentence is a comma used before the conjunction

or? _____

301

Yes

568

The bottle in which the lotion comes costs more than the lotion.

The adjective clause begins with the preposition **in** and ends

with the word _____.

569

---

past

836

To show that something _has been done to_ a person or a
thing, we use a (_present, past_) participle.

837

If

1104

In this and the following frames, eliminate the _if_ in each
adverb clause by changing the word order of the clause:

I should have written Alva _if I had known her address._

I should have written Alva _____

_____.

1105

---

them. Going

1372

**Motorists near Albany   suddenly turned up their car win-
dows   and shifted into reverse gear   when they saw   three
hundred skunks parading across the state highway.**

1373

(to) prove ourselves right. 1640	The teacher can't tell whether an error is caused *by igno-rance* or _____. (whether you were careless) 1641
is 1907	His only source of income (*was, were*) odd jobs. 1908
raised, risen 2174	Just as they r_____ to leave, Suzanne r_____ another problem. 2175
in a lovely manner 2441	The vase of pink and white peonies looked (*nice, nicely*) on the altar. 2442
his 2708	The Martins always insist on (*our, us*) staying for dinner. 2709

capital
 	
2975
	Punctuation and capitals are omitted from the following sentences to avoid revealing the answers.
	    a. **If Ross pitches** *said Bob* **we will surely win**
	    b. **Ross is pitching** *said Bob* **we will surely win**
	In which sentence does *said Bob* stand between two separate sentences? _____
	
	2976

P 33	*S, P,* or *SP?* **a deserted house with broken windows and a sagging roof** _____ 34
b 301	We put a comma before the conjunction **and, but,** or **or** when it connects the two parts of a compound (*sentence, predicate*). 302
comes 569	**The bottle in which the lotion comes costs more than the lotion.** **The bottle** **costs more than the lotion.** When we omit the adjective clause, do we have a complete sentence remaining? (*Yes, No*) 570

past
 	
 837
	To emphasize that the action of a participle has been entirely completed before another action, use *having* before the past participle (*having finished, having seen*).
	
	      a. *Glancing through the paper,* **I laid it aside.**
	      b. *Having glanced through the paper,* **I laid it aside.**
	
	 Which sentence is correct? _____
	
	 838

had I known her address. 1105	*If Stover were willing to run,* **he would win hands down.** _____, **he would** **win hands down.** 1106
This is all one sentence. 1373	**A farmer examined his cow's foot** **to see why she had been limping** **for the past five weeks** **in her hoof he found his wife's diamond ring** **which had disappeared** **exactly five weeks ago.** 1374

(by) carelessness. 1641	Lesson **46** Avoiding *Is When* and *Is Where* Constructions [Frames 1643–1674]
was 1908	Conditions in this hospital (*require, requires*) investigation. 1909
rose, raised 2175	Lesson **61** Keeping Your Tenses Consisten [Frames 2177–2214]
nice 2442	The team felt (*badly, bad*) about the poor attendance at the game. 2443
our 2709	Just suppose that it was (*we, us*) who were starving. 2710
b 2976	Note the difference in the punctuation and capitalization in these sentences: a. "If Ross pitches," said Bob, "we will surely win." b. "Ross is pitching," said Bob. "We will surely win." Sentence *b* is handled differently from sentence *a* because it consists of (*one sentence, two sentences*). 2977

S 34	*S, P,* or *SP?* **a giant explosion with the force of a billion atom bombs sometimes occurs on the sun** _____ 35
sentence 302	**The man fumbled in his pocket and pulled out a letter.** Should a comma be inserted after the word **pocket?** (*Yes, No*) 303
Yes 570	a. **The things (at which the audience laughed) were very silly.** b. **The things at (which the audience laughed) were very silly.** In which sentence is the clause correctly identified? _____ 571
b 838	a. *Having finished his homework,* **Fred went to bed.** b. *Finishing his homework,* **Fred went to bed.** Which sentence is correct? _____ 839
Were Stover willing to run, 1106	**I'll let you know** *if I should change my mind.* **I'll let you know** _____ _____ . 1107
weeks. In 1374	**Alvin Phalen a Canadian trapper caught a wolf by its tail he dragged it over the snow and killed it with one of the skis which he was wearing.** 1375

It is not reasonable to define something as a *time* or *place* when it clearly is *not* a time or a place.

WRONG: **A tragedy** *is when* **a play has an unhappy ending.**
WRONG: **A tragedy** *is where* **a play has an unhappy ending.**

Is a **tragedy** either a *time* or a *place?* (*Yes, No*)

1643

---

require

One of your sleeves (*look, looks*) **shorter than the other.**

1910

Tense means *time.* The tense of a verb shows the time of its action—present, past, or future.

        a. **I** *feel* **good today.**
        b. **I** *felt* **good yesterday.**

The verb is in the past tense in sentence _____.

2177

---

bad

Because it was April Fool's Day, Dick tasted the candy (*suspicious, suspiciously*).

2443

2444

---

we

To (*who, whom*) **did Washington turn for advice?**

2710

2711

---

two sentences

a. **"This is a good story," said Dan. "It holds your interest."**
b. **"This is a good story," said Dan, "it holds your interest."**

Which sentence is correct? _____

2977

2978

S, P, or *SP?*

one of the most successful coaches in the state _____

36

The man fumbled in his pocket and ↓ **pulled out a letter.**

No

Suppose that we added the pronoun **he** at the point indicated by the arrow. Would it then be correct to insert a comma after **pocket?** (*Yes, No*)

303

304

---

a. **We were eager to try the dishes which have made this inn famous.**
b. **We were eager to try the dishes for which this inn is famous.**

a

In which sentence does a preposition precede the relative pronoun which signals the clause? _____

571

572

It is very simple to change a sentence to a past participial phrase when its verb consists of two words—some form of *be* followed by a past participle; for example, *is* **built,** *was* **invited,** *were* **surprised.**

a

It was taken from a plane.

Does the above sentence contain such a verb? (*Yes, No*)

839

840

---

should I change
my mind.

If it were not for the mosquitoes, **camping would be fun.**

_____ ,

camping would be fun.

1107

1108

---

tail. He

Because his truck wouldn't start   on a cold day   a man built a fire under the engine   a barrel of oil exploded   blowing the roof off his garage   and burning his house down   a friend was also injured.

1375

1376

No
 	
1643
	To define a **tragedy** as a *time* or a *place* seems as far off the track as to define an elephant as a kind of vegetable.
	
	    a. **A tragedy** *is when* **a play has an unhappy ending.**
	    b. **A tragedy** *is where* **a play has an unhappy ending.**
	    c. **A tragedy is a** *play* **with an unhappy ending.**
	
	Which definition makes the best sense? _____ 1644

looks 1910	**One important cause of traffic congestion (***is, are***) the huge office buildings.** 1911

b
 	
2177
	a. I *feel* **good today.**
	    b. I *felt* **good yesterday.**
	    c. I *shall feel* **better tomorrow.**
	
	The verb is in the future tense in sentence _____. 2178

suspiciously 2444	**Burning leaves smell very (***pleasant, pleasantly***) in the autumn.** 2445
whom 2711	**Nobody likes to feel that (***he is, they are***) being pushed around.** 2712
a 2978	Supply all necessary punctuation: **You are wrong said Sally Cats do show affection** 2979

S 36	The *predicate* of a sentence makes a statement about the _____. 37
Yes 304	The three conjunctions commonly used to connect the two parts of a compound sentence are **and, but,** and **or.** In a compound sentence, we generally put a comma before the _____ **and, but,** or **or.** 305
b 572	**The conditions . . .** *which we played* **were difficult.** The adjective clause in this sentence requires a preposition. Underline the preposition that would make the best sense: **by under at with** 573
Yes 840	**(It was) taken from a plane.** To change the above sentence to a past participial phrase, start your phrase with the "ready-made" past participle _____, dropping all the words that precede it. 841
Were it not for the mosquitoes, 1108	**We should have started earlier** *if we had known the distance.* **We should have started earlier** _____ _____. 1109
engine. A (barrel) down. A (friend) 1376	**A policeman gave a man a traffic ticket for walking too slowly in front of an automobile and forcing the driver to jam on his brakes the man was Eddie Tolan the former champion runner.** 1377

c 1644	The temptation to use *is when* or *is where* arises whenever you are asked to explain a technical term used in school studies, science, business, sports, fashions, and so on. The first step in defining something is to ask yourself what general type of thing it is. **A tariff is a** (*game, tax, fine*) . . . 1645
is 1911	**Clothes** (*was, were*) **her main topic of conversation.** 1912
c 2178	a. I *feel* **good today.** b. I *felt* **good yesterday.** c. I *shall feel* **better tomorrow.** In which sentence is a change in time shown by a change in the spelling of the verb? ＿＿ 2179
pleasant 2445	**The scheme sounded rather** (*dishonest, dishonestly*) **to me.** 2446
he is 2712	**Pasadena and** (*we, ourselves*) **are tied for first place.** 2713
"You are wrong," said Sally. "Cats do show affection." 2979	Supply all necessary punctuation: **This snapshot isn't good said Dick There wasn't enough sun** 2980

subject 37	Every word in a sentence belongs to either the *complete subject* or the *complete* _____. 38
conjunction 305	**The man fumbled in his pocket and pulled out a letter.** **The movie bored the adults but pleased the children.** **I can call for you or meet you at school.** Not one of these sentences is a compound sentence. Each one is a sentence with a compound (*subject, predicate*). 306
under 573	**The conditions under which we played were difficult.** The adjective clause begins with the preposition **under** and ends with the word _____. 574
taken 841	**This is a picture of our town.** (*It was*) *taken from a plane.* **This is a picture of our town** *taken from a plane.* The participial phrase modifies the noun _____. 842

had we known the distance.
 	
1109
	The adverb **once** can sometimes be used as an adverb clause signal in place of *if, when, after,* or *as soon as.*
	
	   a. **If** *you break the seal,* **you can't return the film.**
	   b. **Once** *you break the seal,* **you can't return the film.**
	
	In which sentence does the condition expressed by the clause seem more emphatic and final? _____
	
	1110

brakes. The (man) 1377	**Disturbed by yowling cats a woman in Maine fired her husband's revolver into the dark to frighten them away she found a dead wildcat the next morning and collected fifteen dollars the state bounty for a wildcat.** 1378

tax 1645	**A tariff is a** *tax* **. . .** After you give the general classification, add a word, phrase, or clause to differentiate the thing you are defining from other things of the same class. **A tariff is a tax** (*charged on income, charged on imports*). <div align="right">1646</div>
were 1912	**Kelly's years of experience** (*qualify, qualifies*) **him for the job.** <div align="right">1913</div>
b 2179	<div align="center">a. I *feel* **good today.** b. I *felt* **good yesterday.** c. I *shall feel* **better tomorrow.**</div> In which sentence is a change in time shown by the addition of a helping verb? _____ <div align="right">2180</div>
dishonest 2446	**Many people felt** (*badly, bad*) **about the results of the election.** <div align="right">2447</div>
we 2713	<div align="center">**The first ones to arrive were Paul and** (*her, she*).</div> <div align="right">2714</div>
"This . . . good," said Dick. "There wasn't enough sun." 2980	Use only one set of quotes ("—") to cover any number of sentences provided that the quotation is not interrupted. Supposing that each line represents a separate sentence, supply the necessary quotation marks: **The chairman said,** _____. _____. _____. <div align="right">2981</div>

predicate 38	The heart of the *complete subject* is the *subject*. The heart of the *complete predicate* is the _____. 39
predicate 306	**The man fumbled in his pocket and pulled out a letter.** **The movie bored the adults but pleased the children.** **I can call for you or meet you at school.** Does any one of these sentences have a comma before the conjunction **and, but,** or **or?** (*Yes, No*) 307
played 574	Although relative pronouns are usually a signal that an adjective clause is starting, the relative pronoun is sometimes omitted. **Most of the things** (*that*) *we fear* **never happen.** Can the clause signal be omitted in the above sentence? (*Yes, No*) 575
picture 842	**The roads were covered with ice.** What is the two-word verb in this sentence? _____ _____. 843
b 1110	Underline the clause signal that makes the clause more emphatic: (*Once, If*) *you feed a stray cat,* **you can't get rid of it.** 1111
away. She 1378	**Benjamin Morris of Kansas City couldn't sleep because the scratching of a branch against his house disturbed him after sawing off the limb he found himself back in bed but this time in a hospital he had sat on the wrong end of the limb while he sawed.** 1379

charged on imports 1646	a. **A tariff is when a tax is charged on imports.** b. **A tariff is where a tax is charged on imports.** c. **A tariff is a tax charged on imports.** Sentence *c* is correct because a **tariff** is not defined as a *when* or a *where*, but as a _____. 1647
qualify 1913	**This article claims that high wages** (*is, are*) **the best way of preventing a business depression.** 1914
c 2180	Do not shift from one tense to another unless there is an actual shift in the time of the action. **Phil** *accepted* **the job and then** *changes* **his mind.** Are both italicized verbs in the same tense? (*Yes, No*) 2181
bad 2447	**A cold shower feels** (*good, well*) **on a hot day.** 2448
she 2714	**We are unable to take a step without** (*them, their*) **complaining of the noise.** 2715
The chairman said, "_____. _____. _____." 2981	Supply the necessary quotation marks. (Note that a colon is generally used to introduce a long or formal quotation.) **As Professor Brown remarked: A people that is ignorant of its history is like an individual without a memory. It can learn nothing from its past experience. It will make the identical mistakes again and again.** 2982

verb *or* simple predicate 39	When we change a sentence from *present* to *past* or from *past* to *present,* the only word that would ordinarily change is the _____. 40
No 307	We do not ordinarily use a comma before the conjunction that connects the two parts of a compound (*predicate, sentence*). 308
Yes 575	We can learn to recognize these "no signal" clauses if we watch for a *subject-verb* combination right after a noun. **Most of the things** *we fear* **never happen.** Here we have a *subject-verb* combination right after the noun _____. 576
were covered 843	**The roads** *were covered* **with ice.** Is one of the words in the two-word verb a past participle? (*Yes, No*) 844
Once 1111	Make this sentence more emphatic by using a "once" clause: *After my tests are over,* **I shall have more time.** _____, **I shall have more time.** 1112
him. After hospital. He 1379	**As he saw a man running from his delivery truck with a crate of eggs a milkman hurled a bottle of milk at the thief and knocked him unconscious the milkman identified himself to the police as Art Wells star pitcher for the Bowman Dairy baseball team.** 1380

tax 1647	a. **Astronomy is the science of the heavenly bodies.** b. **Astronomy is when you study the heavenly bodies.** Sentence *a* is correct because **astronomy** is not defined as a *when,* but as a _____. <div align="right">1648</div>
are 1914	**One in every eight persons in the United States** (*own, owns*) **a dog.** <div align="right">1915</div>
No 2181	a. **Phil** *accepted* **the job and then** *changes* **his mind.** b. **Phil** *accepted* **the job and then** *changed* **his mind.** Which sentence is correct because both verbs are in the same tense? _____ <div align="right">2182</div>
good 2448	**These scissors don't cut as** (*well, good*) **as they once did.** <div align="right">2449</div>
their 2715	(*Who, Whom*) **can a child trust more than his own parents?** <div align="right">2716</div>
remarked: "A people . . . again." 2982	Whenever the speaker changes, begin a new paragraph and use another set of quotes. **It's a burglar said Ron. It's a dog said Ann. It's your** **imagination said Dad.** How many paragraphs and sets of quotes would this mate- rial require? _____ <div align="right">2983</div>

Lesson 2 A Closer Look at Subjects and Verbs

[Frames 42–80]

---

predicate

308

a. **We can't give everybody everything he wants and reduce taxes at the same time.**
b. **The strike was finally settled and the men went back to work.**

Which sentence requires a comma before the conjunction because it is a compound sentence? _____

309

---

things

576

Most of the things we fear never happen.

The subject of the adjective clause is _____, and the verb is _____.

577

Yes

844

(*The roads were*) *covered with ice.* **They were treacherous.**

We can change the italicized sentence to a participial phrase by starting the phrase with the past participle _____.

845

Once my tests are over,

1112

Subordinate the italicized statement by changing it to a "once" clause:

You sign the contract, **and you can't change your mind.**

_____, **you**

can't change your mind.

1113

---

unconscious. The (milkman)

1380

To celebrate the opening of his theater   the owner decided to give a television set   to the person holding the lucky ticket   when the number was called   seventy-two people flocked to the box office   each having the lucky number the printer had made a slight mistake.

1381

page 81

science 1648	**Astronomy is the science of the heavenly bodies.** In defining **astronomy,** first we classify it as a **science.** Then to distinguish it from many other sciences, we add the modifying phrase _____. 1649
owns 1915	**A few drops of oil** (_do, does_) **the trick.** 1916
b 2182	It is perfectly correct to shift tense when we really mean to indicate a change in the time of the action. I _admire_ (_present_) **the courage that Bob** _showed_ (_past_). Because you _admire_ at the present time the courage that Bob _showed_ at a past time, the shift in tenses is (_correct, incorrect_). 2183
well 2449	**Our new radio doesn't sound as** (_well, good_) **as the old one.** (_Note:_ The test for this Unit is combined with the test for Unit 11.) 2450
Whom 2716	**Everybody held** (_his, their_) **breath as the car skidded into the intersection.** 2717

three
 	
2983
	In this and the following frames, circle the letter of the sentence that is correctly punctuated and capitalized:
	
	    a. **The doctor said, "That I needed more sleep."**
	    b. **The doctor said, "You need more sleep, Clyde."**
	
	2984

One or more helping verbs (sometimes called *auxiliary verbs*) are often used with the main verb to express our meaning more exactly.

The rope will break.

The helping verb used with **break** to make its meaning more

exact is _____.

42

---

b

309

a. **A worker must stop for rest but a machine can work continuously.**

b. **I looked into the microscope but saw only a confusing blur.**

Which sentence requires a comma before the conjunction

because it is a compound sentence? _____

310

(subject) we
(verb) fear

577

A good test for a "no signal" adjective clause is to see whether we can insert a relative pronoun before it.

Pete described the kind of boat he expects to build.

Can we insert *which* or *that* before the word **he?** (*Yes, No*)

578

---

covered

845

(*The roads were*) *covered with ice.* **They were treacherous.**
Covered with ice, **they were treacherous.**

In changing the italicized sentence to a participial phrase, we

lost the subject _____.

846

Once you sign
the contract,

1113

Subordinate the italicized statement by changing it to a "once" clause:

A false idea gets into circulation, **and it is difficult to up-root it.**

_____

_____, **it is difficult to uproot it.**

1114

---

ticket. When
number. The
(printer)

1381

A sparrow picked up a lighted cigarette butt   and carried the butt to its nest   on the Henrys' house   a two-story frame structure   which caught on fire   the nest was a total loss   although firemen put out the blaze   before much damage was done to the house.

1382

page 83

of the heavenly bodies 1649	a. **A polygon is where a figure has more than four sides.** b. **A polygon is a figure having more than four sides.** Which definition is correct? _____ 1650
do 1916	**The construction of houses, churches, and schools** (*continue, continues*) **at a high rate.** 1917
correct 2183	**Mr. Clark** *moved* (*past*) **to Omaha, where he now** *manages* (*present*) **a large drugstore.** Because Mr. Clark *moved* to Omaha in the past but *manages* the drugstore at the present time, the shift in tenses is (*correct, incorrect*). 2184
good 2450	**UNIT 11: SOLVING YOUR PRONOUN PROBLEMS** Lesson **69** The Nominative and the Objective Case [Frames 2452–2484]
his 2717	**Paul and** (*myself, I*) **wrote all the invitations.** 2718
b 2984	a. **Will Rogers, the cowboy philosopher, once said, "So live that you wouldn't be afraid to sell the family parrot to the village gossip."** b. **Will Rogers, the cowboy philosopher, once said, "so live that you wouldn't be afraid to sell the family parrot to the village gossip."** 2985

will 42	**The rope <u>will</u> break.** **The rope <u>might</u> break.** The meaning of the first sentence changes when we change the helping verb from **will** to _____. 43
a 310	a. **I just returned from my vacation, and found your letter waiting for me.** b. **Good judgment comes from experience, and experience comes from bad judgment.** From which sentence should the comma be removed because it is not a compound sentence? _____ 311
Yes 578	**Pete described the kind of boat he expects to build.** The adjective clause begins with the word _____ and ends with the word _____. 579
roads 846	(*The roads were*) *covered with ice.* **They were treacherous.** the roads *Covered with ice,* ~~they~~ **were treacherous.** To let the reader know what the sentence is about, we must substitute **the roads** for the pronoun _____ in the main statement. 847

Once a false
idea gets into
circulation,
 	
1114
	Another more unusual type of adverb clause begins with
	now that. These words, similar in meaning to **because,** are
	useful in sentences stating *cause and effect.*
	
	    a. **Because** *you are twenty-one,* **you can vote.**
	    b. **Now that** *you are twenty-one,* **you can vote.**
	
	Which sentence suggests that the cause is recent? _____
	
	1115

fire. The (nest) 1382	Lesson **38** **Pronouns as a Cause of Run-on Sentences** <div align="right">[Frames 1384–1424]</div>

b

1650

a. **Amnesia is when one loses his memory.**
b. **Amnesia is loss of memory.**

Which definition is correct? _____

1651

---

continues

1917

Lesson **54** Recognizing Singular and Plural Subjects

[Frames 1919–1958]

---

correct

2184

a. **The story is about a man who** *achieved* **great wealth but** *loses* **his happiness.**
b. **The story is about a man who** *achieved* **great wealth but** *lost* **his happiness.**

Which sentence is correct? _____

2185

---

a. *Children* **love** *dogs.*   b. *Dogs* **love** *children.*

In sentence *a, Children* is the subject and *dogs* is the direct object.

In sentence *b, Dogs* is the subject and _____ is the direct object.

2452

I

2718

UNIT **12: SKILL WITH GRAPHICS**

Lesson **76** Commas in Compound Sentence

[Frames 2720–2748]

---

a

2985

a. **"We should have won this game," sighed Coach Higgins.**
b. **"We should have won this game", sighed Coach Higgins.**

2986

might 43	**Mary** <u>can bake</u> **a cake.** **Mary** <u>should bake</u> **a cake.** The meaning of the first sentence changes when we change the helping verb from **can** to _____. 44
a 311	**Mr. Trent remained calm and collected and he didn't even raise his voice.** This sentence contains two **and**'s. A comma should be placed before the (*first, second*) **and**. 312
he . . . build 579	**A person is known by the company he keeps.** We could insert the clause signal *which* or *that* before the word _____. 580
they 847	If you lose a noun in making a participial phrase, put this noun back at the *beginning* of your main statement. *The book was autographed by Poe.* **It brought a high price.** Fill in the blank space: *Autographed by Poe,* _____ **brought a high price.** 848
b 1115	a. *Because Dale has a job,* **he takes more interest in his appearance.** b. *Now that Dale has a job,* **he takes more interest in his appearance.** Which sentence suggests that Dale's job is something recent? ——— 1116
	Running one sentence into another without a period (or other end mark) and a capital letter to separate them produces a **run-on** sentence. A run-on sentence is the opposite error of a sentence fragment. A fragment is less than a sentence; a run-on sentence is _____ than a sentence. 1384

Of course, when we are really speaking about *time* or *place*, it is permissible to use *is when* or *is where*.

    a. **Saturday** *is when* **the contest closes.**
    b. **A yearling** *is when* **an animal is one year old.**

In which sentence is the use of *is when* permissible? _____

1652

The following words are singular because they refer to only one person or thing at a time. They require singular verbs.

each	either	neither	any one
each one	either one	neither one	every one

Underline the correct verb:

        Each (*is, are*) **right.**

1919

---

a. **Smith then invested in an oil well in which he lost all his savings.**
b. **Smith then invested in an oil well in which he loses all his savings.**

Which sentence is correct? _____

2186

Children **love** *dogs.* (*Dogs* **love** *children.*)

When we turn this sentence around, do the nouns *children* and *dogs* change in form? (*Yes, No*)

2453

The word **graphics** is one of many English words derived from the Greek word *graphein*, meaning *to write*. We have, for example, *telegraph* (distance writing), *phonograph* (sound writing), and *graphite* (the "lead" in pencils).

The word **graphics,** therefore, applies to (*speaking, writing*).

2720

---

a. **"Nothing great,"** wrote Emerson, **"Was ever achieved without enthusiasm."**
b. **"Nothing great,"** wrote Emerson, **"was ever achieved without enthusiasm."**

2987

should 44	a. **Mary baked a cake.** b. **Mary could have baked a cake.** In sentence *a*, the main verb is used by itself. In sentence *b*, two helping verbs have been added to change its meaning—_____ and _____. 45
second 312	**Food became cheap and plentiful and the automobile came into common use.** A comma should be placed before the (*first, second*) **and.** 313
he 580	**A person is known by the company he keeps.** The "no signal" clause in this sentence consists of two words: _____ _____. 581
the book 848	Put a comma after any participial phrase that comes at the beginning of a sentence. a. *Located near a factory* **the store does a big business.** b. **We visited an old church** *built before the American Revolution.* Which sentence requires a comma? _____ 849
b 1116	In this and the following frames, subordinate the italicized statement by changing it to a "now that" clause: *Christmas is over,* **and life can return to normal.** _____, **life** **can return to normal.** 1117
more 1384	The writer of a run-on sentence doesn't know where a sentence ends. He is like an absent-minded person who reaches the end of a dock and keeps right on walking. WRONG: **The lights were dimmed the concert began.** Here one sentence runs into the next. The first sentence should end with the word _____. 1385

a 1652	a. **A pinch hitter** *is where* **one player bats for another.** b. **The city hall** *is where* **you register to vote.** In which sentence is the use of *is where* permissible? ____ <div align="right">1653</div>
is 1919	The words **each, either,** and **neither** can be used as either pronouns or adjectives. a. *Each* **is right.** *Either* **is right.** *Neither* **is right.** b. *Each* **one is right.** *Either* **answer is right.** *Neither* **answer is right.** The italicized words are used as adjectives in group (*a, b*). <div align="right">1920</div>
a 2186	When you tell a story, it is very easy to make the mistake of shifting back and forth between the past and the present tense. If you start to tell a story in the past tense, you should continue to use the _____ tense consistently throughout the entire story. <div align="right">2187</div>
No 2453	*I* **recognized** *him.* (*He* **recognized** *me.*) When we turn this sentence around, do the pronouns *I* and *him* change in form? (*Yes, No*) <div align="right">2454</div>
writing 2720	In the field of language, *graphics* means the devices that are used only in writing, not in speech. When we speak, is it possible to make an error in punctuation, capitalization, or spelling? (*Yes, No*) <div align="right">2721</div>
b 2987	a. **"We've had no rain," said the farmer. "Crops are drying up."** b. **"We've had no rain," said the farmer, "crops are drying up."** <div align="right">2988</div>

could, have
 	
45
	Learn to recognize these important helping verbs:
	
	HELPING VERBS: **shall, will** **may, can**
	                       could, would, should **must, might**
	          Paul _____ **study.**
	Could each of these helping verbs be used with the main verb **study?** *(Yes, No)*
	<div align="right">46</div>

second 313	**This paint doesn't show brush or roller marks and it dries quickly.** A comma should be placed before *(or, and)*. <div align="right">314</div>
he keeps 581	**The drawer was full of things nobody would ever want.** We could insert the clause signal *which* or *that* before the word _____ . <div align="right">582</div>

a
 	
849
	Put a comma before a participial phrase at the end of a sentence only if it modifies the subject at the beginning of the sentence.
	
	  a. **We stayed at a delightful inn** *operated by the state.*
	  b. **The audience grew restless** *bored by the long speech.*
	
	Which sentence requires a comma? _____
	<div align="right">850</div>

Now that Christmas is over, 1117	*Summer is here,* **and people are planning their vacations.** _____ **, people** **are planning their vacations.** <div align="right">1118</div>

dimmed
 	
1385
	In most run-on sentences, we find a comma between the two run-together sentences.
	
	  a. **After the lights were dimmed, the concert began.**
	  b. **The lights were dimmed, the concert began.**
	
	Which is a run-on sentence? _____
	<div align="right">1386</div>

b 1653	Be on guard against the *is when* and *is where* mistake whenever you are asked to point out the climax, turning point, surprise, or most interesting incident in a book or story. a. **The turning point was where Rita decided to become a nun.** b. **The turning point was Rita's decision to become a nun.** Which sentence is correct? _____ 1654
b 1920	a. <u>Each</u> <u>is</u> right. b. <u>Each</u> <u>one</u> <u>is</u> right. The subject of sentence *a* is the pronoun **Each.** The subject of sentence *b* is the pronoun _____. 1921
past (*or* same) 2187	The following student's summary of "The Necklace," a famous story by the French author Guy de Maupassant, is written mainly—but not entirely—in the past tense. Cross out each verb in the present tense and write the past form of the verb above it. If the sentence contains no error in tense, write *Correct.* (*Turn to the next frame.*) 2188
Yes 2454	NOUNS: *Children* **love** *dogs.* (*Dogs* **love** *children.*) PRONOUNS: *I* **recognized** *him.* (*He* **recognized** *me.*) The words that change in form when their use in the sentence changes are (*nouns, pronouns*). 2455
No 2721	a. **Omission of a capital** b. **Wrong form of verb** Which would be an error in graphics because it could occur only in writing? _____ 2722
a 2988	a. **My Uncle Dan remarked, "I much prefer living in a small town." "Everyone knows everyone else." "People have more time to be courteous and friendly."** b. **My Uncle Dan remarked, "I much prefer living in a small town. Everyone knows everyone else. People have more time to be courteous and friendly."** 2989

Yes 46	The three verbs below may serve as either *main verbs* or *helping verbs*. **be (is, am, are—was, were, been)** **have (has, had)** **do (does, did)** Which verb has the largest number of forms? _____ 47
and 314	**Mr. Sims had accumulated much money and property but he wasn't happy or contented.** A comma should be placed before (*and, but, or*). 315
nobody 582	**The drawer was full of things nobody would ever want.** The "no signal" adjective clause begins with the word _____ and ends with the word _____. 583
b 850	Combine each pair of sentences by changing the italicized sentence to a past participial phrase. Insert a comma wherever needed. **The trainer entered the cage.** *He was armed only with a whip.* _____ _____ 851
Now that summer is here, 1118	*We have spent all our money,* **and we might as well go home.** _____ _____, **we might as well go home.** 1119
b 1386	**The lights were dimmed, and the concert began.** This is *not* a run-on sentence. It is a correct compound sentence formed by combining two simple sentences with the conjunction _____. 1387

b
 	
1654
	Since words such as *climax, turning point, surprise,* and *incident* are nouns, they are best explained by other nouns or gerunds (verbal nouns ending in *-ing*).
	
	  a. **The climax** *was when* **Velvet won the National Derby.**
	  b. **The climax was Velvet's** *victory* **in the National Derby.**
	
	In which sentence is **climax** explained by a noun? _____
	<div align="right">1655</div>

one 1921	<table><tr><td>**each**</td><td>**either**</td><td>**neither**</td><td>**any one**</td></tr><tr><td>**each one**</td><td>**either one**</td><td>**neither one**</td><td>**every one**</td></tr></table>Watch your verb closely when an "of" phrase follows any of these words. A plural verb often tries to slip itself in. <div align="center">**Each one of the answers is right.**</div> The subject of this sentence is (*one, answers*).<div align="right">1922</div>
  2188	Continue to follow the directions for the previous frame: **Mathilde was a pretty French girl who was married to a poor but pleasant clerk in the government service.** <div align="right">2189</div>
pronouns 2455	The change in form of pronouns to show their relationship to other words in the sentence is called **case.** <div align="center">*I* **recognized** *him. He* **recognized** *me.*</div> *I* in sentence *a* and *me* in sentence *b* mean the same person. Are the pronouns *I* and *me* in the same case? (*Yes, No*)<div align="right">2456</div>
a 2722	In this first lesson on graphics, we review the use of the comma in compound sentences. A compound sentence consists of two (or more) main clauses joined by the conjunction **and, but,** or **or.** In a compound sentence there are a subject and a predicate both before and after the _____<div align="right">2723</div>
b 2989	In the remaining frames, punctuate each sentence and supply capitals where necessary. Remember that commas and periods always come *before,* not *after,* quotation marks. **A sign along the highway said remember, telephone poles hit people only in self-defense.**<div align="right">2990</div>

be 47	a. **The <u>weather</u> <u>is</u> bad.** b. **The <u>weather</u> <u>is</u> improving.** Does **is** serve as a helping verb in sentence *a* or *b*? _____ 48
but 315	A sentence that can be separated into two parts—a subject and a predicate—is a (*simple, compound*) sentence. 316
...obody . . . want 583	Now let's review some of the things we have learned about adjective clauses in this and the previous lesson. a. An adjective clause is one that does the work of a single adjective. b. An adjective clause is one that begins with an adjective. Which definition of an adjective clause is correct? _____ 584
The trainer entered the cage, armed only with a whip. 851	Continue to follow the directions for the previous frame: *Baseball was invented by Abner Doubleday in 1839.* **It soon became a favorite sport.** _____ _____ 852
Now that we have spent all our money, 1119	*Mr. Bilby has explained the problem,* **and it seems very simple.** _____ _____, **it seems very simple.** 1120
and 1387	There is another correct way of combining two simple sentences into a compound sentence. **The lights were dimmed; the concert began.** Instead of using the conjunction *and* to combine two simple sentences, we may use a _____. 1388

b 1655	a. **The climax was Velvet's** *winning* **of the National Derby.** b. **The climax** *was when* **Velvet won the National Derby.** In which sentence is **climax** explained by a gerund (a verbal noun ending in *-ing*)? _____ 1656
one 1922	**Each one of the answers . . . right.** We pay no attention to the plural noun **answers** when we select the missing verb. The noun **answers** is not the subject of the sentence but the object of the preposition _____. 1923
Correct 2189	**Because of his small income, her husband is not able to give her the life of luxury and romance for which she had always yearned.** 2190
No 2456	*I* **recognized** *him.* *He* **recognized** *me.* The pronoun *him* in sentence *a* and the pronoun *He* in sentence *b* mean the same thing. Are the pronouns *him* and *He* in the same case? (*Yes, No*) 2457
conjunction 2723	In the following diagrams, a single line represents the subject and a double line the predicate. a. _____ _____ , **and** _____ _____. b. _____ _____ **and** _____. Which diagram represents a compound sentence? _____ 2724
said, "Remember . . . self-defense." 2990	**Education is much more than studying books began the speaker.** 2991

b 48	a. **I have brought my camera along.** b. **I have my camera with me.** Is **have** used as a helping verb in sentence *a* or *b?* _____ 49
simple 316	A compound sentence can be formed by combining two simple sentences with a _____. 317
a 584	An adjective clause, like an adjective, modifies a _____ or a pronoun. 585
Invented by Abner Doubleday in 1839, baseball soon became a favorite sport. 852	**Todd interrupted the pass.** *It was intended for Sanders.* _____ _____ 853
Now that Mr. Bilby has explained the problem, 1120	*We have moved to the city,* **and we miss our farm very much.** _____, **we miss our farm very much.** 1121
semicolon 1388	WRONG: **The lights were dimmed, the concert began.** This sentence is wrong because there is neither a conjunction nor a semicolon to connect the two sentences. Does a comma by itself have the power to connect two simple sentences? (*Yes, No*) 1389

a 1656	a. **The climax was where the tea was dumped into Boston Harbor.** b. **The climax was the dumping of the tea into Boston Harbor.** Which sentence is correct? _____ 1657
of 1923	**Either one of these recipes** (*make, makes*) **a good cake.** We select the verb _____ to agree with the subject _____. 1924
was ~~is~~ 2190	**One day he joyously brings home an invitation to a fancy ball.** 2191
No 2457	A pronoun is in the **nominative case** when it fits *before* an action verb as its subject—*he* laughed; *she* fell; *we* won; *they* lost. Underline the nominative pronoun: *They* **blamed** *us*. 2458
a 2724	a. **John gets high grades and plans to attend college.** b. **John gets high grades, and his teachers urge him to attend college.** Which sentence is compound because there are a subject and a predicate both before and after the conjunction? _____ 2725
"Education . . . books," began the speaker. 2991	**The greatest problem of mankind said Albert Einstein is man himself** 2992

a	a. **Betty did the dishes.** b. **Yes, Betty did wash the dishes.** Is **did** used as a helping verb in sentence *a* or *b*? _____
49	50
conjunction	The three most common conjunctions are *and*, _____, and *or*.
317	318
noun	An adjective clause always comes (*before, after*) the word it modifies.
585	586
Todd interrupted the pass intended for Sanders.	*The candidate was questioned about his policies.* **He gave only vague answers.** _____ _____
853	854
Now that we have moved to the city,	Another unusual type of adverb clause can sometimes be used very effectively in place of an "although" clause. *Cheap as it is,* **the car is no bargain.** This adverb clause is unusual because instead of beginning with a clause signal, it begins with (*a verb, an adjective*).
1121	1122
No	When we incorrectly combine two simple sentences by means of a comma, we produce a _____ sentence, which is considered just as serious an error as a fragment.
1389	1390

b 1657	The coincidence *was when* the brothers met in a German prison camp. Correct the above sentence by writing a gerund in the blank space: The coincidence was the _____ of the brothers in a German prison camp. <div align="right">1658</div>

(verb) makes
(subject) one
 	
1924
	Supply the correct verb in sentence *b*, paying no attention to the object of the preposition.
	
	    a. **Neither fits me.**
	    b. **Neither of the coats** _____ **me.**
	
	<div align="right">1925</div>

brought <s>brings</s> 2191	His wife, however, was not happy because she lacks suitable clothes for such an affair. <div align="right">2192</div>
They 2458	<div align="center">. . . invited John.</div> Underline three pronouns that are in the nominative case because they could serve as the subject in the sentence above: **I** **him** **she** **we** **them** **her** <div align="right">2459</div>
b 2725	Use a comma generally before the conjunction **and, but,** or **or** in a compound sentence. The comma gives each part greater distinctness and makes the sentence easier to read. Insert the necessary comma: **We had only five minutes to play and every second counted.** <div align="right">2726</div>
"The . . . mankind," said Albert Einstein, "is man himself." 2992	**The coffee wasn't too strong commented Uncle Pete the people were just too weak.** <div align="right">2993</div>

b 50	a. I <u>have studied</u> my lesson. b. I <u>should have studied</u> my lesson. c. I <u>should have been studying</u> my lesson. In which sentence does the verb have the largest number of helping verbs? _____ <div align="right">51</div>
but 318	Should a comma be placed before the conjunction that connects the two parts of a compound predicate? (*Yes, No*) <div align="right">319</div>
after 586	If a clause can be shifted from one position to another in a sentence, it is an (*adjective, adverb*) clause. <div align="right">587</div>
Questioned about his policies, the candidate gave only vague answers. 854	*The bandit was surrounded by police.* **He gave himself up.** _____ _____ <div align="right">855</div>
an adjective 1122	a. *although it is cheap* b. *cheap as it is* In which clause is the subject complement *cheap* not in its normal position? _____ <div align="right">1123</div>
run-on 1390	Let us look into a common cause of the sentence collisions that we call run-on sentences. **The <u>motor</u> <u>was wet.</u> The <u>motor</u> <u>refused</u> to start.** Here we have two separate sentences, each with its own _____ and verb. <div align="right">1391</div>

meeting 1658	A simple way to avoid the *is when* or *is where* error is to use such a verb as *occurred, happened,* or *took place,* thus supplying an action verb that your "when" clause can modify. a. **The climax occurred when the submarine was grounded.** b. **The climax was when the submarine was grounded.** Which sentence is correct? _____ 1659
fits 1925	Supply the correct verb in sentence *b,* paying no attention to the object of the preposition. a. **Every one needs washing.** b. **Every one of the windows _____ washing.** 1926
lacked ~~lacks~~ 2192	**Although her husband gave up buying a gun in order to finance a new dress, she was still unhappy because she had no jewels to wear.** 2193
I, she, we 2459	A pronoun is in the **objective case** when it fits *after* an action verb as its direct object—pushed *me;* stopped *him;* asked *her;* beat *us;* called *them.* Underline the objective pronoun: *They* **blamed** *us.* 2460
play, and 2726	Insert the necessary comma: **His eyes were closed but he wasn't sleeping.** 2727
"The . . . strong," commented Uncle Pete. "The . . . weak." 2993	**Miss Morris said, Never offer too many excuses. Too many excuses make people suspicious. People are more likely to believe a single excuse.** 2994

The driver should have been watching the road.

c

The three helping verbs in this frame are _____, _____, and _____.

51

52

No

In a compound sentence, there are a subject and verb both before and after the conjunction. (*True, False*)

319

320

---

adverb

The adjective clause signals **who (whose, whom), which,** and **that** are called *relative* (*adjectives, pronouns*).

587

588

Surrounded by police, the bandit gave himself up.

Eliminate the **and** by changing the italicized statement to a past participial phrase. Insert a comma wherever needed.

The car was forced off the road **and went into a ditch.**

_____

_____

855

856

---

b

a. *cheap as it is*
b. *although it is cheap*

In which clause does the adjective *cheap* occupy a more prominent position? _____

1123

1124

---

subject

It
The motor was wet. ~~The motor~~ **refused to start.**

Since we are still talking about the motor, we do not need to repeat the noun **motor** in the second sentence.

We therefore put the pronoun _____ in place of the noun **motor** as the subject of the second sentence.

1391

1392

a

1659

The turning point *was when* **Silas Marner found Eppie on the hearth.**

This sentence can be corrected by substituting the verb

_____ for the verb **was.**

1660

---

needs

1926

Singular subjects joined by **and** are plural and require a plural verb.

Underline the correct verb:

The air *and* **the water** (*was, were*) **perfect for swimming.**

1927

Correct

2193

She solves her problem by borrowing a diamond necklace from a friend in better circumstances.

2194

---

us

2460

John invited . . .

Underline three pronouns that are in the objective case because they could serve as the direct object in the sentence above:

I   him   we   she   them   her

2461

---

closed, but

2727

Insert the necessary comma:

The clothes must be slightly damp or the wrinkles will not iron out.

2728

Miss Morris said, "Never . . . a single excuse."

2994

Lesson 84 When Quotations Are Questions

[Frames 2996–3028]

should, have, been 52	The *complete* verb in any sentence includes the main verb plus whatever helping verbs it may have. **The driver should have been watching the road.** The *complete* verb in this sentence consists of _____ words. (How many?) 53
True 320	In a compound sentence, the comma should be placed (*before, after*) the conjunction. 321
pronouns 588	When we omit an adjective clause from a sentence, a grammatically (*complete, incomplete*) sentence remains. 589
Forced off the road, the car went into a ditch. 856	Follow the directions given in the previous frame: **A crowd gathered around the excavation, and** *they were fascinated by the steam shovel.* _____ _____ 857
a 1124	a. *Although it is cheap,* **the car is no bargain.** b. *Cheap as it is,* **the car is no bargain.** In which sentence does the clause give more emphasis to the *cheapness* of the price? _____ 1125
It 1392	a. **The motor refused to start.** b. **It refused to start.** Both *a* and *b* are complete sentences. If you were writing only one sentence in isolation, which sentence would you write? _____ 1393

Any one of the following verbs: occurred, took place, came (about) 1660	**The climax** *was when* **Banquo's ghost appeared at the banquet.** Fill in the blank so as to avoid the *was when* construction: **The climax** _____ **when Banquo's ghost appeared at the banquet.** 1661
were 1927	Underline the correct verb: **Her face** *and* **her way of talking** (*remind, reminds*) **me of you.** 1928
solved ~~solves~~ 2194	**After making a great hit at the ball because of her clothes and her beauty, she found, when she arrives home, that the necklace is gone.** 2195
him, them, her 2461	a. **I** **he** **she** **we** **they** b. **me** **him** **her** **us** **them** Which group consists of objective pronouns? _____ 2462
damp, or 2728	**The pilot received a storm warning, and** *he* **moved up to a higher altitude.** If you omitted the italicized pronoun *he* from this compound sentence, would you still retain the comma? (*Yes, No*) 2729
	When a quotation asks a question, you first decide whether you are stating the actual words of the question or merely reporting in your own words what was asked. When you repeat the actual words of the question, your quotation is (*direct, indirect*). 2996

We shall now, for a moment, need to turn our attention to **adverbs,** which most commonly modify verbs.

This has happened frequently.

Because **frequently** modifies the verb **has happened,** it is an

_____.

54

Lesson 9 The Proper Use of the Compound Sentence

[Frames 323–356]

Is a relative pronoun always the first word in an adjective clause? (*Yes, No*)

590

A crowd
gathered around
the excavation,
fascinated by the
steam shovel.
857

The article was written hastily **and contained many inaccuracies.**

_____

_____

858

---

a. *Large as the house is,* **we find it too small for our family.**
b. *Although the house is large,* **we find it too small for our family.**

In which sentence does the clause give more emphasis to the *largeness* of the house? _____

1126

---

a. **The motor refused to start.**
b. **It refused to start.**

If the sentence were to follow another sentence that had already mentioned the **motor,** which sentence would you write? _____

1394

Any one of the following verbs: occurred, took place, came (about) 1661	**The climax** *was* *when* **Banquo's ghost appeared at the banquet.** Fill in the blank so as to avoid the *was* *when* construction: **The climax was the** _____ **of Banquo's** **ghost at the banquet.** 1662
remind 1928	When the two singular subjects joined by **and** mean the same person or thing, a singular verb is proper. a. **The owner** *and* **manager is Mr. Harris.** b. **The owner** *and* **the manager is pleased with each other.** In which sentence is the singular verb **is** correct? _____ 1929
arrived <s>arrives</s> was <s>is</s> 2195	**By going hopelessly into debt, they buy another necklace to replace the one they had lost.** 2196
b 2462	*You* **saw** *it.* (*It* **saw** *you.*) Do the pronouns *You* and *it* change in form when we turn this sentence around? (*Yes, No*) 2463
No 2729	**Coach Blair moved some of his boys around and** ∧ **put several new players into the game.** If you added *he* at the point indicated, would you insert a comma after the word **around?** (*Yes, No*) 2730
direct 2996	a. **Leroy asked, "Where's my ticket?"** b. **Leroy asked where his ticket was.** In which sentence is the question a direct quotation? _____ 2997

adverb 54	a. **This has happened frequently.** b. **This has frequently happened.** In which sentence does the adverb **frequently** break into or interrupt the verb? _____ 55
	A compound sentence is very easy to make. We merely need to combine two simple sentences by using one of these conjunctions: *and,* _____, or _____. 323
No 590	Does an adjective clause always contain a relative pronoun? (*Yes, No*) 591
Written hastily, the article contained many inaccuracies. 858	**Mr. Lee owns a sports car, and** *it was imported from Italy.* _____ _____ 859
a 1126	Sometimes this type of clause begins with an adverb shifted from its usual position at the end of the sentence. a. *Although we came early,* **we got poor seats.** b. *Early as we came,* **we got poor seats.** In which sentence does the clause give more emphasis to the adverb *early?* _____ 1127
b 1394	**The motor was wet. It refused to start.** **It refused to start** is a complete sentence because the reader knows from the previous sentence that the word **It** means _____. 1395

appearance *or* appearing 1662	**The turning point** *is when* **Coach Perry takes charge of the team.** Eliminate the *is when* construction: _____ **when** **Coach Perry takes charge of the team.** 1663

a
 	
1929
	If the two singular subjects joined by **and** are thought of as a single unit, use a singular verb.
	
	    a. **Tea** *and* **coffee is served with every meal.**
	    b. **Bread** *and* **butter is served with every meal.**
	
	In which sentence is the singular verb **is** correct? _____
	
	                                                           1930

bought ~~buy~~ 2196	**For ten years they lived in attics and scrimped and struggled to pay off their enormous debt.** 2197
No 2463	*You* **saw** *it. It* **saw** *you.* Do *you* and *it*—like the other pronouns—have different forms for the nominative and objective case? (*Yes, No*) 2464

Yes
 	
2730
	a. **Our dog often runs away, but he always comes back.**
	    b. **Our dog often runs away, but always comes back.**
	
	From which sentence should the comma be dropped? _____
	
	                                                           2731

a 2997	When you do not repeat the actual words of the question but report it in your own words, your quotation is (*direct, indirect*). 2998

b 55	a. **The game will soon start.** b. **The game will start soon.** In which sentence does the adverb come between the main verb and its helper? _____ 56
but, or 323	Because compound sentences are so easy to make, we must avoid overusing them. Use a compound sentence to combine only *similar* or *related* ideas that are of equal importance. **I study Spanish, and our school has a swimming pool.** Should these two ideas have been combined? (*Yes, No*) 324
No 591	Lesson **16** Choosing Your Relatives [Frames 593–633]
Mr. Lee owns a sports car imported from Italy. 859	*Small boats were warned by the Coast Guard* **and headed for shore.** _____ _____ 860
b 1127	In this and the following frames, make each "although" clause more emphatic by beginning it with an adjective or an adverb: *Although I replied courteously,* **Don took offense.** _____**, Don** **took offense.** 1128
motor 1395	You need have no hesitation in starting a new sentence with the pronoun **It.** Don't let this pronoun trick you into making a run-on sentence error. a. **The motor was wet, it wouldn't start.** b. **The motor was wet. It wouldn't start.** Which is correct? _____ 1396

The turning point occurs (takes place, comes, comes about) 1663	**The turning point** *is where* **Coach Perry takes charge of the team.** Eliminate the *is where* construction: **The turning point is Coach Perry's** _____ **charge of the team.** 1664

b
 	
 1930
	A phrase introduced by **with, along with, together with,** or **as well as** often follows the subject. Do not mistake the noun in such a phrase for part of the subject.
	
	     a. **Mr. Davis and his son are in Alaska.**
	     b. **Mr. Davis, with his son, are in Alaska.**
	
	 In which sentence is the plural verb **are** correct? _____
	
	 1931

Correct 2197	**In the meantime, she loses her beauty and becomes so plain and worn that no one could have recognized her for the beautiful girl she once had been.** 2198
No 2464	Use the nominative case of a pronoun when it is used as the subject of a verb. Underline the correct pronoun: **You and** (*I, me*) **can study together.** (*Note:* The use of the nominative case after forms of the verb **be** will be studied in the following lesson.) 2465
b 2731	a. **New words may become part of our language or they may soon disappear.** b. **New words may become part of our language or may soon disappear.** In which sentence should a comma be inserted after the word **language?** _____ 2732
indirect 2998	**Leroy asked** *where his ticket was.* Are the italicized words the actual words of a question? (*Yes, No*) 2999

One should immediately try artificial respiration.

a

What adverb comes between the main verb and its helper?

_____

56

57

No

a. **I study Spanish, and our school has a swimming pool.**
b. **I study Spanish, and Carol studies French.**

Which compound sentence is better because the ideas are

similar? _____

324

325

Here again are the **relative pronouns** that are used as clause signals to start adjective clauses.

RELATIVE PRONOUNS: **who (whose, whom), which, that**

Are these the same clause signals that start adverb clauses? (*Yes, No*)

593

Warned by the
Coast Guard,
small boats
headed for
shore.

a. **hearing, intending, thinking, falling**
b. **filled, sold, spoken, worn, spent, followed**

Which group of words could be used as past participles?

_____

860

861

Courteously as
I replied,

I had to finish my theme, *although it was late.*

I had to finish my theme, _____.

1128

1129

---

b

Sentences may begin with other pronouns, too.

She will watch the baby.

This is a (*fragment, sentence*).

1396

1397

taking 1664	In this and the following frames, fill in the blank space so as to eliminate the *is when* or *is where* construction: **A pinch hitter is where one player bats for another.** **A pinch hitter** _____ **who bats for another.** 1665

a
 	
1931
	By shifting the prepositional phrase to the end of this sentence, we see that the noun **son** is not part of the subject.
	
	      Mr. Davis, *with his son,* **is in Alaska.**
	      Mr. Davis is in Alaska *with his son.*
	
	This sentence has only one subject, which is _____.
	
	1932

lost ~~loses~~ became ~~becomes~~ 2198	**One day she happens to meet the friend who had lent her the unlucky necklace that had brought them so much misfortune.** 2199
I 2465	Use the objective case of a pronoun when it is used as the object of a verb or a preposition. Underline the correct pronouns: **Several friends save** (*them, they*) **for** (*me, I*). 2466
a 2732	A compound sentence without a comma might sometimes be misread. **We found it too expensive to stay at hotels and motor courts were hard to find.** We can prevent the misreading of this compound sentence by inserting a comma after _____. 2733
No 2999	**Leroy asked** *where his ticket was.* Since the italicized words are not the actual words of a question, do we need to use either a question mark or quotes? (*Yes, No*) 3000

immediately 57	There is something else besides adverbs that can separate a main verb from its helper. STATEMENT: **Judy can drive.** QUESTION: **Can Judy drive?** The verb **can drive** is interrupted in the (*statement, question*). _____ 58
b 325	a. **The road was muddy, and we bought eggs at a farm.** b. **The road was muddy, and we got stuck several times.** Which compound sentence is better because the ideas are related? _____ 326
No 593	Use **who, whose,** and **whom** to refer only to *people.* Underline the correct relative pronoun: **The clerk** (*who, which*) **took my order made a mistake in the bill.** 594
b 861	A phrase built on either a present or a past participle is used as an _____ to modify a noun or pronoun. 862
late as it was. 1129	*Although we tried hard,* **we couldn't make a touchdown.** _____, **we couldn't make a touchdown.** 1130
sentence 1397	a. **Vicky is staying home today. She will watch the baby.** b. **Vicky is staying home today, she will watch the baby.** Which is correct? _____ 1398

is a player	Arson is when someone commits the crime of willfully setting fire to property.
	Arson _____ of willfully setting fire to property.
1665	1666
Mr. Davis	a. **The camera, together with the case, sell for $39.**
	b. **The camera and the case sell for $39.**
	In which sentence is the plural verb **sell** incorrect? _____
1932	1933
happened ~~happens~~	Now that they had finally got out of debt, she decides to tell her friend how she had lost the borrowed necklace and had supplied a substitute for which she had paid such a great price.
2199	2200
them, me	Pronoun errors occur most often when pronouns are used in pairs or when a noun and a pronoun are coupled together.
	a. *He* **refereed the game.**
	b. **Frank and** (*he, him*) **refereed the game.**
	In sentence *b*, which pronoun is correct? _____
2466	2467
hotels	Commas are generally omitted in short compound sentences. The reader can find his way without their help.
	a. **British humor depends on understatement** *but* **American humor is based largely on exaggeration.**
	b. **I knocked** *but* **no one answered.**
	Which compound sentence does not require a comma? _____
2733	2734
No	Punctuation is omitted from the following sentences to avoid revealing the answer.
	a. **The child asked whether our dog bites**
	b. **The child asked Does your dog bite**
	Which sentence contains an indirect question, which requires neither a question mark nor quotes? _____
3000	3001

question 58	STATEMENT: **Dad will want the car tonight.** QUESTION: **Will Dad want the car tonight?** The verb **will want** is interrupted in the (*statement, question*). 59
· b 326	**Our tree is small. It gives very little shade.** Because there is a relationship between the size of a tree and the amount of shade, these sentences would make a (*good, poor*) compound sentence. 327
who 594	Use **which** to refer only to *things* and *animals*. Underline the correct relative pronoun: **The store** (*who, which*) **sells these games is making a fortune.** 595
adjective 862	a. **Frank was raised on a farm.** b. **He knew the problems of the farmer.** Which sentence could be changed to a past participial phrase? _____ 863
Hard as we tried, 1130	In the remaining frames, subordinate each italicized statement by changing it to an adverb clause beginning with an adjective or an adverb. *Webb is able,* **but he is not able enough for this job.** _____, **he is not able enough for this job.** 1131
a 1398	a. **Many advertisements do not state the total price, they merely state the monthly payments.** b. **Many advertisements do not state the total price. They merely state the monthly payments.** Which is correct? _____ 1399

is the crime

1666

Osmosis is where plants absorb moisture from the soil.

Osmosis is the process by which _____

_____ .

1667

---

a

1933

Underline the correct verb:

A tennis court, as well as a swimming pool, (*is, are*) available to guests.

1934

---

decided
~~decides~~

2200

"Oh, my poor Mathilde!" her friend gasps with amazement. "Why, that necklace I lent you was only paste!"

(*End of story*)

2201

---

he

2467

You would never say, "*Him* pushed the car" or "*Me* pushed the car"; so don't make the same mistake by saying, "*Him* and *me* pushed the car."

Underline the correct pronouns:

(*He, Him*) and (*I, me*) **counted the votes.**

2468

---

b

2734

A short compound sentence does not need to be broken into shorter units for the convenience of the reader.

a. **Several parents complained about overcrowding in the schools** *and* **the mayor agreed to take immediate action.**
b. **They rode** *and* **we walked.**

In which sentence would you use a comma before *and*? _____

2735

---

a

3001

Now let's look at a question that is quoted directly:

Leroy asked, "Where's my ticket?"

To show that the quotation is a question, we put the question mark (*inside, outside*) the quotes.

3002

question 59	**Will Dad want the car tonight?** The main verb **want** is separated from its helper **will** by the subject _____. 60
good 327	**Our tree is small. We bought it at a nursery.** Although both these sentences are about a tree, they have little relationship to each other. Therefore, they would make a (*good, poor*) compound sentence. 328
which 595	Underline the correct relative pronoun: **It was the Rosses' dog (*which, who*) tore up our flower bed.** 596
a 863	Lesson **23** Making Use of Gerunds [Frames 865–902]
Able as Webb is, 1131	*Mr. Gross was angry,* **but he didn't show his temper.** _____ , **he didn't show his temper.** 1132
b 1399	a. **Jerry was smiling in a peculiar way. He had apparently been up to some mischief.** b. **Jerry was smiling in a peculiar way, he had apparently been up to some mischief.** Which is correct? _____ 1400

plants absorb moisture from the soil. 1667	The climax is when Tina reveals family secrets on a children's television program. The climax _____ when Tina reveals family secrets on a children's television program. 1668

is
 	
1934
	Singular subjects joined by **or** or **nor** are singular and require a singular verb.
	
	      a. **A doctor** *and* **a nurse ...**
	      b. **A doctor** *or* **a nurse ...**
	
	Which subject is singular because it means only one person —*a* or *b?* _____
	
	1935

gasped
~~gasps~~
 	
2201
	Use the present tense to state facts that are permanently true—for example, the facts of science, mathematics, geography, etc.
	
	      a. **There** *are* **eight quarts in a peck.**
	      b. **There** *are* **eight people in the car.**
	
	Which sentence states a permanent truth? _____
	
	2202

He, I
 	
2468
	When you use pronouns in pairs or when you couple a pronoun with a noun, use the same case that you would use if the pronouns were used singly.
	
	  These flowers are from *Pete.* **These flowers are from** *me.*
	
	Underline the correct pronoun:
	
	    These flowers are from *Pete* **and** (*I, me*).
	
	2469

a 2735	Do not mistake a sentence with a compound predicate for a compound sentence. **The manager <u>was pleased</u>** *and* **<u>raised my salary.</u>** The above sentence is not compound because there is no (*subject, predicate*) after the conjunction *and.* 2736
inside 3002	a. **Roberta asked, "Is this poison ivy"?** b. **Roberta asked, "Is this poison ivy?"** In which sentence is the question mark properly placed to show that the question is a quotation? _____ 3003

Dad 60	Most of the questions we ask begin with a *helping verb*. a. **Will this pen write?** c. **Who borrowed my book?** b. **Is the water boiling?** d. **Does Tom like spinach?** Which is the only one of the above questions that does not begin with a helping verb? _____ 61
poor 328	a. **Our tree is small, and it gives very little shade.** b. **Our tree is small, and we bought it at a nursery.** Which compound sentence is better? _____ 329
which 596	Use **that** to refer to anything—*people, things,* or *animals.* Underline the correct relative pronoun: **Marian wrote a theme about the teacher (*which, that*) had helped her most.** 597
	Present and past participles, as we have seen, are forms of verbs that serve as adjectives. Now we look at verbs that have crossed over into noun territory. **Tennis is good exercise.** *Tennis* is an ordinary noun. It is the subject of the verb _____. 865
Angry as Mr. Gross was, 1132	*The material cost of war is great,* **but the human cost is infinitely greater.** _____, **the human cost is infinitely greater.** 1133
a 1400	A sentence may begin with a pronoun such as *it, he, she,* or *they* even though the noun that the pronoun stands for is in another sentence. (*True, False*) 1401

occurs (takes place, comes, comes about) 1668	**To baste is when you sew with long, loose, temporary stitches.** **To baste is** _____ **with long, loose, temporary stitches.** (*Note:* Don't forget the principle of parallel construction.) <div align="right">1669</div>
b 1935	Underline the correct verb: **A doctor or a nurse** (*is, are*) **always on hand.** <div align="right">1936</div>
a 2202	a. **There** *are* **eight quarts in a peck.** b. **There** *were* **eight quarts in a peck.** In which sentence is the tense of the verb wrong? _____ <div align="right">2203</div>

me
 	
 2469
	You can't blame the *Kirks* **for objecting.**
	    You can't blame *them* **for objecting.**
	
	Underline the correct pronoun:
	
	    You can't blame the *Kirks* **or** (*them, they*) **for objecting.**
	
	<div align="right">2470</div>

subject
 	
 2736
	Do not ordinarily use a comma before the conjunction that connects the two parts of a compound predicate.
	
	    a. **Gary left his salad, but ate his dessert.**
	    b. **Gary left his salad, but he ate his dessert.**
	
	From which sentence should the comma be omitted?
	
	<div align="right">2737</div>

b 3003	Now we shall put the same question at the beginning of the sentence: **"Is this poison ivy?" asked Roberta.** When the quotation is a question, is a comma used between the question and the rest of the sentence? (*Yes, No*) <div align="right">3004</div>

c
 	
61
	A helping verb at the beginning of a sentence is the signal that a question is coming.
	
	    a. **Will this pen write?**
	    b. **Does Tom like spinach?**
	
	In each of these questions, we find the subject between the two parts of the _____.
	
	              62

a 329	The two parts of a compound sentence should be *equal in importance*. **The Mercers have a dog, and it is brown.** The fact that the dog is brown is much less important than the fact that the Mercers have a dog. Is this a good compound sentence? (*Yes, No*) 330

that
 	
597
	The main point to remember is never to use **which** to refer to *people*.
	
	Underline the correct relative pronoun:
	
	    citizens (*who, which*)
	
	              598

is 865	*Tennis* **is good exercise.** *Walking* **is good exercise.** Both *Tennis* and *Walking* are nouns used as subjects of the verb **is.** Which one of these two italicized nouns was formed from a verb? _____ 866
Great as the material cost of war is, 1133	Lesson **30** **Two Useful Adjective Clause Devices** [Frames 1135–1161]

True
 	
1401
	There are several methods of correcting a run-on sentence.
	
	    WRONG: **I approached the squirrel, it ran away.**
	    RIGHT: **I approached the squirrel. It ran away.**
	
	1. Separate the run-together sentences by using a period and a _____. 1402

to sew 1669	The turning point is where Jabez went to Daniel Webster for help. The turning point _____ Jabez went to Daniel Webster for help. 1670
is 1936	Mother *and* Elsie do the dishes. If you changed *and* to *or,* would you need also to change the verb **do?** (*Yes, No*) 1937
b 2203	When a fact permanently true follows an expression in the past tense such as "I didn't know that . . ." or "I forgot that . . . ," you might feel a strong pull to state this fact in the past, instead of the present, tense. **I forgot that there *were* eight quarts in a peck.** Is the verb *were* in the proper tense? (*Yes, No*) 2204
them 2470	The *Smiths* will call for you. *We* will call for you. Underline the correct pronoun: **The *Smiths* or (*us, we*) will call for you.** 2471
a 2737	a. **Shall we buy a new car or shall we repair the old one?** b. **Shall we buy a new car or repair the old one?** Which sentence requires a comma? _____ 2738
No 3004	**"Is this poison ivy?" asked Roberta.** The question mark is placed at the end of the (*question, sentence*). 3005

verb 62	**Does this key fit?** The verb in this sentence consists of the two words: _____ _____ . 63
No 330	a. **The Mercers have a brown dog.** b. **The Mercers have a dog, and it is brown.** Sentence *a* is a *simple* sentence; sentence *b* is a *compound* sentence. The sentence which is better because it doesn't give too much importance to the color of the dog is the (*simple, compound*) sentence. 331
who 598	Underline the correct relative pronoun: **the horse** (*who, which*) 599
Walking 866	*Walking* **is good exercise.** The noun *Walking* was formed by adding _____ to the verb *walk*. 867
	A special type of adjective clause is useful when you wish to state a fact about only a *part* or a *number* of a larger group. **Gloria has three sisters,** *one of whom is a nurse.* The adjective clause states a fact about (*all, one*) of the sisters. 1135
capital 1402	WRONG: **I approached the squirrel, it ran away.** RIGHT: **I approached the squirrel, and it ran away.** 2. Correct the run-on sentence by adding the conjunction _____ . 1403

occurred (took place, came, came about) when 1670	**A straw vote is when an unofficial vote is taken to find out public opinion.** **A straw vote** _____ **taken to find out public opinion.** 1671
Yes 1937	a. **Mother and Elsie do the dishes.** b. **Mother or Elsie do the dishes.** In which sentence is the plural verb **do** incorrect? _____ 1938
No 2204	**I** _forgot_ **that there** _were_ **eight quarts in a peck.** It is the verb _forgot_ in the past tense that influenced the writer of this sentence to use the past tense _were_ to express the permanent truth, instead of the present tense _____. 2205
we 2471	**The reporter snapped a picture of** _her._ **The reporter snapped a picture of** _me._ Underline the correct pronouns: **The reporter snapped a picture of** (_her, she_) **and** (_I, me_). 2472
a 2738	In this and the following frames, insert any necessary commas. If no comma is required, write _None._ **Sue's arm was around the collie's neck and the dog was licking her face affectionately.** 2739
question 3005	When the question comes first, be sure to put the question mark at the end of the question, not at the end of the sentence. a. **"What are we having for dinner?" questioned Don.** b. **"What are we having for dinner," questioned Don?** The question mark is properly placed in sentence (_a, b_). 3006

Does fit 63	**Must the tire be changed?** The verb in this sentence consists of the three words: _____ _____ _____. 64
simple 331	**We have an old apple tree, and it is in our back yard.** Is the second idea equal in importance to the first? (*Yes, No*) 332
which 599	Underline the correct relative pronoun: **any doctor** (*which, that*) 600
ing 867	A noun that is formed by adding -*ing* to a verb is called a **gerund** (pronounced *jare-und*). We can turn any verb into a gerund by adding -*ing* to it (sometimes making minor changes in the spelling). The gerund form of the verb *cook* is _____. 868
one 1135	**Along the coast are many small islands,** *some of which are uninhabited.* The clause states a fact about (*some, all*) of the islands. 1136
and 1403	WRONG: **I approached the squirrel, it ran away.** RIGHT: **I approached the squirrel; it ran away.** 3. The third way to correct a run-on sentence is to insert a _____. 1404

The surprise is where the father demands that the kidnappers pay him to take back his rowdy son.

The surprise is the father's _____ that the kidnappers pay him to take back his rowdy son.

1672

Underline the correct verb:

A thick hedge or a high wall (*give, gives*) a feeling of privacy.

1939

I forgot that there were eight quarts in a peck.

Although this sentence is acceptable in colloquial (conversational) English, it does not meet the more rigid standards of formal speech or writing, which require that a fact that is permanently true should be stated in the (*present, past*) tense.

2206

The *Whittens* and *we* were the first to arrive.

This sentence is correct because if we used each subject separately, we would say:

> **The *Whittens* were the first to arrive.**
> **(*Us, We*) were the first to arrive.**

2473

The waves pound the rocks and gradually break them up into sand.

2740

Here is another type of problem:

> **"Don't handle the fruit."**

Is this quotation a question? (*Yes, No*)

3007

Must be changed
 	
64
	Sometimes, for emphasis, we put the verb ahead of its subject.
	
	    a. **The <u>rain</u> <u>came</u> down.**
	    b. **Down <u>came</u> the <u>rain</u>.**
	
	In which sentence does the verb precede the subject? _____
	
	                                 65

No
 	
332
	a. **We have an old apple tree in our back yard.**
	    b. **We have an old apple tree, and it is in our back yard.**
	
	Sentence *a* is *simple;* sentence *b* is *compound.*
	
	The sentence which is better because it doesn't give too much importance to the location of the tree is the (*simple, compound*) sentence.
	
	                                 333

that
 	
600
	Underline the correct relative pronoun:
	
	          the school (*which, who*)
	
	                                 601

cooking 868	The gerund form of the verb *lie* is _____. 869
some 1136	These adjective clauses begin with such words as **one of whom, several of whom, two of which, most of which.** **The room has three windows,** *one of which is always locked.* The word in the clause that specifies the number to which the statement applies is the (*first, last*) word. 1137

semicolon
 	
1404
	There is sometimes a fourth way to correct a run-on sentence. The best solution may be to subordinate one of the sentences.
	
	    WRONG: **I approached the squirrel, it ran away.**
	    RIGHT: *As I approached the squirrel,* **it ran away.**
	
	4. Change one of the sentences to a phrase or clause. In this case, we used a _____.
	
	                               1405

demand (demanding)	A boondoggler is where a person is hired to do a needless job.
	A boondoggler _____ hired to do a needless job.
1672	1673
gives	**Neither Gary's mother** *nor* **his father was at home.**
	(Neither his mother *was* at home nor his father *was* at home.)
	Because we are thinking of Gary's parents one at a time, we use a (*singular, plural*) verb.
1939	1940
present	In this and the following frames, the first verb in each sentence is in the past tense. Underline the second verb which is in the proper tense. Remember that standard usage requires that a fact permanently true should be expressed in the present tense.
	The article *stated* **that potatoes** (*are, were*) **fattening.**
2206	2207
We	**There will be plenty of room for** *you* **and** *me.*
	This sentence is correct because if we used each pronoun separately, we would say:
	There will be plenty of room for *you.*
	There will be plenty of room for (*me, I*).
2473	2474
None	A pretty face may win friends but it takes character and personality to hold them.
2740	2741
No	**Did you hear the grocer say, "Don't handle the fruit"?**
	The question is the (*quotation, entire sentence*).
3007	3008

b 65	You are more likely to select the right subject if you look for the verb first. **Out jumped the rabbit.** After you find the verb **jumped,** ask yourself, "*Who* or *what* jumped?" The answer will tell you the subject. The subject of this sentence is _____. <div align="right">66</div>
simple 333	a. **Paul made a suggestion, and it was clever.** b. **Paul made a suggestion, and the entire class liked it.** Which compound sentence is better because the ideas are more equal in importance? _____ <div align="right">334</div>
which 601	Underline the correct relative pronoun: <div align="center">**a bumblebee** (*who, which*)</div> <div align="right">602</div>
lying 869	We often wish to talk about actions. We can't talk about *walked, stole,* or *studied,* but we can talk about *walking, stealing,* or _____. <div align="right">870</div>
first 1137	The number of the group that these clauses single out may vary from **none of whom** to **all of whom.** Fill in the missing words to show that *none* of the coins are rare. (*None* may take either a singular or plural verb.) **I have many old coins,** _____ *are rare.* <div align="right">1138</div>
clause 1405	WRONG: **I approached the squirrel, it ran away.** RIGHT: *On my approaching the squirrel,* **it ran away.** Here we used a (*phrase, clause*). <div align="right">1406</div>

page 131

is a person 1673	The climax of the story was when Jeff announced that he would not study law. The climax of the story was _____ _____ that he would not study law. 1674
singular 1940	Underline the correct verb: **Neither Linda nor her sister** (*drive, drives*) **the car.** 1941
are 2207	**The teacher** *reminded* **us that "all right"** (*was, is*) **two separate words.** 2208
me 2474	In this and the following frames, underline the correct pronouns. In each case, choose the form of the pronoun that you would use if the pronoun were used by itself. **The remark made Roxanne and** (*me, I*) **angry.** 2475
friends, but 2741	**Most of us think of taxes as a necessary evil and we seldom think of what we get in return for them.** 2742
entire sentence 3008	**Did you hear the grocer say, "Don't handle the fruit"?** Since the entire sentence and not the quotation is a question, we put the question mark (*inside, outside*) the quotes. 3009

rabbit 66	**This story the class really enjoyed.** First find the verb—**enjoyed.** Then ask yourself, "*Who* or *what* enjoyed?" The subject of this sentence is _____. 67
b 334	a. **The house was attractive. It was too far from any school.** b. **The house was attractive. Rents are high in our city.** Which pair of sentences would make a better compound sentence because their ideas are similar? _____ 335
which 602	Underline the correct relative pronoun: **the nurse** (*who, which*) 603
studying 870	To talk about actions, we must give them names. We give actions names by adding -*ing* to verbs, thus changing the verbs into nouns which we call by the special name of _____. 871
none of which 1138	Fill in the missing words to show that *all* the coins are rare: **I have many old coins,** _____ *are rare.* 1139
phrase 1406	a. **I approached the squirrel; it ran away.** b. **On my approaching the squirrel, it ran away.** c. **I approached the squirrel. It ran away.** d. **I approached the squirrel, it ran away.** e. **As I approached the squirrel, it ran away.** Which is a run-on sentence? _____ 1407

---

drives

1941

If one of the subjects joined by **or** or **nor** is singular and the other plural, the verb should agree with the closer word.

Neither the words nor the music ... very original.

The noun **words** is plural, and the noun **music** is singular. The missing verb should agree with (*words, music*) and should be (*is, are*).

1942

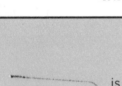
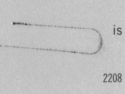

is

2208

The family *moved* to Hollywood, where Verna (*gets, got*) a job as an extra.

2209

---

me

2475

Roger and (*her, she*) disturbed everyone with their talking.

2476

---

evil, and

2742

Nations rise and nations fall.

2743

---

outside

3009

a. **Would any good American want to admit to his child, "I didn't vote because the weather was bad"?**
b. **Would any good American want to admit to his child, "I didn't vote because the weather was bad?"**

The question mark is properly placed in sentence (*a, b*).

3010

class 67	In this and the following frames, underscore the verb with two lines; then underscore the subject with one line: **To this old inn came a strange visitor.** 68
a 335	a. **Brad apologized to Cathy. She was with her sister.** b. **Brad apologized to Cathy. She accepted his apology.** Which pair of sentences would make a better compound sentence because their ideas are related? _____ 336
who 603	How do we choose between **who** and **whom**? Which form we use depends on its use *within* the clause itself. Use **who** when the pronoun is the subject of the verb. Use **whom** when it is the object of a verb or preposition. **Any player** *who can beat Foster* **must be very good.** The pronoun *who* is the subject of the verb _____. 604
gerunds 871	A gerund is a noun that is formed from a _____. 872
all of which 1139	Fill in the missing words to show that *a few* of the coins are rare: **I have many old coins,** _____ *are* *rare.* 1140

d
 	
1407
	Before you correct a run-on sentence, consider the possibility of subordination.
	WRONG: **Illinois has a quarterback, nobody can stop him.**
	  a. **Illinois has a quarterback, and nobody can stop him.**
	  b. **Illinois has a quarterback whom nobody can stop.**
	Which sentence is a better repair—*a* or *b?*_____
	
	1408

Pronouns are generally used in place of nouns to avoid repeating the nouns.

Earl forgot where he had put his keys.

The two pronouns in this sentence are _____ and

_____.

1676

---

music
is

1942

Neither the words nor the music *seems* **very original.**

If we reversed the order of **words** and **music,** would we need to change the verb *seems*? (*Yes, No*)

1943

---

got

2209

Copernicus *believed* **that the earth** (*rotates, rotated*) **around the sun.**

2210

---

she

2476

Neither the Mannings nor (*us, we*) **would sell our land.**

2477

None

2743

The customer upset everything on the counter but finally bought nothing.

2744

---

a

3010

Complete the punctuation at the end of this sentence:

When you get the wrong number, do you say, "I'm sorry

3011

came <u>visitor</u> 68	Underline the verb and its subject: **Up goes his arm for the pitch.** <div align="right">69</div>
b 336	a. **Cars were a luxury in those days, and they did not have self-starters.** b. **Cars were a luxury in those days, and few people could afford them.** Which is a better compound sentence? _____ <div align="right">337</div>
can beat 604	The relative pronoun that starts an adjective clause is not always the subject. **Any player** *whom Ross* <u>*can beat*</u> **must be very poor.** The subject of the verb *can beat* is not the pronoun *whom*, but the noun _____. <div align="right">605</div>
verb 872	Do you remember that we also formed present participles by adding *-ing* to verbs? Could the word *swinging* be either a present participle or a gerund? (*Yes, No*) <div align="right">873</div>
a few of which 1140	In using this type of clause, be careful to use **whom,** and not **which,** to refer to people. **The Kellys have three sons,** *two of (which, whom) are now attending college.* <div align="right">1141</div>

b
 	
 1408
	One of the following sentences is a run-on sentence. Correct this sentence by supplying a period and a capital. Write only the word before and after the period.
	
	    a. **I don't believe this rumor, it can't be true.**
	    b. **If the fan is oiled, it will run more quietly.**
	
	_____
	<div align="right">1409</div>

he, his 1676	**Earl forgot where** *he* **had put** *his* **keys.** The pronouns **he** and **his** refer to the noun _____. 1677
Yes 1943	a. **A few flowers or a plant is a good gift.** b. **A plant or a few flowers is a good gift.** Which sentence is correct? _____ 1944
rotates 2210	**There Cauley** *met* **an editor who** (*urged, urges*) **him to write his life story.** 2211
we 2477	**I understand that Rick told** (*them, they*) **and** (*us, we*) **entirely different stories.** 2478
None 2744	**It took Columbus seventy days to cross the Atlantic but a modern jet makes the trip in less than six hours.** 2745

sorry''?
 	
3011
	When *both* the sentence and the quotation are questions, we use only one question mark, not two. This question mark goes inside the quotation.
	
	        Did the referee ask, "Are you ready?"
	
	Complete the punctuation at the end of this sentence:
	
	        Will Judy ask, "Have you seen Ralph
	
	3012

goes arm 69	Underline the verb and its subject: **Here stands the monument to the Unknown Soldier.** 70
b 337	a. **My birthday was approaching, and I was beginning to think about gifts.** b. **My birthday was approaching, and I had always wanted to go deer hunting.** Which is a better compound sentence? _____ 338
Ross 605	**Any player** *whom Ross can beat* **must be very poor.** Look at the arrow in the above sentence. The relative pronoun *whom* stands for the noun _____. 606
Yes 873	To decide whether an *-ing* word is a present participle or a gerund, we must see how it is used in the sentence. If the *-ing* word is used as an adjective, it is a _____ _____. 874
whom 1141	**Customs officials,** *many of (whom, which) speak English,* **examine your luggage.** 1142
rumor. It 1409	Continue to follow the directions for the previous frame: a. **Whenever we buy a used car, we have a mechanic check it thoroughly.** b. ~~The Smiths didn't come, we waited until 9 o'clock.~~ _____ 1410

Earl 1677	**Earl forgot where** *he* **had put** *his* **keys.** The noun to which a pronoun refers is called its **antecedent.** It is the antecedent that gives a pronoun definite meaning. The antecedent of the pronouns *he* and *his* is the noun _____. 1678
a 1944	**The teacher or the students** (*select, selects*) **the topic.** The singular subject **teacher** requires a singular verb, but the plural subject **students** requires a plural verb. Because the plural subject **students** is closer to the verb, we choose the plural verb _____. 1945
urged 2211	**Franklin's experiment** *proved* **that lightning** (*was, is*) **electricity.** 2212
them, us 2478	**We have decided that Ken and** (*I, me*) **will play against Iris and** (*him, he*). 2479
Atlantic, but 2745	**Are we solving this problem or merely postponing it?** 2746

Ralph?"
 	
3012
	Exclamation points are handled in exactly the same way as question marks.
	
	    "Which tooth hurts?" asked the dentist.
	    "It's another home run!" shouted Pete.
	
	Is a comma used in addition to either a question mark or an exclamation point in these sentences? (*Yes, No*)
	
	3013

<u>stands</u> monument 70	Underline the verb and its subject. Don't overlook the help-ing verb. **Never have I seen a happier face.** 71
a 338	**You can always add salt to your food, but you cannot remove it.** This compound sentence is (*good, poor*). 339
player 606	Keeping in mind that the pronoun *whom* stands for the noun *player,* let us straighten out the clause. (player) (player) *whom <u>Ross</u> <u>can beat</u> = <u>Ross</u> <u>can beat</u> whom* In this clause, the subject of the verb *can beat* is *Ross,* and its direct object is the relative pronoun _____. 607
present participle 874	If the *-ing* word is used as a noun, it is a _____. 875
whom 1142	In this and the following frames, subordinate the italicized statement by changing it to an adjective clause built on the "one of which" or "some of whom" pattern: **We have three clocks,** *and none of them keeps good time.* **We have three clocks,** _____ *keeps good time.* 1143
come. We 1410	a. **This song is not original, it was adapted from a popular piece.** b. **Although Cambridge was a small town, it produced several of our most famous authors.** _____ 1411

Earl 1678	**The break was so small that I could hardly see** *it*. The antecedent of the pronoun *it* is the noun _____. 1679

select
 	
1945
	Though a sentence with a singular and a plural subject joined by **or** or **nor** is correct when the verb agrees with the closer word, careful writers try to avoid such sentences.
	
	    a. **The teacher or the students select the topic.**
	    b. **The teacher selects the topic, or the students do.**
	
	A careful writer would prefer sentence (*a, b*).
	
	1946

is 2212	**The bus driver** *informed* **us that Philadelphia (***is, was***) very close to New York.** 2213
I, him 2479	**Unfortunately, neither (***him, he***) nor Connie remembered to feed the dog.** 2480
None 2746	**The producers must give the program more variety or it will not survive.** 2747
No 3013	a. **"Just look at that sunset!" exclaimed Mother.** b. **"Just look at that sunset," exclaimed Mother!** The exclamation point is properly placed in sentence (*a, b*). 3014

have I seen $\underline{\underline{\text{have}}}$ - $\underline{\underline{\text{seen}}}$ 71	Underline the verb and its subject: **Neither did Pam receive an invitation.** 72
good 339	**Arthur drove most of the way, and we had two flat tires.** This compound sentence is (*good, poor*). 340
whom 607	Here is a quick way to decide whether the clause signal is a subject or an object: When you see no other word before the verb that could possibly serve as its subject, then the relative pronoun is its subject, and **who** is correct. 　*who escaped*　*who were absent*　*who bought our car* The only word that could be the subject here is _____. 608
gerund 875	a. *Swinging* **makes me dizzy.** b. **She went through the** *swinging* **door.** In which sentence is *swinging* a present participle because it is used as an adjective to modify a noun? _____ 876
none of which 1143	**Rita baby-sits with two children,** *and one of them is very mischievous.* **Rita baby-sits with two children,** _____ *is very mischievous.* 1144
original. It 1411	a. **If you will sometimes agree with other people, they will be more likely to agree with you.** b. **Whales do not actually spout water, they merely blow out their moist breath.** _____ 1412

break 1679	**Bananas are harvested while** *they* **are still green.** The antecedent of the pronoun *they* is _____. 1680
b 1946	a. **The kitchen wasn't large enough, and neither were the bedrooms.** b. **Neither the kitchen nor the bedrooms were large enough.** Because each subject has its proper verb, a careful writer would prefer sentence (*a, b*). 1947
is 2213	**The author** *went* **back to Italy, where he** (*visits, visited*) **his birthplace.** 2214
he 2480	**The "Devil's Ride" made Kathy and** (*she, her*) **sick.** 2481
variety, or 2747	**Andy eats like a horse but gains no weight.** 2748
a 3014	a. **Mr. Lutz exclaimed, "What a silly thing to buy!"** b. **Mr. Lutz exclaimed, "What a silly thing to buy"!** The exclamation point is properly placed in sentence (*a, b*). 3015

<u>did</u> Pam <u>receive</u> 72	Underline the verb and its subject: **Must each person bring his own lunch?** 73
poor 340	**We like our new house, but we miss our old neighborhood.** This compound sentence is (*good, poor*). 341
who 608	If, on the other hand, the verb already has a subject, then the relative pronoun must be its object, and **whom** is correct. *whom I admire* *whom we invited* *whom the dog bit* The verbs in the above clauses already have subjects; therefore *whom* must be the (*subject, object*) in each clause. 609
b 876	a. *Swinging* **makes me dizzy.** b. **She went through the** *swinging* **door.** In which sentence is *swinging* a gerund because it is used as a noun to name an action? _____ 877
one of whom 1144	**The air is full of bacteria,** *but most of them are harmless.* **The air is full of bacteria,** _____ *are harmless.* 1145
water. They 1412	In this and the following frames, correct each run-on sentence by adding a conjunction (*and, but, or*), with a comma at the end of the first statement. Write only the word before and after the conjunction. **It wasn't what he said, it was the way he said it.** _____ 1413

Bananas 1680	**Bananas are harvested while *they* are still green.** The noun **Bananas** is the _____ of the pronoun *they*. 1681
a 1947	**A few flowers or a plant is a good gift.** Although this sentence is correct, rewrite it so that each of the two subjects will have its own verb that agrees with it in number. _____ _____ 1948
visited 2214	Lesson **62** Using the Present Perfect Tense [Frames 2216–2245]
her 2481	**The Chandlers and (*they, them*) attend the same church.** 2482
None 2748	Lesson **77** Commas After Introductory Expressions [Frames 2750–2783]
a 3015	In this and the following frames, circle the letter of the sentence that is properly punctuated and capitalized: a. **Our neighbor asked, "If he could borrow our lawnmower?"** b. **Our neighbor asked, "May I borrow your lawnmower?"** 3016

Underline the verb and its subject:

Where does Mother keep the scissors?

74

---

good

341

The car had no lights, and the accident occurred on our corner.

This compound sentence is (*good, poor*).

342

---

object

609

whom I admire   whom we invited   whom the dog bit

When the relative pronoun that stands for a person is the direct object of the verb within the clause, we use the object form (*who, whom*).

610

---

a

877

Although gerunds serve as nouns, they still bear some resemblance to verbs. Like verbs, gerunds may take direct objects or subject complements, as no ordinary noun can do.

Observing ants **is fascinating.**

The noun *ants* is the (*direct object, subject complement*) of the gerund *observing*.

878

---

most of which

1145

The college has eight hundred students, *and many of them come from foreign countries.*

The college has eight hundred students, _____

_____ *come from foreign countries.*

1146

---

said, but it

1413

There will be a thorough inquiry, the truth will come out.

1414

antecedent 1681	The pronouns *I* and *you* require no antecedents because there can be no doubt about to whom they refer. *I* always means the speaker and *you* the person(s) spoken to. If someone should say to you, "I know him" or "You know him," the only pronoun about which there can be any doubt is the pronoun (*I, you, him*). 1682
A few flowers are a good gift, and so is a plant. (*or* a similar sentence) 1948	If you were to add the words printed in parentheses at the point marked by the caret ($_\wedge$), would you need to change the italicized verb? If a change would be necessary, write only the form of the verb that would be required. If the verb would remain the same, write *Correct*. **Neither $_\wedge$ *has* a fur collar. (of my coats)** _____ 1949
	A tense formed by combining a past participle with a form of **have** is called a **perfect tense**. a. **decided** b. **have decided** Which verb is an example of a perfect tense? _____ 2216
they 2482	**Gloria, not (*me, I*), thought up this slogan.** 2483
	For variety or emphasis, we often begin a sentence with an adverbial modifier—a word, a phrase, or a clause. a. **Our team has been winning recently.** b. **Recently our team has been winning.** Which sentence begins with an introductory adverb? _____ 2750
b 3016	a. **"How does the story end?" asked Miss Nolan.** b. **"How does the story end," asked Miss Nolan?** 3017

<u>does</u> <u>Mother</u> <u>keep</u> 74	Underline the verb and its subject: **Can this dress be washed?** 75

poor
 	
342
	Use a compound sentence when you want your reader to think of two ideas in connection with each other.
	  a. **The engine runs smoothly. It uses too much gas.**
	  b. **The engine runs smoothly, but it uses too much gas.**
	Which arrangement brings the two ideas into closer relation-ship—*a* or *b?* _____
	
	343

whom 610	**Mr. Dolby is a person . . .** *worries* *about nothing.* Since the clause has no other subject, the relative pronoun would have to be the subject. We would therefore choose the subject form (*who, whom*). 611
direct object 878	*Being selfish* **is a good way to lose friends.** The adjective *selfish* completes the gerund *Being* and is therefore a (*direct object, subject complement*). 879
many of whom 1146	**The school has twelve rooms,** *and three of them are not used.* **The school has twelve rooms,** _____ *are not used.* 1147
nquiry, and the 1414	**You had better take your time, you might make many mis-takes.** _____ 1415

him
 	
1682
	Pronouns require antecedents whenever there can be any doubt about *whom* or *what* they refer to.
	   a. **As soon as the boys got paid, they spent** *it*.
	   b. **As soon as the boys got their pay, they spent** *it*.
	In which sentence does the pronoun *it* have an antecedent?
	_____ 1683

Correct 1949	∧ **These buses** *go* **to the stadium. (Either of)** ————————— 1950
b 2216	Just as we have three simple tenses—the present, past, and future—we also have three corresponding perfect tenses— the present perfect, the past perfect, and the _____ perfect. 2217
I 2483	**This is something for you and** (*me, I*) **to think about.** 2484

b
 	
2750
	To decide whether to use a comma after an introductory adverb such as *Recently* or *Finally* requires judgment. Using a comma sets the adverb apart and gives it more emphasis.
	   a. *Finally,* **Ted arrived with the refreshments.**
	   b. *Finally* **Ted arrived with the refreshments.**
	In which sentence is *Finally* given more emphasis? _____
	                          2751

a 3017	a. **"Just what I wanted!" exclaimed Ellen as she opened the box.** b. **"Just what I wanted!", exclaimed Ellen as she opened the box.** 3018

<u>Can</u> <u>dress</u> <u>be washed</u> 75	Can a verb consist of more than one word? (*Yes, No*) 76
b 343	a. **You must shut the gate, or the dog will get out.** b. **You must shut the gate. The dog will get out.** Which arrangement brings out the relationship between the two ideas more clearly? _____ 344
who 611	**Mr. Dolby is a person ...** *nothing* *worries*. Since the clause already has the subject *nothing*, the rela- tive pronoun would have to be the object. We would therefore choose the object form (*who, whom*). 612
subject complement 879	The phrases formed by gerunds with their related words are called **gerund phrases.** These phrases can be used in any way that nouns are used. *Reading this book* **changed his entire life.** In this sentence the gerund phrase *Reading this book* is used as the _____ of the verb **changed.** 880
three of which 1147	**Ralph brought his parents,** *and I had met neither of them* *before.* **Ralph brought his parents,** _____ *I had met before.* 1148
time, or you 1415	**The election was close at hand, everyone was discussing** **politics.** _____ 1416

b 1683	a. **Collecting stamps is an interesting hobby if one can afford to buy** *them.* b. **Stamp collecting is an interesting hobby if one can afford to buy** *them.* In which sentence does the pronoun *them* have an antecedent? _____ 1684
goes 1950	**Unseasonable weather** ∧ *forces* **us to cut our prices. (and a heavy stock)** ———————————— 1951
future 2217	Whether a verb is in the present perfect, past perfect, or future perfect tense depends on whether the participle is combined with a present, past, or future form of **have.** Underline the two present forms of **have:** has had have will have 2218
me 2484	Lesson **70** Informal and Formal Pronoun Usage [Frames 2486–2529]
a 2751	The pause at the comma gives the meaning of the introductory adverb more time to "sink in." a. *Fortunately,* **the water was shallow.** b. *Fortunately* **the water was shallow.** The adverb *Fortunately* gets more attention in sentence *a* because it is set off with a _____. 2752
a 3018	a. **Carolyn screamed, "Look out for that child"!** b. **Carolyn screamed, "Look out for that child!"** 3019

Yes 76	a. **shall, could, should, can, must, might** b. **soon, never, now, always, not, surely** Which group of words consists of helping verbs? _____ 77
a 344	a. **I liked the dog. It was a collie.** b. **I liked the dog. The dog liked me.** Which pair of sentences would you connect with *and* to bring the two ideas into closer relationship? _____ 345
whom 612	Underline the correct relative pronoun after deciding whether it is used as the subject or the object of the verb: **People** (*who, whom*) <u>*are*</u> *honest themselves* **usually trust others.** 613
subject 880	**Your mistake was** *enclosing money in a letter.* The gerund phrase completes the linking verb **was** and identifies the subject **mistake.** The gerund phrase is therefore a (*direct object, subject complement*). 881
either of whom 1148	In a similar type of adjective clause, a noun precedes the words **of which**; for example, **the price of which, the result of which, the purpose of which.** **There are many words** *the meanings of which have changed.* What noun precedes *of which*? _____ 1149
hand, and everyone 1416	In this and the following frames, correct the run-on sentence by inserting a semicolon. Write only the word before and after the semicolon. **It isn't the car that kills, it's the driver behind the wheel.** _____ 1417

a. **It is advisable to have farming experience before buying**
   one.
b. **It is advisable to have experience on a farm before buy-**
   ing *one.*

In which sentence does the pronoun *one* have an antece-

dent? _____

The sprayer ∧ *sells* **for two dollars. (with the chemical)**

_____

Using a present form of **have** (*have* or *has*) with a participle
gives us the **present perfect** tense.

Using the past form of **have** (*had*) with a participle gives us
the **past perfect** tense.

a. **have decided**   b. **had decided**

Which verb is in the present perfect tense? _____

Now we consider a rule that holds more rigidly for writing
than it does for speaking:

Use the nominative case for a pronoun that follows any form
of the verb **be** (*is, am, are—was, were, been*).

Underline the correct pronoun:

It must be (*they, them*) **who called.**

An introductory phrase gets more attention, too, when it is
set off with a comma.

a. *For a child* **he was remarkably strong.**
b. *For a child,* **he was remarkably strong.**

Which sentence gives more emphasis to the prepositional

phrase? _____

---

a. **I get tired of being asked, "Is it hot enough for you"?**
b. **I get tired of being asked, "Is it hot enough for you?"**

a 77	A main verb is sometimes separated from its helper by other words. (*True, False*) 78
I liked the dog, and the dog liked me. b 345	Because both parts of the sentence concern the relationship between the person and the dog, this is a (*good, poor*) compound sentence. 346
who 613	Underline the correct relative pronoun: **The speaker (*who, whom*) he introduced was embarrassed by so much praise.** 614
subject complement 881	a. **We paid thirty dollars for repairs.** b. **We paid thirty dollars for repairing the motor.** In which sentence is a gerund phrase the object of the preposition **for?** _____ 882
meanings 1149	**Mr. Kerr bought several stocks** *the value of which is very doubtful.* What noun precedes *of which?* _____ 1150
kills; it's 1417	**Male mosquitoes do not bite people, they live on the juice of plants.** _____ 1418

b 1685	**Pete wants to be a lawyer because *it* interests him.** Can the pronoun *it* be used to refer to the noun **lawyer?** (*Yes, No*) 1686
Correct 1952	∧ **These questions *are* answered in this chapter. (Every one of)** ――――― 1953
a 2219	Using a future form of **have** (*shall have* or *will have*) with a participle gives us the **future perfect** tense. a. **have decided** b. **shall have decided** c. **had decided** Which verb is in the future perfect tense? _____ 2220
they 2486	Why is it that after every other verb in the English language we use an objective pronoun but that after any form of the verb **be** we use a nominative pronoun? **The** *chairman* **was** *he*. (*He* **was the** *chairman*.) Can this sentence be turned around without changing the meaning? (*Yes, No*) 2487
b 2753	*In desperation* **the mayor threatened to resign.** To give more emphasis to the introductory phrase, would you put a comma after *desperation?* (*Yes, No*) 2754
b 3020	a. **Can't you just hear Aunt Emma saying, "I told you so"?** b. **Can't you just hear Aunt Emma saying, "I told you so?"** 3021

True 78	The subject always comes ahead of the verb in every sentence. (*True, False*) 79
good 346	a. **I was born in Utah. Our family soon moved to Oregon.** b. **I was born in Utah. This state has magnificent scenery.** Which pair of sentences could better be combined into a compound sentence? _____ 347
whom 614	Underline the correct relative pronoun: **Robert Frost is the poet** (*who, whom*) **I selected for my report.** 615

b
 	
882
	In this and the following frames, underline each gerund phrase and indicate its use by writing one of the following abbreviations in the parentheses:
	    $S = Subject$ $SC = Subject\ Complement$
	    $DO = Direct\ Object$ $OP = Object\ of\ Preposition$
	    The sign forbids fishing from this dock. (**)**
	
	883

value
 	
1150
	Ordinarily, the relative pronoun **whose** provides a smoother sentence than **of which** and requires fewer words.
	    a. **I read a novel** *the ending of which is disappointing.*
	    b. **I read a novel** *whose ending is disappointing.*
	Sentence *b* is _____ words shorter than sentence *a*. (How many?)
	
	1151

people; they 1418	**It is not enough merely to feel appreciation, one should also express it.** 1419

No 1686	**Pete wants to be a lawyer because *it* interests him.** Does the pronoun *it* have an antecedent to give it meaning? (*Yes, No*) 1687
is 1953	**The janitor** ∧ *helps* **the younger children cross the street. (or an older pupil)** _____ 1954
b 2220	a. **Mr. Frisby *spoke* for an hour.** b. **Mr. Frisby *has spoken* for an hour.** In which sentence is the verb in the present perfect tense? _____ 2221
Yes 2487	**The *chairman* was he. (*He* was the *chairman*.)** This sentence can be turned around because any pronoun that follows a form of **be** means the same person or thing as the subject. In the above sentence, the pronoun *he* means the same person as the subject _____. 2488
Yes 2754	A comma is more frequently used after a long introductory phrase than after a short one. a. **After several weeks of hard and persistent practice the team perfected this play.** b. **For weeks the team practiced this play.** In which sentence would you use a comma? _____ 2755
a 3021	In the remaining frames, punctuate each sentence and supply capitals where necessary. Each sentence requires, among other things, a question mark or an exclamation point. **Are these flowers from your own garden asked Mrs. Sheldon** 3022

False 79	You are less likely to make a mistake in selecting the subject and the verb if you select the _____ first. 80
a 347	**I was born in Utah, but our family soon moved to Oregon.** This is a good compound sentence because both parts concern (*location, growth*). 348
whom 615	When the relative pronoun is the object of a preposition, use the object form **whom**; for example, **to whom, for whom, from whom.** Underline the correct relative pronoun: **Most of the candidates** *for* (*who, whom*) *I voted* **were elected.** 616
fishing from this dock (DO) 883	S = *Subject* SC = *Subject Complement* DO = *Direct Object* OP = *Object of Preposition* **His violation was driving through a red light. (** **)** 884
two 1151	The relative pronoun **whose,** unlike **who** and **whom,** can be used for things as well as for persons. a. **I ordered a French soup** *the name of which I can't pronounce.* b. **I ordered a French soup** *whose name I can't pronounce.* Are both sentences correct? (*Yes, No*) 1152
preciation; one 1419	One of the following sentences is a run-on sentence. In the other, the error was avoided by subordination. a. **After the children left, the cozy home seemed empty and cheerless.** b. **The children left, the cozy home seemed empty and cheerless.** Which sentence is correct? _____ 1420

No 1687	WRONG: **Pete wants to be a lawyer because** *it* **interests him.** RIGHT: **Pete wants to be a lawyer because** *law* **interests him.** This sentence was corrected by (*changing the pronoun to a noun, supplying an antecedent*). 1688
Correct 1954	**A few cookies** ∧ *satisfy* **my hunger after school. (or a sandwich)** _____ 1955

b
 	
2221
	Use the present perfect tense for an action that began in the past but that continues, or whose effect continues, into the present.
	
	    a. **Pat** *lived* **in Chicago for ten years.**
	    b. **Pat** *has lived* **in Chicago for ten years.**
	
	In which sentence is Pat still living in Chicago? _____
	                                        2222

chairman 2488	**The** *chairman* **was** *he.* Since *he* could just as well be the subject of this sentence, we put it in the same case as if it were the subject of the sentence—that is, in the (*nominative, objective*) case. 2489
a 2755	After short introductory phrases that state *time* or *place* (*In June, On Monday, At Buffalo*), commas are usually omitted. a. **On Friday, the Student Council meets.** b. **On the last Friday of each month, the Student Council meets.** The comma might well be omitted in sentence (*a, b*). 2756
"Are . . . garden?" asked Mrs. Sheldon. 3022	**The agent asked is the lady of the house at home** 3023

Lesson 3 Two Sentence Patterns Built on Action Verbs

[Frames 82–126]

---

location

348

Use the conjunction **and** merely to add one idea to another. Use the conjunction **but** to point out a contrast or contradiction between the two ideas.

I didn't want a reward, . . . Mr. Hart made me take it.

Would **and** or **but** make better sense in this sentence?

_____

349

---

whom

616

Most of the candidates *for whom I voted* **were elected.**

We use the object form *whom* because the relative pronoun

is the object of the preposition _____.

617

---

driving through
a red light (SC)

884

$S = Subject$ $SC = Subject\ Complement$
$DO = Direct\ Object$ $OP = Object\ of\ Preposition$

Saving the precious topsoil is one of the aims of conservation. (   )

885

Yes

1152

Even though **whose** may be used for things, there are times when you might prefer the **of which** construction. Change the **whose** to the **of which** construction:

She makes pastry *whose preparation takes an entire day.*

She makes pastry _____

_____ *takes an entire day.*

1153

---

a

1420

a. **We hiked through a dense woods, the sunlight hardly penetrated the thick foliage.**
b. **We hiked through a dense woods, where the sunlight hardly penetrated the thick foliage.**

Which sentence is correct? _____

1421

changing the pronoun to a noun 1688	WRONG: **Pete wants to be a lawyer because** *it* **interests him.** RIGHT: **Pete wants to study** *law* **because** *it* **interests him.** This sentence was corrected by (*changing the pronoun to a noun, supplying an antecedent*). 1689
satisfies 1955	**A pedigreed cocker spaniel** ∧ *goes* **to the winner. (, as well as a year's supply of dog food,)** _____ 1956
b 2222	If a past action or its effect continues into the present time, use the (*present perfect, present*) tense. 2223
nominative 2489	WRONG: **The** *chairman* **was** *him.* If we used the objective pronoun *him* after the verb **was,** could we turn this sentence around without changing the pronoun? (*Yes, No*) 2490
a 2756	Use a comma after an adverb clause that comes at the beginning of a sentence, ahead of the main clause. a. **You will change your mind** *when you hear all the facts.* b. *When you hear all the facts* **you will change your mind.** Which sentence requires a comma because the adverb clause comes first? _____ 2757
The agent asked, "Is . . . home?" 3023	**Stop shouted the bandleader** 3024

Nearly every simple sentence that we make falls into one of three basic patterns. Two of these patterns involve *action verbs.*

Underline the one verb which indicates an *action:*

was   pushed   seemed

82

---

but

349

Use the conjunction **or** to express a choice between two ideas.

a. **I steered for the shore, . . . the wind kept turning the boat.**
b. **The course is getting harder, . . . I am getting lazier.**

In which sentence would **or** make good sense? _____

350

---

for

617

Underline the correct relative pronoun:

My grandfather was a man to (*whom, who*) **everyone came for advice.**

618

Saving the precious topsoil (S)

885

$S = Subject$ $SC = Subject\ Complement$
$DO = Direct\ Object$ $OP = Object\ of\ Preposition$

The clerk made an error in adding the figures. (   )

886

---

the preparation of which

1153

Change the **whose** to the **of which** construction:

The minister told a story *whose point most people missed.*

The minister told a story _____

most people missed.

1154

---

b

1421

a. **The restaurant being crowded, we decided not to wait.**
b. **The restaurant was crowded, we decided not to wait.**

Which sentence is correct? _____

1422

supplying an antecedent 1689	When a pronoun lacks an antecedent, we can correct the sentence in either of two ways: (1) Eliminate the pronoun; (2) supply an _____ to give the pronoun meaning. 1690
Correct 1956	∧ **The boys** *are* **very willing to help. (Each of)** _____ 1957
present perfect 2223	**Mr. Frisby** *spoke* **for an hour.** This could mean that Mr. Frisby spoke yesterday, last year, or ten years ago. The action belongs entirely to the past. To show that Mr. Frisby is still speaking, we must replace *spoke* with the present perfect verb _____ *spoken.* 2224
No 2490	Underline the correct pronoun—the one that you could use if you turned the sentence around: **The culprits were** (*they, them*). 2491
b 2757	**Shorthand is difficult** *unless you are a good speller.* *Unless you are a good speller,* **shorthand is difficult.** Only one of the above sentences contains a comma. The comma is used when the adverb clause comes (*first, last*). 2758
"Stop!" shouted the bandleader. 3024	**Will all these new inventions** **asked the speaker** **make people any happier** 3025

pushed
 	
82
	Some action verbs indicate actions of the *body;* others indicate actions of the *mind.*
	
	   a. **worked, drove, washed, wrote, lifted**
	   b. **thought, hoped, believed, decided, understood**
	
	Which group of verbs indicates actions of the mind—*a* or *b?*
	
	_____ 83

b 350	**Our school is small, . . . we have good teams.** Which conjunction would bring out the meaning more clearly—**and** or **but?** _____ 351

whom
 	
618
	a. **Everyone values a friend . . . is dependable.**
	   b. **Everyone values a friend upon . . . he can depend.**
	
	In which sentence would **whom** be correct? _____
	
	                  619

adding the
figures (OP)
 	
886
	S = Subject *SC = Subject Complement*
	  DO = Direct Object *OP = Object of Preposition*
	
	Being a road hog increases the likelihood of automobile accidents. ( )
	
	                  887

the point of which 1154	Change the **whose** to the **of which** construction: **The doctor recommended a cough medicine** *whose name I can't recall.* **The doctor recommended a cough medicine** _____ _____ *I can't recall.* 1155

a
 	
1422
	a. **Having no one to play with, the child turned to books for companionship.**
	   b. **The child had no one to play with, she turned to books for companionship.**
	
	Which sentence is correct? _____
	
	                  1423

antecedent 1690	*It* is sometimes used not as a pronoun, but as an introductory word to get a sentence started—especially in remarks about *time* or the *weather*. This usage is perfectly correct. a. *It* **was ten o'clock, and** *it* **was starting to rain.** b. **I guess I'm not musical because I've never enjoyed** *it.* In which sentence is *it* correctly used? _____ 1691
is 1957	**The superb acting** ∧ *makes* **this an outstanding movie. (and the fine directing)** _____ 1958
has (spoken) 2224	a. **Carl** *built* **a fire.** b. **Carl** *has built* **a fire.** One sentence means that the fire is past history. The other means that, although the fire was built in the past, the effect of the action continues into the present moment. Which sentence means that the fire is still burning? _____ 2225
they 2491	Underline the correct pronoun: **The only other girl in the class was** (*her, she*). 2492
first 2758	a. **Most voters have made up their minds before the campaign starts.** b. **Before the campaign starts most voters have made up their minds.** Which sentence requires a comma? _____ 2759
"Will . . . inventions," . . . speaker, "make . . . happier?" 3025	**The people behind him were shouting sit down** 3026

b 83	Action verbs can sometimes make complete statements about their subjects without the need of any other words. a. **Harvey stumbled.** b. **Harvey sharpened** . . . Does the action verb make a complete statement about its subject in *a* or *b?* _____ 84
but 351	**Hockey originated in Canada, . . . many of the best players are Canadians.** Which conjunction would bring out the meaning more clearly—**and** or **but?** _____ 352
b 619	When a phrase such as **I think, I suppose, we hope** follows the relative pronoun, choose the same form of the pronoun you would choose if the phrase were not there. **It is John** *who* I think *should apologize.* Disregarding the phrase *I think,* we choose *who* because it is the subject of the verb _____ _____. 620
Being a road hog (S) 887	**Railroads are still one of the cheapest means of hauling heavy loads. ( )** 888
the name of which 1155	In this and the following frames, subordinate each italicized statement to an **of which** construction, preceded by a noun ("the cause of which," "the price of which"): **Our school had an assembly,** *and the purpose was to improve sportsmanship.* **Our school had an assembly** _____ _____ *was to improve sportsmanship.* 1156
a 1423	a. **Ruth looked admiringly at Bob, she was impressed with his handsome uniform.** b. **Ruth looked admiringly at Bob, impressed with his handsome uniform.** Which sentence is correct? _____ 1424

<table>
<tr>
<td>

a

1691
</td>
<td>

We often move a word group used as a subject to the end of the sentence and use an introductory *It* to fill the gap. (Such a subject, by the way, is called a *delayed subject*.)

   a. *To walk* **would be fun.**   b. *It* **would be fun** *to walk.*

In sentence *b*, the subject *to walk* has been moved to the end, and the gap is filled by the word _____.

1692
</td>
</tr>
<tr>
<td>

make

1958
</td>
<td>

Lesson 55 An Agreement Problem in Adjective Clauses

[Frames 1960–1989]
</td>
</tr>
<tr>
<td>

b

2225
</td>
<td>

The present perfect tense always ties up the action in some way with the present. If the action is not still continuing, it at least has some effect upon a present situation.

Underline the correct verb:

   If Dad (*took, has taken*) **the car, we shall have to walk.**

2226
</td>
</tr>
<tr>
<td>

she

2492
</td>
<td>

Why is this rule so frequently disregarded in informal English? It is because after every verb except **be,** we are accustomed to hearing and seeing the *objective* form of pronouns.

Tom knows *me.*   **The police stopped** *him.*   **Colby beat** *us.*

The verb in each of the above sentences is followed by (*a nominative, an objective*) pronoun.

2493
</td>
</tr>
<tr>
<td>

b

2759
</td>
<td>

a. **As the number of cars increases, many highways become inadequate.**
b. **Many highways become inadequate, as the number of cars increases.**

From which sentence should the comma be omitted? _____

2760
</td>
</tr>
<tr>
<td>

shouting, "Sit down!"

3026
</td>
<td>

It was Cain who asked   am I my brother's keeper

3027
</td>
</tr>
</table>

a 84	a. **Our guest brought** b. **Our guest arrived** Does the action verb make a complete statement about its subject in *a* or *b*? _____ 85
and 352	**Machinery is supposed to make life easier, . . . people seem to be busier than ever.** Which conjunction would bring out the meaning more clearly—**and** or **but**? _____ 353
should apologize 620	Underline the correct relative pronoun in each sentence: a. **Briggs is the man** (*who, whom*) *will be elected.* b. **Briggs is the man** (*who, whom*) I suppose *will be elected.* 621
hauling heavy loads (OP) 888	**The next step is removing the tire from the rim. ( )** 889
the purpose of which 1156	**My tropical fish contracted a disease,** *and the cause of it is not known.* **My tropical fish contracted a disease** _____ _____ *is not known.* 1157
b 1424	Lesson **39** **Adverbs as a Cause of Run-on Sentences** [Frames 1426–1459]

It 1692	Move the italicized subject to the end of the sentence and put the introductory word *It* in its place: *To take chances* **is foolish.** _____ 1693
	In an adjective clause, a verb should agree with its subject—often the relative pronoun **who, which,** or **that.** Whether these pronouns are singular or plural depends on whether their antecedents are singular or plural. **I like a dog** *that is friendly.* The antecedent of the pronoun *that* is the noun _____. 1960
has taken 2226	a. **Mr. Perkins** *was* **our postman for twelve years.** b. **Mr. Perkins** *has been* **our postman for twelve years.** Which sentence would mean that Mr. Perkins is still your postman? _____ 2227
an objective 2493	People find it difficult to make a single exception to the general pattern of our language and often say, "It was *us*" or "It was *them*"—just as they say, "It followed *us*" or "It followed *them.*" Underline the pronouns that are *formally* correct: **It was** (*we, us*). **It was** (*they, them*). 2494
b 2760	If an introductory adverb clause is shifted to the end of a sentence, a comma is usually (*necessary, unnecessary*). 2761
asked, "Am . . . keeper?" 3027	**Wasn't it P. T. Barnum who said there's a sucker born every minute** 3028

b 85	The action verb that makes a complete statement about its subject gives us our first sentence pattern: PATTERN I: *Subject—Action Verb* a. **Our guest brought . . .** b. **Our guest arrived.** Which word group represents **Pattern I?** _____ 86
but 353	It is not a good idea to begin a sentence with a conjunction. Let the conjunction stand between the two parts of the sentence where it can do its job of connecting. a. **It was a hot day. And all the windows were open.** b. **It was a hot day, and all the windows were open.** The conjunction **and** is properly used in (*a, b*). 354
a. who b. who 621	**There are some customers . . .** *you can never please.* Because *you* is the subject of the verb *can please* in the adjective clause, the missing relative pronoun would be its direct object. We would therefore choose the relative pronoun (*who, whom*). 622
removing the tire from the rim (SC) 889	**Norman dreaded going to the dentist. ( )** 890
the cause of which 1157	**Our television set has a knob,** *and I have never discovered its purpose.* **Our television set has a knob** _____ _____ *I have never discovered.* 1158
	There is a special group of *adverbs* that we use to lead the reader smoothly from one sentence to the next: then besides furthermore otherwise therefore however consequently nevertheless As a rule, would one of these adverbs be the very first word of something you wrote? (*Yes, No*) 1426

It is foolish to take chances. 1693	Move the italicized subject to the end of the sentence and put the introductory word *It* in its place: *That he forgot his own birthday* **seems strange.** _____ _____ 1694
dog 1960	**I like a dog** *that is friendly.* Because the pronoun *that* stands for the singular noun **dog,** it requires the singular verb _____. 1961
b 2227	a. **From that day on, I always** *feared* **the water.** b. **From that day on, I always** *have feared* **the water.** Which sentence is correct because the fear continues to exist at the present time? _____ 2228
we, they 2494	The use of objective pronouns after **be** has been gaining ground in informal usage. "It's *me*" is now generally accepted as correct speech. "It's *us*" is trailing close behind. Although "It's *me*" violates the formal rule, it is acceptable in free-and-easy conversation. (*True, False*) 2495
unnecessary 2761	An adverb clause that comes at the end of a sentence does not usually require a comma. However, when the end clause begins with **for** (meaning **because**), a comma is needed to prevent misreading. **She had to wait** *for* **the doctor was out.** Without a comma, might this sentence be puzzling? (*Yes, No*) 2762
said, "There's . . . minute"? 3028	Lesson **85** Pinning Down the Apostrophe [Frames 3030–3070]

b
 	
86
	Any sentence is **Pattern I** if the action verb *by itself* makes a complete statement about its subject—no matter how many other words and phrases may be present.
	
	    a. **Our guest arrived.**
	    b. **Our guest from Ohio arrived by plane this morning.**
	
	Both *a* and *b* are **Pattern I** sentences. (*True, False*) 87

b 354	a. **I dropped the light bulb, but it didn't break.** b. **I dropped the light bulb. But it didn't break.** The conjunction **but** is properly used in (*a, b*). 355
whom 622	**There are some customers** *whom you can never please.* Now insert the phrase *I suppose* after the clause signal *whom.* Underline the correct relative pronoun: **There are some customers** (*who, whom*) I suppose *you can never please.* 623
going to the dentist (DO) 890	We can sometimes improve a weak compound sentence by changing one of its statements to a gerund phrase used as the object of a preposition. *Dave watched the men work,* **and he learned about motors.** By *watching the men work,* **he learned about motors.** We change the verb *watch* to the gerund _____. 891
the purpose of which 1158	**The county constructed a road,** *and the need for it was very great.* **The county constructed a road** _____ _____ *was very great.* 1159
No 1426	**then** **besides** **furthermore** **otherwise** **therefore** **however** **consequently** **nevertheless** These words usually refer to something previously said. Besides pointing back to something previously said, do these adverbs lead on to the next idea? (*Yes, No*) 1427

It seems strange
that he forgot
his own birthday.

1694

Although such expressions as **"It says"** are commonly used, they are rather roundabout and clumsy.

It says **in the Bible that all men are brothers.**

Is there any noun in this sentence that tells you *who* or *what* the mysterious *It* is? (*Yes, No*)

1695

---

is

1961

---

a. **I like a dog** *that is friendly.*
b. **I like dogs** *that are friendly.*

In which sentence does the relative pronoun *that* have a

plural antecedent? _____

1962

---

b

2228

---

a. **Archie** *has lost* **his voice.**
b. **Archie** *lost* **his voice.**

Which sentence would you use to indicate that Archie's

voice is still gone? _____

2229

True

2495

Many people who accept "It's *me*" and perhaps "It's *us*" draw the line at "It's *him*," "It's *her*," and "It's *them*."

You are less likely to be criticized for saying "It's *me*" than for saying "It's *them*." (*True, False*)

2496

Yes

2762

---

a. **I did not apply for the job was in another town.**
b. **I did not apply because the job was in another town.**

In which sentence is a comma needed to prevent misread-

ing? _____

2763

Fred Sims misplaces and loses keys and other things and then blames his brothers.

How many words in this sentence end with **s**? _____

3030

---

page 174

True 87	**Our guest from Ohio arrived by plane this morning.** This is a **Pattern I** sentence because **Our guest arrived** is (*complete, incomplete*) in its meaning. 88
a 355	a. **You must follow the recipe precisely. Or the fudge will be a failure.** b. **You must follow the recipe precisely, or the fudge will be a failure.** The conjunction **or** is properly used in (*a, b*). 356
whom 623	Underline the correct relative pronoun in this and the following frames: **It is the parents** (*who, whom*) **I believe are responsible.** 624
watching 891	*Dave watched the men work,* **and he learned about motors.** **By** *watching the men work,* **he learned about motors.** After changing the verb *watch* to the gerund *watching,* we put an appropriate preposition before it—in this case, the preposition _____. 892
the need for which 1159	**We studied a poem by Robert Frost,** *and its meaning was very difficult.* **We studied a poem by Robert Frost** _____ _____ *was very difficult.* 1160
Yes 1427	then besides furthermore otherwise therefore however consequently nevertheless Because these special adverbs point both backward and forward, they are useful steppingstones between sentences. Which of these adverbs would fit in best below? **I enjoy movies.** _____, **I seldom go.** 1428

No

1695

a. **It says in the Bible that all men are brothers.**
b. **The Bible says that all men are brothers.**

Which sentence is more direct and to the point? _____

1696

---

b

1962

I like dogs *that are friendly.*

Because the pronoun *that* stands for the plural noun **dogs,** it requires the plural verb _____.

1963

---

a

2229

Underline the correct verb:
When I was a small child, I (*disliked, have disliked*) **spinach.**

2230

True

2496

Is there general agreement about informal usage after forms of the verb **be?** (*Yes, No*)

2497

---

a

2763

Use a comma before **for** whenever you can put **because** in its place.

a. **They sold us two** *for* **the price of one.**
b. **We didn't stop** *for* **the light had turned green.**

Which sentence requires a comma before *for?* _____

2764

---

eight

3030

Fred Sims misplaces and loses keys and other things and then blames his brothers.

Every word in this sentence is correctly spelled.

Is there an apostrophe before any one of the eight final **s's?** (*Yes, No*)

3031

complete 88	a. **Heavy black <u>clouds</u> <u>appeared</u> on the horizon.** b. **Heavy black <u>clouds</u> <u>covered</u> the airport.** Read just the *subject* and *verb* in each sentence. Which sentence is **Pattern I** because the verb makes a statement that is *complete* in meaning? _____ 89
b 356	Lesson **10** **The Compound Predicate as a Word-saver** [Frames 358–390]
who 624	**Most of the girls (*who, whom*) take our business course get excellent jobs.** 625
By 892	*Dave watched the men work,* **and he learned about motors.** <div align="center">**Dave**</div>**By** *watching the men work,* ~~he~~ **learned about motors.** Since we lost the subject *Dave*, we put it back at the beginning of the main statement in place of the pronoun _____. 893
the meaning of which 1160	**We camped at the foot of Silver Mountain,** *and its top is snow-capped.* **We camped at the foot of Silver Mountain** _____ _____ *is snow-capped.* 1161
However, r Nevertheless,) 1428	**then besides furthermore otherwise** **therefore however consequently nevertheless** These adverbs modify the entire word group to which they are attached rather than a single word. <div align="center">**I enjoy movies.** *However,* **I seldom go.**</div>The adverb *However* modifies (*go, I seldom go*). 1429

b	a. **The sign said that hunting was not allowed.** b. **It said on the sign that hunting was not allowed.** Which sentence is more direct and to the point? _____
1696	1697

are	**Rex paid for the book** *which was damaged.* If you changed the noun **book** to **books,** would you also need to change the verb that follows it? (*Yes, No*)
1963	1964

disliked	Underline the correct verb: **Ever since I was a small child, I** (*disliked, have disliked*) **spinach.**
2230	2231

No	What are we to do while we wait for time to settle this problem of pronoun usage? One solution might be to use whatever pronoun seems natural and comfortable to us in our everyday speech (as many people do). If you adopted this policy, would you be entirely free from criticism? (*Yes, No*)
2497	2498

b	When an introductory adverb clause is short, you may omit the comma, as you do in short compound sentences. a. **When I saw the price, I changed my mind.** b. **When I saw that the price was unreasonably high, I changed my mind.** From which sentence might the comma be omitted? _____
2764	2765

No	Should you put an apostrophe before the final **s** in every word that ends in **s?** (*Yes, No*)
3031	3032

a. **Heavy black clouds appeared**
b. **Heavy black clouds covered**

Which group of words requires the addition of other words

to complete its meaning? _____

a

89

90

In a compound sentence, the conjunction **and, but,** or **or** stands between two word groups, each with a subject and a predicate.

Hank swung at the ball, but he missed it by a foot.

What is the subject of the part of the sentence that follows

the conjunction **but?** _____

358

---

who

Most of the girls (*who, whom*) **we train get excellent jobs.**

625

626

He sent a check, and *he didn't sign his name.*
He sent a check   *signing his name.*

he

After you've changed the verb *sign* to the gerund *signing,* what preposition would make good sense in the blank space?

_____

893

894

---

the top
of which

Lesson **31** Noun Clause Devices

[Frames 1163–1191]

1161

---

then   besides   **furthermore**   **otherwise**
therefore   **however**   **consequently**   **nevertheless**

Because of their usefulness in leading smoothly from one idea to the next, these special adverbs listed above are called **conjunctive adverbs.** Do adverbs have the power of conjunctions to form compound sentences? (*Yes, No*)

I seldom go

1429

1430

a 1697	**It shows in the diagram how to adjust the carburetor.** Rewrite the above sentence, eliminating the introductory **It.** _____ _____ 1698
Yes 1964	a. **Banks will not hire people** _who gamble._ b. **Banks will not hire a person** _who gambles._ In which sentence would you consider _who_ a plural pronoun? _____ 1965
have disliked 2231	Underline the correct verb: **We don't want to move because we** (_lived, have lived_) **in our present house for many years.** 2232
No 2498	Another solution might be to use the nominative case on "dress-up" occasions or when we are with people who observe the traditional rule. a. **It must have been** _them._ b. **It must have been** _they._ Which sentence would be preferred by people who strictly follow the traditional rules of English? _____ 2499
a 2765	Use a comma wherever it is needed to prevent misreading—regardless of the length of the introductory phrase or clause. Insert a comma to prevent misreading of this sentence: **If you can get some information about campus life.** 2766
No 3032	An apostrophe is not an ornament for decorating a final **s.** One of its main uses is to show ownership. To own something means to possess it. We say, therefore, that a word that shows ownership is in the **possessive case.** Underline two nouns that are in the possessive case: **Another boy's name was in Paul's book.** 3033

b

Heavy black clouds covered . . . (What?)

What did the clouds cover—the moon, the mountain, or the airport? We don't know.

Until we answer this question, the meaning of the sentence is (*complete, incomplete*). _____

90

91

---

he

Hank swung at the ball, but (he) missed it by a foot.

Would this sentence still make good sense if we omitted the subject **he** that follows the conjunction? (*Yes, No*)

358

359

---

whom

It was the principal (*who, whom*) issued the order.

626

627

---

without

Eliminate the **and** by changing each italicized statement to a gerund phrase used as the object of a preposition.
(Prepositions: *by, for, of, on, before, after, without*)

Jerry has an annoying habit, and *it is slamming doors.*

_____

_____

894

895

A noun clause is one that is used as a _____.

1163

No

Many run-on sentences result from mistaking conjunctive adverbs for conjunctions. It is easy to prove that these words are not conjunctions.

The line broke, *and* the fish got away.

Can the conjunction *and* be shifted to any other position in this sentence? (*Yes, No*)

1430

1431

The diagram shows how to adjust the carburetor. 1698	**In this movie it shows how flour is manufactured.** Rewrite the above sentence, eliminating the introductory **It**. _____ _____ 1699
a 1965	Ordinarily we have no trouble in making the subject and verb of an adjective clause agree. When the relative pronoun stands for a singular noun, we use a singular verb. When the relative pronoun stands for a plural noun, we use a _____ verb. 1966
have lived 2232	Underline the correct verb: **Before entering law school, my brother** (_spent, has spent_) **three years in the Navy.** 2233

b
 	
2499
	Or you can play safe by putting your sentence in a way that avoids the problem altogether (and offends no one).
	    a. **It was** _we_ **who made the suggestion.**
	    b. **We were the** _ones_ **who made the suggestion.**
	Which sentence sidesteps the problem of whether to use the nominative or the objective case after a form of **be?** _____
	2500

can, get 2766	Insert a comma to prevent misreading: **To help the government started an extensive relief program.** 2767

boy's, Paul's
 	
3033
	To form the possessive case of a singular noun, add an apostrophe _s_ (**'s**) without making any change in the spelling.
	
	    a boy's haircut **the boss's desk**
	    a lady's dress **Miss Jones's room**
	
	Look at the word that precedes each apostrophe.
	
	Each of these words is (_singular, plural_).
	3034

incomplete 91	**Heavy black clouds covered the airport.** Now we know what the clouds covered, and the meaning of our sentence is complete. Which word follows the verb **covered** to complete the meaning of the sentence? _____ 92
Yes 359	**Hank <u>swung</u> at the ball but <u>missed</u> it by a foot.** This is no longer a compound sentence because, after the conjunction **but,** we now have only a (*subject, predicate*). 360
who 627	**The major under** (*who, whom*) **he served was a strict disciplinarian.** 628
Jerry has an annoying habit of slamming doors. 895	(Prepositions: *by, for, of, on, before, after, without*) *We used the old lumber* **and saved a lot of money.** _____ _____ 896
noun 1163	Many noun clauses begin with the clause signal **that.** *That I had saved the receipt* **was fortunate.** The noun clause is the _____ of the verb **was.** 1164
No 1431	WRONG: **The line broke,** *therefore* **the fish got away.** WRONG: **The line broke, the fish** *therefore* **got away.** Can the adverb *therefore* be shifted from its position between the two statements? (*Yes, No*) 1432

This movie shows how flour is manufactured. 1699	We often use the pronoun *you* to mean people in general. It is best to avoid this usage when it leads to absurdity. **You should remove all lipstick for a photograph.** This sentence becomes absurd when it is addressed to (*a girl, your father*). 1700
plural 1966	However, in sentences that contain expressions like "one of those fellows who . . . ," people are sometimes confused as to which of two words the relative pronoun stands for. **Roy was one of those fellows** *who . . . always in debt.* If *who* stands for **one**, we would say *who is*; if *who* stands for **fellows,** we would say *who* _____. 1967
spent 2233	Now we shall consider a problem that sometimes arises when we use infinitives. Infinitives, too, have a present perfect form in which they are combined with the verb **have.** a. **to write** b. **to have written** Which infinitive is in the present perfect tense? _____ 2234
b 2500	a. **It was Irene who answered the phone.** b. **It was she who answered the phone.** c. **She was the one who answered the phone.** The two sentences that are so worded as to avoid the problem of case after the verb **be** are _____ and _____. 2501
help, the 2767	Insert a comma to prevent misreading: **With Ernie Cook formed a business partnership.** 2768
singular 3034	To form the possessive case of a plural noun that ends in **s** (as most plural nouns do), add only an apostrophe. the boys' voices the players' uniforms the ladies' coats the Joneses' cottage Look at the word that precedes each apostrophe. Each of these words is (*singular, plural*). 3035

airport 92	A word that follows a verb and completes the meaning of a sentence is known as a **complement,** which is the grammar name for a *completer.* A complement, or completer, is sometimes needed after a verb to _____ the meaning of a sentence. 93
predicate 360	**Hank swung at the ball but missed it by a foot.** This sentence has two predicates. Each predicate makes a statement about the same subject, _____. 361
whom 628	**All the young people** (*who, whom*) **the company hires must have high school diplomas.** 629
By using the old lumber, we saved a lot of money. 896	(Prepositions: *by, for, of, on, before, after, without*) **The customer left the store, and** *he didn't wait for his change.* _____ _____ 897
subject 1164	Using a "that" noun clause at the beginning of a sentence sounds rather stiff and formal for ordinary conversation. a. *That I had saved the receipt* **was fortunate.** b. **It was fortunate** *that I had saved the receipt.* Which sentence sounds more informal? _____ 1165
Yes 1432	WRONG: **The line broke,** *therefore* **the fish got away.** WRONG: **The line broke, the fish** *therefore* **got away.** If *therefore* had the power of the conjunction *and* to bind these two sentences together, could it be shifted from its position between the two statements? (*Yes, No*) 1433

your father 1700	**You should remove all lipstick for a photograph.** **One should remove all lipstick for a photograph.** **Girls should remove all lipstick for a photograph.** Because **You** does not apply to the person spoken to, we can substitute the pronoun _____ or the noun _____. <div align="right">1701</div>
are 1967	**Roy was one of those fellows** _who . . . always in debt._ Does _who_ stand for **one** or **fellows?** Let's reason it out: Roy is just one of many fellows. What kind of fellows? Fellows _who are_ always in debt. Since _who_ refers to the plural noun **fellows,** we use the plural verb (_is, are_) in our problem sentence.<div align="right">1968</div>
b 2234	Can you hope, plan, expect, or intend to do something in time that is already past? (_Yes, No_)<div align="right">2235</div>

a, c
 	
2501
	In all formal speech or writing, remember to use a nomina-tive pronoun after any form of the verb **be** (_is, am, are—was, were, been_).
	
	    a. **I** **he** **she** **we** **they**
	    b. **me** **him** **her** **us** **them**
	
	The pronouns to be used after forms of **be** are in group (_a, b_).<div align="right">2502</div>

Ernie, Cook 2768	This and the following frames review the main points of this lesson. _In England_ **motor traffic keeps to the left-hand side of the road.** Would inserting a comma after the italicized phrase make this phrase more emphatic? (_Yes, No_)<div align="right">2769</div>
plural 3035	a. **boy's** **lady's** **teacher's** **player's** b. **boys'** **ladies'** **teachers'** **players'** The plural possessive pronouns are those that end with an (_apostrophe, apostrophe s_).<div align="right">3036</div>

complete	**The police <u>blocked</u> the road.**

Because the noun **road** is needed to complete the meaning of this sentence, it is a _____. |
| 93 | 94 |

	a. **Hank <u>swung at the ball</u>, but he <u>missed it by a foot</u>.** b. **Hank <u>swung at the ball</u> but <u>missed it by a foot</u>.**
Hank	Sentence _a_ is a compound sentence because the conjunction **but** connects two sentences.

Sentence _b_ is a simple sentence with a compound predicate because the conjunction **but** connects two _____. |
| 361 | 362 |

whom	**This water color was painted by a girl** (_who, whom_) **I think has unusual talent.** (Pay no attention to the explanatory words **I think.**)
629	630

| | (Prepositions: _by, for, of, on, before, after, without_)

I consulted a number of people **and decided to become a chemist.**

_____

_____ |
|---|---|
| The customer left the store without waiting for his change. | |
| 897 | 898 |

| | _That I had saved the receipt_ **was fortunate.**
was fortunate _that I had saved the receipt._

Moving the noun clause to the end of the sentence leaves a gap that must be filled before the verb _____. |
|---|---|
| b | |
| 1165 | 1166 |

| | WRONG: **The line broke,** _therefore_ **the fish got away.**

The above sentence is a run-on sentence because there is no (_adverb, conjunction_) to hold the two statements together. |
|---|---|
| No | |
| 1433 | 1434 |

(pronoun) One (noun) Girls 1701	**Mother, you can't play football without getting a few scratches.** Substitute another word for **you:** **Mother, _____ can't play football without getting a few scratches.** 1702
are 1968	Underline the correct verb: **Roy was one of those fellows** *who (is, are) always in debt.* 1969
No 2235	After verbs that point to the future, such as **hope, plan, expect,** and **intend,** use a present infinitive (*to go, to see*), not a present perfect infinitive (*to have gone, to have seen*). Underline the correct infinitive: **I intended** (*to write, to have written*) **you about my operation.** 2236
a 2502	In this and the following frames, underline the *two* pronouns in each group that are in the proper case, according to the standard of formal usage. Be sure to select only nominative pronouns when they follow forms of the verb **be.** **If I were** (*he, her, them, she, him*)**, I should accept the offer.** 2503
Yes 2769	*Recently* **complaints about rising taxes have been increasing.** Inserting a comma after *Recently* would give this adverb (*more, less*) emphasis. 2770
apostrophe 3036	a. **the boy's room** b. **the boys' room** Which means the room of *one* boy because the word that precedes the apostrophe is the singular noun **boy?** _____ 3037

complement *or* completer 94	The kind of complement that *receives the action* of the verb or *shows the result* of this action is called a **direct object**. **The teacher will correct the tests.** Which word is a direct object because it *receives the action* of the verb **will correct**? _____ 95

predicates
(*or* verbs)
 	
362
	A careful writer streamlines his writing by eliminating all useless words. Words that add nothing to the meaning, clearness, or interest of a sentence should be dropped.
	
	  a. **Hank swung at the ball, but he missed it by a foot.**
	  b. **Hank swung at the ball but missed it by a foot.**
	
	Which sentence says the same thing in fewer words? _____
	
	363

who 630	**The magician called up a boy** (*who, whom*) **I suppose he had planted in the audience.** 631
After consulting a number of people, I decided to become a chemist. 898	Continue to follow the directions for the previous frame: **Mother has a handy gadget, and** *it slices vegetables.* _____ _____ 899
was 1166	*It* **was fortunate** *that I had saved the receipt.* We fill the gap left as a result of moving the noun clause with the *introductory* word _____. 1167
conjunction 1434	a. **The line broke,** *therefore* **the fish got away.** b. **The line broke, and** *therefore* **the fish got away.** Which sentence is correct because a conjunction connects the two statements? _____ 1435

one, a boy, a player (*or a similar word*) 1702	In this and the following frames, if the italicized pronoun needs an antecedent, cross out the pronoun and write in the parentheses the word or words it is supposed to mean. Where the pronoun is correctly used, write *Correct*. **I seldom cook because I don't enjoy** *it*. (_____) 1703
are 1969	On the other hand, our meaning might be different so that the pronoun refers to the singular word **one,** and not to the plural noun that follows it. **Fred was the only** *one* **of those fellows** *who was hired.* Several fellows applied for the job, but only _____ was hired. 1970
to write 2236	Underline the correct infinitive: **Mother had hoped** (*to have baked, to bake*) **a cake for your birthday.** 2237
he, she 2503	**Howard drove Phil and** (*I, us, she, they, her*) **to the game.** 2504
more 2770	**Plants grew on our earth** *long before man appeared on the scene.* If you shifted the italicized clause to the beginning of the sentence, would you insert a comma after the word *scene?* (*Yes, No*) 2771
a 3037	a. **the boy's room** b. **the boys' room** Which means the room of *more than one* boy because the word that precedes the apostrophe is the plural noun **boys?** ——— 3038

tests 95	**The cashier made a slight mistake.** Which word is a direct object because it *shows the result* of the action of the verb **made?** _____ 96
b 363	**Bobby frightened the bird, and it flew up into a tree.** What is the subject of the part of the sentence which follows the conjunction **and?** _____ 364

whom
 	
631
	In free-and-easy conversation, **who** has largely driven out **whom.** In formal speech and writing, however, **whom** should be used for all objects.
	    a. INFORMAL: **I just met a fellow . . . you know.**
	    b. FORMAL: **Our director is a man . . . citizens respect.**
	The pronoun **who** would be considered an error in (*a, b*).
	
	632

Mother has a handy gadget for slicing vegetables. 899	*Sue got out of the car* **and turned her ankle.** _____ _____ 900
It 1167	*That anyone should believe this story* **seems absurd.** *It* **seems absurd** *that anyone should believe this story.* After moving the noun clause to the end of the sentence, we put the *introductory* word *It* in the (*subject, object*) position. 1168
b 1435	then besides furthermore otherwise therefore however consequently nevertheless If you mistake these conjunctive adverbs for conjunctions, you are likely to write many run-on sentences. **Al shut off the alarm,** *then* **he went back to sleep.** This sentence is a (*run-on, correct*) sentence. 1436

cooking 1703	Continue to follow the directions for the previous frame: **Typing would make your paper look neater if you can borrow** *one*. (_____) 1704
one 1970	**Fred was the only** *one* **of those fellows** *who was hired*. If we said ". . . **fellows** *who were hired*," we should be stating something that isn't true. Because only *one* of the fellows was hired, the pronoun *who* stands for the noun (*one, fellows*). 1971
to bake 2237	Underline the correct infinitive: **I meant** (*to pay, to have paid*) **this bill on time.** 2238
us, her 2504	**Bob and** (*me, him, her, I, he*) **secured most of the advertisements.** 2505
Yes 2771	*On Tuesday* **the new semester begins.** *In Europe* **gasoline is more expensive.** Is a comma necessary after a short introductory phrase that states *time* or *place*? (*Yes, No*) 2772

b
 	
3038
	There are a small number of plural nouns that do not end in **s**, as nearly all plural nouns do.
	
	    a. **boy** **doctor** **student** **engineer**
	    b. **men** **women** **children** **people**
	
	In neither group do the nouns end in **s**.
	
	Which group consists of plural nouns? _____
	
	3039

mistake 96	a. **The campers covered the fire.** b. **The campers started a fire.** In one sentence the direct object **fire** receives the action of the verb; in the other it shows the result of the action. The direct object *receives the action* in sentence (*a, b*). _____ 97
it 364	**Bobby** <u>frightened</u> **the bird, and (it)** <u>flew</u> **up into a tree.** Would this sentence still make good sense if we omitted the subject **it,** which follows the conjunction? (*Yes, No*) 365
b 632	a. **It is the original thinker . . . the world needs today.** b. **Is Dick the boy . . . you invited?** In which sentence would *who* be acceptable as informal usage? _____ 633
In (on, *etc.*) getting out of the car, Sue turned her ankle. 900	**Paul parked the car on a hill, and** *he didn't pull the brake.* _____ _____ 901
subject 1168	*That the weather affects people's moods* **has been proved.** Supply the missing words, using the introductory word *It:* _____ *that the weather affects people's moods.* 1169
run-on 1436	WRONG: **Al shut off the alarm,** *then* **he went back to sleep.** We know that *then* is not a conjunction because it (*can, cannot*) be shifted to another position. 1437

a typewriter (a machine) 1704	The straight and narrow path would not be so narrow if more people traveled *it*. (_____) 1705
one 1971	Underline the correct verb: **Fred was the only** *one* **of those fellows** *who* (*was, were*) *hired*. 1972
to pay 2238	On the other hand, you can be happy or unhappy about an action that has already been completed. a. **I intended** *to have seen* **this game.** b. **I am happy** *to have seen* **this game.** In which sentence does the present perfect infinitive make good sense because it refers to a completed action? _____ 2239
I, he 2505	**How can you be sure that it was** (*we, us, me, they, her*)? 2506
No 2772	*Whenever you are in doubt about manners,* **do what seems reasonable to you.** If you shifted the italicized clause to the end of the sentence, would this sentence still require a comma? (*Yes, No*) 2773
b 3039	Of the nouns having irregular plurals that do not end in **s,** the most frequently used are— **men women children people** These plural nouns look like singular nouns. We make them possessive in the same way that we make singular nouns possessive: by adding an (*apostrophe, apostrophe s*). 3040

The sentence that contains a direct object gives us our second sentence pattern.

PATTERN II: *Subject—Action Verb → Direct Object*

A sentence in Pattern II has three basic parts.

The third basic part is the _____ *object.*

a

97

98

No

Bobby frightened the bird, and (it) flew up into a tree.

Our word-saving device does not work here because each predicate makes a statement about (*a different, the same*) subject.

365

366

---

b

633

Lesson **17** Subordination by Adjective Clauses

[Frames 635–673]

Paul parked the car on a hill without pulling the brake.

901

Beth had not yet completed her commercial course, **and she was offered a good job.** (Try *before.*)

_____

_____

902

It has been proved

1169

Make the following sentence more informal by moving the noun clause to the end:

That Norma won both prizes **seems unfair.**

_____

_____

1170

---

can

1437

a. **Al shut off the alarm. Then he went back to sleep.**
b. **Al shut off the alarm; then he went back to sleep.**
c. **Al shut off the alarm, then he went back to sleep.**

Which is a run-on sentence? _____

1438

Correct 1705	**If you park there,** *they* (_____) **will tow away your car.** 1706
was 1972	Suppose that you have several library books that *are* overdue and that *The Yearling* is one of these books. Underline the correct verb: *The Yearling* **is one of my library books that** (*is, are*) **overdue.** 1973
b 2239	a. **Roberta was disappointed** *to have sold* **so few tickets.** b. **Roberta hoped** *to have sold* **many more tickets than she did.** In which sentence is the perfect infinitive correctly used because it refers to a completed action? _____ 2240
we, they 2506	**My brother divided his stamp collection between Cliff and** (*she, me, him, he, I*). 2507
No 2773	**We had to cut our speed** *because* **the road suddenly became very rough.** If you changed *because* to *for,* would you insert a comma after the word **speed?** (*Yes, No*) 2774

apostrophe s
 	
3040
	To form the possessive of the few plural nouns that do not end in **s,** add **'s**—just as you do with any singular noun.
	
	    the men's lounge the children's program
	    women's fashions the people's choice
	
	We know that each of these possessive nouns is plural because the word that precedes each apostrophe is (*singular, plural*).
	3041

direct 98	**PATTERN II: The speaker showed a movie of his travels.** Notice that the action begins with the subject and ends with the direct object. The direct object of an action verb is the goal of its action. Which word is the *direct object* in the example above? _____ 99
a different 366	**Hank swung at the ball, but (he) missed it by a foot.** We can change this compound sentence to a sentence with a *compound predicate* because both predicates make statements about the same person, _____. 367
	The adjective clause is useful in combining sentences when one sentence states an explanatory fact about a noun or pronoun in the previous sentence. **Our yearbook comes out in June.** *It sells for one dollar.* The italicized sentence states an explanatory fact about the noun _____ in the first sentence. 635
Before completing her commercial course, Beth was offered a good job. 902	**Lesson 24 Making Use of Infinitives** [Frames 904–938]
It seems unfair that Norma won both prizes. 1170	Make the following sentence more informal by moving the noun clause to the end: *That snakes have the power to hypnotize* **is a false idea.** _____ _____ 1171
c 1438	**His parents needed his help, or** *otherwise* **Ken would have gone to college.** If you omitted the conjunction **or,** the above sentence would then be a (*compound, run-on*) sentence. 1439

the police (*or whoever it might be*) 1706	Although Mr. Neville was very wealthy, he made poor use of *it*. (_____) 1707
are 1973	Now suppose that you have several library books but that only one of them *is* overdue. Underline the correct verb: *The Yearling* is the only *one* of my library books that (*is, are*) overdue. 1974
a 2240	Underline the correct infinitive: We are happy (*to be, to have been*) of service to you in the recent sale of your home. 2241
me, him 2507	Marge and (*me, I, her, him, we*) were in charge of the decorations. 2508
Yes 2774	When I read *long and tiresome descriptions of nature,* I get drowsy. If you omitted the italicized words, would it be all right to omit the comma? (*Yes, No*) 2775
plural 3041	a. all singular nouns b. plural nouns ending in s c. plural nouns not ending in s To form the possessive case, add an 's to all nouns except those in group _____. 3042

movie 99	Don't mistake another word that may follow an action verb for a direct object. To be a **direct object,** a word must either receive the action of the verb or show the result of this _____. 100
Hank 367	**Bobby frightened the bird, and (it) flew up into a tree.** We *cannot* change this compound sentence to a sentence with a *compound predicate* because the first predicate makes a statement about **Bobby,** and the second predicate makes a statement about _____. 368
yearbook 635	**Our yearbook comes out in June.** *It sells for one dollar.* Which word in the italicized sentence means the same thing as the noun **yearbook** in the first sentence? _____ 636
	Infinitives are the forms of verbs most commonly listed in the dictionary. If you should look up the words *grew* and *broken,* the dictionary would refer you to the words *grow* and _____. 904
It is a false idea that snakes have the power to hypnotize. 1171	Combine each pair of sentences into a single sentence by changing the italicized sentence to a noun clause. Begin your sentence with *It* and put the noun clause at the end. *I took along a flashlight.* **This was very lucky.** _____ _____ 1172
run-on 1439	WRONG: **His parents needed his help,** *otherwise* **Ken would have gone to college.** You can repair this run-on sentence either by inserting a period after the word *help* and then using a capital letter or by inserting a _____. (What punctuation mark?) 1440

his wealth (his money) 1707	*It* (—————————————) **is always cool in the evening.** 1708
is 1974	There are many factors that cause war. Greed is one of them. Underline the correct verb: **Greed is one of the many factors that** (*cause, causes*) **war.** 1975
to have been 2241	Underline the correct infinitive: **Jim had hoped** (*to receive, to have received*) **a college recommendation.** 2242
I, we 2508	**The evidence indicates that it was** (*he, them, her, they, me*) **who divulged this secret information.** 2509
Yes 2775	**While we tour we eat lightly.** Is a comma necessary after the word **tour**? (*Yes, No*) 2776
b 3042	A simple way to apply these rules is to look at the word you have written and ask yourself, "Who is the owner?" Then put the apostrophe right after the word that answers this question. **this boys jacket** (Who is the owner? **boy**) Now go back and put the apostrophe after **boy**. 3043

action 100	a. **Mr. Price returned** *recently*. b. **Mr. Price returned the** *money*. Does the word *recently* or *money* receive the action of the verb **returned?** _____ 101
it *or* bird 368	We can change a compound sentence to a sentence with a compound predicate only when both predicates make statements about the _____ subject. 369
It 636	*which* **Our yearbook comes out in June.** ~~It~~ *sells for one dollar.* To change the italicized sentence to an adjective clause, we put the relative pronoun _____ in place of *It*. 637
break 904	An **infinitive** is the basic form of a verb from which all other forms are derived. The infinitive is usually combined with the preposition *to;* for example, *to walk, to drive, to sleep.* The infinitive from which the verbs *flew, flying,* and *flown* are derived is _____. 905
t was very lucky that I took along a flashlight. 1172	Continue to follow the directions for the previous frame: *Mrs. Hicks never left her house.* **This seemed strange to the neighbors.** _____ _____ 1173
semicolon 1440	**It was his own fault.** *Nevertheless,* **I felt sorry for him.** **It was his own fault;** *nevertheless,* **I felt sorry for him.** Are both arrangements correct? (*Yes, No*) 1441

Correct 1708	**We found a delightful souvenir shop where** *they* (_____ _____) **spoke English.** 1709
cause 1975	Your friend has had many pictures taken, but you think that only one of them looks at all like him. Underline the correct verb: **This is the only one of the pictures that** (*look, looks*) **at all like you.** 1976
to receive 2242	Underline the correct infinitive: **Alison intended** (*to apply, to have applied*) **for this job.** 2243
he, they 2509	**The car missed Donna and** (*him, we, he, me, she*) **by only a hair's breadth.** 2510
No 2776	**If Jim doesn't tell the truth will never be known.** Is a comma necessary in this sentence? (*Yes, No*) 2777
this boy's jacket 3043	**these boys grades** (Who is the owner? **boys**) Now go back and put the apostrophe after **boys**. 3044

money

101

a. **Mr. Price returned** *recently.*
b. **Mr. Price returned the** *money.*

Which sentence contains a direct object? _____

102

---

same

369

The students went to England by boat. They returned by plane.

In combining these two sentences, which word would you omit? _____

370

---

which

637

which
Our yearbook comes out in June. ~~It~~ *sells for one dollar.*

The clause *which sells for one dollar* should be inserted in the sentence right after the noun (*yearbook, June*), which it modifies.

638

---

to fly

905

An infinitive—like a gerund—is often used to name an action. It is often interchangeable with a gerund.

GERUND: *Walking* **is good exercise.**
INFINITIVE: *To walk* **is good exercise.**

Both the gerund and the infinitive are used as nouns. Each is the _____ of the verb **is.**

906

---

seemed strange
to the neighbors
that Mrs. Hicks
never left her
house.
1173

Children pick up a foreign language very fast. **This is a well-known fact.**

_____

_____

1174

Yes

1441

a. **If you don't care about your appearance,** *then* **nobody else will.**
b. **The salesman neglected his appearance,** *then* **he began to lose business.**

Which sentence is a run-on sentence? _____

1442

page 203

the clerks, the owners (*or whoever it might have been*) 1709	**Our friends fished all morning but didn't catch a single** *one.* (_____) 1710
looks 1976	Another situation that invites trouble is the sentence in which we use an expression like "one of the best games that . . ." or "one of the worst floods that. . . ." We solve this problem in the same way: If the relative pronoun refers to **one,** we choose a singular verb; if it refers to a plural noun, we choose a _____ verb. 1977
to apply 2243	Underline the correct infinitive: **Our town seems** (*to change, to have changed*) **a lot during the past five years.** 2244
him, me 2510	**It was** (*us, they, him, me, she*) **who objected to the new policy.** 2511
Yes 2777	In this and the following frames, insert any necessary commas. If no comma is required, write *None.* **In the theater of Shakespeare's day the farthest spectator was only fifty-five feet from the stage.** 2778
these boys' grades 3044	In this and the following frames, ask yourself, "Who is the owner?" or "Who are the owners?" Underline the part of the possessive noun that answers this question and insert an apostrophe at this point; for example, **one <u>man</u>'s car, both <u>men</u>'s cars.** **these girls voices** 3045

b 102	a. **The rain stopped the** game. b. **The rain stopped** suddenly. Which sentence contains a direct object? _____ 103
They 370	a. **The coach went to the blackboard, and he drew a diagram of the play.** b. **The curtain went up, and the show began.** Which compound sentence can be changed to a sentence with a compound predicate because both predicates make statements about the same subject? _____ 371
yearbook 638	a. **Our yearbook,** *which sells for one dollar,* **comes out in June.** b. **Our yearbook comes out in June,** *which sells for one dollar.* In which sentence is the adjective clause properly placed? _____ 639
subject 906	Fill the blank with the infinitive form of *traveling:* GERUND: *Traveling* **broadens the mind.** INFINITIVE: _____ **broadens the mind.** 907
t is a well-known act that children ɔick up a foreign ɩguage very fast. 1174	A noun clause is often used as an appositive after the words **the fact.** **The fact** *that the door was open* **made me suspicious.** The clause *that the door was open* is an appositive because it explains the noun _____. 1175
b 1442	a. **All our bills were paid,** *consequently* **we had little to worry about.** b. **Because all our bills were paid, we** *consequently* **had little to worry about.** Which sentence is a run-on sentence? _____ 1443

fish 1710	*It* (_____) **is very strange that Briggs refused the promotion.** 1711
plural 1977	**The wheel was one of the greatest inventions** *that* **. . . ever made.** The antecedent of *that* is **inventions,** not **one,** for we surely do not mean to say that only *one* great invention was ever made. Since the relative pronoun *that* stands for **inventions,** it requires a (*singular, plural*) verb. 1978
to have changed 2244	Underline the correct infinitive: **I meant** (*to mail, to have mailed*) **this card on my way home from school.** 2245
they, she 2511	**The entire incident was no surprise to the Sampsons or** (*us, we, them, I, they*). 2512
day, the 2778	**If dogs and cats have such a remarkable sense of direction why do so many get lost only a block or two away from their homes?** 2779
<u>girls'</u> 3045	**my doctors opinion** 3046

a 103	*Pattern I* is built around a two-part framework: a *subject* and an *action verb*. *Pattern II* is built around a three-part framework: a *subject,* an *action verb,* and a _____ _____. 104
a 371	**The coach went to the blackboard, and he drew a diagram of the play.** **The coach went to the blackboard and drew a diagram of the play.** When we change a compound sentence to a sentence with a compound predicate, we (*keep, drop*) the comma. 372
a 639	a. **Our yearbook comes out in June, and it sells for one dollar.** b. **Our yearbook, which comes out in June, sells for one dollar.** One sentence is *compound;* the other is *complex.* The sentence that is complex because it contains a subordinate clause is (*a, b*). 640
To travel 907	Fill the blank with the infinitive form of *hunting:* GERUND: **His favorite sport is** *hunting.* INFINITIVE: **His favorite sport is** _____. 908
fact 1175	"The fact that . . ." construction sometimes proves useful in tightening up a loose compound sentence. *I ate the stew,* **but that doesn't mean that I liked it.** Supply "the fact that" construction: _____ *I ate the stew* **doesn't mean that I liked it.** 1176
a 1443	a. **We printed our own programs,** *thus* **saving considerable expense.** b. **We printed our own programs,** *thus* **we saved considerable expense.** Which sentence is a run-on sentence? ____ 1444

Correct 1711	In British traffic *they* (_____) keep to the left. 1712
plural 1978	Underline the correct verb: The wheel was one of the greatest inventions that (*was, were*) ever made. 1979
to mail 2245	Lesson **63** Using the Past Perfect and the Future Perfect Tenses [Frames 2247–2282]
us, them 2512	It could not have been (*us, them, we, I, him*) who broke the window. 2513
direction, why 2779	When he tries he succeeds. 2780
doctor's 3046	both parents consent 3047

direct object 104	a. **All good citizens vote on Election Day.** b. **All good citizens cast their vote on Election Day.** Which sentence is **Pattern II** because the verb is followed by a direct object? _____ 105
drop 372	a. **We won our first game, but we lost the second.** b. **We won our first game but lost the second.** No comma is used before a conjunction that connects the two parts of a compound (*sentence, predicate*). 373
b 640	a. **Our yearbook comes out in June, and it sells for one dollar.** b. **Our yearbook, which comes out in June, sells for one dollar.** The two facts are brought into closer relationship by the (*compound, complex*) sentence. 641
to hunt 908	Like participles and gerunds, infinitives may take direct objects and subject complements, as no ordinary noun can do. *To waste food* **is sinful.** The noun *food* is the (*direct object, subject complement*) of the infinitive *to waste*. 909
The fact that 1176	In this and the following frames, improve each compound sentence by changing the italicized statement to "the fact that" construction: *Fred's dad is a dentist,* **and that influenced him to study dentistry.** _____ _____ 1177
b 1444	If the second word group begins with a conjunctive adverb, supply a period and a capital. If it begins with a conjunction, merely add a comma. Write only the word before and after your punctuation mark. **The play was dull besides, the acting was mediocre.** 1445

cars, automobiles, drivers, people (*or similar words*) 1712	Mr. Krause is bald, but his partner is well-supplied with *it*. (_____) 1713
were 1979	Suppose that someone made a list of the most unusual stories that *were* ever written. It is likely that Stevenson's "The Bottle Imp" would be one of these. Underline the correct word: **Stevenson's "The Bottle Imp" is one of the most unusual stories that** (*was, were*) **ever written.** 1980
	The past perfect tense is formed by combining **had** (the past tense of **have**) with the past participle of a verb (*seen, walked, taken*). a. **had decided** b. **has decided** Which verb is in the past perfect tense? _____ 2247
we, I 2513	In this and the following frames, the italicized pronouns are correct. If a person should find them awkward to say, how could he change the wording to eliminate the pronoun after the form of the verb **be**? "May I speak to Paul?" "This is *he* speaking." "May I speak to Paul?" "This is _____ speaking." 2514
None 2780	**To unite the Colonies needed to forget their local interests and rivalries.** 2781
parents' 3047	**some peoples property** 3048

a. **Each student keeps a list of every misspelled word.**
b. **The wheezing motor finally stopped completely.**

Which sentence is **Pattern II** because the verb is followed by a direct object? _____

106

---

predicate

373

a. **We heard a voice, but we couldn't recognize it.**
b. **We heard a voice, but couldn't recognize it.**

In which sentence should the comma before the conjunction be dropped because it is not a compound sentence?

————

374

---

complex

641

Our yearbook comes out in June, and it sells for one dollar.

By using a compound sentence we give (*equal, unequal*) emphasis to the two facts that the conjunction **and** connects.

642

---

direct object

909

To be healthy **is a great advantage.**

Because the adjective *healthy* completes the linking verb *be*, it is a (*direct object, subject complement*).

910

The fact that
Fred's dad is a
ntist influenced
him to study
dentistry.
1177

Smith knew Madden. **That doesn't make him a party to the crime.**

_____

_____

1178

---

dull. Besides,

1445

Continue to follow the directions for the previous frame:

We play one game for several weeks   then we tire of it and take up another.

_____

1446

Lesson 48 Making Pronoun Reference Clear

---

were

1980

Underline the correct verb:

Dad caught one of the largest catfish that (*was, were*) **ever caught in Mud Lake.**

1981

---

a

2247

Ellen *bought* **a dress but later** *returned* **it.**

There are two verbs in this sentence.

Does the order of the verbs represent the order in which the actions occurred? (*Yes, No*)

2248

Paul

2514

It might have been *we* **who were hurt.**

We might have been the _____.

2515

---

unite, the

2781

The messenger kept feeling his pocket for the papers were very valuable.

2782

---

people's

3048

the boys locker room

3049

The pitcher threw George a fast curve.

After the verb **threw,** we have two nouns—**George** and **curve.**

To decide which is the **direct object,** ask yourself, "What did the pitcher throw?"

The direct object is the noun _____.

a

106

107

---

a. **A large tree had fallen and was blocking traffic.**
b. **A large tree had fallen and traffic was slowed down.**

In which sentence should a comma be inserted before the conjunction? _____

b

374

375

You have learned that to *subordinate* a fact or an idea means to put it into a word group that is (*more, less*) than a sentence.

equal

642

643

Since an infinitive is a mixture of both a verb and a noun, it may be modified by an adverb.

Test pilots like *to live dangerously.*

The adverb *dangerously* modifies the infinitive _____.

subject
complement

910

911

The fact that Smith knew Madden doesn't make him a party to the crime.

The lights were on, **and that made me think that the Orrs were at home.**

_____

_____

1178

1179

---

weeks. Then

It had rained all night   and consequently the field was muddy.

_____

1446

1447

The meaning of a pronoun usually depends upon its antecedent, the word to which it refers. This referring to another word is known as the **reference** of a pronoun.

When a pronoun has no antecedent to give it meaning, we say the pronoun lacks _____.

1715

---

were

1981

In this and the following frames, underline the correct verb after you think over each sentence to decide whether the relative pronoun (*who, which, that*) refers to **one** or to the plural noun that follows it.

Mr. Slocum is one of those speakers who never (*seem, seems*) **to come to the point.**

1982

Yes

2248

    a. **Ellen** *bought* **a dress but later** *returned* **it.**
    b. **Ellen** *returned* **the dress that she** *had bought.*

In which sentence is the last action mentioned first and the first action mentioned last? _____

2249

---

ones who were
hurt.

2515

I'm sure that it was *she* **in the front seat.**

I'm sure that _____.

2516

---

pocket, for

2782

I know that Jack can keep a secret because he has never told me anything confidential about anyone else.

2783

---

boys'

3049

    SINGULAR: **lady**   PLURAL: **ladies**
When you write a possessive noun, be sure that you have the correct spelling of the owner(s) before the apostrophe.
    a. **a ladie's coat**   b. **a lady's coat**
Which is correct because the word before the apostrophe is correctly spelled? _____

3050

curve 107	**The pitcher threw George a fast curve.** What does the noun **George** do? It shows *to whom* the pitcher threw the **curve**. We call such a noun (or pronoun) an **indirect object**. **Curve** is the *direct object;* **George** is the _____ *object.* 108
b 375	**The teacher liked the movie. She urged her classes to see it.** If you were to combine these two sentences, it would be better to use a compound (*sentence, predicate*). 376
less 643	a. **It sells for one dollar.** b. **which sells for one dollar** Both word groups state a fact about *price.* The word group that *subordinates* the fact about *price* is the (*clause, sentence*). 644

to live
 	
911
	The phrases formed by infinitives with their related words are called **infinitive phrases.** These phrases can be used in most of the ways that nouns are used.
	
	   To teach a dog tricks **requires endless patience.**
	
	The infinitive phrase is used as the _____ of the verb **requires.**
	
	    912

The fact that the lights were on made me think that the Orrs were at home.
 	
1179
	We shall now learn to avoid a common error that is sometimes made when using noun clauses.
	
	   I knew *that the cement would harden.*
	
	This sentence contains a _____ clause.
	
	    1180

night, and 1447	**People once considered the night air poisonous therefore they kept their windows tightly closed.** _____ 1448

reference 1715	When we say that a pronoun lacks reference, we mean that there is no word that serves as its _____ 1716
seem 1982	**Hawley's is the only one of the gas stations that** (*stay, stays*) **open all night.** 1983
b 2249	a. **Ellen** *bought* **a dress but later** *returned* **it.** b. **Ellen** *returned* **the dress that she** *had bought.* In which sentence do you find a verb. in the past perfect tense? _____ 2250
she was (the one) in the front seat. 2516	*WHO* AND *WHOM* AS INTERROGATIVE PRONOUNS **Who** is nominative; **whom** is objective. *Who* **was the inventor of wireless telegraphy?** The nominative pronoun *Who* is correct because it is the subject of the verb _____. 2517
None 2783	Lesson **78** **Commas to Separate Items in a Series** [Frames 2785–2820]
b 3050	SINGULAR: **baby** PLURAL: **babies** a. **the babies' mothers** b. **the babys' mothers** Which is correct because the word before the apostrophe is correctly spelled? _____ 3051

indirect 108	**The pitcher threw George a fast curve.** The indirect object **George** comes (*before, after*) the direct object **curve.** _____ 109
predicate 376	**The teacher liked the movie and urged her classes to see it.** Should a comma be inserted before the conjunction **and?** (*Yes, No*) 377
clause 644	a. **Our yearbook,** *which sells for one dollar,* **comes out in June.** b. **Our yearbook comes out in June, and it sells for one dollar.** In which sentence is the *price* of the yearbook subordinated? _____ 645
subject 912	**My plan is** *to save enough money for college.* The infinitive phrase is used as a (*direct object, subject complement*). 913
noun 1180	**I knew** *that the cement would harden if I didn't hurry.* Besides a noun clause, this sentence now has a second clause, which is an (*adverb, adjective*) clause. 1181
poisonous. Therefore 1448	**The plane took off an hour late or otherwise we should have missed it.** _____ 1449

antecedent
 	
1716
	In the previous lesson we repaired sentences in which the pronouns had no antecedents to make their meaning clear.
	
	   a. **Terry sang and everyone enjoyed** *it*.
	   b. **Terry sang a song, and everyone enjoyed** *it*.
	
	Which sentence is faulty because the pronoun *it* lacks reference? _____
	
	1717

stays 1983	**The Netherlands was one of the many neutral countries that** (*was, were*) **invaded by the Nazis.** 1984
b 2250	Use the past perfect tense of a verb for an earlier action that is mentioned after a later action. Suppose that John *picked* an apple and then *ate* it. You would put the verb *picked* in the past perfect tense if you mentioned it (*first, last*). 2251
was 2517	*Whom* **did the Duke of Wellington defeat at Waterloo?** **(The Duke of Wellington did defeat** *whom* **at Waterloo?)** The objective pronoun *Whom* is correct because it is the direct object of the verb _____ _____. 2518
	A series is a number of similar things that follow one after another. We speak of a series of games, accidents, or coincidences. In a sentence, a series is *three or more* words, phrases, or clauses all used in the same way. **There was sand** *on the floor, in our beds,* **and** *in our food.* This sentence contains a series of (*words, phrases, clauses*). 2785
a 3051	Here is another problem that concerns apostrophes: WRONG: **the dentist who pulled my tooth's office** This sentence is wrong because the apostrophe is not in the right word. The owner of the office is not **tooth** but _____ 3052

before 109	a. **The pitcher threw George a fast curve.** b. **The pitcher threw him a fast curve.** In which sentence is the indirect object a pronoun? _____ 110
No 377	**We have good traffic laws. They are strictly enforced.** If you were to combine these two sentences, you would need to use a compound (*sentence, predicate*). 378
a 645	To subordinate a fact or an idea is like taking an article from the front of a showcase and putting it in the back, where it is less conspicuous. A fact or an idea gets less emphasis when we put it in a (*sentence, clause*). 646
subject complement 913	**A good citizen does not refuse** *to be a witness.* The infinitive phrase is used as a (*direct object, subject complement*). 914
adverb 1181	a. **I knew** *that the cement would harden if I didn't hurry.* b. **I knew** *that if I didn't hurry the cement would harden.* In which sentence is the adverb clause inserted between parts of the noun clause? _____ 1182
late, or 1449	Continue to follow the directions for the previous frame, with only one change: Use a semicolon where you have previously been using a period and a capital. Both are equally correct. **I had paid my bill however, I could not find my receipt.** 1450

a 1717	Sentences are even more confusing when it is not clear to which of two words a pronoun refers. Suppose that while staying at a summer cottage, you received the following message. **Take the motor off the boat and sell** *it*. Could *it* refer to either the **motor** or the **boat**? (*Yes, No*) 1718
were 1984	**His boss was one of those employers who** (*don't, doesn't*) **welcome suggestions from their employees.** 1985
last 2251	**John** *ate* **the apple that he** *had picked*. Are the actions mentioned in the order in which they occurred? (*Yes, No*) 2252
did defeat 2518	**To** *whom* **will the President entrust this responsibility?** The objective form *whom* is correct because it is the object of the preposition _____. 2519
, phrases 2785	It takes at least _____ items to form a series. (How many?) 2786
dentist 3052	The apostrophe should be placed in the word that shows the owner, not in a word that belongs to a modifying phrase or clause. WRONG: **the dentist who pulled my tooth's office** Can you correct this error by moving the **'s** to the word **dentist**? (*Yes, No*) 305

b
 	
110
	An indirect object can show **to what,** as well as **to whom,** something was done.
	
	        You should give this story more suspense.
	
	The noun **suspense** is the _____ *object.*
	The noun **story** is _____ *object.*
	
	                111

sentence 378	**We have good traffic laws and they are strictly enforced.** Should a comma be inserted before the conjunction **and?** (*Yes, No*) 379
clause 646	**Our yearbook,** *which comes out in June,* **sells for one dollar.** This complex sentence states two facts: one about *price* and another about *time of issue.* This sentence gives greater emphasis to the fact about (*price, time of issue*). 647

direct object
 	
914
	In addition to being used as nouns, infinitives are also used as modifiers—both as adjectives and as adverbs.
	
	    I want a chance *to work.* **I want a chance** *to play.*
	    I want a chance *to rest.* **I want a chance** *to travel.*
	
	Each sentence means a different kind of **chance** because the _____ is different in each sentence.
	
	                915

b
 	
1182
	We often interrupt a noun clause after the clause signal *that* to insert an adverb phrase or clause.
	
	Put parentheses around the adverb clause that interrupts the noun clause:
	
	    I knew *that if I didn't hurry the cement would harden.*
	
	              1183

bill; however, 1450	**I wrote down my answer** **and then I changed my mind.** ――――――――――――――――――――― 1451

Yes 1718	**Take the motor off the boat and sell** *it.* Because this sentence has two possible meanings, we say that it is **ambiguous,** which means "having more than one possible meaning." The word that makes this sentence ambiguous is the pronoun _____.　　　　　　　　　　　　　　　1719
don't 1985	**Are you one of those newspaper readers who** (*read, reads*) **only the headlines?** 　　　　　　　　　　　　　　　1986
No 2252	Use the past perfect tense when the first action is mentioned (*first, last*). 　　　　　　　　　　　　　　　2253
To 2519	a. ... **was Lincoln's Secretary of State?** b. ... **did Lincoln appoint as his Secretary of State?** In which sentence would **Whom** be correct because it is the direct object of the verb? _____　　　　2520
three 2786	a. **Many friends and relatives were invited.** b. **Many friends, relatives, and neighbors were invited.** Which sentence contains a series of nouns? _____　　2787
No 3053	WRONG: **the dentist who pulled my tooth's office** To avoid this error, it is necessary to show the ownership of the office by using an **of** phrase. 　　RIGHT: **the office of the dentist who pulled my tooth** Instead of using an **'s** to show ownership, we use the preposition phrase _____. 　　　　　　　　　　　　　　　3054

uspense) direct (story) indirect 111	Besides showing *to whom* (or *to what*) something was done, an **indirect object** can also show *for whom* (or *for what*) something was done. **Aunt Jane knitted Fred some socks.** *For whom* did Aunt Jane knit the socks? For _____. 112
Yes 379	**The crowded bus stopped. It took on still more people.** If you were to combine these two sentences, it would be better to use a compound (*sentence, predicate*). 380
price 647	a. **Our yearbook,** *which comes out in June,* **sells for one dollar.** b. **Our yearbook,** *which sells for one dollar,* **comes out in June.** One sentence emphasizes the *price;* the other, the *time of issue.* Which emphasizes the *time of issue?* _____ 648
infinitive 915	**I want a chance** *to work.* **I want a chance** *to play.* **I want a chance** *to rest.* **I want a chance** *to travel.* Each infinitive in the above sentences modifies the noun _____. 916
I didn't hurry) 1183	When we interrupt a noun clause in this way, we must guard against a common error. WRONG: **I knew** *that (if I didn't hurry) that the cement would harden.* The sentence above is incorrect because the clause signal _____ is repeated. 1184
answer, and 1451	**The two essays were judged equally good therefore the prize was divided between us.** _____ 1452

it 1719	**Take the motor off the boat and sell** *it*. This sentence is ambiguous because there are *two* nouns before the pronoun *it* that could serve as its antecedent. These nouns are _____ and _____. 1720
read 1986	**This was one of the worst floods that** (*has, have*) **ever occurred in the South.** 1987
last 2253	a. **Howard . . . off the alarm and went back to sleep.** b. **Howard went back to sleep after he . . . off the alarm.** In which sentence should the past perfect verb **had shut** be used? _____ 2254
b 2520	In ordinary conversation, the nominative form **who** is generally used even though it may be the object of a verb or a preposition. INFORMAL: *Who* **did you see at church today?** This violates the rule for formal usage because *Who* is the direct object of the verb _____ _____. 2521
b 2787	Use commas *between* the items in a series but not before or after the series (unless a comma is required for another reason). Punctuate the following sentence: **Many of the world's greatest books paintings and inventions were produced by people past sixty.** 2788
of the dentist 3054	a. **the wife of the man in the other car** b. **the man in the other car's wife** Which is correct? _____ 3055

Fred 112	**Aunt Jane knitted Fred some socks.** The direct object is _____. The indirect object is _____. 113
predicate 380	In this and the following frames, combine each pair of sentences, using a compound predicate whenever possible. Indicate your answer by writing the conjunction and the two words surrounding it. Insert any necessary comma. **Lee made a two-base hit. The ball game was over.** _____ 381
b 648	The type of sentence we use depends on the emphasis we wish to give various facts or ideas. If we wish to give two facts equal emphasis, we would use a (*compound, complex*) sentence. 649
chance 916	**I want a chance** *to work.*　　**I want a chance** *to play.* **I want a chance** *to rest.*　　**I want a chance** *to travel.* Because each infinitive modifies the noun **chance,** it is used as an _____. 917
that 1184	It is easy to forget that you have already written the word *that* and repeat it when you continue the clause. a. **I decided that after I graduated I would go to college.** b. **I decided that after I graduated that I would go to college.** Which sentence is correct? _____ 1185
good; therefore 1452	**The doctor was exhausted　but nevertheless he kept on working.** _____ 1453

motor, boat 1720	a. **Take the** *motor* **off the** *boat* **and sell it.** b. **Sell the** *motor* **after you take** *it* **off the** *boat.* Which sentence is clear because there is only *one* noun before the pronoun *it* that could serve as its antecedent? ——— 1721
have 1987	**This is just one more of those stupid prejudices that** (*is, are*) **passed on from one generation to another.** 1988
b 2254	a. **The police captured the prisoner who . . . .** b. **The prisoner . . . but the police captured him.** In which sentence should the past perfect verb **had escaped** be used? —— 2255
did see 2521	The widespread use of **who** instead of **whom** is due to the fact that it comes in the subject position at the head of the sentence, and position is an important factor in our language. Can a word occupy the subject position and still not be the subject of the sentence? (*Yes, No*) 2522
books, paintings, 2788	Make a count to see how, in a series, the number of commas compares with the number of items: ————, ————, **and** ———— ————, ————, ————, **and** ———— The number of commas is always one (*more, less*) than the number of items in a series. 2789
a 3055	Rewrite the following sentence correctly: **The girl in the front seat's name is Linda.** ———————————————— ———————————————— 3056

(direct object) socks (indirect object) Fred 113	**Aunt Jane knitted Fred some socks.** The indirect object comes (*before, after*) the direct object. 114
hit, and the 381	Follow the directions given in the previous frame. Be sure to select a conjunction that expresses the meaning most clearly. **Paul wanted a date. He was too timid to ask.** _____ 382
compound 649	If we wish to subordinate one idea to another, we would use a (*compound, complex*) sentence. 650
adjective 917	**I learned a new way** *to play checkers.* The infinitive phrase *to play checkers* modifies the noun _____. 918
a 1185	a. **We knew that if we appeared too eager that the price would be raised.** b. **We knew that if we appeared too eager the price would be raised.** Which sentence is correct? _____ 1186
exhausted, but 1453	**The job provided me with spending money furthermore, it built up my self-confidence.** _____ 1454

b 1721	*the motor* **Take the motor off the boat and sell ~~it~~.** Another very simple way to clear up the meaning of this sentence is to eliminate the pronoun *it* by repeating the noun _____. 1722
are 1988	**Milner was the only one of our players who** (*was, were*) **selected for the all-state team.** 1989
a 2255	After you decide which action came first, underline the preferred verb: **The witness made this statement but later** (*denied, had denied*) **it.** 2256

Yes
 	
2522
	In formal writing or speaking, use **whom** if the interrogative pronoun is the object of a verb or a preposition.
	    a. *Who* **did Earl take to the prom?**
	    b. *Who* **will the party select for its candidate?**
	Your use of the pronoun *Who* instead of *Whom* would be less subject to criticism in sentence (*a, b*).
	
	2523

less 2789	In a series of *three* items, we would use *two* commas. In a series of *four* items, we would use _____ commas. 2790
The name of the girl in the front seat is Linda. 3056	Rewrite the following sentence correctly: **The family next door's dog tears up our lawn.** _____ _____ 3057

before 114	**The club bought the church a new organ.** The indirect object is the noun _____. 115
date but was 382	**It was getting late. The children were growing restless.** _____ 383
complex 650	Now let's look into the process of subordinating an idea by changing it to an adjective clause. **Tony read some notices.** *Few students heard them.* The italicized sentence provides information about the noun _____ in the first sentence. 651
way 918	**I learned a new way** *to play checkers.* Because the infinitive phrase modifies the noun **way,** it is used as an _____. 919
b 1186	a. **I am sure that if we don't buy the car someone else will.** b. **I am sure that if we don't buy the car that someone else will.** Which sentence is correct? _____ 1187
money; furthermore, 1454	Copy each pair of sentences, inserting the word in parentheses between them. Show by your punctuation whether they form one sentence or two. **The trip takes all day. The scenery is interesting.** (*but*) _____ _____ 1455

motor 1722	**After Mother left Eve at camp,** *she* **felt lonesome.** This sentence is ambiguous because *she* might refer to either _____ or _____. 1723
was 1989	Lesson **56** A Few Remaining Problems [Frames 1991–2030]
denied 2256	Underline the preferred verb: **The witness later denied the statement that he** (*made, had made*)**.** 2257
a 2523	In this and the following frames, underline the pronoun that is proper for formal usage: (*Who, Whom*) **will be in favor of this new tax?** 2524
three 2790	a. **We export, food, cotton, and machinery to many countries.** b. **We export food, cotton, and machinery to many countries.** c. **We export food, cotton, and machinery, to many countries.** Which sentence is correctly punctuated? _____ 2791
The dog of the family next door tears up our lawn. 3057	Be sure to recognize possessive nouns when the thing that is owned is understood but not expressed. **Your voice sounds just like Mary's (voice).** We put an apostrophe in the word **Mary's** because the noun _____ is understood. 3058

church 115	An **indirect object** shows *to whom* or *what* or _____ *whom* or *what* something is done. 116
late, and the 383	**Most Americans want their children to attend college. They will make great sacrifices to send them.** _____ 384
notices 651	**Tony read some notices.** *Few students heard them.* Which word in the italicized sentence means the same thing as **notices** in the first sentence? _____ 652
adjective 919	**I learned a new way** *to play checkers.* The fact that the infinitive *to play* takes the direct object *checkers* shows that besides being used as an adjective, an infinitive also has the characteristics of a _____. 920
a 1187	Copy each sentence, inserting the word group in parentheses after the clause signal **that**. Do not repeat *that* when you continue the interrupted clause. **I was afraid that I would not be ready.** *(when my turn came)* _____ _____ 1188
The trip takes all day, but the scenery is interesting. 1455	**The trip takes all day. The scenery is interesting.** *(however)* _____ _____ 1456

Mother, Eve 1723	You can often get rid of ambiguity by shifting the "false" antecedent to a position *after* the pronoun, where it can't confuse the reader. **Mother felt lonesome after *she* left Eve at camp.** Now we know that *she* means **Mother** and not **Eve** because the noun _____ has been put after the pronoun *she*. <div style="text-align:right">1724</div>

	To make sentences more forceful, we often start them with the words **There is, There are,** or **Here is, Here are.**
	
	    a. **A spot is on your coat.**
	    b. **There is a spot on your coat.**
	
	In which sentence is the usual order of the subject and verb turned around? _____
	<div style="text-align:right">1991</div>

had made 2257	Underline the preferred verb: **I read the article and (*made, had made*) a summary of it.** <div style="text-align:right">2258</div>
Who 2524	**By (*who, whom*) will this new tax be favored?** <div style="text-align:right">2525</div>
b 2791	Punctuate the following sentence: **Immediate pursuit quick arrest and certain conviction reduce crime.** <div style="text-align:right">2792</div>
voice 3058	Supply the missing apostrophe: **A porpoise's brain is as large as a mans.** <div style="text-align:right">3059</div>

<table>
<tr><td>

for

116
</td><td>

An **indirect object**—if one is present—always comes *before* the **direct object,** and the word *to* or *for* is understood but never used.

    a. **I offered** *Frank* **my ticket.**
    b. **I offered my ticket to** *Frank.*

Is *Frank* an indirect object in sentence *a* or *b?* _____

117
</td></tr>
</table>

---

college and will

384

You must be completely satisfied. We will return your money.

_____

385

---

them

652

                                             which
Tony read some notices. *Few students heard* ~~*them.*~~

To change the italicized sentence to an adjective clause, we put the relative pronoun _____ in place of *them.*

653

---

verb

920

    a. **I learned a new way** *to play checkers.*
    b. **I learned a new way of** *playing checkers.*

One sentence contains a gerund phrase; the other an infinitive phrase.

Which sentence contains an infinitive phrase? _____

921

I was afraid that
when my turn
came I would
not be ready.

1188

Continue to follow the directions for the previous frame:

Many believe that they could write a song hit. (*if they took the time*)

_____

_____

1189

---

day. However,
or
day; however,

1456

The dogs growled at each other. They began to fight. (*then*)

_____

_____

1457

Eve 1724	**Hank backed the car out of the garage and cleaned** *it*. This sentence is ambiguous because we don't know whether *it* refers to the **car** or to the _____. 1725
b 1991	In sentences that begin with **There is, There are,** or **Here is, Here are,** the verb precedes the subject. There <u>is</u> a <u>spot</u> on your coat. We use the singular verb **is** because its subject _____ is singular. 1992
made 2258	Underline the preferred verb: **I remembered what the coach** (*said, had said*) **about forward passes.** 2259
whom 2525	(*Who, Whom*) **will the President appoint to this new post?** 2526
pursuit, arrest, 2792	Punctuate the following sentence: **The bellboy stopped me asked me my name and handed me a telegram.** 2793
man's 3059	In this and the following frames, supply the necessary apostrophes. Remember that possessive pronouns are never written with apostrophes—*yours, hers, its, ours, theirs*. If no apostrophes are required, write *None*. **Eleanors theme was more original than either Pats or hers.** 3060

a. **This machine will save much time.**
b. **This machine will save the company much time.**

The noun **time** is the direct object in both sentences. Which
sentence also contains an indirect object? _____

a

117

118

---

satisfied, or we

**My father can play several instruments. His favorite is the
violin.**

_____

385

386

---

which

which
Tony read some notices. *Few students heard* ~~them.~~
Tony read some notices, *which few students heard.*

Since a relative pronoun usually starts an adjective clause,
we move **which** to the front of the clause, before the word

_____ .

653

654

Lyle ran *to catch the bus.*

a

The infinitive phrase *to catch the bus* explains **why** about
the verb _____ .

921

922

Many believe that
if they took the
time they could
write a song hit.

The study shows that school grades drop sharply. (*when
students get their own cars*)

_____

_____

1189

1190

---

other. Then
or
other; then

The college is small. Its school spirit is excellent.
(*nevertheless*)

_____

_____

1457

1458

garage 1725	We can always reconstruct a faulty sentence to make the reference of a pronoun perfectly clear. **Hank cleaned the car after backing** *it* **out of the garage.** **Hank cleaned the garage after backing out the car.** Does either sentence leave any doubt as to what was cleaned? (*Yes, No*) 1726
spot 1992	**There are spots on your coat.** We use the plural verb **are** because its subject _____ is plural. 1993
had said 2259	Even though the actions are mentioned in the order of their occurrence, we sometimes use the past perfect tense to emphasize that the first action was completed before the second action began. **After we** *had washed* **the car, it** *rained* **very hard.** Was the washing completed when it began to rain? (*Yes, No*) 2260
Whom 2526	(*Who, Whom*) **was the patriot who said, "Give me liberty or give me death"?** 2527
me, name, 2793	Three or more short and closely related sentences may be written in series as a single sentence without being considered a run-on sentence error. Punctuate the following sentence: **The toast burned the coffee boiled over and Bobby spilled his orange juice.** 2794
Eleanor's, Pat's 3060	**Both suspects fingerprints were in the police departments files.** 3061

Mother made the boys some sandwiches.

b

The direct object is _____.

The indirect object is _____.

118

119

---

instruments,
but his

Shall I write a new theme? Shall I revise the old one?

_____

386

387

---

few

Tony read some notices, *which few students heard.*

The adjective clause is in its proper position right after the

word _____, which it modifies.

654

655

---

ran

Lyle ran *to catch the bus.*

Because the infinitive phrase modifies the verb **ran,** it is used

as an _____.

922

923

---

he study shows
that when
students get
their own cars
school grades
drop sharply.
1190

Employers find that production increases. (*when rest periods are allowed*)

_____

_____

1191

---

small.
Nevertheless,
or
small;
nevertheless,
1458

The college is small. Its school spirit is excellent. (*but*)

_____

_____

1459

No 1726	a. **Stan was out of practice when Jack beat** *him*. b. **Stan beat Jack when** *he* **was out of practice.** c. **Jack was out of practice when Stan beat** *him*. In which sentence is the reference of the italicized pronoun confusing because we can't tell to whom the pronoun refers? ———— 1727
spots 1993	**There is no stamp on this letter.** If you changed the noun **stamp** to **stamps,** you would need to change the verb **is** to —————. 1994
Yes 2260	PAST: I *finished* **my work when Jim arrived.** PAST PERFECT: I *had finished* **my work when Jim arrived.** Do both sentences have the same meaning? (*Yes, No*) 2261
Who 2527	(*Who, Whom*) **does the law hold responsible in such cases?** 2528
burned, over, 2794	a. **I looked at the dog, the dog looked at me, and we immediately became friends.** b. **I looked at the dog, the dog looked at me.** Which is a correct series of sentences and not a run-on sentence? ———— 2795
suspects' department's 3061	**The girls study hall is right next to the boys.** 3062

(direct object) sandwiches (indirect object) boys 119	**The dog found itself a warm place in the kitchen.** The direct object is _____. The indirect object is _____. 120

theme or revise
 	
387
	Sometimes we want the balanced effect of a compound sentence even though a compound predicate would express our meaning in fewer words.
	
	    a. **Fashions come and fashions go.**
	    b. **Fashions come and go.**
	
	Which sentence gives a more balanced effect? _____
	
	388

notices 655	**Several of Don's friends play college football.** *He went to high school with them.* The pronoun *them* is the object of the preposition *with*. Underline the clause signal you would put in place of *them* in changing the italicized sentence to an adjective clause: **which whose whom who** 656
adverb 923	We can sometimes combine two sentences by changing one sentence to an infinitive phrase. **Larry gave a cough.** (*This was*) *to prove that he was sick.* **Larry gave a cough** *to prove that he was sick.* To change the italicized sentence to an infinitive phrase, we drop the words before the _____. 924
Employers find that when rest periods are allowed production increases. 1191	Lesson **32** **Three Effective Sentence Devices** [Frames 1193–1224]
small, but its 1459	Lesson **40** **Review: The Sentence Unit** [Frames 1461–1480]

b 1727	In this and the following frames, one of each pair of sentences is clear. The other is ambiguous because the pronoun has two possible antecedents. Circle the letter of the correct sentence. a. **When our bus reached the station, it was almost empty.** b. **Our bus was almost empty when it reached the station.** <div align="right">1728</div>
are 1994	In sentences that begin with **There is, There are,** or **Here is, Here are,** don't choose your verb until you look ahead to see whether a singular or a plural subject is coming. <div align="center">**There . . . several ways of making frosting.**</div> Before we supply **is** or **are** in this sentence, we must look ahead to the subject _____. <div align="right">1995</div>
No 2261	<div align="center">a. I *finished* my work when Jim arrived. b. I *had finished* my work when Jim arrived.</div> In which sentence was your work already completed at the time of Jim's arrival? _____ <div align="right">2262</div>
Whom 2528	**To** (*who, whom*) **can small nations appeal for protection?** <div align="right">2529</div>
a 2795	If there is a comma *before* a series, it is not used because of the series but for another reason. **When I arrived home from school, Louis, Ron, and Steve were waiting for me.** The comma after the word **school** is correct because it follows (*an introductory, a main*) clause. <div align="right">2796</div>
girls' boys' 3062	**His father buys and sells all kinds of stamps and coins.** <div align="right">3063</div>

(direct object) place (indirect object) itself 120	A sentence in **Pattern II** always contains a direct object. Does it always contain an indirect object? (*Yes, No*) 121
a 388	a. **He couldn't eat and couldn't sleep.** b. **He couldn't eat, and he couldn't sleep.** Which sentence is more effective because of the repetition of the subject? _____ 389
whom 656	**Several of Don's friends play college football.** *He went to* whom *high school with* ~~them.~~ We choose *whom* rather than *who* because it is the object of the preposition _____. 657
infinitive 924	Change the italicized sentence to an infinitive phrase: **Wendy touched the flowers.** *She wanted to see if they were* *real.* _____ _____ 925
	1. The "no sooner . . . than" device: a. **When we sat down to eat, company arrived.** b. *No sooner* **had we sat down to eat** *than* **company arrived.** Which sentence shows more effectively that one event followed the other almost immediately? _____ 1193
	In this and the following frames, one of each pair of items is a sentence; the other is a fragment. Circle the letter of the complete sentence. a. **A good citizen helps with the work of his community.** b. **A good citizen who helps with the work of his community.** 1461

b 1728	Continue to circle the letter of the correct sentence: a. **As soon as Larry gets a kennel, he is going to keep the dog in it.** b. **Larry is going to keep the dog in a kennel as soon as he gets one.** 1729
ways 1995	Underline the correct verb: **There (*is, are*) several ways of making frosting.** 1996
b 2262	a. **We *had* just *finished* scrubbing the floor when Larry came in with his muddy shoes.** b. **We just *finished* scrubbing the floor when Larry came in with his muddy shoes.** Which sentence emphasizes the fact that the first action had been completed when the second action occurred? _____ 2263
whom 2529	Lesson **71** A Number of Pronoun Problems [Frames 2531–2569]
an introductory 2796	If there is a comma *after* a series, it is not used because of the series but for another reason. **For better schools, better roads, and clean government, cast your vote for Mrs. Henshaw.** The comma after **government** is used because it follows an introductory (*phrase, clause*). 2797
None 3063	**These childrens bad manners reflect on their parents training at home.** 3064

No
 	
121
	In this and the following frames, *S = Subject, V = Verb, IO = Indirect Object, DO = Direct Object.*
	
	Fill in the missing word:
	
	This bakery makes the best doughnuts in town.
	
	   S *V* *DO*
	
	 bakery **makes** _____
	                                          122

b 389	Except where we wish to produce a special effect, we should try to save words by using a compound (*sentence, predicate*). 390

with
 	
657
	Several of Don's friends play college football. *He went to*
	                         whom
	high school with ~~them~~.
	
	After we move *with whom* to the front of the clause, we should insert it in the sentence after the word (*friends, football*), which it modifies.
	                                      658

Wendy touched the flowers to see if they were real. 925	Change the italicized sentence to an infinitive phrase: **Vic's dad set the clock ahead.** *This was to prevent Vic from being late.* _____ _____ 926
b 1193	*No sooner* **had we sat down to eat** *than* **company arrived.** The words *no sooner* must be followed later in the sentence by the word _____. 1194
a 1461	Circle the letter of the complete sentence: a. **Posted in the most conspicuous place on the bulletin board.** b. **The notice was posted on the bulletin board.** 1462

a 1729	a. **The Red Sox will play the Yankees. They have a great team.** b. **The Red Sox will play the Yankees, who have a great team.** 1730
are 1996	a. **Here . . . the key to the car.** b. **Here . . . the keys to the car.** Which sentence requires the plural verb **are?** _____ 1997
a 2263	Here is a sentence with an "if" clause that states a condition under which something could have or would have happened: **If I** *had seen* **the light, I** *would have stopped.* The past perfect verb is used in the part of the sentence that states the (*condition, result*). 2264
	PRONOUNS IN COMPARISONS When we use the word **than** or **as** to make a comparison, we generally shorten our sentence by omitting one or more unnecessary words. **The Smiths have a larger house than we (have).** The omitted word in this sentence is _____. 2531
phrase 2797	Although it's not wrong to omit the comma between the last two items of a series, many writers prefer to use this comma —especially in formal writing. a. **Gas, electricity, and water are included in the rent.** b. **Gas, electricity and water are included in the rent.** Are both sentences punctuated correctly? (*Yes, No*) 2798
children's parents' 3064	**Mr. Barrys young son knows all the players batting averages.** 3065

Anyone can show you the way to the bridge.

DO doughnuts 122	Fill in the missing words: S V IO DO **Anyone** _____ _____ **way.** 123

predicate

390

Lesson 11 The Semicolon as a Connector
[Frames 392–434]

---

friends

658

a. **Several of Don's friends play college football** *with whom he went to high school.*

b. **Several of Don's friends** *with whom he went to high school* **play college football.**

In which sentence is the clause properly placed? _____

659

Vic's dad set
the clock ahead
to prevent Vic
from being late.

926

After changing the italicized sentence to an infinitive phrase, insert it in the sentence next to the noun it modifies:

Johnny's ambition was typical of a small boy. *It was to become a fireman.* _____

_____

927

---

a. **When I last saw Ben, he was looking for a job.**
b. **When the picnic table was set, it began to rain.**

than

Which of the above sentences could best be put into the "no sooner . . . than" arrangement because the two events

1194

occurred at about the same time? _____

1195

Continue to circle the letter of the complete sentence:

b

a. **Which was Mr. Egan's way of getting us to read a book.**
b. **This was Mr. Egan's way of getting us to read a book.**

1462

1463

b 1730	a. **If you find any worms in the cabbages, destroy them.** b. **Destroy any worms that you find in the cabbages.** 1731

b
 	
1997
	Since **There's** and **Here's** are contractions of **There is** and **Here is,** they should be used only before singular subjects.
	
	        a. **. . . no battery in this flashlight.**
	        b. **. . . no batteries in this flashlight.**
	
	In which sentence would **There's** be correct? _____
	
	1998

condition 2264	**If I** *had seen* **the light, I** *would have* **stopped.** Notice that *would have* is used in only one part of the sentence—the part that shows what *would have* happened if an earlier action (past perfect) *had* occurred. Are the words *would have* used in the "if" clause? (*Yes, No*) 2265
have 2531	**Mr. Metz gave Fred just as good a grade as (he gave) me.** The omitted words in this sentence are _____. 2532
Yes 2798	Do not omit the comma between the last two items of a series if there is any chance of misunderstanding. **We served** *coffee, salad, cheese* **and** *egg* **sandwiches.** Can you be sure whether one or two kinds of sandwiches were served? (*Yes, No*) 2799
Mr. Barry's players' 3065	**Peoples ages are nobodys business but their own.** 3066

V
can show
IO
you

123

The alumni bought the school a new organ.

Fill in the missing words:

S	V	IO	DO
alumni	bought	_____	_____

124

We have seen that two *similar* or *related* sentences that are *equal in importance* can be combined into a compound sentence by using the _____ **and, but,** or **or.**

392

---

b

659

A local firm got the order. *Its bid was the lowest.*

Underline the clause signal you would put in place of *Its* in changing the italicized sentence to an adjective clause:

who   whose   that   which

660

Johnny's
ambition to
become a
fireman was
typical of a
small boy.
927

Jerry pounded the table once again. *This showed that he was his own boss.*
Jerry pounded the table once again *to show that he was his own boss.*

We changed the italicized sentence to an infinitive phrase by changing the verb *showed* to the infinitive _____.

928

---

b

1195

a. **When the picnic table was set, it began to rain.**
b. *No sooner* **was the picnic table set** *than* **it began to rain.**

Which sentence is more novel and forceful? _____

1196

---

b

1463

a. **Walter Johnson was a great pitcher.**
b. **Walter Johnson, the greatest pitcher in the history of baseball.**

1464

b 1731	a. **Father said to Bobby, "Your hands are always dirty."** b. **Father told Bobby that his hands were always dirty.** 1732
a 1998	a. **. . . some scraps for your dog.** b. **. . . a bone for your dog.** In which sentence would **Here's** be correct? _____ 1999
No 2265	Be sure not to use the words *would have* in the "if" clause. a. **If I** *would have* **seen the light, I** *would have* **stopped.** b. **If I** *had seen* **the light, I** *would have* **stopped.** Which sentence is correct? _____ 2266
he gave 2532	When a pronoun follows the word **than** or **as** in a comparison, think of the missing words and you will have no trouble in deciding which case of the pronoun to use. **Don can print much better than** *I* **(can print).** We use the nominative pronoun *I* because it is the subject of the omitted verb _____ _____. 2533
No 2799	**These sports shoes are available in** *green, red, brown* **and** *white.* If four different kinds of shoes are available, would you insert a comma after *brown*? (*Yes, No*) 2800
People's nobody's 3066	**Sudden starts and stops wear out tires and brakes very rapidly.** 3067

10
school
DO
organ
124
	The white paint gives a new look to the house.
	
	Fill in the missing words:
	
	    S *V* *DO*
	
	paint gives _____
	
	                                          125

conjunction
 	
392
	Another useful device for holding two sentences together is the semicolon (;). In many compound sentences, we can use a semicolon in place of the conjunction.
	
	    The ceiling was low, *and* **all planes were grounded.**
	    The ceiling was low; all planes were grounded.
	
	The semicolon replaces the conjunction _____.
	
	                                        393

whose
 	
660
	whose
	A local firm got the order. ~~*Its*~~ *bid was the lowest.*
	
	    a. **A local firm** *whose bid was the lowest* **got the order.**
	    b. **A local firm got the order** *whose bid was the lowest.*
	
	In which sentence is the clause properly placed? _____
	
	                                        661

to show 928	Change the italicized sentence to an infinitive phrase: **We boiled our drinking water.** *This killed all the bacteria.* _____ _____ 929

b
 	
1196
	a. *No sooner* <u>**was**</u> **the picnic** <u>**table**</u> <u>**set**</u> *than* **it began to rain.**
	    b. **The picnic** <u>**table**</u> <u>**was**</u> *no sooner* <u>**set**</u> *than* **it began to rain.**
	
	In which arrangement does the subject **table** come between the two parts of the verb? _____
	
	                                        1197

a
 	
1464
	a. **Mother considers spinach good for our health.**
	    b. **Because Mother considers spinach good for our health.**
	
	                                        1465

a 1732	a. **At the time of Clem's birth, his father was a bandleader.** b. **Clem's father was a bandleader at the time of his birth.** 1733
b 1999	The problem of subject-verb agreement is the same when a sentence begins with **There was, There were, There has been, There have been.** Underline the correct verb: **There** (*was, were*) **sixteen lighted candles on the cake.** 2000
b 2266	a. **If it had rained another ten minutes, the game would have been called off.** b. **If it would have rained another ten minutes, the game would have been called off.** Which sentence is correct? _____ 2267
can print 2533	**The noise didn't bother Dad as much as (it bothered)** *her*. We use the objective pronoun *her* because it is the direct object of the omitted verb _____. 2534
Yes 2800	Do not use commas when all the items in a series are connected by *and, or,* or *nor.* **The heat** *and* **the noise** *and* **the confusion were too much for my mother.** Does this sentence require any commas? (*Yes, No*) 2801
None 3067	**Their guests cars were blocking the Donaldsons driveway.** 3068

DO
look

125

The white paint gives the house a new look.

Fill in the missing words:

S	V	IO	DO
paint	gives	_____	_____

126

---

and

393

The ceiling was low; all planes were grounded.

After the semicolon, the compound sentence continues with a (*small, capital*) letter.

394

---

a

661

A local firm *whose bid was the lowest* **got the order.**

The adjective clause is properly placed because it comes after the noun _____, which it modifies.

662

We boiled our
drinking water
to kill all the
bacteria.

929

Change the italicized sentence to an infinitive phrase:

Always keep receipts. *They will prove that you have paid your bills.*

_____

_____

930

---

a

1197

In a "no sooner . . . than" sentence, we usually need a helping verb such as **was, did,** or **had** with the main verb.

a. **The two boys met, and they began to argue.**

b. **No sooner had the two boys met than they began to argue.**

The verb **met** in sentence *a* becomes _____ in *b*.

1198

---

a

1465

---

a. **In time to save the fireman from being crushed by the toppling wall.**

b. **He shouted his warning in time to save the fireman's life.**

1466

a 1733	a. Whenever Dad discusses politics with Mr. Hart, he gets very excited. b. Dad gets very excited whenever he discusses politics with Mr. Hart. 1734
were 2000	Underline the correct verb: There (*has, have*) been too many accidents lately. 2001
a 2267	Sometimes the "if" clause comes at the end of the sentence. Underline the correct verb: It is very likely that they would have struck oil if only they (*had drilled, would have drilled*) twenty feet more. 2268
bothered 2534	Sometimes the meaning of a sentence depends on whether we use the nominative or objective case of a pronoun. Hank owes Roy more money than *I* (owe him). Hank owes Roy more money than (he owes) *me*. Do the sentence with *I* and the sentence with *me* have the same meaning? (*Yes, No*) 2535
No 2801	a. Jerry couldn't decide whether to add, or subtract, or multiply the numbers. b. Jerry couldn't decide whether to add or subtract or multiply the numbers. Which sentence is correct? _____ 2802
guests' Donaldsons' 3068	Todays paper tells about these boys experience in Sundays blizzard. 3069

Lesson 4 — The Sentence Pattern Built on Linking Verbs

[Frames 128–166]

---

small

394

The committee discussed the problem, *but* they reached no conclusions.

The committee discussed the problem; they reached no conclusions.

The semicolon replaces the conjunction _____.

395

---

firm

662

We can often strengthen a weak compound sentence by changing one of the statements to an adjective clause.

We have a neighbor, and he has his own private plane.
We have a neighbor *who has his own private plane.*

The two facts are brought into closer relationship by the (*compound, complex*) sentence.

663

Always keep receipts to prove that you have paid your bills.

930

Don't nag a child to practice. **It does no good.**
To nag a child to practice **does no good.**

Here we have replaced the words *Don't nag* with the infinitive

_____.

931

---

had met

1198

a. **When I sit down to study, someone usually disturbs me.**
b. **No sooner do I sit down to study than someone usually disturbs me.**

The verb **sit** in sentence *a* becomes _____ in sentence *b*.

1199

---

b

1466

a. **This surprised even his closest friends.**
b. **A fact that surprised even his closest friends.**

1467

---

b 1734	Sentences that report someone's remark often leave the reader guessing as to which person the pronoun *he* or *she* means. **The doctor told Dad that *he* needed a vacation.** This sentence is ambiguous because *he* could mean either the _____ or _____. 1735
have 2001	In interrogative sentences, too, the verb (or part of the verb) usually precedes the subject, and we must look ahead to see whether a singular or a plural subject is coming. a. **Where . . . your father? How . . . your father?** b. **Where . . . your parents? How . . . your parents?** Which sentences require the plural verb **are?** _____ 2002
had drilled 2268	Underline the correct verb: **I'm certain Frank would not have bought the car if he (*would have known, had known*) the reputation of the dealer.** 2269
No 2535	a. **Sue wrote Bob more often than *I*.** b. **Sue wrote Bob more often than *me*.** Each of the above sentences has a different meaning. Which sentence means that Sue wrote to Bob more often than she wrote to you? _____ 2536
b 2802	Use a comma between two adjectives—even though they are not a series—when they modify the same noun and are not connected by a conjunction. **Sanding rust off a car is a *messy* and *tiresome* job.** If you omitted the conjunction **and,** would you insert a comma after the adjective *messy?* (*Yes, No*) 2803
Today's boys' Sunday's 3069	**Ladies fashions change more frequently than mens.** 3070

Suppose that you wish to point out that your friend Henry is happy. You would not be likely to say—

Happy Henry
Henry happy

Is either of these pairs of words a sentence? (*Yes, No*)

128

---

but

395

The deadline was rapidly approaching; we worked furiously to meet it.

In this sentence, the semicolon replaces the conjunction

_____.

396

---

complex

663

In this and the following frames, convert each *compound* sentence into a *complex* sentence by changing the italicized sentence to an adjective clause:

We parked next to a fireplug, and *nobody had noticed it.*

_____

_____

664

To nag

931

Change the italicized sentence to an infinitive phrase:

Don't start eating before your host. **It is bad manners.**

_____

_____

932

---

do sit

1199

Put this sentence into the "no sooner . . . than" arrangement. Count your sentence right whether the *no sooner* comes at the beginning of your sentence or later.

When I saw him, I recognized him.

_____

_____

1200

---

a

1467

a. **We stood at the door and waited for the store to open.**
b. **Standing at the door and waiting for the store to open.**

1468

doctor, Dad 1735	**The doctor told Dad that *he* needed a vacation.** Usually the only way to eliminate the ambiguity in a sentence like this is to use a direct quotation. **The doctor told Dad, "You need a vacation."** This means that (*the doctor, Dad*) needs a vacation. 1736
b 2002	Underline the correct verb: **How much (*is, are*) the tickets?** 2003
had known 2269	Supply the proper tense of the verb **see:** **You too would have bought the dress if you _____ it.** 2270
b 2536	**Sue wrote Bob more often than (she wrote) *me*.** The objective pronoun *me* is the direct object of the omitted verb _____. 2537
Yes 2803	Insert the necessary comma: **There are long dreary stretches of desert in the West.** 2804
Ladies' men's 3070	Lesson **86** Apostrophes for Contractions and Special Plurals [Frames 3072–3106]

No 128	a. **Happy Henry** b. **Henry happy** c. **Henry is happy.** Which one of these groups of words is a sentence? _____ 129
and 396	**I could see them; they couldn't see me.** In this sentence, the semicolon replaces the conjunction _____. 397
We parked next to a fireplug, which (that) nobody had noticed. 664	**Mr. Berg equipped the playground, and** *he is very fond of children.* (Be sure to put the clause after the word it modifies.) _____ _____ 665
To start eating before your host is bad manners. 932	A sentence with an infinitive phrase as subject may sound stiff and formal. We can move the phrase to the end of the sentence, putting an introductory *It* in its place. a. *To change one's mind* **is no crime.** b. **It is no crime** *to change one's mind.* Which sentence sounds more informal? _____ 933
No sooner had I seen him than I recognized him. *or* I no sooner saw him than I recognized him. 1200	Continue to follow the directions for the previous frame. (*Note:* Be sure to follow the "no sooner" construction with "than," not "when.") **When the concert started, the lights went out.** _____ _____ 1201
a 1468	a. **Each family taking a favorite dish to the church supper.** b. **Each family took a favorite dish to the church supper.** 1469

Dad 1736	**The doctor told Dad, "You need a vacation."** If it were the doctor who needed the vacation, we would change **You** to _____. 1737
are 2003	Underline the correct verb: (*Has, Have*) **there been any complaints about the service?** 2004
had seen 2270	The future perfect tense is formed by combining **will have** or **shall have** with the past participle of a verb. a. **will save** b. **had saved** c. **will have saved** Which verb is in the future perfect tense? _____ 2271
wrote 2537	a. **Sue wrote Bob more often than** *I.* b. **Sue wrote Bob more often than** *me.* Which sentence means that Sue wrote Bob more often than you wrote Bob? _____ 2538
long, dreary 2804	Insert the necessary comma: **Their smiling friendly faces gave me confidence.** 2805
	As a short cut, we frequently run two separate words together by omitting one or more letters; for example, **we've** (*we have*), **doesn't** (*does not*). These two-in-one words are called **contractions.** **Let's** is a contraction of the two words _____ _____. 3072

<table>
<tr><td>c</td><td>

a. **Henry happy**
b. **Henry <u>is</u> happy.**

The adjective **happy** by itself cannot make a statement about **Henry**.

We change *a* to a sentence by adding the verb _____.

</td></tr>
<tr><td>129</td><td>130</td></tr>
</table>

<table>
<tr><td>but</td><td>

The bottle should be tightly closed; the perfume will evaporate.

In this sentence, the semicolon replaces the conjunction

_____.

</td></tr>
<tr><td>397</td><td>398</td></tr>
</table>

<table>
<tr><td>

Mr. Berg, who is very fond of children, equipped the playground.

</td><td>

Mrs. Doty owned a canary, and *she was very much attached to it.* (Try *to which.*)

_____

_____

</td></tr>
<tr><td>665</td><td>666</td></tr>
</table>

<table>
<tr><td>b</td><td>

To beat a dead horse **does no good.**

Rewrite this sentence, moving the infinitive phrase to the end of the sentence and putting an introductory *It* in its place.

_____

_____

</td></tr>
<tr><td>933</td><td>934</td></tr>
</table>

<table>
<tr><td>

The concert had no sooner started than the lights went out.

</td><td>

We got to the corner, and the engine stopped.

_____

_____

</td></tr>
<tr><td>1201</td><td>1202</td></tr>
</table>

<table>
<tr><td>b</td><td>

In this and the following frames, label each item according to the following key:

S = *Correct Sentence*; F = *Fragment*;
$R\text{-}S$ = *Run-on Sentence*

Although cotton is still an important crop in the South. _____

</td></tr>
<tr><td>1469</td><td>1470</td></tr>
</table>

I 1737	**Paula told Doris that *her* friend was waiting.** Complete this sentence with a direct quotation to show that *Doris's* friend was waiting: **Paula told Doris, "**_____ _____." 1738
Have 2004	The nouns **kind, sort,** and **type** are singular and require singular verbs. **The other kind of cookies *is* easier to make.** We use the singular verb *is* because the subject in the above sentence is (*kind, cookies*). 2005
c (will have saved) 2271	Use the future perfect tense for an action that *will have been completed* at a specified future time. **By tomorrow night, this car *will have traveled* one hundred thousand miles.** What is the specified future time at which the action will have been completed? _____ 2272
a 2538	**Sue wrote Bob more often than *I* (wrote Bob).** The nominative pronoun *I* is the subject of the omitted verb _____. 2539
smiling, friendly 2805	Do not put a comma after the last adjective in a series of adjectives. Put commas only *between* the adjectives, just as you do in any other series. **Irish terriers are friendly, intelligent, and obedient dogs.** Should a comma be inserted after the adjective **obedient**? (*Yes, No*) 2806

Let us
 	
3072
	Put an apostrophe in place of the omitted letter or letters in a contraction.
	
	  a. **it ɪ̸s = it's** d. **we wi̸ll = we'll**
	  b. **who i̸s = who's** e. **I ha̸ve = I've**
	  c. **I wo̸u̸l̸d = I'd** f. **you a̸re = you're**
	
	In which of the above contractions does the apostrophe take the place of the largest number of letters? _____
	
	3073

is 130	**Henry happy** **Henry is happy.** The verb **is** helps to turn the adjective **happy** into a statement about the subject _____. 131

or
 	
398
	A semicolon can also take the place of **because,** which is not a regular conjunction such as **and, but,** or **or.**
	
	  a. **Doris had made up her mind; nothing could change it.**
	  b. **Virginia didn't vote; she couldn't make up her mind.**
	
	In which sentence does the semicolon take the place of
	
	because? _____
	
	399

Mrs. Doty owned a canary to which she was very much attached. 666	**I have a friend, and** *his father is an inventor.* _____ _____ 667
It does no good to beat a dead horse. 934	In this and the following frames, eliminate the **and** by changing the italicized statement to an infinitive phrase: **I have a job, and** *I must finish it before dinner.* _____ _____ 935
No sooner had we got to the corner than the engine stopped. 1202	**When I reached the dentist's office, my tooth stopped aching.** _____ _____ 1203
F 1470	*S = Correct Sentence; F = Fragment;* *R-S = Run-on Sentence* **You can't run away from a problem, it has a way of trailing you.** _____ 1471

"Your friend is waiting." 1738	**Paula told Doris that *her* friend was waiting.** Complete this sentence with a direct quotation to show that *Paula's* friend was waiting: **Paula told Doris, "**_____ _____." 1739
kind 2005	Underline the correct verb: **The newer type of automatic machines (*wash, washes*) the clothes faster.** 2006
(By) tomorrow night 2272	a. **When Mother unwraps the gift, she *will have discovered* who sent it.** b. **After I buy gas, I *shall have spent* my last cent.** In which sentence is the future perfect tense correctly used because the action will have been completed at a specified future time? _____ 2273
wrote 2539	Underline the correct pronoun: **Sandy is jealous because Dad praises Boyd more than (*he, him*).** 2540
No 2806	Insert the necessary commas: **The company needs an honest reliable and experienced salesman with a thorough understanding of cars and people.** 2807

c *or* I'd
 	
3073
	The adverb **not**, shortened to **n't**, is part of many contractions.
	
	    isn't don't hasn't couldn't
	    aren't doesn't wasn't shouldn't
	
	The apostrophe always comes between the **n** and the **t** because it takes the place of the missing letter _____.
	
	3074

Henry 131	a. <u>Henry</u> <u>washed</u> the car. b. <u>Henry</u> <u style="border-bottom:double">is</u> happy. Which sentence does *not* contain an *action* verb? _____ 132
b 399	a. **The child fell asleep; he was tired out from playing.** b. **We listened very carefully; we could hear nothing.** In which sentence does the semicolon take the place of *because?* _____ 400
I have a friend whose father is an inventor. 667	**Some friends arrived suddenly, and** *we were not expecting them.* (Be sure to put the clause after the word it modifies.) ———————————————— ———————————————— 668
I have a job to finish before dinner. 935	**We sent out cards, and** *these reminded members of the meeting.* ———————————————— ———————————————— 936
No sooner had I reached the dentist's office than my tooth stopped aching. 1203	**We raised the price, and our sales dropped.** ———————————————— ———————————————— 1204
R-S 1471	*S = Correct Sentence; F = Fragment;* *R-S = Run-on Sentence* **We hunted for night crawlers, using our pocket flashlights.** ————— 1472

The cashier told the clerk that *she* had made a mistake.

Rewrite this sentence with a direct quotation to show that the *clerk* had made a mistake:

_____

_____

1740

---

washes

2006

Because the nouns **kind, sort,** and **type** are singular, use the singular adjectives **this** and **that** (not the plural adjectives **these** and **those**) to point them out.

    a. **This kind of berries is better for shipping.**
    b. **These kind of berries are better for shipping.**

Which sentence is correct—*a* or *b?* _____

2007

---

b

2273

Underline the correct verb:

By next week, I (*shall save, shall have saved*) **enough money for a vacation.**

2274

---

him

2540

Underline the correct pronoun:

Since Jack always feeds the dog, it obeys him better than (*me, I*).

2541

---

honest, reliable(,)

2807

Sometimes an adjective is used so commonly with a noun that we think of it as part of the noun—for example, *old man, little boy, gold watch, fresh air, wild animal.*

a. **gold watch**   **fur coat**   **brick house**
b. **expensive watch**   **worn-out coat**   **comfortable house**

We think of the adjectives as part of the nouns after (*a, b*).

2808

---

o

3074

    a. **is'nt**   **does'nt**   **was'nt**   **should'nt**
    b. **isn't**   **doesn't**   **wasn't**   **shouldn't**

The apostrophes are correctly placed in group (*a, b*).

3075

b 132	**Henry is happy.** The verb **is** does not show action—like *washed* or *fixed*. What does it do? The verb **is** ties up or *links* the adjective **happy** with the subject _____, which it *describes*. 133
a 400	a. **Few people attended the game because of the bad weather.** b. **Frank didn't worry because he was well-prepared for the test.** In which sentence could a semicolon take the place of **because?** _____ 401
Some friends whom (that) we were not expecting arrived suddenly. 668	**The teacher asked a question, and** *nobody could answer it.* _____ _____ 669
We sent out ards to remind nembers of the meeting. 936	**The city issued a request, and** *it was to refrain from wasting water.* _____ _____ 937
No sooner had we raised the price than our sales dropped. 1204	2. The "not only . . . but also" device: a. **Wilma cooked the dinner and washed the dishes.** b. *Not only* **did Wilma cook the dinner,** *but* **she** *also* **washed the dishes.** Which sentence is more forceful in emphasizing how much work Wilma did? _____ 1205
S 1472	*S, F, or R-S?* **Never paying the least attention to how he dressed or what people thought of him.** _____ 1473

The cashier told the clerk (*or* said to the clerk), "You have made a mistake." 1740	Clear up the meaning of this sentence by substituting a noun for the ambiguous pronoun: **If the lids won't fit the jars, throw** *them* **out.** **If the lids won't fit the jars, _____** **_____.** 1741
a 2007	Underline the correct words: (*This, These*) **sort** (*is, are*) **much harder to grow.** 2008
shall have saved 2274	In this and the following frames, underline the verb whose tense expresses the time relationship in the sentence more accurately: **Lincoln felt that his speech at Gettysburg** (*had been, was*) **a failure.** 2275
me 2541	PRONOUNS AS APPOSITIVES Pronouns are frequently used as appositives; that is, they are set after nouns to explain more precisely to whom the nouns refer. Underline the pronoun used as an appositive: **Both players, Greg and he, were penalized.** 2542
a 2808	Do not use a comma between two adjectives when you think of the second adjective as part of the noun it modifies. **The moose is a ferocious** *wild animal.* We do not use a comma between the adjectives *ferocious* and *wild* because we think of the adjective *wild* as part of the noun _____. 2809
b 3075	Insert the needed apostrophes: **It wouldnt burn because it wasnt dry enough.** 3076

Henry 133	Henry was the chairman. In this sentence, the verb **was** ties up or *links* the noun _____ with the subject **Henry,** which it *identifies.* 134
b 401	We can combine two simple sentences into a compound sentence by using either a conjunction or a _____. 402
The teacher asked a question that which) nobody could answer. 669	**Roxanne made a rude remark, and** *there was no excuse for it.* (Try *for which.*) _____ _____ 670
The city issued a request to refrain from wasting water. 937	**We are planning a pageant, and** *it will dramatize the history of our town.* _____ _____ 938
b 1205	a. *Not only* **did Wilma cook** the dinner, *but* she *also* **washed the dishes.** b. **Wilma** *not only* **cooked** the dinner, *but* she *also* **washed the dishes.** In which sentence is the subject **Wilma** put between two parts of the verb? _____ 1206
F 1473	*S, F,* or *R-S?* **Some drugs quicken the heartbeat, others slow it down.** _____ 1474

throw the lids (the jars) out 1741	Clear up the meaning of this sentence by substituting a noun for the ambiguous pronoun: **When Fred saw Bruce,** *he* **was in uniform.** _____ 174?
This, is 2008	Underline the correct words: (*That, Those*) **type** (*seems, seem*) **sturdier to me.** 200?
had been 2275	**The fire inspector eventually found the short circuit that** (*had caused, caused*) **the fire.** 2276
he 2542	When you use a pair of pronouns (or a noun and a pronoun) as appositives after a noun, use the same pronouns that you would use if you omitted the noun they explain. Underline the correct pronoun: ~~Two girls,~~ **Diane and** (*she, her*), **made all the posters.** 2543
animal 2809	a. **All of us respected this dignified old man.** b. **All of us respected this dignified elderly man.** In which sentence would you insert a comma after the adjective **dignified?** _____ 2810
wouldn't wasn't 3076	When you write contractions, don't change any letters in the original words. (The contractions *won't* for *will not* and *can't* for *cannot* are the exceptions.) Merely substitute an apostrophe for the letter or letters you omit. The contraction for **does not** is (*doesn't, dosen't*). 3077

chairman 134	Henry is happy. Henry was the chairman. A verb like **is** or **was** is called a **linking verb** because it *links* a noun, pronoun, or adjective that follows it with the _____ of the sentence. 135
semicolon 402	When might we use a semicolon in preference to a conjunction? If there are too many *and*'s in a sentence, we may get rid of one by substituting a semicolon. **The patient asked for steak and potatoes, and the doctors and nurses were astonished.** How many **and**'s are there in this sentence? _____ 403
Roxanne made a rude remark for which there was no excuse. 670	**My sister works for Dr. Mack, and** *his office is downtown.* _____ _____ 671
We are planning a pageant to dramatize the history of our town. 938	Lesson **25** Subordination by Appositives [Frames 940–979]
a 1206	**The food was expensive and poor.** Supply the missing words to complete the "not only . . . but also" device: **Not only** _____, **but** _____. 1207
R-S 1474	*S, F,* or *R-S?* **The only one in our family who plays a musical instrument.** _____ 1475

Bruce (*or* Fred) 1742	Clear up the meaning of this sentence by substituting a noun for the ambiguous pronoun: **If there are any misspelled words in your themes, copy** *them* **correctly.** **If there are any misspelled words in your themes,** _____ _____ 1743

That, seems
 	
2009
	A noun that means a group or collection of persons or animals is called a **collective noun.**
	
	    a. **member, child, student, chairman, goat**
	    b. **team, family, class, audience, flock**
	
	Which group of words consists of collective nouns? _____
	2010

had caused 2276	**Mr. Dawson wrote an angry letter and then** (*tore, had torn*) **it up.** 2277
she 2543	Underline the correct pronoun: **All the posters were made by** ~~two girls,~~ **Diane and** (*she, her*). 2544
b 2810	In this and the following frames, insert the necessary commas. If no commas are required, write *None.* **The child's blond hair blue eyes and pink cheeks make her an artist's dream.** 2811
doesn't 3077	The contraction for **are not** is (*aren't, arn't*). 3078

subject 135	**Be** is by far the most common *linking verb*. Be sure that you can recognize its various forms. FORMS OF *BE:* **is, am, are—was, were, been** The crops . . . good. Which two forms of *be* could be used to link **good** with **crops** in the above sentence? _____ , _____ 136
three 403	**The patient asked for steak and potatoes, and the doctors and nurses were astonished.** To get rid of one of the three **and**'s, we can substitute a semicolon for the **and** which follows the word _____. 404
My sister works for Dr. Mack, whose office is downtown. 671	a. **The man** *who owns the lot* **lives across the street.** b. **The man** *who lives across the street* **owns the lot.** Which of the above sentences emphasizes where the man lives—*a* or *b?* _____ 672
	Joseph Priestley discovered oxygen. Because most people might not know who **Joseph Priestley** was, it would be well to add an explanation. **Joseph Priestley,** *an English minister,* **discovered oxygen.** The noun *minister* explains the noun _____ _____ . 940
(Not only) was the food expensive, (but) it was also poor. 1207	**The food was expensive and poor.** This sentence can be changed to the "not only . . . but also" arrangement in still another way. Supply the missing words: **The food** _____ but _____ poor. 1208
F 1475	*S, F,* or *R-S?* **I cleaned and adjusted all the spark plugs, then I replaced them in the motor.** _____ 1476

copy the words (*or* themes) correctly. 1743	Rewrite each sentence so that the italicized pronoun can mean only the underlined word. Do not merely substitute nouns for pronouns. (Count any answer correct if the antecedent of the pronoun is entirely clear.) **If the <u>blouse</u> doesn't match the skirt, you can return *it*.** 1744
b 2010	A collective noun takes a singular verb when the group acts together *as a single unit;* a plural verb when the members of the group act *individually*. a. **The class *is* now in the library.** b. **The class *are* giving their talks on famous inventors.** We think of the class *as a single unit* in sentence (*a, b*). 2011
tore 2277	**Fortunately, Mr. Dawson tore up the angry letter that he** (*wrote, had written*). 2278
her 2544	Underline the correct pronouns: **The article mentioned only two players,** (*he, him*) **and** (*I, me*). 2545
hair eyes(,) 2811	**Bob and Leslie came to the test without paper or pens or pencils.** 2812
aren't 3078	The contraction for **were not** is (*weren't, were'nt*). 3079

(any two) are, were, have been, had been 136	FORMS OF *BE:* **is, am, are—was, were, been** **I . . . the first speaker.** Which two forms of be could be used to link **speaker** with **I** in the above sentence? _____, _____ 137
potatoes 404	**The weather was hot and sticky, and the boys and girls were listless.** To get rid of one of the three **and**'s, we can substitute a semicolon for the **and** which follows the word _____. 405
a 672	**Ron's mother,** *who bandaged my arm,* **is a graduate nurse.** Rewrite this sentence so as to emphasize the fact that Ron's mother *bandaged my arm* and to subordinate the fact that she is a *graduate nurse.* _____ _____ 673
oseph Priestley 940	A noun or pronoun—often with modifiers—that is set after another noun or pronoun to explain it is called an **appositive.** **Joseph Priestley,** *an English minister,* **discovered oxygen.** The appositive is the noun _____. 941
(The food) was not only expensive (but) also poor. 1208	a. **The food was** *not only* **expensive** *but also* **poor.** b. **The food was** *not only* **expensive** *but* **poor.** Both sentences are correct. In which sentence do we omit the word *also* from our device? _____ 1209
R-S 1476	*S, F,* or *R-S?* **While he was looking for his lost nickel, Harvey found a quarter.** _____ 1477

You can return the blouse (the skirt) if it doesn't match the skirt (the blouse). 1744	**Whenever Miss Ross talks to Sally,** *she* **seems embarrassed** _____ _____ (*Note: She* will become *her* in your revised sentence.) 174
a 2011	a. **The class** *is* **now in the library.** b. **The class** *are* **giving their talks on famous inventors.** We think of the members of the class as acting *individually* in sentence (*a, b*). 201
had written 2278	**Loren would probably have driven more carefully if Peggy** (*would have, had*) **suggested it.** 227
him, me 2545	To decide between **we** and **us** in expressions like "*we* (or *us* fellows" or "*we* (or *us*) girls," omit the appositive *fellows* or *girls,* and you will see instantly which pronoun is right. Underline the correct pronoun: (*We, Us*) ~~boys~~ **can get our own lunch.** 254
None 2812	**Mr. Kress plopped into a chair pulled out a handkerchief and mopped his brow.** 281
weren't 3079	Write in the contractions for the italicized words: **It** *does not* (_____) **taste good when it** *is no* (_____) **ripe.** 308

(any two)
am, was,
had been
 	
137
	We have seen that some *action verbs* make complete statements about their subjects and that others do not.
	
	    a. **The engine started.**
	    b. **The engine uses . . .**
	
	In which sentence does the action verb make a complete statement? _____ 138

sticky 405	**The gold and the silver finally gave out, and many miners settled down and became farmers.** To get rid of one of the three **and**'s, we can substitute a semicolon for the **and** which follows the word _____. 406
Ron's mother, o is a graduate rse, bandaged my arm. 673	Lesson **18** A Final Attack on *And* [Frames 675–699]
minister 941	**Harold won the first prize,** *a trip to Washington.* The noun *trip* explains the noun _____. 942

b
 	
1209
	Put each sentence into the "not only . . . but also" arrangement, omitting the *also* if you wish. Count your answer right so long as the words *not only* and *but* are present.
	
	    Steve is a good student and a good athlete.
	
	_____
	
	_____
	         1210

S 1477	*S, F,* or *R-S?* **The dodo, a large, clumsy bird that was unable to fly.** _____ 1478

Sally seems embarrassed whenever Miss Ross talks to her. 1745	**When Fred saw <u>Bruce</u>,** *he* **was in uniform.** _____ (*Note: He* will become *him* in your revised sentence.) 174
b 2012	Underline the correct verb in each sentence: a. **The class** (*is, are*) **now in the library.** b. **The class** (*is, are*) **giving their talks on famous inventors** 201
had 2279	**If we** (*had urged, would have urged*) **him a little more** **Tony would have sung for us.** 228
We 2546	Underline the correct pronoun: **The lady asked** (*we, us*) **fellows to push her car.** 254
chair, handkerchief(,) 2813	**It was a gray cold cheerless morning in February.** 281
doesn't, isn't 3080	Write in the contractions for the italicized words: **Edward** *did not* (_____) **come because he** *was no* (_____) **invited.** 308

page 277

a 138	However, a linking verb cannot by itself make a complete statement about its subject. Since the purpose of a *link* is to connect two things, a *linking verb* must be followed by a complement that it can link with the _____ of the sentence. 139

out
 	
406
	If you have a good ear for the sound of sentences, you have noticed that a semicolon produces a quicker, brisker rhythm than a conjunction.
	
	  a. **You need your church, and your church needs you.**
	  b. **You need your church; your church needs you.**
	
	Which sentence is more brisk and forceful? _____
	
	407

	And is a good word to use when you wish merely to *add* one idea to another equal idea.
	
	  a. **I recognized Joe, and he recognized me.**
	  b. **I recognized Joe, and I hadn't seen him for years.**
	
	In which sentence is **and** more appropriate—*a* or *b?* _____
	
	675

prize 942	**Harold won the first prize, *a trip to Washington.*** The appositive is the noun _____. 943
eve is not only good student but (also) a good athlete. *or* Not only is , but (also) ... 1210	Continue to follow the directions for the previous frame: **The article misspelled my name and gave a wrong age.** _____ _____ 1211
F 1478	*S, F,* or *R-S?* **We had been eating sweets, therefore we had no appetite for dinner.** _____ 1479

Bruce was in uniform when Fred saw him. 1746	**My uncle heard Heifetz play when** *he* **was a child.** _____ _____ 174
a. is b. are 2013	Underline the correct verb in each sentence: a. **The team** (*has, have*) **not yet worn their new uniforms.** b. **The team** (*has, have*) **won every game this season.** 201
had urged 2280	**By the time my sister Dorothy is ready for college, sh** (*will save, will have saved*) **a thousand dollars.** 228
us 2547	Underline the correct pronouns: **The lifeguard had warned** (*we, us*) **boys, but** (*we, us*) **boy** **wouldn't listen.** 254
gray, cold, 2814	**Grange went dodging and twisting and bucking through th** **Buckeye tackles.** 28
didn't, wasn't 3081	Write in the contractions for the italicized words: *Let us* (_____) **see if** *they will* (_____) **help us** 30

subject 139	**The paint was . . . (What?)** Was the paint wet, dry, or sticky? Until we add a word that the linking verb **was** can connect with the subject, the meaning of the sentence is (*complete, incomplete*). 140
b 407	a. **You can sell your home; you can't sell rent receipts.** b. **You can sell your home, but you can't sell rent receipts.** Which sentence is more brisk and forceful? _____ 408
a 675	a. **I recognized Joe,** *and* **I hadn't seen him for years.** b. **I recognized Joe** *although* **I hadn't seen him for years.** Which word brings the two facts into closer relationship— *and* or *although*? _____ 676
trip 943	**Both parties, the Republicans and the Democrats, favored the bill.** This sentence contains _____ appositives. (How many?) 944
he article not ly misspelled my name but (also) gave a wrong age. 1211	**Insulation saves fuel and keeps a house more comfortable.** _____ _____ 1212
R-S 1479	*S, F,* or *R-S?* **Many settlers headed back to the East, discouraged by all the hardships of pioneer life.** _____ 1480

When Heifetz was a child, my uncle heard him play.	**If you use high-grade oil in your <u>motor</u>,** *it* **will last longer.**
1747	_____ _____ 174
a. have b. has 2014	It is sometimes difficult to decide whether a group is acting as a single unit or as individuals. Whatever you decide, be sure to keep your pronoun consistent with the verb. a. **The class <u>was</u>** (*singular*) **ready for <u>their</u>** (*plural*) **test** b. **The class <u>was</u>** (*singular*) **ready for <u>its</u>** (*singular*) **test.** The pronoun is consistent with the verb in sentence (*a, b*) 201
will have saved 2281	**When I sell two more tickets, I** (*shall sell, shall have sold*) **my quota for the game.** 228
us, we 2548	a. **... girls can meet at my house.** b. **All of ... girls can meet at my house.** In which sentence would the objective pronoun **us** be correct? _____ 254
None 2815	**Heavy drapes rugs and overstuffed furniture are giving way to simpler streamlined furnishings.** 281
Let's, they'll 3082	Do not confuse contractions with possessive pronouns which are pronounced the same. CONTRACTIONS: **it's you're they're who's** POSSESSIVE PRONOUNS: **its your their whose** To show ownership you would choose one of the above word (*with, without*) an apostrophe. 308

incomplete 140	**The <u>paint</u> <u>was</u> sticky.** We have now completed our sentence by adding the complement **sticky.** The complement **sticky** describes the subject _____. 141
a 408	a. **Clyde sat right in front of me, and we soon became close friends.** b. **The brakes failed, and the car crashed into the truck.** In which sentence is the action more exciting? _____ 409
although 676	a. **Her mother wasn't home. Mona started the dinner.** b. **Mona started the dinner. Her mother finished it.** Which pair of sentences would it be better to combine by **and** to form a compound sentence—*a* or *b?* _____ 677
two 944	**Both parties, the Republicans and the Democrats, favored the bill.** The two appositives are the words _____ and _____. 945
Insulation not only saves fuel but (also) keeps a house more comfortable. 1212	**Franklin was a great statesman and a distinguished scientist.** _____ _____ 1213
S 1480	UNIT 7: THE SMOOTH-RUNNING SENTENCE Lesson **41** Placing Modifiers Sensibly [Frames 1482–1520]

Your motor will last longer if you use high-grade oil in it. 1748	**Mom doesn't like Diane to practice when _she_ is tired.** _____ _____ 1749
b 2015	Underline the correct words: **The audience** (_was, were_) **rattling** (_its, their_) **programs.** 2016
shall have sold 2282	Lesson **64** Using Active Verbs for Directness [Frames 2284–2318]
b 2549	A very common error often made is the expression "Let's you and _I_ . . . ," which should be "Let's you and _me._ . . ." _Let's_ is a contraction of _Let us._ Since _us_ is the object of the verb _Let,_ the pronouns that explain whom we mean by the objective pronoun _us_ should also be in the (_nominative, objective_) case. 2550
drapes, rugs(,) simpler, 2816	**After we planted the corn potatoes and cabbages we had little room for anything else.** 2817
without 3083	a. **it's** **you're** **they're** **who's** b. **its** **your** **their** **whose** From which group would you choose your word if you could put two words in its place? _____ 3084

paint 141	**Fred was** . . . (What?) **Fred was the driver.** The complement **driver** completes the meaning of the sentence and identifies the subject _____. 142
b 409	a. **Clyde sat right in front of me, and we soon became close friends.** b. **The brakes failed, and the car crashed into the truck.** Which sentence, because of its more exciting action, would benefit more from the brisk effect of a semicolon? _____ 410
b 677	**Mona started the dinner, and her mother finished it.** This is a good compound sentence because the **and** connects two *similar* ideas of (*equal, unequal*) importance. 678
Republicans Democrats 945	An appositive generally comes (*before, after*) the noun or pronoun it explains. 946
Franklin was not only a great statesman but (also) a distinguished scientist. 1213	**Ellen wrote the words and composed the music.** _____ _____ 1214
	The meaning of a sentence often depends on where we place adverbs such as *only, just, merely, almost, nearly,* and *even.* a. **Steve** *only* **glanced at the advertisements.** b. **Steve glanced** *only* **at the advertisements.** Which sentence means that Steve did not read the advertisements thoroughly? _____ 1482

When Mom is tired, she doesn't like Diane to practice. 1749	**Vern couldn't notify <u>Earl</u> because _he_ has no telephone.** _____ (_Note:_ Use an adjective clause beginning with _who_.) 1750
were, their 2016	Weights, measurements, periods of time, and amounts of money generally take singular verbs because they are thought of as single quantities rather than separate units. **Fifty feet of hose** _is_ **enough. Ten dollars** _seems_ **a fair price.** Although the subjects of these sentences are plural in form, they take (_singular, plural_) verbs. 2017
	a. **The catcher dropped the ball.** b. **The ball was dropped by the catcher.** In one sentence, the subject of the verb performs an action; in the other, the subject is acted upon. The subject performs an action in sentence (_a, b_). 2284
objective 2550	For the same reason that we say "Let _me_," we should also say, "Let's you and (_I, me_)." 2551
corn, potatoes(,) cabbages, 2817	**Mr. Jayne has a story to prove or disprove almost any political economic or educational theory.** 2818
a 3084	a. **. . . lunch is ready.** b. **. . . making a mistake.** The contraction **You're** would be correct in sentence (_a, b_). 3085

Fred 142	A complement that follows a linking verb and describes or identifies the subject is sometimes called a *predicate nominative, predicate adjective,* or *subject complement.* In this text, we shall use the term **subject complement.** It is called a **subject complement** because it *describes* or *identifies* the _____. 143
b 410	a. **The strike was called, and five thousand men laid down their tools.** b. **The game was very slow, and many fans left the stadium.** In which sentence would the use of a semicolon reinforce the excitement of the action? _____ 411
equal 678	**Her mother wasn't home. Mona started the dinner.** Here the first sentence explains *why* about the second sentence. Which word would bring out this relationship more clearly— *and* (before **Mona**) or *because* (before **Her**)? _____ 679
after 946	**Our principal, Mr. Rayfield, attends every game.** **Mr. Rayfield, our principal, attends every game.** Is the appositive the same in both sentences? (*Yes, No*) 947
Ellen not only wrote the words but (also) composed the music. 1214	3. The "the more . . . the more" or "the more . . . the less" device: *The more* **you eat,** *the more* **you want.** Does this sentence have any connecting word between the two word groups? (*Yes, No*) 1215
a 1482	a. **Steve** *only* **glanced at the advertisements.** b. **Steve glanced** *only* **at the advertisements.** Which sentence means that Steve paid no attention to the news articles or editorials? _____ 1483

Vern couldn't notify Earl, who has no telephone. 1750	**Mr. Brock said to <u>Dad</u> that *he* needed more insurance.** _____ _____ 1751
singular 2017	a. **Five minutes is enough time for my announcement.** b. **Four yards of material are enough for a dress.** In which sentence is the verb correct? _____ 2018

a
 	
2284
	A verb is said to be **active** when its subject performs an action.
	
	    a. **The catcher *dropped* the ball.**
	    b. **The ball *was dropped* by the catcher.**
	
	In which sentence is the verb *active* because its subject performs an action? _____
	
	2285

me 2551	Underline the correct pronoun: **Let's you and (*me*, *I*) exchange letters.** 2552
political, economic(,) 2818	**A neat little girl with curly red hair was bouncing a big rubber ball on the sidewalk.** 2819
b 3085	a. **I wonder if . . . ready.** b. **Which is . . . house?** The contraction **they're** would be correct in sentence (*a, b*). 3086

subject
 	
143
	The **subject complement** brings us to our third sentence pattern:
	
	PATTERN III: *Subject—Linking Verb ← Subject Complement*
	
	    a. **A forest ranger guards our forests.**
	    b. **A forest ranger's life is rather lonely.**
	
	Which sentence is an example of **Pattern III?** _____ 144

a
 	
411
	Don't use a comma without a conjunction to connect sentences. Only a semicolon has the power to hold two sentences together without the help of **and, but,** or **or.**
	
	    a. **Bob shook the branches, the apples came tumbling down.**
	    b. **Bob shook the branches; the apples came tumbling down.**
	
	Which sentence is correctly punctuated? _____ 412

because 679	a. **Her mother wasn't home,** *and* **Mona started the dinner.** b. *Because* **her mother wasn't home, Mona started the dinner.** Which sentence is better because it makes clear the relationship between the two facts—*a* or *b?* _____ 680
No 947	The modifiers of an appositive may consist of words, phrases, and clauses. **Alfred Nobel,** *the inventor of dynamite,* **established the Nobel prizes.** The appositive *inventor* is modified by a (*phrase, clause*). 948
No 1215	This sentence device is useful to show that as one thing increases or decreases, something else increases or decreases. *The more* **you eat,** *the more* **you want.** As your eating increases, your wanting (*increases, decreases*). 1216
b 1483	a. **Tom's Shop** *just* **repairs radios.** b. **Tom's Shop repairs** *just* **radios.** Which sentence means that the shop repairs radios but not other appliances? _____ 1484

Lesson **49** Incorrect Omission of Words

[Frames 1753–1791]

| a

2018 | **One dollar seems too much to pay for this cake.**

If you changed **One dollar** to **Three dollars,** would you need to change the verb **seems?** (*Yes, No*)

2019 |

| a

2285 | a. **The catcher** *dropped* **the ball.**
b. **The ball** *was dropped* **by the catcher.**

In which sentence is the subject of the verb acted upon?

———

2286 |

| me

2552 | POSSESSIVE PRONOUNS BEFORE GERUNDS

A gerund, as you have learned, is a special kind of noun that is formed by adding *-ing* to a verb.

I enjoy all *sports,* **but I like** *skiing* **best.**

Which of the two italicized words is a gerund? ———

2553 |

| None

2819 | **Because it was the day before Thanksgiving planes trains and buses were filled to capacity.**

2820 |

| a

3086 | a. **I think . . . boiling.**
b. **I like . . . design.**

The contraction **it's** would be correct in sentence (*a, b*).

3087 |

b 144	**Some cameras are very expensive.** The subject complement that follows the linking verb in this sentence is _____. 145
b 412	a. **The weather was raw, and the field was muddy.** b. **The weather was raw, the field was muddy.** In which sentence is the comma correctly used? _____ 413

b
 	
680
	And is objectionable only when it steals the job of words such as **who, which, as, when, because,** and **although,** which show exactly *how* two ideas are related to each other.
	
	  a. **The water boils** *and* **the kettle whistles.**
	  b. *As soon as* **the water boils, the kettle whistles.**
	
	Which of the above sentences gives more specific information—*a* or *b?* _____
	
	681

phrase 948	**Alfred Nobel,** *the chemist who invented dynamite,* **established the Nobel prizes.** The appositive *chemist* is modified by a (*phrase, clause*). 949
increases 1216	*The more* **one learns,** *the less* **positive one becomes.** This means that as one's learning increases, one's positiveness (*increases, decreases*). 1217
b 1484	a. **Tom's Shop** *just* **repairs radios.** b. **Tom's Shop repairs** *just* **radios.** Which sentence means that the shop repairs radios but does not sell them? _____ 1485

When the same form of a word fits in two places in a sentence, we may avoid repetition by using it only once and taking it for granted in the other position.

You *have* **four and I** *have* **three.**

May we omit the second *have?* (*Yes, No*)

1753

No

2019

In this and the following frames, underline the correct verb. Remember that a verb ending in *s* in the present tense is always singular.

There (*is, are*) **about twenty-four electric light bulbs in the average car of today.**

2020

---

b

2286

A verb is said to be **passive** when its subject is acted upon.

    a. **The catcher** *dropped* **the ball.**
    b. **The ball** *was dropped* **by the catcher.**

In which sentence is the verb *passive* because its subject is acted upon? _____

2287

---

skiing

2553

    a. **I was surprised at** *his* **behavior.**
    b. **I was surprised at** *his* **offering a tip.**

In which sentence is the possessive pronoun *his* followed by a gerund? _____

2554

Thanksgiving,
planes, trains(,)

2820

Lesson 79   Commas for Interrupting Expressions

[Frames 2822–2857]

---

a

3087

    a. **. . . ringing the doorbell?**
    b. **. . . ticket is this?**

The pronoun **Whose** would be correct in sentence (*a, b*).

3088

expensive
 	
145
	FORMS OF *BE:* **is, am, are—was, were, been**
	
	Although a form of **be** can be used by itself as a linking verb, it is often used as a *helper* with the main verb.
	
	   a. **The leaves are green.** b. **The leaves are falling.**
	
	In which sentence is **are** used as a helper? _____
	
	   146

a
 	
413
	a. **The weather was raw, the field was muddy.**
	   b. **The weather was raw; the field was muddy.**
	
	Which sentence is correctly punctuated? _____
	
	   414

b
 	
681
	You will greatly improve your writing if you use **and** only when you are sure that no *more specific* relationship exists.
	   a. *After* **Steve visited the club, he decided to join.**
	   b. **Steve visited the club,** *and* **he decided to join.**
	The relationship between the two facts is clearer in (*a, b*).
	
	   682

clause
 	
949
	An appositive with its modifiers forms an **appositive phrase.**
	
	   Pete, *their youngest son,* **has just started college.**
	   Pete **has just started college.**
	
	When we omit the appositive phrase, does a complete sentence remain? (*Yes, No*)
	
	   950

decreases
 	
1217
	a. *The more* **one learns,** *the less* **positive one becomes.**
	   b. **As one learns more, one becomes less positive.**
	
	Which sentence makes the relationship between the two facts more striking? _____
	
	   1218

a
 	
1485
	Wherever misunderstanding might occur, place the adverb *only, just, merely, almost, nearly,* or *even* as near as possible to the word it modifies and generally before it.
	
	      We ___(a)___ wash ___(b)___ the towels.
	
	To mean that you wash the towels, but not the sheets or pillowcases, put the word *only* in space (*a, b*).
	
	   1486

Yes

1753

a. **You** *have* **four and I . . . three.**
b. **You** *have* **four and he . . . three.**

In which sentence would the verb *have* not fit in the blank space? _____

1754

---

are

2020

(*Here's, Here are*) **the list of contributors.**

2021

---

b

2287

a. **The catcher** *dropped* **the ball.**
b. **The ball** *was dropped* **by the catcher.**

In sentence *a,* the performer of the action is shown by the subject.

In sentence *b,* the performer of the action is shown by the prepositional phrase _____.

2288

---

b

2554

a. **I was surprised at** *his* **behavior.**
b. **I was surprised at** *his* **offering a tip.**

In which sentence might you sometimes hear the objective pronoun *him* used instead of the possessive pronoun *his?*

_____

2555

We often interrupt a sentence to insert an expression that is aside from our main thought. In speech, we keep such expressions in the background by dropping our voice and pausing before and after; in writing, we use commas.

Punctuate the interrupting expression:

The stories *on the whole* **are lacking in originality.**

2822

---

b

3088

In this and the following frames, underline the correct word in each pair. Be sure to choose the contraction whenever you can substitute two words:

(*It's, Its*) **trying to escape from** (*it's, its*) **cage.**

3089

146

b

a. **The leaves are green.**   b. **The leaves are falling.**

Which sentence contains a subject complement? _____

147

---

b

414

If you omit the conjunction from a compound sentence, put a (*comma, semicolon*) in its place.

415

---

a

682

By using fewer **and's** and more clause signals such as **which, whose, since, whenever,** and **although,** you will show the relationship between your ideas (*more, less*) clearly.

683

Yes

950

An appositive is useful for avoiding an "I-forgot-to-tell-you" type of sentence that explains something you have just named in the previous sentence.

Mr. Cross is the editor. *He is a friend of my father's.*

The second sentence explains _____ in the first sentence.

951

---

a

1218

In this and the following frames, put each sentence into "the more . . . the more" or "the more . . . the less" arrangement:

As he earns more, he spends more.

_____

_____

1219

---

b

1486

We ___(a)___ wash ___(b)___ the towels.

To mean that you wash the towels but do not iron them, put the word *only* in space (*a, b*).

1487

b 1754	WRONG: **You** *have* **four and he three.** This sentence is wrong because with **You** we use *have*, but with **he** we need (*have, has*). 1755
Here's 2021	**License statistics show that there** (*is, are*) **more fishermen than hunters in the United States.** 2022
by the catcher 2288	a. **The band** *played* **a march.** b. **A march** *was played* **by the band.** Which sentence contains an active verb? _____ 2289
b 2555	a. **I was surprised at** *his* **behavior.** b. **I was surprised at** *his* **offering a tip.** Since you would never use the objective pronoun *him* before the noun **behavior,** it would seem reasonable not to use *him* before the gerund _____. 2556
, on the whole, 2822	There are several types of interrupting expressions. Any of them can be omitted without damaging the meaning or completeness of your sentence. Underline and put commas around three words that form an interrupting expression: **The refreshments by the way were excellent.** 2823
It's, its 3089	(*It's, Its*) **lightness is** (*it's, its*) **greatest advantage.** 3090

a 147	**The fans were** *cheering.* **The fans were** *enthusiastic.* One of the italicized words is part of an action verb; the other is a subject complement. The subject complement is the word _____. 148
semicolon 415	There are a number of adverbs that are sometimes mistaken for conjunctions. ADVERBS: **however** **otherwise** **nevertheless** **therefore** **consequently** **furthermore** Since these words are adverbs, they do not have the power of _____ to combine sentences. 416
more 683	a. **This part controls the shutter,** *and* **it is very delicate.** b. **This part,** *which* **controls the shutter, is very delicate.** Which sentence is tighter because it brings the two facts into closer relationship—*a* or *b?* _____ 684
Mr. Cross 951	**Mr. Cross is the editor.** *He is a friend of my father's.* **Mr. Cross,** *a friend of my father's,* **is the editor.** We changed the italicized sentence to an appositive and put it next to the noun _____, which it explains. 952
The more he earns, the more he spends. 1219	Sometimes a comparative form (*-er*) of an adjective or an adverb is used in these arrangements. **When you drive faster, you see less.** _____ _____ 1220
a 1487	**Vic can ___(a)___ play ___(b)___ any instrument.** To mean that Vic can play many instruments, put *almost* in space (*a, b*). 1488

has 1755	a. **You** *have* **four and he three.** b. **You** *have* **four and I three.** Which sentence is correct? _____ 1756
are 2022	**How much** (*are, is*) **those pads of paper?** 2023
a 2289	ACTIVE: **The band** *played* **a march.** ↓ PASSIVE: **A march** *was played* **by the band.** What happens to the direct object **march** when we change the verb from active to passive? It becomes the _____ of the passive verb *was played.* 2290
offering 2556	INFORMAL: **I was surprised at** *him* **offering a tip.** Although an objective pronoun before a gerund is frequently heard in conversation, a possessive pronoun is more appropriate for careful writing and speaking. Underline the preferred pronoun: **The likelihood of** (*them, their*) **winning the game is slight.** 2557
, by the way, 2823	PARENTHETICAL EXPRESSIONS Turn to the following frame, in which you will find some common interrupters known as **parenthetical expressions.** We often add these words and phrases to sentences to make their meaning clearer or more emphatic or to tie them up with the preceding sentences. (*Turn to the next frame.*) 2824
Its, its 3090	(*It's, Its*) **tongue hangs out when** (*it's, its*) **thirsty.** 3091

enthusiastic 148	**Be** is not the only linking verb. Among other verbs that can serve as linking verbs are **seem, become, appear, look, feel,** and **get** (when it means **become**). **The candidate appeared cheerful.** The linking verb in this sentence is _____. 149
conjunctions 416	a. **The air is humid, therefore the paint dries slowly.** b. **The air is humid, and therefore the paint dries slowly.** Which sentence is incorrect because there is no conjunction to connect its two parts? _____ 417
b 684	Eliminate the **and** in each sentence by changing the italicized idea to either an adverb or adjective clause, as the meaning requires. Write the full sentence. **Grandmother has many friends, and** *they visit her often.* _____ _____ 685
Mr. Cross 952	a. **Mr. Cross is the editor.** *He is a friend of my father's.* b. **Mr. Cross,** *a friend of my father's,* **is the editor.** Which arrangement is better because it puts the explanation of **Mr. Cross** where it belongs—directly after the noun it explains? _____ 953
The faster you drive, the less you see. 1220	**If a car is heavier, it rides more smoothly.** _____ _____ 1221
b 1488	**Vic can __(a)__ play __(b)__ any instrument.** To mean that Vic really can't quite play any one instrument, put *almost* in space (*a, b*). 1489

b 1756	a. **Sue** *goes* **to high school, and he . . . to college.** b. **Sue** *goes* **to high school, and I . . . to college.** In which sentence do we not need to repeat the verb *goes* because the same form would fit in the blank space? _____ <div align="right">1757</div>
are 2023	**There** (*hasn't, haven't*) **been any changes in the rules.** <div align="right">2024</div>
subject 2290	ACTIVE: **The band** *played* **a march.** PASSIVE: **A march** *was played* **by the band.** Follow the arrow to see what happens to the subject **band** when we change the verb from active to passive. The subject **band** becomes the object of the preposition <div align="right">2291</div>
their 2557	Underline the preferred pronoun: **Political experts now see many reasons for** (*his, him*) **winning the election.** <div align="right">2558</div>

2824	however of course for example after all
	therefore by the way nevertheless if possible
	     a. **The cake was a failure** *after all* **her efforts.**
	     b. **Freddy** *after all* **is only ten years old.**
	In which sentence should *after all* be set off with commas
	
	because it is an interrupter? _____
	<div align="right">2825</div>

Its, it's 3091	(*You're, Your*) **circulation slows down when** (*you're, your*) **asleep.** <div align="right">3092</div>

appeared 149	**The animals . . . cold.** Underline the two words that can be used as *linking verbs* in the above sentence: **feel** **like** **look** **avoid** 150
a 417	**The air is humid, and therefore the paint dries slowly.** The word **therefore** is not a conjunction and has no connecting power. For this reason, we need to use the conjunction _____ in this sentence. 418
Grandmother has many friends who visit her often. 685	Follow the directions given in the previous frame. Count your sentence right if it makes good sense even if you did not use the same clause signal given in the answer. **I got a poor seat, and** *I arrived very early.* _____ _____ 686
b 953	Watch your writing for a weak sentence explaining something you have just written. If it contains the verb **is, are, was,** or **were,** followed by a noun, change it to an appositive phrase and fit it into the previous sentence. **a. Mr. Lee urged us to win.** **b. He is our new coach.** Which sentence can be changed to an appositive? _____ 954
The heavier a car is, the more smoothly it rides. 1221	**As a person gets older, he has more responsibilities.** _____ _____ 1222
a 1489	**Joe __(a)__ earned __(b)__ ten dollars.** To mean that Joe came close to earning this money but that he didn't get the job, put *nearly* in space (*a, b*). 1490

a 1757	WRONG: **Sue** *goes* **to high school, and I to college.** This sentence is wrong because with **Sue** we use *goes*, but with **I** we need _____. 1758
haven't 2024	(*Those, That*) **type of scissors** (*are, is*) **made for cutting hair.** 2025
by 2291	A passive verb always consists of a past participle combined with one of the tense forms of the verb **be.** Underline two passive verbs: **took** **was taken** **will give** **will be given** 2292
his 2558	Underline the preferred pronoun: **The principal has no objection to** (*us, our*) **using his name.** 2559

b
 	
2825
	Here are other parenthetical expressions:
	
	perhaps **you know** **on the whole** **on the other hand**
	it seems **I suppose** **on the contrary** **generally speaking**
	
	    a. **The coach** *I suppose* **was very pleased.**
	    b. *I suppose* **that the coach was very pleased.**
	
	I suppose should be set off with commas in sentence (*a, b*).
	
	2826

Your, you're 3092	(*You're, Your*) **not in** (*you're, your*) **right seat.** 3093

feel, look 150	**The animals . . . cold.** Underline the two words that can be used as *linking verbs* in the above sentence to make **cold** describe **animals**. **fear become prefer get** 151
and 418	**The air is humid; therefore the paint dries slowly.** This sentence is correct because a semicolon has the power of a _____ to connect the two parts of a compound sentence. 419
I got a poor seat although I arrived very early. 686	**The mayor made a statement, and** *many people disagreed with it.* (Try *with which.*) _____ _____ 687
b 954	**He is our new coach.** It is easy to change this sentence to an appositive phrase because it contains the verb **is,** which is followed by the noun _____. 955
The older a person gets, the more responsibilities he has. 1222	**You go out farther, and the water gets deeper.** _____ _____ 1223
a 1490	**Joe __(a)__ earned __(b)__ ten dollars.** To mean that Joe earned slightly less than ten dollars, put *nearly* in space (*a, b*). 1491

go 1758	**I never have *eaten* and never will *eat* an oyster.** Does the same form of the verb *eat* follow both **have** and **will?** (*Yes, No*) 1759
That, is 2025	(*This, These*) **kind** (*wears, wear*) **much longer than the cheaper ones.** 2026
was taken, will be given 2292	Underline two passive verbs: **sees is seen has sent has been sent** 2293
our 2559	In this and the following frames, underline the correct pronouns or, in some cases, the pronouns appropriate for formal usage. (*We, Us*) **boys saw no good reason for** (*them, their*) **postponing the game.** 2560
a 2826	Insert the necessary commas: **She plays the radio for example after everyone has gone to bed.** 2827
You're, your 3093	(*You're, Your*) **eyes show that** (*you're, your*) **tired.** 3094

become, get 151	You can be sure that a verb is a linking verb if you can put some form of **be (is, am, are—was, were, been)** in its place. a. **The customer** *feels* **the material.** b. **The weather** *feels* **muggy.** In which sentence can you substitute **is** for **feels?** _____ 152
conjunction 419	a. **It rained all day, nevertheless everyone had a good time.** b. **It rained all day, but everyone had a good time.** Which sentence is correct because its two parts are connected by a conjunction? _____ 420
...e mayor made a statement with which many people disagreed. 687	*Cars become more complicated,* **and mechanics require more training.** ———————————————————— ———————————————————— 688
coach 955	**Mr. Lee once played college football.** (*He is*) *our new coach.* **Mr. Lee,** *our new coach,* **once played college football.** In changing the italicized sentence to an appositive phrase, we dropped everything except the noun _____ and its modifiers. 956
...he farther out you go, the deeper the water gets. 1223	**Traveling has made me appreciate my own town more.** ———————————————————— ———————————————————— 1224
b 1491	**The man paid the bill with a** *worthless* **check.** **The man paid the bill with a check** *that was worthless.* The adjective *worthless* comes before the noun **check,** which it modifies. The adjective clause *that was worthless* comes (*before, after*) the noun **check,** which it modifies. 1492

No

1759

---

a. **I never have *eaten* and never will *eat* an oyster.**
b. **I never have and never will *eat* an oyster.**

Which sentence is correct—*a* or *b?* _____

1760

This, wears

2026

The entire Indian tribe (*was, were*) **moved to another reservation.**

2027

---

is seen,
has been sent

2293

A sentence with an active verb is shorter, stronger, and more direct than one with a passive verb.

ACTIVE: **Paul *found* a dollar.**
PASSIVE: **A dollar *was found* by Paul.**

The sentence that gives a clumsy, roundabout effect is the one with the (*active, passive*) verb.

2294

We, their

2560

Most of (*we, us*) **boys are just as busy as** (*him, he*).

2561

, for example,

2827

Sometimes there is so little interruption—if any—that commas would only tend to make the reading jerky.

Of course **I'm going.**   *Perhaps* **you will find it.**

a. **We *therefore* sent a telegram.**
b. **We decided *therefore* to send a telegram.**

In which sentence would you use commas? _____

2828

Your, you're

(*They're, Their*) **delicious when** (*they're, their*) **toasted.**

3095

a. **The customer** *feels* **the material.**
b. **The weather** *feels* **muggy.**

b

In one sentence **feels** is used as an *action* verb; in the other it is used as a *linking* verb.

In which sentence is it used as a *linking* verb? _____

152   153

---

a. **It rained all day, nevertheless everyone had a good time.**
b. **It rained all day; nevertheless everyone had a good time.**

b

Which sentence is correctly punctuated? _____

420   421

---

s cars become
e complicated,
hanics require
more training.

A friend recommended this book, and *I value his opinion highly.* (Try *whose.*)

_____

_____

688   689

Mr. Lee once played college football. (*He is***) *our new coach.*
Mr. Lee, *our new coach,* **once played college football.**

coach

Then we put the appositive phrase directly after the noun

_____, which it explains.

956   957

The more I
avel, the more
appreciate my
own town.

1224

Lesson **33** The Useful Noun–Participle Phrase

[Frames 1226–1255]

Unless an adjective clause is placed directly *after* the word it modifies, your reader is likely to connect it with the wrong thing.

after

The pill came from this bottle *that the baby swallowed.*

The adjective clause is meant to modify **pill,** but it appears

to modify the noun _____.

1492   1493

page 305

a 1760	WRONG: **I never have and never will** *eat* **an oyster.** This sentence is wrong because with **will** we use *eat,* but with **have** we need _____. 176
was 2027	**The band** (*was, were*) **tuning up their instruments.** 202
passive 2294	a. **The pitcher** *took* **a chance and** *threw* **the ball to first base** b. **A chance** *was taken* **by the pitcher, and the ball** *wa* *thrown* **to first base.** Which sentence is better because it is more direct? _____ 229
us, he 2561	**Let's you and** (*me, I*) **insist on** (*his, him*) **paying his own way** 256

b
 	
 2828
	When the word **well, why, yes,** or **no** is used as a sentenc opener, it is generally followed by a comma.
	
	 Punctuate the following sentences:
	
	       Well maybe you're right.
	       Why this is a surprise!
	
	 282

They're, they're 3095	(*They're, Their*) **fenders prove that** (*they're, their*) **poo drivers.** 309

b 153	a. **The restaurant** *looked* **crowded.** b. **The speaker** *looked* **at his watch.** In which sentence can you substitute **was** for **looked?** _____ <div align="right">154</div>
b 421	a. **Our team was overconfident; consequently we lost.** b. **Our team was overconfident, and consequently we lost.** c. **Our team was overconfident, consequently we lost.** Which one of these three sentences is incorrectly punctuated? _____ <div align="right">422</div>
A friend whose opinion I value highly recommended this book. 689	*The score was tied,* **and we had to play another game.** _____ _____ <div align="right">690</div>
Mr. Lee 957	a. **Mr. Lee once played college football.** *He is our new coach.* b. **Mr. Lee,** *our new coach,* **once played college football.** In which arrangement does the explanation of **Mr. Lee** sound less like an afterthought? _____ <div align="right">958</div>
	A **noun-participle** phrase consists of a noun followed by a present or past participle that modifies this noun. *Knees trembling,* **Dick stepped up to the stage.** In the italicized phrase, the noun *Knees* is modified by the (*present, past*) participle *trembling.* <div align="right">1226</div>
bottle 1493	a. **The pill came from this bottle** *that the baby swallowed.* b. **The pill** *that the baby swallowed* **came from this bottle.** Which sentence is better because the adjective clause comes right after the noun it modifies? _____ <div align="right">1494</div>

eaten 1761	We always have *paid* and always will *pay* our bills on time. Can we omit the verb *paid*? (*Yes, No*) 1762
were 2028	Five tons (*were, was*) too big a load for the truck. 202?
a 2295	a. This play was practiced by the team until it was perfect b. The team practiced this play until it was perfect. Which sentence is better? _____ 229?
me, his 2562	(*Us, We*) girls think that this shade of red suits you better than (*her, she*). 256?
Well, Why, 2829	Punctuate the following sentences: Yes I agree with you. No I didn't see Paul. 283?
Their, they're 3096	(*They're, Their*) bringing out (*they're, their*) new models in October. 309?

a 154	a. **The restaurant** *looked* **crowded.** b. **The speaker** *looked* **at his watch.** In which sentence is there a linking verb that is followed by a subject complement? _____ 155

c
 	
422
	ADVERBS: **however** **otherwise** **nevertheless**
	              therefore **consequently** **furthermore**
	It is equally correct to start a new sentence with one of these adverbs. Many writers prefer to do so.
	    Our team was overconfident. Consequently we lost.
	This sentence is (*correct, incorrect*).
	
	423

Because the score was tied, we had to play another game. 690	*This was my first speech,* **and I wasn't nervous at all.** _____ _____ 691
b 958	Do not confuse an appositive phrase with an adjective clause. An appositive phrase consists only of a noun (or pronoun) with its modifiers. An adjective clause always has a subject and a _____. 959
present 1226	*The dinner prepared,* **Mother waited for her guests.** In the italicized phrase, the noun *dinner* is modified by the (*present, past*) participle *prepared.* 1227
b 1494	**We sold our car to a used-car dealer** *that had a cracked cylinder head.* This sentence is absurd because the adjective clause appears to modify the noun **dealer** when it is really meant to modify the noun _____. 1495

a. **Did you put** *a* **pear or** *a* **peach in my lunch?**
b. **Did you put** *a* **pear or** *an* **apple in my lunch?**

We use the article **a** before a consonant sound (**a** *fish*) and the article **an** before a vowel sound (**an** *eel*).

In which sentence could we omit the article *a* because the same form of the article fits in both places? _____ 176

Two hours (*seems, seem*) **hardly enough time to see all the sights.**

203

Unless you have a good reason for not doing so, always use (*an active, a passive*) verb.

229

I intend to ask both our neighbors, Mr. Doyle and (*he, him*) **if they object to** (*me, my*) **using their names for references**

256

We often use a "not" phrase to show what we do *not* mean in contrast to what we do mean. Such phrases require commas because they are strong interrupters.

> **The company,** *not the salesman,* **is to blame.**

Punctuate the following sentence:

> **Graphite not oil should be used on locks.**

283

Let's decide (*who's, whose*) **going in** (*who's, whose*) **car.**

309

a 155	We have now studied two kinds of complements: *direct objects* and *subject complements*. With a little reasoning, we can avoid confusing the two. A *direct object* can follow only an *action verb*. A *subject complement* always follows a _____ verb. 156
correct 423	a. **I lost my car keys; otherwise I would have driven.** b. **I lost my car keys, otherwise I would have driven.** c. **I lost my car keys. Otherwise I would have driven.** Which one of these three sentences is incorrectly punctuated? _____ 424
Although this was my first speech, I wasn't nervous at all. 691	**My uncle had a tent, and** *he had no further use for it.* _____ _____ 692
verb (*or* predicate) 959	a. **Mr. Lee,** *our new coach from Notre Dame,* **played college football.** b. **Mr. Lee,** *who is our new coach from Notre Dame,* **played college football.** Which sentence contains an appositive phrase? _____ 960
past 1227	A noun-participle phrase has no grammatical connection with the rest of the sentence. *Knees trembling,* **Dick stepped up to the stage.** Is there any connecting word such as *when, because, who,* or *which* to connect the phrase with the main statement? (*Yes, No*) 1228
car 1495	a. **We sold our car** *that had a cracked cylinder head* **to a used-car dealer.** b. **We sold our car to a used-car dealer** *that had a cracked cylinder head.* Which sentence is better because the adjective clause comes directly after the noun it modifies? _____ 1496

a 1763	**Did you put** *a* **pear or** *an* **apple in my lunch?** We cannot omit the *an* before **apple** because with **pear** we use *a*, but with **apple** we need to use _____. 1764
seems 2030	Lesson **57** Review: Agreement of Subject and Verb [Frames 2032–2056]
an active 2297	**The nomination will be accepted by Nolan.** To change this sentence to one with an active verb, you would make _____ the subject of your revised sentence. 2298
him, my 2564	**I couldn't understand** (*him, his*) **wanting to pay for all** (*us, we*) **fellows.** 2565
, not oil, 2831	Punctuate the following sentence: **It is the motion of the cloth not the red color that excites the bull.** 2832
who's, whose 3098	(*Who's, Whose*) **the girl** (*who's, whose*) **taking the part of the grandmother?** 3099

linking 156	Usually the subject and direct object are two *different* things, and the action passes from one to the other. 1 ————————→ 2 **The heavy downpour flooded many basements.** The action passes from **downpour** to _____ 157
b 424	a. **Education must include the whole person; otherwise it is not true education.** b. **Education must include the whole person. Otherwise it is not true education.** Both *a* and *b* are correct. (*True, False*) 425
My uncle had a tent for which he had no further use. (*Or which he had no further use for.*) 692	*You switch the tires around,* **and they will wear longer.** _____ _____ 693
a 960	a. **We visited Monticello,** *which was the home of Thomas Jefferson.* b. **We visited Monticello,** *the home of Thomas Jefferson.* Which sentence contains an appositive phrase? _____ 961
No 1228	In the participial phrases we studied earlier, the participle modified a noun or pronoun in the main statement. *Trembling with excitement,* **Bert stepped up to the stage.** In the above sentence the present participle *Trembling* modifies the noun _____ in the main statement. 1229
a 1496	a. **The book is very modern that we use in our literature class.** b. **The book that we use in our literature class is very modern.** Which sentence is better because the adjective clause comes directly after the noun it modifies? _____ 1497

an 1764	a. **Shall I make** *an* **apple or apricot pie?** b. **Shall I make** *an* **apple or pumpkin pie?** Which sentence is correct? _____ 1765
	If you were to add the words printed in parentheses at the point marked by the caret (∧), would you need to change the italicized verb? If a change would be necessary, write only the form of the verb that would be required. If the verb would remain the same, write *Correct*. ∧ **Those records** *belong* **to Maxine. (One of)** _____ 2032
Nolan 2298	a. **The nomination** *will be accepted* **by Nolan.** b. **Nolan** *will accept* **the nomination.** The verb in sentence *b* is active because its subject **Nolan** (*acts, is acted upon*). 2299
his, us 2565	**The other boys, Louis and (***he, him***), were envious because Mr. Ringler didn't pay them as much as (***I, me***).** 2566
, not the red color, 2832	APPOSITIVES An appositive is a noun or pronoun—often with modifiers—that follows another noun or pronoun to explain it. **Fred Kemp,** *a senior,* **spoke for the teen-agers.** Can the italicized appositive be omitted without damaging the meaning or completeness of this sentence? (*Yes, No*) 2833
Who's, who's 3099	(*Who's, Whose*) **mother is the lady** (*who's, whose*) **driving them to school?** 3100

basements 157	A subject complement, however, always *means the same thing* as the subject or *describes* the subject. We are dealing with *one* thing—not *two*. 1———→ 2 1←——— 1 a. **Mr. Ford hired a lawyer.** b. **Mr. Ford is a lawyer.** The noun **lawyer** is a subject complement in sentence (*a, b*). 158
True 425	In this and the following frames, insert the proper punctuation between the two word groups. Copy the word *before* the punctuation and *after* the punctuation. If a conjunction is present, insert a comma. If a conjunction is missing, insert a semicolon. **The field was muddy it didn't stop the Rangers.** _____ 426
If you switch e tires around, they will wear longer. 693	A sentence consisting of a main statement and an adverb or adjective clause is a (*compound, complex*) sentence. 694
b 961	An appositive phrase should be set off from the rest of the sentence by two commas (or a single comma if it ends the sentence) because it is an "extra" that could be omitted. Punctuate the following sentence: **Only one other team the New York Giants did as well.** 962
Bert 1229	*Knees trembling,* **Bert stepped up to the stage.** In the noun-participle phrase, however, the present participle *trembling* does not modify a word in the main statement. It modifies the noun _____ in the phrase itself. 1230
b 1497	a. **No joke** *that hurts our feelings* **amuses us.** b. **No joke amuses us** *if it hurts our feelings.* One sentence contains an adverb clause; the other, an adjective clause. Which sentence contains the adverb clause? _____ 1498

a
 	
1765
	Repeat an article (*a, an, the*) or a possessive pronoun (*my, your, his,* etc.) if there is any chance of misunderstanding.
	
	    a. **The McCanns have** *a* **black and white dog.**
	    b. **The McCanns have** *a* **black and** *a* **white dog.**
	
	Which sentence means two dogs? _____ 1766

belongs 2032	**A friendly note** ∧ *doesn't* **take much time. (or a telephone call)** _____ 2033
acts 2299	Change the following sentence to one with an active verb: **These souvenirs** *will be appreciated* **by the children.** _____ _____ 2300
he, me 2566	(*Us, We*) **girls get out of school earlier than** (*her, she*). 2567
Yes 2833	Set off an appositive and its modifiers with commas because it is not an essential part of the sentence. Punctuate the following sentence: **Our principal an enthusiastic football fan attends every game.** 2834
Whose, who's 3100	APOSTROPHES FOR SPECIAL PLURALS You have learned not to use apostrophes with ordinary plural nouns that do not show ownership. **Several** *girls'* **took** *boys'* **parts.** The plural noun in this sentence that should not be written with an apostrophe is (*girls, boys*). 3101

b 158	a. **The owner of the restaurant hired a new cook.** b. **The owner of the restaurant is the cook.** In which sentence is the noun **cook** a subject complement because it means the same person as the subject? _____ 159
muddy; it 426	Follow the directions given in the previous frame: **The wise are so uncertain the ignorant are so positive.** _____ 427
complex 694	The exact relationship between two facts or ideas is more clearly brought out by a (*compound, complex*) sentence. 695
team, Giants, 962	Punctuate the following sentence: **The car belongs to Howard the oldest of the Ross boys.** 963
Knees 1230	a. *Trembling with excitement,* **Bert stepped up to the stage.** b. *Knees trembling,* **Bert stepped up to the stage.** In which sentence does the participle *trembling* modify a word in the main statement, thus connecting it grammatically with that statement? _____ 1231
b 1498	a. **No joke** *that hurts our feelings* **amuses us.** b. **No joke amuses us** *if it hurts our feelings.* The clause that can be shifted to other positions in the sentence is the (*adjective, adverb*) clause. 1499

b 1766	a. **Harvey ordered** *a* **cheese and** *a* **ham sandwich.** b. **Harvey ordered** *a* **cheese and ham sandwich.** Which sentence means two sandwiches? _____ 1767
Correct 2033	**The shortage of goods** ∧ *makes* **prices skyrocket. (and the abundance of money)** _____ 2034

The children
will appreciate
these souvenirs.
 	
2300
	Although you should generally try to use active verbs, there are times when passive verbs are very useful; for example, when the doer of an action is not known.
	
	    a. **Our dog** *was stolen* **last night.**
	    b. **The game** *was won* **by the Mustangs.**
	
	In which sentence is the doer of the action not known? _____
	2301

We, she 2567	**Let's you and** (*me, I*) **see if Miss Haines won't let** (*we, us*) **girls prepare a Christmas program for the class.** 2568
, an enthusiastic football fan, 2834	Punctuate the following sentence: **The antelope the fastest animal in existence has been known to achieve a speed of sixty-two miles per hour.** 2835

girls
 	
3101
	However, there are a few special cases where there is a good reason for using apostrophes to form ordinary plurals.
	
	    a. **Your os look like as.**
	    b. **Your o's look like a's.**
	
	Which sentence is easier to figure out? _____
	3102

b 159	**The owner of the restaurant is energetic.** Because the adjective **energetic** describes the subject **owner** and is not something apart from it, **energetic** is a (*subject complement, direct object*). 160
uncertain; the 427	**There are thirteen dogs on our block and all of them seemed to be barking at once.** _____ 428
complex 695	In changing a compound sentence to a complex sentence, you (*drop, add*) the conjunction *and, but,* or *or.* 696
Howard, 963	Punctuate the following sentence: **The Icelanders immigrants from Norway colonized their island in the ninth century.** 964
a 1231	Because a noun-participle phrase has no grammatical connection with the rest of the sentence, it is often called an **absolute** phrase, *absolute* meaning *independent.* An example of an absolute phrase is a (*participial, noun-participle*) phrase. 1232
adverb 1499	a. *If it hurts our feelings,* **no joke amuses us.** b. **No joke,** *if it hurts our feelings,* **amuses us.** c. **No joke amuses us** *if it hurts our feelings.* Does an adverb clause, like an adjective clause, need to come directly after the word it modifies? (*Yes, No*) 1500

a 1767	a. *My* **cousin and best friend will go with me.** b. *My* **cousin and** *my* **best friend will go with me.** Which sentence means two persons? _____ 1768
make 2034	**His father** ∧ *plays* **the piano. (, as well as his mother,)** _____ 2035
a 2301	a. **The test** *had been passed* **by the student.** b. **The kitten** *had been left* **at our door.** In which sentence is a passive verb preferable because the doer of the action is not known? _____ 2302
me, us 2568	**My two friends, Walt and** (*him, he*)**, were disappointed be- cause Mr. Hill didn't give them as good parts in the play as** (*me, I*)**.** 2569
, the fastest animal in existence, 2835	DIRECT ADDRESS Direct address is a noun or other identifying words with which we sometimes interrupt a sentence to show to whom we are speaking. **You know,** *Nancy,* **that you're always welcome.** Is the noun *Nancy* essential to the sentence? (*Yes, No*) 2836
b 3102	Use apostrophes to form the ordinary plurals of letters, numbers, signs, and words referred to as words. **There are two 3***'s* **and two 5***'s* **in our number.** **The +***'s* **should be changed to −***'s.* Insert the needed apostrophes: **The temperature is usually in the 70s or 80s.** 3103

subject complement 160	$S = Subject, LV = Linking\ Verb, SC = Subject\ Complement$ **Some players get nervous just before a game.** Fill in the missing words: S LV SC **players** _____ _____ 161
block, and 428	**Much of the soil is poor consequently the Japanese farmer depends greatly upon fertilizers.** _____ 429
drop 696	Every compound sentence can be improved by changing it to a complex sentence. (*True, False*) 697
Icelanders, Norway, 964	Punctuate the following sentence: **A fierce battle of World War II was fought on Iwo Jima a tiny island in the Pacific.** 965
noun-participle 1232	Because a noun-participle phrase, unlike a participial phrase, is related to the rest of the sentence only by our thought, it is classified as an ab _____ phrase. 1233
No 1500	Modifiers—words, phrases, and clauses—sometimes get in one another's way and produce an awkward or absurd sentence. When this happens, you can often solve your problem by shifting the (*adverb, adjective*) clause to the beginning of the sentence. 1501

b 1768	a. **We invited** *our* **coach and** *our* **math teacher to the picnic.** b. **We invited** *our* **coach and math teacher to the picnic.** Which sentence means two persons? _____ 1769
Correct 2035	∧ **These stories** *deal* **with sports. (Every one of)** _____ 2036

b
 	
2302
	Passive verbs are also useful when the doer of an action is obvious or unimportant.
	    a. **The package** *will be delivered* **tomorrow.**
	    b. **The deliveryman** *will deliver* **the package tomorrow.**
	Which sentence is better because the doer of the action is unimportant and had better be omitted? _____
	2303

he, me 2569	Lesson **72** Reflexive, Intensive, Demonstrative, and Possessive Pronouns [Frames 2571–2608]
No 2836	Use commas to set off direct address because it interrupts the sentence and is not essential to its meaning. Underline and set off the direct address with commas: **Our team fellow students needs your full support.** 2837
70's, 80's 3103	Insert the needed apostrophes: *Bookkeeping* **is the only English word having three double letters in a row—two os, two ks, and two es.** 3104

161

LV
get

SC
nervous

$S = Subject, LV = Linking\ Verb, SC = Subject\ Complement$

Mercury was the speedy messenger of the old Roman gods.

Fill in the missing words:

S	LV	SC
Mercury	_____	_____

162

---

poor;
consequently

429

Mrs. Merrill may be old   however, she is not old-fashioned.

_____

430

False

697

For combining two similar or related ideas of equal importance, a (*compound, complex*) sentence is better.

698

Iwo Jima,

965

Change each italicized sentence to an appositive phrase,
and insert it in the first sentence right after the word it explains. Supply the necessary commas.

La Paz is the highest capital in the world. *It is the capital of*
Bolivia. _____

_____

966

---

absolute

1233

To change a sentence to a noun-participle phrase is very
simple.

SENTENCE: **The fuel** *was running* **low.**
NOUN-PARTICIPLE PHRASE: **The fuel** *running* **low . . .**

We change the verb *was running* to a present participle by

dropping the helping verb _____.

1234

---

adverb

1501

**Grace couldn't say good-by to her uncle who was leaving the
country because she had measles.**

Did Grace's uncle leave the country because of her measles?
This amusing sentence contains an adjective clause beginning with the word **who** and an adverb clause beginning with

the word _____.

1502

a
 	
1769
	Do not omit a word required by the meaning or grammatical construction of a sentence or by customary usage.
	
	    Bob made fun . . . my suggestion.
	    Bob made fun . . . and ridiculed my suggestion.
	
	What preposition is missing from both sentences? _____
	<div align="right">1770</div>

deals 2036	**The vacuum cleaner** ∧ *sells* **for $69. (and all its attachments)** _____ <div align="right">2037</div>

a
 	
2303
	Use a passive verb when you wish to avoid naming the person who made a mistake or did something wrong.
	
	  a. **My mother** *threw* **out this important letter.**
	  b. **This important letter** *was thrown* **out by mistake.**
	
	Which sentence would you use to avoid embarrassing your mother? _____
	<div align="right">2304</div>

	REFLEXIVE AND INTENSIVE PRONOUNS Pronouns that end with *-self* or *-selves* can be used as either *reflexive* or *intensive* pronouns. When they reflect or turn back the action of the verb to the doer of the action, they are **reflexive** pronouns. A reflexive pronoun always ends with *-self* or _____. <div align="right">2571</div>
, fellow students, 2837	Punctuate the following sentence: **Let me know you lucky fellow how you manage to get such high grades.** <div align="right">2838</div>

o's, k's, e's
 	
3104
	Apostrophes make reading easier when we write the plurals of words referred to as words.
	
	    a. **Tony has spelled all his toos wrong.**
	    b. **Tony has spelled all his too's wrong.**
	
	Which sentence is easier to read? _____
	<div align="right">3105</div>

LV was SC messenger 162	*S = Subject, LV = Linking Verb, SC = Subject Complement* **An officer should feel responsible for the men in his unit.** Fill in the missing words: *S* *LV* *SC* _____ **should feel** _____ 163
old; however 430	**Fruit trees must be sprayed at the right time or the fruit will be wormy.** _____ 431
compound 698	As a person develops greater writing skill and sees the relationship between his ideas more clearly, he tends to use (*more, fewer*) compound sentences. 699
La Paz, the capital of Bolivia, is the highest capital in the world. 966	Continue to follow the directions for the previous frame: **The dahlia is named after Dahl.** *He was a Swedish botanist.* _____ _____ 967
was 1234	Sometimes we need to change a one-word verb to a present participle. SENTENCE: **The fuel** *ran* **low.** NOUN-PARTICIPLE PHRASE: **The fuel** *running* **low . . .** Here we change the verb *ran* to the present participle _____. 1235
because 1502	**Grace couldn't say good-by to her uncle who was leaving the country because she had measles.** **Because she had measles, Grace couldn't say good-by to her uncle who was leaving the country.** We get rid of the absurdity by shifting the (*adjective, adverb*) clause to the beginning of the sentence. 1503

of 1770	The team had no respect . . . their coach. The team had no respect . . . or confidence in their coach. What preposition is missing from both sentences? _____ 1771
sell 2037	The vacuum cleaner ʌ *sells* for $69. (, with all its attach- ments,) _____ 2038
b 2304	a. **The room** *had* **not** *been cleaned* **after the party.** b. **Virginia** *had* **not** *cleaned* **the room after the party.** Which sentence is more tactful because it would not embar- rass Virginia? _____ 2305
-selves 2571	a. **Frank blamed** *me* **for his failure.** b. **Frank blamed** *himself* **for his failure.** Which sentence contains a reflexive pronoun that turns the action back to the doer of the action? _____ 2572
, you lucky fellow, 2838	Punctuate the following sentence: **I wonder Fred if you have heard about Bob Chapman.** 2839
b 3105	Insert the needed apostrophes: **Too many ands and sos make writing sound childish.** 3106

S
officer
 	
SC
responsible
 	
163
	Sled dogs are an indispensable part of any Arctic expedition.
	Fill in the missing words:
	
	      S *LV* *SC*
	
	   dogs _____ _____
	                                                         164

time, or 431	**Fruit trees must be sprayed at the right time otherwise the fruit will be wormy.** _____ 432
fewer 699	Lesson **19** Recognizing Noun Clauses [Frames 701–740]
The dahlia is named after Dahl, a Swedish botanist. 967	**Two great composers died at an early age.** *They were Schubert and Mozart.* _____ _____ 968
running 1235	**The fuel** running **low...** This is a noun-participle phrase because the present participle *running* modifies the noun _____. 1236
adverb 1503	Underline the adverb phrase that could be shifted to the beginning of the sentence to get rid of its absurdity: **Dad glued together the vase that Chuck had broken with remarkable skill.** 1504

for 1771	The teacher referred . . . a book. The book . . . which the teacher referred was not in the library. What preposition is missing from both sentences? _____ 1772
Correct 2038	Greene's is ∧ one of the groceries that *deliver*. (the only) _____ 2039
a 2305	When you have a good reason for not mentioning the doer of an action or when you wish to focus attention on the person(s) or thing(s) acted upon, use (*an active, a passive*) verb. 2306

b
 	
2572
	When pronouns that end with *-self* or *-selves* are used after a noun or another pronoun to emphasize or intensify it, they are called **intensive** pronouns.
	
	    a. **The manager** *himself* **waited on me.**
	    b. **The manager blamed** *himself* **for the mistake.**
	
	Is *himself* used as an intensive pronoun in *a* or *b*? _____
	2573

, Fred, 2839	DATES AND ADDRESSES The date in the following sentence consists of three parts: **On** *Sunday, July 9, 1961,* **the new church was dedicated.** After the first part of the date, is there a comma both before and after each additional part? (*Yes, No*) 2840
and's, so's 3106	Lesson **87** Controlling Your Capitals [Frames 3108–3139]

LV are SC part 164	**The young children in the back seat were becoming very restless.** Filling in the missing words: *S* *LV* *SC* _____ _____ _____ 165
me; otherwise 432	**Up to twenty-one a girl tries to look older** **after twenty-one she tries to look younger.** _____ 433
	We have now completed our study of adverb and adjective clauses. We turn next to the third (and last) type of clause—the **noun clause.** As its name suggests, a noun clause is a clause that is used as a _____. 701
Two great composers, Schubert and Mozart, died at an early age. 968	**John's father gave him his first lessons in reporting.** *He was the editor of a country paper.* _____ _____ 969
fuel 1236	a. *Running low,* **the fuel was insufficient to carry the plane to its destination.** b. *The fuel running low,* **the pilot made an emergency landing.** Which sentence contains a noun-participle phrase? _____ 1237

th remarkable skill
 	
1504
	a. **We almost know everyone in town.**
	       b. **We know almost everyone in town.**
	
	In which sentence is the adverb **almost** placed more sensibly?
	
	_____
	                          1505

to 1772	a. **We** *did* **many things that were fun.** b. **We swam, fished, and many other things that were fun.** What word is missing from sentence *b?* _____ 177
delivers 2039	**The yield of corn** ∧ *has* **been increased. (and wheat)** _____ 204
a passive 2306	In this and the following frames, make each sentence more direct by changing the verb from passive to active. To do so, make the object of the preposition **by** the subject of your revised sentence. **Nothing** *had been said* **by the teacher about a test.** _____ _____ 230
a 2573	a. **The manager** *himself* **waited on me.** b. **He** *himself* **waited on me.** In which sentence does the intensive pronoun emphasize another pronoun? _____ 257
Yes 2840	The address in the following sentence consists of three parts: **The Atlas Company of** *240 Oak Street, Dayton 17, Ohio,* **will send you a catalogue.** After the first part of the address, is there a comma both before and after each additional part? (*Yes, No*) 284
	The eleven rules for capitals presented in this and the next lesson are all based upon one general principle: Use a capital letter for a proper noun—a name that fits only *one particular* person, group of people, place, or thing. Use a small letter for a common noun—a name that fits *any one* of its kind. (*Turn to the next frame.*) 310

S children LV were becoming SC restless 165

The coach of the other team was looking worried.

Fill in the missing words:

S	LV	SC
_____	_____	_____
		166

---

older; after

433

Athletics keep a person physically fit   and furthermore they develop a sense of teamwork.

_____

434

---

noun

701

We have seen that adverb and adjective clauses offer almost endless possibilities for showing the various kinds of

rel_____ that exist among our ideas.

702

John's father, the editor of a country paper, gave him his first lessons in reporting.

969

Thursday is named after Thor. *He is the god of thunder in Norse mythology.*

970

---

b

1237

The fuel running low, **the pilot made an emergency landing.**

This is a noun-participle phrase because the participle *running* modifies the noun *fuel,* which is (*inside, outside*) the phrase.

1238

---

b

1505

a. **With trembling knees, Bill walked into the office where the principal was sitting.**

b. **Bill walked into the office where the principal was sitting with trembling knees.**

In which sentence are the modifiers placed more sensibly?

_____

1506

did 1773	a. **The author has lived** *among* **the Eskimos.** b. **The author has lived, as well as written about, the Eskimos** What word is missing from sentence *b?* _____ 177
Correct 2040	**The team** *was* ∧ **in the gym. (weighing themselves)** _____ 204
The teacher had said nothing about a test. 2307	Continue to follow the directions for the previous frame: **All your worries** *will be forgotten* **by you at this gay comedy** _____ _____ 230
b 2574	Be sure that you know the correct forms of the variou reflexive and intensive pronouns: SINGULAR: **myself** **himself** **itself** **yourself** **herself** **oneself** PLURAL: **ourselves, yourselves, themselves.** Is there such a word as **hisself?** (*Yes, No*) 257
Yes 2841	After writing the first part of a date or an address, pu a comma both before and after each additional part. Punctuate the following sentence: **On Monday August 7 we left Phoenix Arizona and heade** **for El Paso Texas.** 284
	1. Capitalize geographical names that apply to *particula* countries, sections of countries, states, cities, oceans rivers, lakes, etc. **Canada** **North Dakota** **Pacific Ocean** **Hudson Rive** Copy one italicized word that requires a capital: **He lives in a** *city* **not far from** *cleveland.* 310

Lesson 5 Reviewing Basic Sentence Patterns

[Frames 168–190]

---

fit, and

434

UNIT 3: THE COMPLEX SENTENCE TO SHOW RELATIONSHIP

Lesson 12 Recognizing Adverb Clauses

[Frames 436–477]

---

relationship

702

Noun clauses do not begin to have the usefulness of the other clauses for sentence improvement. We use noun clauses so naturally that we study them mainly to complete our picture of the three kinds of clauses that we find in (*compound, complex*) sentences.

703

Thursday is
named after
Thor, the god
of thunder in
se mythology.

970

Eliminate the **and** by changing the italicized sentence to an appositive phrase and inserting it in the first sentence right after the word it explains.

Bermuda consists of 360 small islands, and *it is a British colony.* _____

_____

971

---

inside

1238

Now let's change a sentence to a noun-participle phrase that contains a past participle:

SENTENCE: **Her test** *was completed.*
NOUN-PARTICIPLE PHRASE: **Her test** *completed . . .*

We change the verb *was completed* to the past participle *completed* by dropping the helping verb _____.

1239

---

a

1506

a. **They moved the chairs on which they were sitting closer to the fire.**
b. **They moved the chairs closer to the fire on which they were sitting.**

Which sentence is better? _____

1507

among 1774	Do not omit *that* from a noun clause used as a subject com plement after any form of the linking verb *be*. RIGHT: **His excuse was that he didn't see the stop sign.** WRONG: **His excuse was he didn't see the stop sign.** What word is missing from the sentence that is labeled WRONG? _____ 1775
were 2041	ʌ **These doors** *lead* **to the basement. (Either of)** _____ 2042
You will forget all your worries at this gay comedy. 2308	**After a long voyage, Tahiti** *was reached* **by the mutineers.** _____ _____ 2309

No
 	
2575
	Underline the correct intensive pronoun:
	
	       Fred built the entire boat (*himself, hisself*).
	
	                          2576

Monday, August 7, Phoenix, Arizona, El Paso, 2842	Punctuate the following sentence: **In Hardin County Kentucky Abraham Lincoln was born on** **February 12 1809.** 2843

Cleveland
 	
3109
	Copy one italicized word that requires a capital:
	
	   Are there more *lakes* **in** *wisconsin* **or in our** *state*?
	
	                          3110

An action verb is (*always, sometimes*) followed by a direct object.

168

---

a. **The whistle blew.**
b. **When the whistle blew**

Although both word groups have a subject and a verb, only one word group makes sense by itself.

Which word group makes sense by itself? _____

436

---

complex

703

Since noun clauses are used exactly as nouns, let us review the various ways in which nouns are used.

His *remark* **puzzled us.**

The noun *remark* is the *subject* of the verb _____.

704

Bermuda, a
British colony,
consists of 360
small islands.

971

Continue to follow the directions for the previous frame:

My mother made cream puffs, and *they are my favorite dessert.*

_____

_____

972

---

was

1239

Her test *completed* . . .

This is a noun-participle phrase because the past participle *completed* modifies the noun _____ within the phrase.

1240

---

a

1507

a. **The postman has to walk all day without sitting down to rest in the slushy snow.**
b. **The postman has to walk all day in the slushy snow without sitting down to rest.**

Which sentence is better? _____

1508

that 1775	In this and the following frames, if the omission is incorrect, add the necessary word. If the omission is allowable, write *Correct.* **I *was* on one side and my two friends _____ on the other.** 1776
leads 2042	**In many parts of the world, the opportunity for education** ∧ *does* **not exist. (and personal development)** _____ 2043
After a long voyage, the mutineers reached Tahiti. 2309	**The high cost of medical service *is pointed* out by this article.** _____ _____ 2310
himself 2576	SINGULAR: **myself** **himself** **itself** **yourself** **herself** **oneself** PLURAL: **ourselves, yourselves, themselves** Is there such a word as **theirselves?** (*Yes, No*) 2577
Hardin County, Kentucky, February 12, 2843	A one-part address is set off with commas only when there is no preposition such as *of, at,* or *on* to connect it with the sentence. a. **Andy Shaw** *of* **778 Montclair Avenue was the winner.** b. **Andy Shaw 778 Montclair Avenue was the winner.** The one-part address requires commas in sentence (*a, b*) 2844
Wisconsin 3110	Copy only the words to which capitals should be added: **The Mississippi river begins at lake Itasca in minnesota.** 3111

sometimes 168	**The price of steel rose as a result of the strike.** Does the verb **rose** require a complement to complete the meaning of the sentence? (*Yes, No*) 169
a 436	a. **The whistle blew.** b. **When the whistle blew** Which word group is a sentence because it makes sense by itself? _____ 437
puzzled 704	a. **His** *remark* **puzzled us.** b. *What he said* **puzzled us.** The clause *What he said* does the same job in sentence *b* that the noun *remark* does in sentence *a*. It is therefore a _____ clause. 705
y mother made eam puffs, my vorite dessert. 972	**Kitty Hawk is in North Carolina, and** *it was the birthplace of aviation.* _____ _____ 973
test 1240	a. *Her test completed,* **Carol turned in her paper.** b. *Completing her test,* **Carol turned in her paper.** Which sentence contains a noun-participle phrase? _____ 1241
b 1508	a. **The car was taken for investigation to the factory where it had been made after the crash.** b. **After the crash, the car was taken for investigation to the factory where it had been made.** Which sentence is better? _____ 1509

were 1776	I *was* on one side and my friend _____ on the other. 1777
Correct 2043	ʌ The sparrows *wake* me every morning. (The noisy chirping of) _____ 2044
This article points out the high cost of medical service. 2310	This event *will* always *be remembered* by our family. _____ _____ 2311
No 2577	Underline the correct reflexive pronoun: The Lamberts have bought (*theirselves, themselves*) a boat. 2578
b 2844	The Speedy Cleaners *at* 600 Main Street give three-hour service on request. If you omitted the preposition *at*, would you set off 600 Main Street with commas? (*Yes, No*) 2845

River, Lake,
Minnesota
 	
3111
	Capitalize north, east, south, and west when they name geographical sections of a country or of the world. Use small letters when they indicate directions on the compass.
	
	     a. The road turns *south.*
	     b. The *south* is quite industrial.
	
	Capitalize *south* in sentence (*a, b*). 3112

No 169	a. **The price of steel rose as a result of the strike.** b. **The price rose.** Although sentence *a* provides more detail than sentence *b*, the verb **rose** makes a (*complete, incomplete*) statement about the subject in both sentences. 170
a 437	a. **The whistle blew.** b. **When the whistle blew** Word group *b* is not a sentence because the word _____ has been added. 438
noun 705	We have seen that when we omit an adverb or adjective clause, we still have a grammatically complete sentence remaining. *What he said* **puzzled us.** When we omit the noun clause in this sentence, does a complete sentence remain? (*Yes, No*) 706
Kitty Hawk, the birthplace of aviation, is in North Carolina. 973	**The game drew a crowd of 1,500, and** *it was the largest attendance of the year.* _____ _____ 974
a 1241	*Her test completed,* **Carol turned in her paper.** This is a noun-participle phrase because the past participle *completed* modifies the noun *test*, which is (*inside, outside*) the phrase. 1242
b 1509	In this and the following frames, rewrite each sentence to improve the placement of the modifiers: **The branch suddenly broke that he was climbing on.** _____ 1510

Correct 1777	Alva never has _____ and never will *join* a sorority 177
wakes 2044	If making the change indicated after each sentence would make it necessary to change the italicized verb, write only the form of the verb that would be required. If the verb would remain the same, write *Correct*. **Where *is* your ticket?** (Change **ticket** to **tickets**.) _____ 204
Our family will always remember this event. 2311	**The rushing life of big cities *was* never *enjoyed* by my father** _____ _____ 231

themselves
 	
2578
	All the *-self* pronouns are solid words. Do not split them!
	
	  a. **my self, your self, her self, our selves, them selves**
	  b. **myself, yourself, herself, ourselves, themselves**
	
	The pronouns are printed correctly after (*a, b*).
	
	257

Yes
 	
2845
	In line with the modern tendency to eliminate unnecessary commas, many publications omit commas in dates when *only* the month and the year are stated.
	
	  a. **In May 1961 construction of the bridge was started.**
	  b. **On May 27 1961 construction of the bridge was started**
	
	Which sentence can do without commas? _____
	
	284

b 3112	a. **Our house is on the *West* side of the street.** b. **The movie industry is in the *West*.** The word *west* should not be capitalized in sentence (*a, b*) 311

complete 170	$S–V$ = Subject–Action Verb $S–V–DO$ = Subject–Action Verb → Direct Object **Several athletes from our school competed.** The pattern of this sentence is ($S–V$, $S–V–DO$). 171

When
 	
438
	A word group that has a subject and a verb but does not make sense by itself is a **clause.**
	
	   a. **The road was rough.**
	   b. **Because the road was rough**
	
	Which word group is a clause? _____
	
	439

No 706	(*What he said*) **puzzled us.** If we omitted the noun clause, the sentence would lack a (*subject, direct object*). 707
he game drew owd of 1,500, the largest attendance of the year. 974	**Joe Sims discovered the fire, and** *he is the night watchman.* _____ _____ 975
inside 1242	*Her eyes shining with joy,* **Judy showed me her new dress.** **Judy,** *her eyes shining with joy,* **showed me her new dress.** **Judy showed me her new dress,** *her eyes shining with joy.* Can a noun-participle phrase be shifted from one position to another in a sentence? (*Yes, No*) 1243
he branch that e was climbing on suddenly broke. 1510	Continue to follow the directions for the previous frame: **Every student passed to whom the test was given.** _____ _____ 1511

joined	I must find *a* book or _____ article about politics.
1778	1779
are	Selecting the right color *is* very important. (Change **color** to **colors**.) _____
2045	2046
My father (has) never enjoyed the rushing life of big cities.	Change the verb from active to passive to eliminate the present subject, which is obvious, unimportant, or tactless. Start your sentence with the thing or things *acted upon* and omit the doer of the action. **Someone *took* the injured man to the hospital.** _____
2312	2313
b	Underline the correct reflexive pronoun: **Try to put** (*yourself, your self*) **in my place.**
2579	2580
a	In this and the following frames, insert the necessary commas. If no commas are required, write *None*. **It is doubtful however whether any good will result from the change.**
2846	2847
a	2. Capitalize the names of nationalities, languages, races, religions, and the adjectives formed from these names. **American Negro Catholic Protestant** **Italian Indian Methodist Jew (Jewish)** Copy the words that require capitals: **There is an ancient catholic church in this spanish town.**
3113	3114

S—V 171	$S-V = Subject-Action\ Verb$ $S-V-DO = Subject-Action\ Verb \rightarrow Direct\ Object$ **Henry Thoreau filled many notebooks with his careful obser-vations of nature.** The pattern of this sentence is ($S-V$, $S-V-DO$). 172
b 439	**Because the road was rough** This word group would become a sentence if we dropped the word _____. 440
subject 707	**We raise** *vegetables.* In this sentence the noun *vegetables* is the direct object of the verb _____. 708
Joe Sims, the ight watchman, discovered the fire. 975	An appositive generally comes (*before, after*) the noun it explains. 976
Yes 1243	a. **The audience grew restless, their patience exhausted.** b. **Their patience exhausted, the audience grew restless.** In which sentence does the noun-participle phrase come at the end of the sentence? _____ 1244
Every student to whom the test was given passed. 1511	**Bert was given the part in the school play of the cranky old farmer.** _____ 1512

an 1779	Dr. Shorr is looking for *a* typist and _____ receptionist. (Two persons) 1780
Correct 2046	This is the finest stock car that *was* ever built. (Change **the finest stock car** to **one of the finest stock cars.**) _____ 2047
The injured man was taken to the hospital. 2313	Continue to follow the directions for the previous frame: **People *should* not *keep* bananas in a refrigerator.** _____ _____ 2314
yourself 2580	Supply the proper reflexive pronoun: **The Marines hid** _____ **behind some large rocks.** 2581
, however, 2847	**Send me word Virginia when you are well enough to have visitors.** 2848
Catholic, Spanish 3114	Copy the words that require capitals: **The author had lived on several indian reservations in the west.** 3115

S—V—DO 172	a. **Our teacher will return in a few days.** b. **Our teacher will return the test papers.** Which sentence is in the *S—V—DO* pattern? _____ 173
Because 440	Every clause is used like a single word—like an *adverb*, an *adjective*, or a *noun*. Since no adverb, adjective, or noun makes sense by itself, it follows that no clause that is used like one of these words makes sense by itself either. Only a (*clause, sentence*) makes sense by itself. 441
raise 708	a. **We raise** *vegetables.* b. **We raise** *whatever we need.* The noun clause *whatever we need* in sentence *b* is used just like the direct object _____ in sentence *a*. 709
after 976	Does an appositive phrase, like a clause, contain a subject and a verb? (*Yes, No*) 977
a 1244	a. **His eyelids drooping with sleepiness, Bob struggled through the last chapter.** b. **Bob struggled through the last chapter, his eyelids drooping with sleep.** In which sentence does the noun-participle phrase come at the end of the sentence? _____ 1245
Bert was given the part of the cranky old farmer . . . *or* In the school play Bert . . . 1512	**I saw people waiting for the bus that looked frozen.** _____ _____ 1513

a 1780	Cliff *is* seventeen and his sister _____ sixteen. 178
were 2047	The principal and the assistant principal *attend* every game (Change **and** to **or**.) _____ 204
Bananas should not be kept in a refrigerator. 2314	Sally *had left* the iron on all night. _____ _____ 2315
themselves 2581	Supply the proper reflexive pronoun: **We can set our stove to turn _____ off.** 2582
, Virginia, 2848	Mr. Higgins my counselor understood how I a new student felt on my first day in high school. 284
Indian, West 3115	Copy the words that require capitals: **There are negroes of both the catholic and protestant faiths.** 311

b 173	a. **The principal spoke a few words.** b. **The principal spoke briefly.** Which sentence is in the *S—V—DO* pattern? _____ 174
sentence 441	In this lesson you will study **adverb clauses.** As its name suggests, an adverb clause is a clause that is used as an (*adjective, adverb*). 442
vegetables 709	**We raise** *whatever we need.* When we omit the noun clause in this sentence, does a complete sentence remain? (*Yes, No*) 710
No 977	When an appositive phrase is omitted from a sentence, does a grammatically complete sentence remain? (*Yes, No*) 978
b 1245	A noun-participle phrase is a rather mature construction used by experienced writers to combine ideas. In this and the following frames, combine the sentences by changing each italicized sentence to a noun-participle phrase. **I stood in the icy water.** *My teeth were chattering.* **I stood in the icy water,** _____. 1246
I saw people that looked frozen waiting for the bus. 1513	**You should not put a glass into hot water that is cold.** _____ _____ 1514

Correct 1781	Our country must be strong *on* the sea and _____ the air. 1782
attends 2048	Neither his hands nor his face *was* clean. (Reverse the positions of **hands** and **face**.) _____ 2049
The iron had been left on all night. 2315	They *guarantee* these batteries for one year. _____ _____ 2316
itself 2582	Supply an intensive pronoun to emphasize the subject **students:** **The students** _____ **patrol the corridors.** 2583
, my counselor, , a new student, 2849	**The famous Dionne quintuplets were born on May 28 1934 in Callander Ontario.** 2850
Negroes, Catholic, Protestant 3116	3. Capitalize the entire names of organizations, companies, buildings, theaters, and institutions such as schools, clubs, churches, libraries, and hospitals. a. **Evanston high school** b. **Evanston High School** Which is correctly capitalized? _____ 3117

a
 	
174
	In addition to a *direct* object, the *S—V—DO* sentence some-times contains an *indirect* object, which explains *to whom* (or *to what*) or *for whom* (or *for what*) something is done.
	
	   a. **Mr. Harvey sold his stamp collection.**
	   b. **Mr. Harvey sold my brother his stamp collection.**
	
	Which sentence contains an indirect object? _____ 175

adverb 442	An ordinary adverb modifies a verb by answering questions such as **When? Where?** or **How?** about its action. **Our sales increased** *recently.* The word *recently* is an adverb because it tells **when** about the verb _____. 443
No 710	**We raise** (*whatever we need*). If we omitted the noun clause, the sentence would lack a (*subject, direct object*). 711
Yes 978	An appositive phrase, because it is an "extra," should be set off from the rest of the sentence by commas. (*True, False*) 979
my teeth chattering. 1246	Continue to follow the directions for the previous frame: *The band was playing.* **The team rushed onto the field.** _____, **the team rushed onto the field.** 1247

You should not put a glass that is cold into hot water.
 	
1514
	Write the numbers of the three word groups to show in which order you would combine them. Be careful to avoid giving your sentence a ridiculous meaning.
	
	   1. a movie will be shown
	   2. on how to play football
	   3. in the public library _____ _____ _____
	
	1515

in 1782	The steak *was* tough and the potatoes _____ overcooked. 1783
were 2049	This kind of rice *cooks* very fast. (Change **rice** to **beans**.) _____ 2050
These batteries are guaranteed for one year. 2316	The voters *will vote* upon this proposal at the next election. _____ _____ 2317
themselves 2583	Do not use a reflexive pronoun in place of a simple pronoun like *I, he,* or *we*—especially in careful speech or in formal writing. a. *I* **went fishing.** b. **Dad and *I* went fishing.** In which sentence might you sometimes hear *myself* instead of *I?* _____ 2584
May 28, 1934, Callander, 2850	Yes we must realize my young friends that failure is often a steppingstone to success. 2851
b 3117	Copy and capitalize the words that require capitals: **The Rotary club made a donation to the Hillside children's hospital.** 3118

b 175	**Mr. Harvey sold my brother his stamp collection.** The indirect object in this sentence is _____. 176
increased 443	a. **Our sales increased** *recently.* b. **Our sales increased** *when we lowered our price.* Both the adverb clause in sentence *b* and the adverb *recently* in sentence *a* tell (*where, when, how*) about the verb **increased.** 444
direct object 711	An *indirect* object precedes the *direct* object and shows *to whom* (or *to what*) or *for whom* (or *for what*) something is done. **She will pay the finder a reward.** The indirect object in the above sentence is the noun _____. 712
True 979	Lesson **26** The Process of Reduction [Frames 981–1016]
The band playing, 1247	**The dog was shivering on the doorstep.** *His rough coat was covered with snow.* **The dog was shivering on the doorstep,** _____ _____. 1248

Either of these is correct:
3–1–2
1–3–2
 	
1515
	Continue to follow the directions for the previous frame:
	
	    1. **we bought an ashtray**
	    2. **at the souvenir stand**
	    3. **made of shells** ____ ____ ____
	
	1516

were 1783	In this and the following frames, insert any word that has been *incorrectly* omitted. If the omission of the word is allowable, write *Correct*. **My sister takes Latin and I Spanish.** 1784
Correct 2050	**Gambling** *was* **his downfall.** (Change **gambling** to **horses**.) _____ 2051
This proposal will be voted upon at the next election. 2317	Mother *had put* **the letter in the wrong envelope.** _____ _____ 2318
b 2584	a. *I* **went fishing.** b. **Dad and** *I* **went fishing.** Since you would never use *myself* in sentence *a,* it would seem just as unreasonable to use *myself* in sentence *b.* In both sentences, *I* is used as the _____ of the verb **went.** 2585
Yes, , my young friends, 2851	**It is human failure not mechanical failure that is responsible as a matter of fact for most of the slaughter on our highways.** 2852
Club, Children's Hospital 3118	Such words as *company, building, theater, college, high school, church,* and *hospital* are not capitalized unless they are a part of a particular name. **a Baptist church** Is this the special name of one particular church at a particular location? (*Yes, No*) 3119

page 352

brother 176	**Mr. Harvey sold my brother his stamp collection.** When an indirect object is present, it always comes (*before, after*) the direct object. 177
when 444	a. **Our sales increased** *recently.* b. **Our sales increased** *when we lowered our price.* Because the clause in sentence *b* does the same job as the adverb in sentence *a*, it is an _____ *clause.* 445
finder 712	a. **She will pay the finder a reward.** b. **She will pay whoever finds the dog a reward.** Write the four-word noun clause in sentence *b* that takes the place of the indirect object **finder** in sentence *a*. _____ 713
	When we substitute a simpler word group for a longer and more complicated word group, we say that we *reduce* the longer word group. To reduce a word group means to (*simplify, complicate*) it. 981
his rough coat covered with snow. 1248	**Refugees wandered about aimlessly.** *Their homes were destroyed.* **Refugees wandered about aimlessly,** _____ _____. 1249
2-1-3 1516	1. **my aunt flew to Florida** 2. **after Claude went to college** 3. **to bask in the sunshine** ___ ___ ___ 1517

I *take* Spanish 1784	**The truck was turning left and our car right.** 1785
were 2051	**Potatoes** *are* **our main crop.** (Reverse the positions of **potatoes** and **our main crop.**) _____ 2052
The letter had been put in the wrong envelope. 2318	Lesson **65** Review: Using Verbs Correctly [Frames 2320–2352]
subject 2585	Do not use a reflexive pronoun unless the word it stands for appears earlier in the sentence. **Corey excused** *himself* **and left early.** The pronoun *himself* is correctly used because it stands for the noun _____ earlier in the sentence. 2586
, not mechanical failure, , as a matter of fact, 2852	**The Liberty Bell cracked on July 8 1835 when it was tolled for the death of John Marshall Chief Justice of the United States.** 2853
No 3119	a. **a new Baptist church** b. **Calvary Baptist church** In which item should **church** be capitalized because it is part of the special name of a particular church? _____ 3120

before 177	**The charcoal gives the meat a tangy flavor.** The indirect object in this sentence is _____. <div align="right">178</div>
adverb 445	Think of an adverb clause as a "stretched-out" adverb consisting of a number of words and having a *subject* and a _____. <div align="right">446</div>
whoever finds the dog 713	**She will pay** *whoever finds the dog* **a reward.** An indirect object is not an essential part of the sentence framework. If we omit the clause in the above sentence, does a complete sentence remain? (*Yes, No*) <div align="right">714</div>
simplify 981	In general, express your idea in the simplest word group you can without sacrificing clearness. A good sentence, like a good machine, has no useless parts. If you can express your idea in a prepositional phrase, don't use (*a sentence, an adjective*). <div align="right">982</div>
their homes destroyed. 1249	**Hundreds of persons work on each car.** *Each person performs one small operation.* **Hundreds of persons work on each car,** _____ _____. <div align="right">1250</div>
2–1–3 1–3–2 1517	1. clean your hands 2. after you paint 3. with turpentine _____. <div align="right">1518</div>

Correct 1785	The branch of medicine which Dr. Nelson specializes is skin diseases. 1786
is 2052	One hour hardly *seems* enough time for this job. (Change **One hour** to **Two hours**.) _____ 2053
	In this and the following frames, write the correct forms of the verbs in parentheses: **If the chairman had** _____ (*give*) **me a chance, I** **would have** _____ (*speak*). 2320
Corey 2586	a. **The two brothers put** *themselves* **through college.** b. **Ralph and** *himself* **paid their own way through college.** In which sentence is the reflexive pronoun used correctly? ____ 2587
July 8, 1835, Marshall, 2853	Well the interview by the way lasted for over an hour. 2854
b 3120	a. **the Kirby oil company** b. **a large oil company** In which item should the words **oil company** be capitalized because they are part of the name of a particular company? ____ 3121

meat 178	a. **Shirley read** *Cynthia* **her letter.** b. **Shirley read her letter to** *Cynthia.* In which sentence is *Cynthia* an indirect object? _____ 179
verb (*or* predicate) 446	**Our farm begins** *here.* The word *here* is an adverb because it tells **where** about the verb _____. 447
Yes 714	a. **This is my** *recipe* **for fudge.** b. **This is** *how I make fudge.* Both the noun clause *how I make fudge* in sentence *b* and the noun *recipe* in sentence *a* complete the linking verb **is.** Both are used as (*subject complements, direct objects*). 715
a sentence 982	1. Sentence 3. Phrase (verbal, appositive, prepositional) 2. Clause 4. Single word (adjective, adverb) As we proceed through this list from 1 to 4, the sentence elements become more (*simple, complicated*). 983
each person performing one small operation. 1250	In this and the following frames, eliminate the **and** by chang- ing the italicized statement to a noun-participle phrase. (Rewrite the complete sentence.) *Their money was spent,* **and the children left the carnival.** _____ _____ 1251
2–1–3 1–3–2 1518	1. **many people came** 2. **to see the game** 3. **from nearby towns** ____ ____ ____ 1519

medicine *in* which *or* specializes *in* 1786	**Tony would not take any advice except his father.** 1787
Correct 2053	**What color *is* its hair? (Change hair to eyes.)** _____ 2054
given, spoken 2320	**The window was _____ (*break*) when I _____ (*see*) it.** 2321
a 2587	Underline the correct pronoun: **I hope that your mother and (*you, yourself*) can attend my commencement.** 2588
Well, , by the way, 2854	**I wonder Phyllis if you ever see our old neighbors the Bur- gesses at church.** 2855
a 3121	4. Capitalize the names of the days of the week, months, and holidays, but *not* the names of the seasons. **Wednesday** **Christmas** **spring** **February** **Memorial Day** **fall** Copy the words that require capitals: **In the autumn we look forward to thanksgiving day.** 3122

a 179	A linking verb is (*always, sometimes*) followed by a subject complement. 180
begins 447	a. **Our farm begins** *here.* b. **Our farm begins** *where the road turns.* The adverb clause in sentence *b* does the same job as the adverb *here* in sentence *a.* Both tell (*where, when, how*) about the verb **begins.** 448
subject complements 715	**This is** (*how I make fudge*). We cannot omit the noun clause because we should lose an essential part of the sentence framework. The part we would lose is the (*subject, direct object, subject complement*). 716

simple
 	
983
	The process of reducing a word group to a simpler word group is called **reduction.**
	
	    a. Changing a sentence to an appositive phrase.
	    b. Changing a single word to a clause.
	
	Which is an example of reduction—*a* or *b?* _____ 984

Their money spent, the children left the carnival. 1251	*No guides were available,* **and we had to depend on ourselves.** (Change *were* to *being.*) _____ _____ 1252
1–3–2 2–1–3 3–1–2 1519	1. she gave the cookies 2. to the children 3. that had stuck to the pan ____ ____ ____ 1520

except *from* his *or* his father's 1787	**Next year we lose our best pitcher and hitter.** (one person) 1788
are 2054	**This is the best fair that** *was* **ever held here.** (Change **the best fair** to **one of the best fairs.**) _____ 2055
broken, saw 2321	**Bob might have _____** (*become*) **ill from all the ice water that he _____** (*drink*). 2322
you 2588	DEMONSTRATIVE PRONOUNS Demonstrative pronouns (or adjectives) are used to point out. There are only four demonstrative words: **this that these those** Do you find the word *them* among these words? (*Yes, No*) 2589
, Phyllis, , the Burgesses, 2855	**Mr. Knox the principal pointed out that the boys after all were only children not adults.** 2856
Thanksgiving Day 3122	a. **Our winter sale begins after New Year's.** b. **Our Winter sale begins after new year's.** Which sentence is correctly capitalized? _____ 3123

always 180	a. **are, were, seemed, became** b. **ate, took, studied, listened** Would you expect to find a subject complement after the words in group *a* or group *b*? _____ 181
where 448	a. **Mr. Crane spoke** *seriously.* b. **Mr. Crane spoke** *as if he meant business.* Both the adverb clause in sentence *b* and the adverb *seriously* in sentence *a* tell (*when, where, how*) about the verb **spoke.** 449
subject complement 716	**We were still ten miles from our** *destination.* The noun *destination* is the object of the preposition _____. 717
a 984	a. Changing a sentence to an appositive phrase. b. Changing a single word to a clause. Which change would be preferable in your writing? _____ 985
No guides being available, we had to depend on ourselves. 1252	**Mrs. Koss entered the store, and** *her three children were trailing after her.* _____ _____ 1253
1-3-2 2-1-3 1520	Lesson **42** Recognizing Dangling Word Groups [Frames 1522–1554]

Correct 1788	**A dachshund's body is long and its legs very short.** 1789
were 2055	**There** *was* **only one street between our house and the park.** (Change **one street** to **three streets**.) _____ 2056
become, drank 2322	**When Connie** _____ (*come*) **into the house, her ears** **were** _____ (*freeze*). 2323
No 2589	The word *them* is not a demonstrative pronoun. It is the (*objective, nominative*) form of the personal pronoun **they**. 2590
, the principal, , after all, , not 2856	**The Chinese Telephone Exchange 743 Washington Street San Francisco 3 California welcomes visitors.** 2857
a 3123	5. Capitalize the brand names of particular products, but *not* the types of products that they identify. **Sunkist oranges** **Chrysler car** **Protecto paint** Copy the words that require capitals: **The makers of broadway shirts recommend that you use swish detergent.** 3124

a 181	$S—LV—SC$ = Subject—Linking Verb ← Subject Complement $1\longrightarrow 2$ a. **Larry lost his voice.** $1\longleftarrow\!\!—1$ b. **Larry became hoarse.** Which sentence is in the $S—LV—SC$ pattern? _____ 182
how 449	Besides telling **when, where,** and **how** about verbs, as adverbs can do, adverb clauses can also tell **why.** a. **We moved** *because our house was too small.* b. **We moved** *where there were very few other houses.* In which sentence does the adverb clause tell **why** about the verb **moved?** _____ 450
from 717	a. **We were still ten miles from our** *destination.* b. **We were still ten miles from where we were going.** In sentence *a*, the noun *destination* is the object of the preposition **from.** Write the noun clause in sentence *b* that is the object of the preposition **from.** _____ 718
a 985	When you reduce a word group, you generally improve your writing by using (*fewer, more*) words. 986
Mrs. Koss entered the store, her three children trailing after her. 1253	**Shirley came to the door, and** *her hair was done up in pin curls.* (Insert the noun-participle phrase after **Shirley.**) _____ _____ 1254
	You have seen that it is a good idea, now and then, to begin a sentence with an introductory phrase or clause. PRESENT PARTICIPIAL PHRASE: *Climbing the ladder,...* ADVERB CLAUSE: *As Jim climbed the ladder,...* The word group that doesn't tell **who** climbed the ladder is the (*phrase, clause*). 1522

legs *are* very 1789	Cathy's reason for breaking the date was she had a bad headache. 1790
were 2056	UNIT 9: SOLVING YOUR VERB PROBLEMS Lesson **58** **A Group of Similar Three-Part Verbs** [Frames 2058–2093]
came, frozen 2323	Terry had _____ (*grow*) so much that you would hardly have _____ (*know*) him. 2324

objective
 	
 2590
	Use the demonstrative pronoun (or adjective) *those*, not the personal pronoun *them*, to point out persons or things.
	
	   a. *Them* **are good cookies. I like** *them* **cookies.**
	   b. *Those* **are good cookies. I like** *those* **cookies.**
	
	 The correct sentences follow the letter (*a, b*). 2591

743 Washington Street, San Francisco 3, California, 2857	Lesson **80** **Commas for Nonrestrictive Clauses** [Frames 2859–2892]
Broadway, Swish 3124	a. **Blue Star Gasoline** b. **Blue Star gasoline** Which item is correctly capitalized? _____ 3125

b 182	a. **Larry became a . . .** b. **Larry found a . . .** Which sentence would be completed by a subject complement? _____ <div align="right">183</div>

a
 	
 450
	An adverb clause can also answer the question **On what condition?** or **Under what condition?** about the verb.
	    a. **Our car will start** *if you push it.*
	    b. **Our car will start** *when you turn the key.*
	In which sentence does the adverb clause tell **on what condition** the car will start? _____
	<div align="right">451</div>

where we were going 718	**We were still ten miles from** (*where we were going*). We cannot omit the noun clause because the preposition **from** would then be without an _____. <div align="right">719</div>
fewer 986	We have spent many frames on reducing sentences to subordinate word groups—to clauses and various kinds of phrases. Now we shall practice other types of reduction. **Ann stumbled** *while she was coming down the stairs.* Which two words can you omit from the adverb clause without changing the meaning? _____ _____ <div align="right">987</div>
hirley, her hair done up in in curls, came to the door. 1254	**Ten scouts stood on the stage,** *and each was holding a different flag.* (Insert the phrase after **scouts.**) _____ _____ <div align="right">1255</div>
phrase 1522	PAST PARTICIPIAL PHRASE: *Packed in straw, . . .* ADVERB CLAUSE: *When this clock is packed in straw, . . .* The word group that doesn't tell **what** was packed in straw is the (*phrase, clause*). <div align="right">1523</div>

was *that* she 1790	We can learn from almost everyone whom we come in contact. 1791
  	The three basic forms of a verb from which all its various tenses are formed are called the **principal parts** of the verb. PRESENT PAST PAST PARTICIPLE **talk** **talked** **(have) talked** Both the *past* and the *past participle* of this verb end with the two letters _____. 2058
grown, known 2324	I have _____ (*write*) a letter to the company, complaining that the dress has _____ (*shrink*). 2325
b 2591	Underline the correct word: Why don't we ask (*those, them*) **fellows to help us?** 2592
  	Adjective clauses begin with the relative pronouns **who (whose, whom), which,** and **that.** An adjective clause, like an adjective, modifies a noun or a _____. 2859
b 3125	6. Capitalize the names of governmental bodies, agencies, departments, and offices. **Senate** **Board of Education** **City Council** **Supreme Court** **Treasury Department** **Department of Health** Copy the words that require capitals: **The congress referred the matter to the state department.** 3126

a

183

---

a. **The boys** *are getting* **their own lunch.**
b. **The boys** *are getting* **hungry.**

In which sentence is the verb *are getting* used as a *linking* verb? _____

184

---

a

451

---

a. **Vern went to school** *because a test was scheduled.*
b. **Vern went to school** *although he had a bad cold.*

In which sentence does the adverb clause tell **under what condition** Vern went to school? _____

452

---

object

719

An *appositive* is a noun or pronoun set after another noun or pronoun to explain it.

His last hope, <u>*rescue* by the Marines,</u> **was soon to be realized.**

The appositive *rescue,* with its modifiers, follows and explains the noun _____.

720

---

she was

987

Ann stumbled *while (she was) coming down the stairs.*

The two words that we can omit from the adverb clause are the subject and a part of the _____.

988

Ten scouts, each holding a different flag, stood on the stage.

1255

Lesson **34** **Review: Devices for Sentence Variety**

[Frames 1257–1273]

---

phrase

1523

PREPOSITIONAL GERUND PHRASE: *After biting six children,* ...
ADVERB CLAUSE: *After the dog had bitten six children,* ...

The phrase doesn't tell you **who** or **what** bit the children, but the clause tells you that it was a _____.

1524

Lesson **50** Making Logical Comparisons

[Frames 1793–1830]

---

ed

2058

The past participle of a verb is the form we use in combina-tion with any form of the helping verb **have** or **be**.

PRESENT	PAST	PAST PARTICIPLE
talk	**talked**	**(have) talked**

In the case of the verb **talk,** is there any difference between the past and past participle form? (*Yes, No*)

205

---

written, shrunk

2325

You would not have _____ (*eat*) it if you had _____ (*see*) it made.

232

---

those

2592

POSSESSIVE PRONOUNS

Possessive pronouns show possession without the use of apostrophes. *Your's* or *our's* is just as incorrect as *hi's*.

POSSESSIVE PRONOUNS: **yours, his, hers, its, ours, theirs**

Yours **is just like** *ours.*

Do the italicized pronouns require apostrophes? (*Yes, No*)

259

---

pronoun

2859

To decide whether or not to set off an adjective clause with commas, ask yourself what purpose it serves.

    a. **all students**
    b. **all students** *who can typewrite*

The adjective clause in *b* makes the noun **students** refer to (*more, fewer*) students.

286

Congress, State Department

3126

    a. **Federal Bureau of Investigation**
    b. **Federal bureau of investigation**

Which item is correctly capitalized? _____

312

b 184	**The boys are getting hungry.** The word **hungry** is a (*direct object, subject complement*). <div align="right">185</div>
b 452	Learn to recognize the clause signals that tell us that an adverb clause is beginning. They are grouped according to the kind of information that the clauses supply. WHEN? **while, when, whenever, as, as soon as, before, after, since, until** Look for adverb clauses (*before, after*) these words. <div align="right">453</div>
hope 720	a. **His last hope,** *rescue by the Marines,* **was soon to be realized.** b. **His last hope,** *that the Marines would rescue him,* **was soon to be realized.** The noun clause in sentence *b* does the same job as the appositive _____ in sentence *a*. <div align="right">721</div>
verb (*or* predicate) 988	The word *elliptical* means "having words omitted." An adverb clause from which words have been omitted is an **elliptical clause.** **Ann stumbled** *while (she was) coming down the stairs.* In the above sentence, using an elliptical clause eliminates _____ words. (How many?) <div align="right">989</div>

	Each sentence lettered *a* represents one of the devices you have studied in this unit. Rewrite each sentence lettered *b*, putting it in the same arrangement as *a*.
	
	    a. **This fact no sensible person will deny.**
	    b. **The dog refused to eat these biscuits.**
	
	_____
	
	_____
	<div align="right">1257</div>

dog 1524	INFINITIVE PHRASE: *To get more business,...* ADVERB CLAUSE: *If a company wants to get more business,...* The phrase doesn't tell you **who** or **what** is to get more business, but the clause tells you that it is a _____. <div align="right">1525</div>

Make comparisons only between things of the same class.

WRONG: **Tommy's** *vocabulary* **is like an** *adult.*

This comparison is faulty because Tommy's *vocabulary* is not like an *adult.* It is like an adult's _____.

1793

No

2059

English verbs fall into two general classes: **regular** and **irregular** verbs. Verbs are classified as regular when both their past and past participle forms end with *-ed.*

PRESENT	PAST	PAST PARTICIPLE
talk	**talked**	**(have) talked**

The verb **talk** is (*regular, irregular*).

2060

---

eaten, seen

2326

When I _____ (*run*) to the window, the car had already _____ (*drive*) **away.**

2327

No

2593

Because apostrophes are needed to make nouns possessive, it is a natural and common mistake to use them with pronouns, too.

Underline the italicized word which requires an apostrophe to show possession:

We parked *ours* **in** *Stanleys* **driveway.**

2594

---

fewer

2860

a. **people**
b. **people** *who fail to vote*

People means *all* people.

By adding the clause *who fail to vote,* we (*increase, limit*) the number of people we are talking about.

2861

---

a

3127

In this and the following frames, copy only the words in each sentence to which capitals need to be added, according to the rules presented in this lesson:

Memorial day comes in the spring, not in the fall.

3128

subject complement 185	a. **The quality of the programs** *is* **excellent.** b. **The quality of the programs** *is* **improving.** In one of the sentences *is* serves as a helper to the main verb. In the other, it is a linking verb followed by a subject complement. Which sentence contains a subject complement? _____ 186
after 453	There are only two clause signals which can start adverb clauses that answer the question **Where?** WHERE? **where, wherever** **Mother hid the candy** *where no one could find it.* The adverb clause modifies the word (*hid, candy*). 454
rescue 721	**His last hope,** *that the Marines would rescue him,* **was soon to be realized.** **His last hope . . . was soon to be realized.** When we omit the noun clause used as an appositive, does a complete sentence remain? (*Yes, No*) 722
two 989	**Crackers will stay crisp** *if they are kept in a tin box.* Write the elliptical clause to which the italicized adverb clause can be reduced: _____. 990
These biscuits the dog refused to eat. 1257	a. **For a person of his age, such exercise seems much too strenuous.** b. **Mr. Walsh held the interest of his audience from his very first sentence.** _____ _____ 1258

company
 	
1525
	CLAUSES: *As Jim climbed the ladder, . . .*
	    When this clock is packed in straw, . . .
	    After the dog had bitten six children, . . .
	    If a company wants to get more business, . . .
	Do clauses have subjects that tell **whom** or **what** they are about? (*Yes, No*)
	1526

vocabulary 1793	a. **Tommy's** *vocabulary* **is like an** *adult.* b. **Tommy's** *vocabulary* **is like the** *vocabulary* **of an adult.** Which comparison is correct? _____ <div align="right">1794</div>

regular
 	
2060
	Of the thousands of verbs in our language, fewer than 150 are irregular. A verb is classified as irregular when its past and past participle forms do not end with *-ed.*
	
	    work **worked** **(have) worked**
	    drive **drove** **(have) driven**
	
	The irregular verb is (*work, drive*).
	
	<div align="right">2061</div>

ran, driven 2327	**Sam** _____ (*give*) **the police a description of the** **bicycle that had been** _____ (*steal*). <div align="right">2328</div>
Stanley's 2594	a. *Carols* **coat is newer than** *Virginias.* b. *Yours* **is newer than** *hers.* Which sentence is correct without apostrophes? _____ <div align="right">2595</div>
limit 2861	**To restrict** means "to limit the number." When we say the use of a parking lot is *restricted* to cus- tomers, we mean that its use is _____ to customers and that not everyone can park there. <div align="right">2862</div>
Day 3128	**The hurricane veered west on monday night and struck** **several states along the atlantic ocean.** <div align="right">3129</div>

a	**Gwen felt . . . about the run in her stocking.** The missing word in this sentence would be a _____
186	187

---

hid	Only two clause signals can start adverb clauses that answer the question **How?**
	
	HOW? **as if, as though**
	
	    a. **Mr. Kay frowned** *as we told him our plan.*
	    b. **Mr. Kay frowned** *as if he were doubtful.*
	
	The clause in sentence (*a, b*) tells **how** Mr. Kay frowned.

454	455

Yes	A noun clause is generally an essential part of the sentence framework and cannot be omitted. The only exceptions are noun clauses used as indirect objects or as appositives. If a noun clause is used as a subject, direct object, subject complement, or object of a preposition, it (*can, cannot*) be omitted.
722	723

---

if kept in a tin box.	*While he was looking for a job,* **Ted had many disappointments.** Write the elliptical clause to which the italicized adverb clause can be reduced: _____.
990	991

From his very first sentence, Mr. Walsh held the interest of his audience.	a. **The land, dry and rocky, is useless for farming.** b. **The old, dingy city hall was being remodeled.** _____ _____
1258	1259

Yes	PHRASES: *Climbing the ladder,* . . .
	              Packed in straw, . . .
	              After biting six children, . . .
	              To get more business, . . .
	
	Do phrases have subjects that tell **whom** or **what** they are about? (*Yes, No*)

1526	1527

b 1794	a. **Tommy's** *vocabulary* **is like the** *vocabulary* **of an adult.** b. **Tommy's** *vocabulary* **is like** *that* **of an adult.** Each of these sentences is correct because *vocabulary* is compared with *vocabulary*. In sentence *b*, the word that stands for *vocabulary* is the pronoun _____. <div align="right">1795</div>
drive 2061	There is great variety among irregular verbs because they came into English from other languages and their forms have changed over the centuries without following any set pattern. **drive** **drove** **(have) driven** **do** **did** **(have) done** Are the forms of these two irregular verbs similar? (*Yes, No*) <div align="right">2062</div>
gave, stolen 2328	**The bell was** _____ (*ring*) **just after Walter had** _____ (*begin*) **his talk.** <div align="right">2329</div>
b 2595	No blunder is more common than confusing the possessive pronoun **its** (belonging to *it*) with the contraction **it's** (= *it is*). RIGHT: *It's* (= *It is*) **waiting for** *its* (*possessive*) **meal.** Underline the correct words in the following sentence: (*It's, Its*) **mother knows when** (*it's, its*) **hungry.** <div align="right">2596</div>
limited 2862	A clause that restricts or limits the number of the word it modifies is called a **restrictive clause.** A restrictive clause makes the word it modifies mean (*less, more*) than it would mean without the clause. <div align="right">2863</div>
Monday, Atlantic Ocean 3129	**The Studio theater on Madison avenue features english, italian, and other foreign films.** <div align="right">3130</div>

subject complement	**Mother moved the . . . to the kitchen.** The missing word in this sentence would be a _____ _____.
187	188

b	Several clause signals can start adverb clauses that answer the question **Why?**
	
	WHY? **because, since, as, so that**
	
	   a. **I couldn't concentrate** *because of the noise.*
	   b. **I couldn't concentrate** *because the room was noisy.*
	
	In which sentence does *because* start a clause? _____

455	456
cannot	A noun clause is a clause that is used in any way that a _____ can be used.
723	724

While looking for a job,	An adverb clause can often be reduced to a present participial phrase.
	
	   When I saw the child, **I put on the brakes.**
	   Seeing the child, **I put on the brakes.**
	
	This reduction eliminates _____ words. (How many?)

991	992
The city hall, old and dingy, was being remodeled.	a. **The job would have been simple had I used the right tools.** b. **Helen would have sung if we had urged her.** _____ _____
1259	1260

No	Since a phrase leaves your reader in the dark, you must answer the question **Who?** or **What?** at the beginning of the main statement that follows.
	
	   a. *Going up the ladder,* **a branch hit Jim's head.**
	   b. *Going up the ladder,* **Jim hit his head on a branch.**
	
	Which sentence answers the question **Who?** _____

1527	1528

that 1795	**Tommy's** *vocabulary* **is like an** *adult's.* This comparison is correct because the possessive noun *adult's* implies an adult's _____ 1796
No 2062	A small number of verbs such as **bet, hit, put,** and **shut** have only one form for all uses. These verbs that have reached the limit of simplification are called *one-part* verbs. **see** **saw** **(have) seen** **hit** **hit** **(have) hit** The one-part verb is (*see, hit*). 2063
rung, begun 2329	In this and the following frames, underline the correct verb. **The dog** (*lay, laid*) **down under the chair where Noreen was** (*sitting, setting*). 2330
Its, it's 2596	Do not write the word **it's** unless you can put the words _____ _____ in its place. 2597
less 2863	**Students** *who do failing work* **may not participate in sports.** This sentence does not make a statement about *all* students. It makes a statement only about those *who* _____ _____ 2864
Theater, Avenue, English, Italian 3130	**A crowd was gathered around a ford truck, where a man** **was giving away free samples of snowflake crackers.** 3131

direct object 188	**The house seemed strangely empty without the children.** The word **empty** is a _____ _____. 189
b 456	WHY? **because, since, as, so that** 　**The man moved over . . . Doris and I could sit together.** The clause signal needed in this sentence would consist of (*one word, two words*). 457
noun 724	The words **that, whether, what, how,** and **why** are often used as clause signals to start noun clauses. 　*That anyone should believe this rumor* **is absurd.** The noun clause begins with the word _____ and ends with the word _____. 725
two 992	Fill in the present participial phrase to which the adverb clause can be reduced: *Because I wanted experience,* **I fixed the radio myself.** _____, **I fixed the** **radio myself.** 993
Helen would have sung had we urged her. 1260	a. **Now that Jack has a driver's license, he wants to drive all the time.** b. **I have a typewriter, and my work looks neater.** _____ _____ 1261
b 1528	WRONG: *Going up the ladder,* **a branch hit Jim's head.** Since there is no word for the italicized phrase to modify, it appears to modify the noun **branch.** Is it the **branch** that is *going up the ladder?* (*Yes, No*) 1529

vocabulary 1796	a. **Tony's vocabulary is like the vocabulary of an adult.** b. **Tony's vocabulary is like that of an adult.** c. **Tony's vocabulary is like an adult.** d. **Tony's vocabulary is like an adult's.** The only incorrect comparison is in sentence _____. 1797
hit 2063	**burst** **burst** **(have) burst** **cost** **cost** **(have) cost** **find** **found** **(have) found** **hurt** **hurt** **(have) hurt** All the above verbs are one-part verbs except _____. 2064
lay, sitting 2330	**When the curtain** (*raised, rose*), **a body was** (*lying, laying*) **on the floor of the living room.** 2331
it is 2597	Underline the correct words: (*It's, Its*) **not in** (*it's, its*) **usual place.** 2598
do failing work 2864	**Students** *who do failing work* **may not participate in sports.** Because the clause *who do failing work* restricts or limits the number of students we are talking about, it is a re_____ clause. 2865
Ford, Snowflake 3131	**Our high school will open on september 5, the day after labor day.** 3132

subject complement **189**	**Franklin's experiments in the field of electricity brought him international fame.** The word **him** is an _____ _____. **190**
two words (so that) **457**	Several clause signals can start adverb clauses that answer the question **On (or under) what condition?** These are **if, unless, though, although, provided that.** **The cake might burn** *unless you watch it.* The adverb clause explains **under what condition** the cake _____ _____. **458**
That . . . rumor **725**	*That anyone should believe this rumor* **is absurd.** The noun clause in the above sentence is used as the _____ of the verb **is.** **726**

Wanting experience, **993**	An adverb clause that starts with the clause signal **so that** can often be reduced to an infinitive phrase.
	
	      I set the alarm *so that it would wake me at six.*
	      I set the alarm *to wake me at six.*
	
	This reduction eliminates _____ words. (How many?)
	
	994

Now that I have a typewriter, my work looks neater. **1261**	a. **Once a forest fire starts, it is hard to control.** b. **After you play a card, you can't take it back.** _____ _____ **1262**
No **1529**	A phrase that has no word to modify or appears to modify the wrong word is a **dangling phrase.** It is like a plane circling in the air with no place to land. a. *Going up the ladder,* **Jim hit his head on a branch.** b. *Going up the ladder,* **a branch hit Jim's head.** Which sentence contains a dangling phrase? _____ **1530**

c 1797	a. **Our customs are different from the customs of Mexico.** b. **Our customs are different from Mexico.** c. **Our customs are different from Mexico's.** d. **Our customs are different from those of Mexico.** The only incorrect comparison is in sentence _____. 1798
find 2064	Many irregular verbs have the same form for both their past and past participles. These are called *two-part* verbs. **bring** **brought** **(have) brought** **spread** **spread** **(have) spread** One of the above verbs has one part; the other has two parts. The two-part verb is _____. 2065
rose, lying 2331	**I had (*lain, laid*) there reading for about an hour but then had (*rose, risen*) to answer the telephone.** 2332
It's, its 2598	In this and the following frames, underline the correct pronouns or, in some cases, the pronouns appropriate for formal usage: **At a buffet dinner, the guests serve (*themselves, theirselves*).** 2599
restrictive 2865	A sentence usually becomes untrue or absurd when you omit a restrictive clause. Because a restrictive clause is very essential to the meaning of a sentence, do *not* set it off with commas. **Visitors *who stay too long* are not welcome.** Does the italicized clause require commas? (*Yes, No*) 2866
September, Labor Day 3132	**Next fall Arlene plans to attend some women's college in the east.** 3133

Lesson 6 One-word Modifiers: Adjectives and Adverbs

[Frames 192–234]

---

might burn

458

The adverb clause, just like the adverb it resembles, can generally be moved from one position to another in a sentence.

    a. **Lucille changed her mind** *when she saw the price.*
    b. *When she saw the price,* **Lucille changed her mind.**

The adverb clause comes first in sentence (*a, b*).

459

---

subject

726

A lie detector shows *whether you are telling the truth.*

The noun clause begins with the word _____

and ends with the word _____.

727

---

three

994

He adjusted the carburetor *so that it would use less gas.*

Fill in the infinitive phrase to which the adverb clause can be reduced:

He adjusted the carburetor _____

_____.

995

Once you play
card, you can't
take it back.

1262

    a. **Good as the play was, many did not appreciate it.**
    b. **The book was long, but it held my interest.**

_____

_____

1263

---

b

1530

Going up the ladder, **Jim hit his head on a branch.**

Now the phrase no longer dangles because the question

Who? is answered by the noun _____.

1531

b 1798	Always make sure that your comparisons are logical. WRONG: **Montreal is larger than** *any city* **in Canada.** Does *any city* include the city of Montreal? (*Yes, No*) 1799

bring
 	
2065
	PRESENT PAST PAST PARTICIPLE
	  bring **brought** **(have) brought**
	  catch **caught** **(have) caught**
	  swing **swung** **(have) swung**
	In two-part verbs, the past and _____ _____
	forms are the same. 2066

lain, risen 2332	**We had** (*set, sat*) **a bench under a tree and had** (*lain, laid*) **our picnic baskets on it.** 2333
themselves 2599	**Why did the clerk put** (*hisself, himself*) **in this embarrassing position?** 2600
No 2866	**A newspaper should not publish news** *that has not been checked.* Would you use a comma to set off the italicized clause in the above sentence? (*Yes, No*) 2867
East 3133	**Surrounding Shady Grove park are an episcopal church, an elementary school, and a library.** 3134

Until this point, we have been dealing mainly with only the framework of sentences—subjects, verbs, and sometimes complements.

Brakes cause accidents.

Does this sentence contain any words that are not a part of its framework? (*Yes, No*)

192

---

b

459

a. **Lucille changed her mind** *when she saw the price.*
b. *When she saw the price,* **Lucille changed her mind.**

A comma is needed when the adverb clause comes (*before, after*) the main statement of the sentence.

460

---

nether . . . truth

727

A lie detector shows *whether you are telling the truth.*

The noun clause is used as the _____ of the verb **shows.**

728

---

to use less gas.

995

Adjective clauses, too, can often be reduced to the same kind of verbal phrases. See how we change an adjective clause to a present participial phrase:
a. **The house was built on a hill** *that overlooked a lake.*
b. **The house was built on a hill** *overlooking a lake.*

The present participle in sentence *b* is _____.

996

Long as the book (it) was, (the book) held my interest.

1263

a. **A lady asked me to baby-sit with her two children, neither of whom I had ever seen before.**
b. **Ann applied to two colleges, and both of them accepted her.**

_____

_____

1264

Jim

1531

Packed in straw, **you can ship this clock anywhere.**

Is the introductory phrase followed closely by a word that tells **what** is *packed in straw?* (*Yes, No*)

1532

Yes 1799	WRONG: **Montreal is larger than** *any city* **in Canada.** Since *any city* includes Montreal, this sentence states that Montreal is larger than itself. Therefore, this comparison is (*logical, illogical*). 1800

past participle
 	
2066
	Most irregular verbs have a special form for the past participle. These are the *three-part* verbs that are responsible for most verb trouble.
	
	    see **saw** **(have) seen**
	    catch **caught** **(have) caught**
	
	The three-part verb is (*see, catch*). 2067

set, laid 2333	**Herman moved to Appleton, where he** (*bought, buys*) **a small newspaper.** 2334
himself 2600	**Coach Fry told us that we might lose the game if we are too sure of** (*our selves, ourselves*). 2601

No
 	
2867
	Suppose that a druggist were to put a sign in his window to advertise for a boy.
	
	    a. **A boy is wanted.**
	    b. **A boy** *who has a car* **is wanted.**
	
	Which statement would restrict or limit the number of applicants for the job—*a* or *b*? _____ 2868

Park, Episcopal 3134	**The Civil Aeronautics administration appealed to congress for new legislation.** 3135

No 192	To supply additional information about the various parts of the sentence framework, we use *modifiers*. **Poor <u>brakes</u> <u>cause</u> many accidents.** This sentence contains two modifying words that are not part of its framework. These two words are: _____ and _____.　　　193
before 460	a. **Although we were tired, we finished the job.** b. **We finished the job although we were tired.** The adverb clause comes first in sentence (*a, b*). 　　461
object *or* direct object 728	**You can depend on whatever he tells you.** The noun clause begins with the word _____ and ends with the word _____. 　　729
overlooking 996	**Books may be borrowed by anyone** *who has a library card.* Fill in the present participial phrase to which the adjective clause can be reduced: **Books may be borrowed by anyone** _____ _____.　　997
Ann applied to two colleges, both of which accepted her. 1264	a. **The union held a meeting, the outcome of which was not announced.** b. **He was struck by a car, and the owner was not insured.** _____ _____ 　　1265
No 1532	*Packed in straw,* **you can ship this clock anywhere.** The italicized phrase is a (*dangling, correct*) phrase. 　　1533

illogical 1800	a. **Montreal is larger than** *any* **city in Canada.** b. **Montreal is larger than** *any other* **city in Canada.** Which comparison is correct? _____ 1801
see 2067	The main danger with three-part verbs is confusing their two past forms—the simple past and the past participle. PRESENT PAST PAST PARTICIPLE **see** **saw** **(have) seen** The past form of the verb **see** that may be used by itself without a helping verb is (*saw, seen*). 2068
bought 2334	**The play is about a woman who came to live with a family and** (*tries, tried*) **to take over.** 2335
ourselves 2601	**Harvey and** (*you, yourself*) **can ride with us.** 2602
b 2868	**A boy** *who has a car* **is wanted.** Not any boy would apply for this job—only a boy *who has a car.* The clause *who has a car* is therefore a _____ clause. 2869
Administration, Congress 3135	**The program is sponsored jointly by the makers of zip soap and polar bear freezers.** 3136

Poor, many 193	**Poor brakes cause many accidents.** The word **Poor** modifies the noun _____. The word **many** modifies the noun _____. 194
a 461	a. **Although we were tired, we finished the job.** b. **We finished the job although we were tired.** A comma is needed when the adverb clause comes (*before, after*) the main statement. 462
whatever . . . you 729	**You can depend on whatever he tells you.** The noun clause is used as the object of a (*verb, preposition*). 730
having a library card. 997	Now we shall reduce an adjective clause to a past participial phrase: **We bought some corn** *that was picked this morning.* Which two words in the adjective clause can be omitted without changing the meaning? _____ _____ 998
He was struck by a car, the owner of which was not insured. 1265	a. **The fact that Andy plays the accordion makes him very popular.** b. **Miss Daly has gray hair, but that doesn't make her old.** _____ _____ 1266
dangling 1533	a. *Packed in straw,* **you can ship this clock anywhere.** b. *Packed in straw,* **this clock can be shipped anywhere.** Which sentence is correct because the introductory phrase is followed closely by the word it modifies—the word that answers the question **What?** _____ 1534

b 1801	WRONG: **Montreal is the largest of** *any other city* **in Canada.** The words *any other city* mean only *one* city. Can Montreal be the largest of *one* city? (*Yes, No*) 1802
saw 2068	To avoid misusing the past and past participle forms of a verb, observe two rules: 1. Never use the past participle by itself without some form of the helping verb **have** or **be.** a. I *seen* **the accident.** b. I *saw* **the accident.** Which sentence is wrong? _____ 2069
tried 2335	**Johnny couldn't understand why a fourth (*was, is*) larger than a fifth.** 2336
you 2602	**The British and (*ourselves, we*) are united by the bond of a common language.** 2603
restrictive 2869	A clause that is essential to the meaning of a sentence (*is, is not*) set off with commas. 2870
Zip, **Polar Bear** 3136	**The auditorium of the Utley high school is used for jewish religious services on saturdays and for christian services on sundays.** 3137

(Poor) brakes (many) accidents 194	Words that modify *nouns* and *pronouns* are **adjectives.** Adjectives modify _____ different classes of words. (How many?) 195
before 462	a. **A child appreciates nothing if he is given too much.** b. **If a child is given too much he appreciates nothing.** Which sentence requires a comma—*a* or *b?* _____ 463
preposition 730	**This tiny spring is what powers the watch.** The noun clause begins with the word _____ and ends with the word _____. 731
that was 998	**We bought some corn** *that was picked this morning.* Fill in the past participial phrase to which the adjective clause can be reduced: **We bought some corn** _____. 999
The fact that Miss Daly has gray hair doesn't make her old. 1266	a. **It was fortunate that the fire broke out after school.** b. **The child was traveling alone, and this seemed strange.** _____ _____ 1267
b 1534	*After biting six children,* **a policeman shot the dog.** Since this introductory phrase is not followed by a word that sensibly answers the question **Who?** or **What?** it suggests that a _____ bit the children. 1535

No 1802	WRONG: **Montreal is the largest of all the** *other* **cities in Canada.** Since Montreal is not among the *other* cities, can it be the largest of them? (*Yes, No*) 1803
a 2069	WRONG: **I** *seen* **the accident.** This sentence is wrong because the past participle *seen* is used without the helping verb *have*. Supply the correct form of **see:** RIGHT: I _____ **the accident.** 2070
is 2336	**The doctor said that too much salt** (*is, was*) **bad for people.** 2337
we 2603	(*Those, Them*) **dishes are exactly like** (*our's, ours*). 2604
is not 2870	Less frequently, an adjective clause is used merely to provide an additional fact about the word it modifies. Such a clause may be omitted without destroying the truth or accuracy of your statement. **Cliff Miles,** *who plays first base,* **is only a sophomore.** Is this sentence true without the clause? (*Yes, No*) 2871
High School, Jewish, Saturdays, Christian, Sundays 3137	**Heroes of both the north and the south are buried in Arlington national cemetery.** 3138

two 195	An **adjective** makes the meaning of a noun or pronoun more exact by telling *what kind, which one(s)*, or *how many*. Underline the adjective that tells *what kind*: *these* **roads** *wide* **roads** *three* **roads** 196
b 463	a. **Mr. Tate becomes hard-of-hearing, when anyone asks him for money.** b. **When anyone asks Mr. Tate for money, he becomes hard-of-hearing.** In which sentence should the comma be dropped? _____ 464
what . . . watch 731	**This tiny spring is what powers the watch.** The noun clause in this sentence follows the linking verb **is** and is used as a (*subject complement, direct object*). 732

picked this
morning.
 	
999
	An adjective clause can sometimes be reduced to an infinitive phrase.
	
	    You need more facts *that will prove your argument.*
	    You need more facts *to prove your argument.*
	
	In the second sentence we changed the verb *will prove* to the infinitive _____.
	1000

It seemed strange that the child was traveling alone. 1267	a. **The article explains that, as time has gone on, football has become more complicated.** b. **Mother insisted that I had to invite Martha because she is my cousin.** (Insert the adverb clause after *that*.) _____ _____ 1268
policeman 1535	a. **After biting six children, the dog was shot by a policeman.** b. **After biting six children, a policeman shot the dog.** Which sentence is wrong because it contains a dangling phrase? _____ 1536

No 1803	WRONG: **Montreal is the largest of all the other cities in Canada.** To make this comparison logical, we must omit the word _____. 1804
saw 2070	2. Never use the simple past form of a three-part verb after any form of the helping verb **have** or **be**. PRESENT PAST PAST PARTICIPLE **write** **wrote** **(have) written** The form of **write** that must be used with the helping verb **have** is (*wrote, written*). 2071
is 2337	**Cooking is an art that always** (*has appealed, appealed*) **to me.** 2338
Those, ours 2604	**Mrs. Kemp parked** (*hers, her's*) **next to** (*theirs, their's*). 2605
Yes 2871	a. **Any number** *which can be divided by two* **is an even number.** b. **Crater Lake,** *which is two thousand feet deep,* **has no inlet or outlet.** In which sentence can the clause be omitted without damaging the meaning of the sentence? _____ 2872
North, South, National Cemetery 3138	**The Union bank is in the Keystone building on the south side of Main street.** 3139

wide 196	Underline the adjective that points out *which one:* *comfortable* **chair** *one* **chair** *this* **chair** 197
a 464	**The maple trees are still green** *after the ash trees have shed their leaves.* If you moved the adverb clause to the beginning of the sentence, would you put a comma after *leaves*? (*Yes, No*) 465
subject complement 732	Some of the same clause signals that start adverb and adjective clauses can also start noun clauses; for example, **if, when, where, who,** and **which.** If the clause is an essential part of the sentence that cannot be omitted, it is (*an adverb, an adjective, a noun*) clause. 733
to prove 1000	**We are planning a program** *that will stimulate an interest in science.* Fill in the infinitive phrase to which the adjective clause can be reduced: **We are planning a program** _____ _____. 1001
Mother insisted that, because Martha is my cousin, I had to invite her. 1268	a. **No sooner had I turned in my test paper than I realized my mistake.** b. **It began to pour as soon as we stepped out of the house.** _____ _____ 1269

b
 	
1536
	Of course, if your introductory word group has a subject to explain **whom** or **what** it is about, you do not need to explain this again in the main statement that follows it.
	
	    a. **While I was pushing the car, I ripped my coat.**
	    b. **While I was pushing the car, my coat ripped.**
	
	Are both sentences correct? (*Yes, No*)
	
	1537

other 1804	a. **Montreal is the largest of any other city in Canada.** b. **Montreal is the largest of all the other cities in Canada.** c. **Montreal is the largest of all the cities in Canada.** Which comparison is correct? _____ 1805
written 2071	PRESENT PAST PAST PARTICIPLE **write** **wrote** **(have) written** a. **I** *have wrote* **a letter.** b. **I** *have written* **a letter.** Which sentence is wrong? _____ 2072
has appealed 2338	**Uncle Pete** (*has smoked, smoked*) **for twenty years and then suddenly quit.** 2339
hers, theirs 2605	(*Yours, Your's*) **must be in one of** (*those, them*) **drawers.** 2606
b 2872	A clause which merely adds a fact that is not essential to the meaning of the sentence is called a **nonrestrictive clause.** A nonrestrictive clause is (*more, less*) important than a restrictive clause. 2873
Bank, Building, Street 3139	Lesson **88** **Further Uses of Capitals** [Frames 3141–3178]

this 197	Underline the adjective that tells *how many:* *modern* **houses** *these* **houses** *several* **houses** 198
Yes 465	**This book begins where the other leaves off.** The adverb clause in this sentence starts with the clause signal _____ and ends with the word _____. 466
a noun 733	a. **The bus** *that the train delayed* **was an hour late.** b. **We found** *that a train had delayed the bus.* One clause is an adjective clause that can be omitted; the other is a noun clause that is an essential part of the sentence framework. Which sentence contains the noun clause? _____ 734
to stimulate an interest in science. 1001	By understanding the various types of subordinate word groups, you not only save words but also give more interesting variety to your sentences. If you had several adjective clauses close together, would it generally be a good idea to change one of them to a participial phrase? (*Yes, No*) 1002
No sooner had we stepped out of the house than it began to pour. 1269	a. **Not only did George pass the course, but he also received an A.** b. **Phil borrowed my book, and he lost it.** _____ _____ 1270

Yes
 	
 1537
	Do you remember that an elliptical clause is an adverb clause from which the subject and part of the verb have been omitted?
	
	     a. **While I was pushing the car,** . . .
	    b. **While pushing the car,** . . .
	
	 Which is an elliptical (incomplete) clause? _____
	
	 1538

c 1805	Now we shall look at another type of comparison. Supply the missing word that completes the comparison: **Greg earns** *as much* _____ **his brother.** 1806
a 2072	WRONG: I *have wrote* **a letter.** This sentence is wrong because the simple past instead of the past participle is used with the helping verb *have.* Supply the correct form of the verb **write:** RIGHT: I *have* _____ **a letter.** 2073
smoked 2339	**Electric home appliances** (*have made, made*) **the housewife's chores much easier.** 2340
Yours, those 2606	(*It's, Its*) **looking for** (*it's, its*) **nest.** 2607
less 2873	Because a nonrestrictive clause is an "extra" that may be omitted—just like parenthetical expressions, appositives, and direct address—we set it off with commas. Punctuate the following sentence: **My birthday** *which is on Christmas* **receives very little attention.** 2874
	In this lesson we complete our study of capitals. 7. Capitalize titles that show a person's profession, rank, office, or family relationship *when they are used with personal names.* a. **the mayor of the city** b. **for mayor Jensen** **Mayor** should be capitalized in sentence (*a, b*). 3141

several 198	**Three students received perfect scores on this test.** How many adjectives does this sentence contain? _____ 199
where . . . off 466	**Fred looks tall until he stands beside his father.** The adverb clause in this sentence starts with the clause signal _____ and ends with the word _____. 467
b 734	**We found** *that a train had delayed the bus.* The noun clause cannot be omitted because it is the (*subject, direct object*) of the verb **found.** 735
Yes 1002	If you thought that you had repeated the word *because* too many times, how could you change the adverb clause in the following sentence? **I threw away the box** *because I thought it was empty.* **I threw away the box,** _____ *it was empty.* 1003
ot only did Phil orrow my book, but he also lost it. 1270	a. **The more one reads, the more interested one becomes in the characters.** b. **As he argued more, he convinced me less.** _____ _____ 1271
b 1538	a. **While I was pushing the car, . . .** b. **While pushing the car, . . .** After which clause would you need to tell **who** in order to avoid a dangling word group? _____ 1539

as 1806	Supply the missing word that completes the comparison: **Greg earns** *more* _____ **his brother.** 1807
written 2073	This and the following frames will present twenty-two three-part verbs whose past participles all end with *-n* or *-en*. Their similarity should help you to remember them. In each frame, fill in the correct forms of the verbs in parentheses. Be sure to use the past participle with any form of the helping verb **have** or **be**. (*Turn to the next frame.*) 2074
have made 2340	**We had hoped** (*to have visited, to visit*) **Williamsburg on our trip East last summer.** 2341
It's, its 2607	(*It's, Its*) **quills stiffen when** (*it's, its*) **frightened.** 2608
birthday, Christmas, 2874	a. **Anyone** *who lives in Bedford* **knows Uncle Joe.** b. **Uncle Joe** *who lives in Bedford* **knows everyone in town.** In which sentence should the clause be set off with commas because it is not essential to the meaning of the sentence and is therefore nonrestrictive? _____ 2875
b 3141	a. **Does superintendent Stern approve the plan?** b. **A new superintendent will be selected.** In which sentence should **superintendent** be capitalized because it is used with a personal name? _____ 3142

three (Three— perfect—this) 199	**Three students received perfect scores on this test.** Each adjective comes (*before, after*) the noun that it modifies. 200
until . . . father 467	**A poor sport does not enjoy a game unless he can win.** The adverb clause in this sentence starts with the clause signal _____ and ends with the word _____. 468
direct object 735	a. *Where Captain Kidd buried his treasure* **remains a mystery.** b. **No one has yet discovered the place** *where Captain Kidd buried his treasure.* Which sentence contains a noun clause? _____ 736
thinking 1003	If you thought that you had used too many clauses beginning with "*When you . . . ,*" how could you change the adverb clause in the following sentence? *When you train a dog,* **always use the same commands.** *In* _____**, always use the same commands.** 1004
The more he argued, the less e convinced me. 1271	a. **The nights being cold, we took along our sweaters.** b. **The inn was expensive, and we stayed only one day.** _____ _____ 1272
b 1539	a. **While pushing the car, my coat ripped.** b. **While pushing the car, I ripped my coat.** Which sentence is wrong because it suggests that the coat was pushing the car? _____ 1540

than 1807	WRONG: **Greg earns as much,** *if not more than,* **his brother.** Omit the italicized phrase and you will see what is wrong with the above sentence. The trouble is that **as much** is followed by *than* instead of by _____. 1808
2074	PRESENT PAST PAST PARTICIPLE **blow** **blew** **(have) blown** **tear** **tore** **(have) torn** **A gale had** _____ (*blow*) **down our sign, and it was badly** _____ (*tear*). 2075
to visit 2341	**How could Gordon ever have expected** (*to have memorized, to memorize*) **his speech in one evening?** 2342
Its, it's 2608	Lesson **73** **Keeping Person and Number Consistent** [Frames 2610–2645]
b 2875	a. **Rich people** *who pretend to be poor* **disgust me.** b. **Mr. Wetherby** *who pretends to be poor* **is really very rich.** Which sentence requires commas because the clause is nonrestrictive? _____ 2876
a 3142	**Wendy is staying with our Uncle Steve and Aunt Jane.** Would you capitalize **Uncle** and **Aunt** if you omitted the names **Steve** and **Jane**? (*Yes, No*) 3143

before 200	Besides coming right before the nouns they modify, adjectives are sometimes found in another position. **The car is blue. The eggs are fresh. The house looks new.** The adjectives in these sentences follow *linking verbs* and are therefore (*subject complements, direct objects*). 201
unless . . . win 468	**Donna seldom eats sweets although she enjoys them very much.** The adverb clause in this sentence starts with the clause signal _____ and ends with the word _____. 469
a 736	*Where Captain Kidd buried his treasure* **remains a mystery.** The noun clause is the _____ of the verb **remains.** 737
training a dog, 1004	As I got off the bus, I saw fire engines. After the above sentence, which of the following sentences would offer greater variety—*a* or *b*? _____ a. **As I looked down the street, I saw clouds of smoke.** b. **Looking down the street, I saw clouds of smoke.** 1005
The inn being expensive, we stayed only one day. 1272	a. **The two boys were playing together, their recent quarrel forgotten.** b. **We looked up the old house, and its porch was still unrepaired.** _____ _____ 1273
a 1540	a. **While pushing the car, my coat ripped.** b. **While pushing the car, I ripped my coat.** Which sentence is right because the elliptical clause is followed by a word that answers the question **Who?** _____ 1541

as 1808	In combining an "as" and a "than" comparison, first complete the "as" comparison. Then add the "if" phrase at the end, where it need not be completed. a. **Greg earns as much, if not more than, his brother.** b. **Greg earns as much as his brother, if not more.** Which sentence is correct? _____ 1809

blown, torn
 	
2075
	PRESENT PAST PAST PARTICIPLE
	  give **gave** **(have) given**
	  fall **fell** **(have) fallen**
	
	The farmer _____ (*give*) **us the apples that had**
	
	_____ (*fall*) **from the tree.** 2076

to memorize 2342	**Columbus thought that he** (*had reached, reached*) **the East Indies.** 2343

	Personal pronouns show by their form whether they mean the person *speaking, spoken to,* or *spoken about.*
	
	A pronoun in the **first person** indicates the person *speaking* or his group.
	
	Underline the two pronouns in the *first person:*
	
	         you **I** **he** **we**
	                                         2610

b 2876	a. **It is against the law to use a stamp,** *which has been canceled.* b. **Shakespeare died at fifty-two,** *which was considered an advanced age at that time.* In which sentence should the comma be omitted because the clause is restrictive? _____ 2877
No 3143	a. **The flowers were from my Cousin.** b. **The flowers were from my Cousin Glenn.** **Cousin** should not be capitalized in sentence (*a, b*). 3144

<table>
<tr>
<td>subject complements

201</td>
<td>The car is blue. The eggs are fresh. The house looks new.

When adjectives are subject complements, they come (*before, after*) the nouns they modify.

202</td>
</tr>
<tr>
<td>although . . . much

469</td>
<td>**The actor hesitated as though he had forgotten his lines.**

The adverb clause starts with the two-word clause signal

_____ _____ and ends with the word _____.

470</td>
</tr>
<tr>
<td>subject

737</td>
<td>a. **The dress** *which I liked best* **was too expensive.**
b. **I could not decide** *which I liked best.*

Which sentence contains a noun clause? _____

738</td>
</tr>
<tr>
<td>b

1005</td>
<td>In this and the following frames, reduce each italicized clause to the type of word group indicated in parentheses:

If they are overcooked, **vegetables lose their flavor.** (elliptical clause)

_____, **vegetables lose their flavor.**

1006</td>
</tr>
<tr>
<td>We looked up the old house, its porch still unrepaired.

1273</td>
<td>UNIT **6: RECOGNIZING THE SENTENCE UNIT**

Lesson **35** **Some Typical Sentence Fragments: Clauses and Verbal Phrases**

[Frames 1275–1311]</td>
</tr>
<tr>
<td>b

1541</td>
<td>After an introductory word group that lacks a subject, do not use the possessive form of a noun or pronoun to answer the question **Who?** or **What?**

While standing in the crowd, *Pam's* **purse was stolen.**

This sentence is wrong because the person standing in the crowd was not *Pam's purse,* but _____.

1542</td>
</tr>
</table>

b 1809	a. **The new school will be as large, if not larger, than ours.** b. **The new school will be as large as ours, if not larger.** Which sentence is correct? _____ 1810
gave, fallen 2076	PRESENT PAST PAST PARTICIPLE **fly** **flew** **(have) flown** **drive** **drove** **(have) driven** **We have _____ (*fly*) to Miami, and we have also** **_____ (*drive*) there.** 2077
had reached 2343	**The campers discovered that they (*used, had used*) their last match.** 2344
I, we 2610	A pronoun in the **second person** indicates the person or persons *spoken to.* Underline the one pronoun in the *second person:* **she you I they** 2611
a 2877	Occasionally, the same clause can be either restrictive or nonrestrictive, depending on what you mean to say. **Mr. Crump sold his land** *which was unprofitable.* If you mean that Mr. Crump sold only that part of his land *which was unprofitable,* you would make the clause restrictive by (*using, omitting*) a comma. 2878
a 3144	**My grandmother speaks French.** If you inserted the name **Gervaise** after **grandmother**, would you capitalize **grandmother**? (*Yes, No*) 3145

after 202	a. **Virginia has an <u>excellent</u> idea.** b. **Virginia's idea is <u>excellent</u>.** Does the adjective **excellent** come after the noun it modifies in sentence *a* or *b?* _____ 203
as though . . . lines 470	**The dog chewed up the letter before we had read it.** The adverb clause in this sentence starts with the clause signal _____ and ends with the word _____. 471

b
 	
738
	When *that* starts an adjective clause, it is a relative pronoun.
	When *that* starts a noun clause, it is an "empty" word that
	merely signals the start of a noun clause.
	
	    a. **I have a tame crow** *that* (*=crow*) *can talk.*
	    b. **Mother said** *that she was ready.*
	
	Which sentence contains a noun clause? _____
	
	739

If overcooked, 1006	**A violin will deteriorate** *if it is not played occasionally.* (elliptical clause) **A violin will deteriorate** _____ _____. 1007

	To be a sentence, a word group must pass two tests:
	
	    1. Does it have a subject and verb?
	    2. Does it make sense by itself?
	
	      If you change your mind
	
	This word group fails to pass test (*1, 2*).
	
	1275

Pam 1542	a. **While standing in the crowd, Pam's purse was stolen.** b. **While standing in the crowd, Pam had her purse stolen.** Which sentence is correct because the elliptical clause is followed by a word that answers the question **Who?** _____ 1543

b 1810	**This is one of the best,** *if not the best,* **hotel in town.** Omit the italicized phrase and you will see what is wrong with the above sentence. The trouble is that **one of the best** requires **hotels** (plural) and *the best* requires _____ (singular). 1811

flown, driven
 	
2077
	PRESENT PAST PAST PARTICIPLE
	  choose chose (have) chosen
	  draw drew (have) drawn
	
	The design that was _____ (*choose*) **by the judges**
	
	was _____ (*draw*) **by Vera.** 2078

had used 2344	**If we** (*had offered, would have offered*) **Henry the nomination, he might have accepted.** 2345
you 2611	Does the second-person pronoun **you** have different forms for singular and plural? (*Yes, No*) 261
omitting 2878	**Mr. Crump sold his land** *which was unprofitable.* If you mean that all of Mr. Crump's land was unprofitable and that he therefore sold all of it, you would make the clause nonrestrictive by (*using, omitting*) a comma. 287

Yes
 	
3145
	As a mark of respect, the titles of high government official are capitalized even when used without personal names.
	  a. The President consulted the Secretary of State.
	  b. The Corporal hoped to become a Sergeant.
	The capitalization is correct in sentence (*a, b*). 314

b 203	Adjectives normally come before the nouns they modify except when they are _____ *complements.* 204
before . . . it 471	A sentence that contains a clause is called a **complex sentence.** It is more complex (or complicated) than a simple sentence. a. **My friend often telephones at dinnertime.** b. **My friend often telephones** *while we are eating dinner.* Which is a complex sentence—*a* or *b?* _____ 472
b 739	The "empty" word *that,* which starts many noun clauses, is often omitted when the clause is a direct object. **I knew** *(that) we would win.* **I hope** *(that) you can go.* Is the clause signal *that* a relative pronoun that stands for any noun in the other part of the sentence? (*Yes, No*) 740
if not played occasionally. 1007	*As I walked through the tall grass,* **I suddenly heard the rattle of a snake.** (present participial phrase) _____, **I suddenly heard the rattle of a snake.** 1008

2
 	
1275
	Tests for a sentence:
	
	    1. Does it have a subject and verb?
	    2. Does it make sense by itself?
	
	    A touchdown in the third quarter
	
	This word group fails to pass test (*1, 2, 1 and 2*).
	
	1276

b 1543	a. **Raised in Georgia, Sally had a Southern accent.** b. **Raised in Georgia, Sally's accent was Southern.** Which sentence is correct? _____ 1544

hotel 1811	**This is one of the best, if not the best, hotel in town.** **This is one of the best hotels in town, if not the best.** We repaired this sentence as we did the others. We completed the first statement and then added the "if" phrase at the _____ of our sentence. 1812

chosen, drawn
 	
2078
	PRESENT PAST PAST PARTICIPLE
	  freeze **froze** **(have) frozen**
	  wear **wore** **(have) worn**
	
	If I had not _____ (*wear*) **my sweater, I would**
	
	have _____ (*freeze*).
	
	2079

had offered 2345	**I would certainly have written to you from Hawaii if I** (*had remembered, would have remembered*) **your address.** 2346
No 2612	A pronoun in the **third person** indicates the person or persons *spoken about.* Underline three pronouns in the *third person:* **he** **I** **she** **they** **you** **we** 2613
using 2879	a. **Do not use string,** *which is too weak.* b. **Do not use string** *which is too weak.* Which sentence suggests that all string is too weak and that you use rope, or something stronger? _____ 2880
a 3146	**The courageous** *captain* **was decorated by the** *governor.* Which italicized word should be capitalized? _____ 3147

subject 204	**Most people are honest.** How many adjectives does this sentence contain? _____ 205
b 472	**My friend often telephones** *while we are eating dinner.* We know that this is a complex sentence because it contains a _____. 473
No 740	Lesson **20** The *Who–Whom* Problem in Noun Clauses [Frames 742–781]
alking through the tall grass, 1008	*Since I don't understand Spanish,* **I was at a serious disadvantage.** (present participial phrase) _____, **I was at a serious disadvantage.** 1009
1 and 2 1276	1. Does it have a subject and verb? 2. Does it make sense by itself? If you cannot answer "Yes" to both questions, the word group is not a complete sentence but a **fragment.** A handle broken off a cup is to a cup what a fragment is to a _____. 1277
a 1544	In this and the following frames, circle the letter of the correct sentence—the one in which the introductory word group does *not* dangle: a. **Being barefooted, the stones cut our feet.** b. **Because we were barefooted, the stones cut our feet.** 1545

<table>
<tr>
<td>end

1812</td>
<td>a. **Cookie is one of the smartest dogs I know, if not the smartest.**
b. **Cookie is one of the smartest, if not the smartest, dog I know.**

Which sentence is correct? _____

1813</td>
</tr>
<tr>
<td>worn, frozen

2079</td>
<td>

PRESENT	PAST	PAST PARTICIPLE
know	knew	(have) known
steal	stole	(have) stolen

The dealer must have _____ (*know*) that the car was _____ (*steal*).

2080</td>
</tr>
<tr>
<td>had remembered

2346</td>
<td>**In a few more months, we (*shall live, shall have lived*) in our present house for twenty years.**

2347</td>
</tr>
<tr>
<td>he, she, they

2613</td>
<td>*I* (first person) speak to *you* (second person) about *him* or *her* (third person).
Write the word *first, second,* or *third* in each blank to indicate the person of the italicized pronouns:
They (_____ person) told *us* (_____ person) about *you* (_____ person).

2614</td>
</tr>
<tr>
<td>a

2880</td>
<td>a. **Do not use string,** *which is too weak.*
b. **Do not use string** *which is too weak.*

Which sentence suggests that it is all right to use string, but not string that is weak? _____

2881</td>
</tr>
<tr>
<td>Governor

3147</td>
<td>Copy the words that require capitals:

The chairman of the meeting sent a telegram of congratulation to senator Hollis and the president.

3148</td>
</tr>
</table>

two (Most—honest) 205	**Most people are honest.** The two adjectives—**Most** and **honest**—modify the noun _____. 206
clause _or_ adverb clause 473	**I always drive as though everyone else were crazy.** Because this sentence contains a clause, it is called a _____ sentence. 474
	Few people notice the _sign_. The noun _sign_ is the direct object of the verb _____. 742
Not understanding Spanish, 1009	**We went to the lake** so that we could escape the heat. (infinitive phrase) **We went to the lake** _____. 1010
sentence 1277	The various types of clauses and phrases you have used to subordinate ideas fail to meet the two tests of a sentence. If you detach them from the sentences with which they are grammatically connected, you have (_fragments, sentences_). 1278
b 1545	Circle the letter of the correct sentence: a. **Going down the drain, the chemical made a boiling sound.** b. **Going down the drain, I heard the chemical make a boiling sound.** 1546

a 1813	Do not omit words needed to prevent ambiguity (double meaning). a. **Andy enjoys television more than his friends.** b. **Andy enjoys television more than he enjoys his friends.** c. **Andy enjoys television more than his friends enjoy it.** Could sentence *a* mean either *b* or *c*? *(Yes, No)* 1814

known, stolen
 	
2080
	PRESENT PAST PAST PARTICIPLE
	  grow grew (have) grown
	  see saw (have) seen
	
	How Steve has _____ *(grow)* **since I last**
	
	_____ *(see)* **him!** 2081

shall have lived 2347	**By this time next year, you** *(will have cast, will cast)* **your first vote.** 2348
They (third) *us* (first) *you* (second) 2614	Write the word *first, second,* or *third* in each blank to indicate the person of the italicized pronouns: *You* (_____ person) told *her* (_____ person) to invite *me* (_____ person). 2615
b 2881	Participial phrases, as well as adjective clauses, can be either restrictive or nonrestrictive. a. **All cars** *leaving Lewiston* **were stopped by the police.** b. **Maxine** *excusing herself politely* **went upstairs to study.** In which sentence would you use commas because the participial phrase is not essential to the meaning? _____ 2882
Senator, President 3148	When a title is used alone, without a name, to refer to a particular person, it may be capitalized. a. **A** *principal* **has many responsibilities.** b. **The** *principal* **will address the parents' meeting.** In which sentence would it be permissible to capitalize *principal?* _____ 3149

people 206	We very seldom use adjectives before pronouns as we do before nouns. We say "a *pretty* girl," but not "a *pretty* she"; "a *new* book," but not "a *new* it." **She looks very pretty. It is new.** In these sentences, the adjectives come (*before, after*) the pronouns they modify. 207
complex 474	Unlike a sentence, a clause (*does, does not*) make sense by itself. 475
notice 742	a. **Few people notice the *sign*.** b. **Few people notice *who directs a movie*.** The clause *who directs a movie* in sentence *b* does the same job as the noun *sign* in sentence *a*. Both are _____ _____ of the verb **notice.** 743
to escape the heat. 1010	**It is a tedious job** *which requires much patience.* (present participial phrase) **It is a tedious job** _____ _____ . 1011
fragments 1278	WRONG: **The class starts.** *When the bell rings.* "*When the bell rings*" is an adverb clause. Although it has a subject and verb, does it make sense by itself? (*Yes, No*) 1279
a 1546	Circle the letter of the correct sentence: a. **In opening the can, Amy's finger was badly cut.** b. **In opening the can, Amy cut her finger badly.** 1547

Yes 1814	**The dealer made Dad a better offer than Ed.** Add the necessary words to mean that the dealer's offer to Dad was better than Ed's offer to Dad: **The dealer made Dad a better offer than** _____ _____. 1815

grown, saw
 	
2081
	PRESENT PAST PAST PARTICIPLE
	  take **took** **(have) taken**
	  throw **threw** **(have) thrown**
	
	Someone had _____ (*take*) **the letter and had**
	
	_____ (*throw*) **it away.**
	2082

will have cast 2348	Rewrite this sentence, changing the verb from passive to active: **The Segals' paper** *had been left* **at our door by mistake by the newsboy.** _____ _____ 2349
You (second) *her* (third) *me* (first) 2615	Since a noun is something that you talk *about*, every noun is ordinarily in the (*first, second, third*) person. 2616
b 2882	In this and the following frames, supply the necessary commas. If the clause is restrictive because it is essential to the meaning of the sentence, add no commas and write *None*. **St. Nicholas** *who is identified with Santa Claus* **was an actual saint.** 2883

b
 	
3149
	When you use *mother, father, dad,* etc., in place of personal names, you may capitalize them or not—as you prefer.
	
	    I hope that Mother can get Dad's consent.
	    I hope that mother can get dad's consent.
	
	Are both sentences correct? (*Yes, No*)
	3150

after 207	We have seen that adjectives answer the questions *What kind? Which one(s)?* and *How many?* about nouns and _____. 208
does not 475	An adverb clause is so called because it does the work of an _____. 476
direct objects 743	a. **Few people notice the** *sign.* b. **Few people notice** *who directs a movie.* Because the clause *who directs a movie* in sentence *b* is used just like the noun *sign* in sentence *a,* it is a _____ clause. 744
requiring much patience. 1011	**The union published a full-page advertisement** *which stated their viewpoint on the strike.* (present participial phrase) **The union published a full-page advertisement** _____ _____. 1012
No 1279	SENTENCE: **The bell rings.** ADVERB CLAUSE: *When the bell rings* Which word in the clause makes the clause depend on something else for its full meaning? _____ 1280
b 1547	Continue to circle the letter of the correct sentences: a. **If neatly written, more attention will be paid to your letter.** b. **If neatly written, your letter will get more attention.** 1548

Ed made (*or* did) 1815	**The dealer made Dad a better offer than Ed.** Add the necessary words to mean that the dealer's offer to Dad was better than the dealer's offer to Ed: **The dealer made Dad a better offer than** _____ _____. 1816

taken, thrown
 	
2082
	PRESENT PAST PAST PARTICIPLE
	  shake shook (had) shaken
	  break broke (had) broken
	
	The collision had _____ (*shake*) **up the box, and**
	
	many dishes were _____ (*break*). 2083

The newsboy (had) left the Segals' paper at our door by mistake. 2349	Rewrite this sentence, changing the verb from passive to active: **The star** *could be seen* **clearly by us through the telescope.** _____ _____ 2350

third
 	
2616
	Underline three words (nouns or pronouns) that are in the third person:
	
	    I **team** **you** **it** **story** **we**
	
	     2617

St. Nicholas, Santa Claus, 2883	**It is the policy of our restaurant to serve no food** *which we would not eat ourselves.* 2884

Yes
 	
3150
	On the other hand, when you use *mother, father, dad,* etc., merely to show family relationship, always use small letters.
	
	      His *mother* **is a** *cousin* **of my** *father.*
	
	Should the italicized words be capitalized? (*Yes, No*)
	
	     3151

pronouns
 	
208
	We need another class of words to answer the questions that we might ask about the action of verbs.
	
	      George drove. *(When? Where? How? How much?*
	                        How often?)
	
	Are the questions in parentheses about **George** or **drove?**
	
	_____ 209

adverb 476	Any clause that modifies a verb is an _____ clause. 477

noun
 	
744
	The choice between **who** and **whom,** when they start noun clauses, depends upon their use *within the clause.*
	
	                who directs a movie
	
	The clause signal *who* is the subject of the verb _____.
	                                             745

stating their viewpoint on the strike. 1012	**Every nail** *that was used in the old fort* **was made by hand.** (past participial phrase) **Every nail** _____ **was made by hand.** 1013

When
 	
1280
	WRONG: **The class starts.** *Promptly.*
	You would never think of separating the adverb *promptly* from the sentence that contains the word it modifies.
	
	          The class starts. *When the bell rings.*
	
	Is it correct to separate an adverb clause from the sentence that contains the verb it modifies? *(Yes, No)*
	                                       1281

b 1548	a. **To get an honor diploma, a student must maintain a B average or better.** b. **To get an honor diploma, a B average or better must be maintained.** 1549

he made (*or* did) to Ed 1816	**I know Sally better than Evelyn.** Add the necessary words to mean that you are better acquainted with Sally than you are with Evelyn: **I know Sally better than** _____. 1817

shaken, broken
 	
 2083
	PRESENT PAST PAST PARTICIPLE
	    eat ate (have) eaten
	    ride rode (have) ridden
	 If we had _____ (*eat*) **our lunch, we would have**
	 _____ (*ride*) **further.**
	 2084

We could see the star clearly through the telescope. 2350	Change the verb from active to passive by eliminating the present subject: **My dad** *had not paid* **our telephone bill.** _____ _____ 2351
team, it, story 2617	A shift in person confuses the viewpoint within a sentence. You begin by talking about one person and end up by talking about another. Underline the pronoun that continues the same viewpoint: **As we looked around us, (** *you, we* **) could see that spring was near.** 2618
None 2884	**Caffeine** *which is present in both tea and coffee* **stimulates the heart and raises blood pressure.** 2885
No 3151	When *father, mother, dad,* etc., are used with articles (*a, an, the*) or possessive pronouns (*my, his, your*), they show family relationship and should not be capitalized. **The** *mother* **of one of my friends knew my** *dad* **at college.** Should the italicized words be capitalized? (*Yes, No*) 3152

drove 209	George drove *safely.* Underline the question that the word *safely* answers: **When? Where? How? How much? How often?** 210
adverb 477	Lesson **13** **Expressing the Exact Relationship** [Frames 479–520]
directs 745	Use the subject form **who** for subjects and subject complements; use the object form **whom** for objects of verbs and prepositions. *who directs a movie* We use the subject form *who* because it is the (*subject, direct object*) of the verb *directs.* 746
used in the old fort 1013	**Most of the articles** *that were advertised in the paper* **were sold out.** (past participial phrase) **Most of the articles** _____ **were sold out.** 1014
No 1281	**The class starts** *when the bell rings.* Now the adverb clause makes sense because it is in the same sentence with the verb _____, which it modifies. 1282
a 1549	a. **Questioned about the check, the man's answers were very evasive.** b. **Questioned about the check, the man answered very evasively.** 1550

I know (*or* do) Evelyn 1817	**I know Sally better than Evelyn.** Add the necessary words to mean that Evelyn is not as well-acquainted with Sally as you are: **I know Sally better than** _____. 1818
eaten, ridden 2084	PRESENT swear speak PAST swore spoke PAST PARTICIPLE (have) sworn (have) spoken **The witness** _____ (*swear*) **that he had never** _____ (*speak*) **to the accused man.** 2085
Our telephone bill had not been paid. 2351	Change the verb from active to passive by eliminating the present subject: **The mailman** *delivers* **our mail around ten o'clock.** _____ 2352
we 2618	SHIFT IN PERSON: *I* **liked this story because it kept** *you* **guessing until the very last page.** This sentence is faulty because *I* is in the first person and *you* is in the _____ person. 2619
Caffeine, coffee, 2885	**Gilbert Stuart** *who painted most of the portraits of George Washington* **was one of the outstanding painters of his day.** 2886
No 3152	**I want my** *dad* **and** *uncle* **Frank to meet your** *grandfather.* The only one of the italicized words that should be capitalized is _____. 3153

How?	**George drove** *yesterday*.
	Underline the question that the word *yesterday* answers:
	When? Where? How? How much? How often?
210	211

	In this lesson you will study **subordination** as a way of building sentences.
	Subordinate means "of lower rank." A *clerk,* for example, is subordinate to a *manager.*
	In the army, a *sergeant* is subordinate to a (*private, general*).
	479

	Few people notice *who directs a movie.*
subject	Be careful to avoid the mistake of thinking that the clause signal is the direct object of the verb **notice** and therefore requires the object form *whom.*
	The direct object of the verb **notice** is not the clause signal
746	but the entire noun _____. 747

advertised in the paper	**Frank had little money** *that he could spend on entertainment.* (infinitive phrase)
	Frank had little money _____
	_____.
1014	1015

	WRONG: **Dad went to Ohio.** *Leaving me in charge of the farm.*
starts	*"Leaving me in charge of the farm"* is a present participial phrase.
	Does it have a subject and verb, and does it make sense by itself? (*Yes, No*)
1282	1283

b	a. **After winning three games, the school keeps the trophy permanently.**
	b. **After winning three games, the trophy is kept permanently by the school.**
1550	1551

Evelyn knows her (Sally) *or* Evelyn does 1818	In this and the following frames, put a circle around the letter of the sentence which states the comparison logically: a. **Our traffic laws are different from Oregon's.** b. **Our traffic laws are different from Oregon.** 1819
swore, spoken 2085	Whenever you are doubtful about the past participle form of a verb, ask yourself, "Is there a form of this verb that ends with -*n* or -*en?*" If there is, use it after any form of **have** or **be**. Underline two verbs that have forms ending with -*n* or -*en:* **freeze think speak work** 2086
Our mail is delivered around ten o'clock. 2352	UNIT **10:** USING ADVERBS AND ADJECTIVES Lesson **66** Using Adverbs to Describe Action [Frames 2354–2392]
second 2619	a. *I* **liked this story because it kept** *you* **guessing.** b. *I* **liked this story because it kept** *me* **guessing.** Which sentence is correct because the person of the pronouns is consistent? _____ 2620
Stuart, Washington, 2886	**We seldom interrupt a person** *who is praising us.* 2887
uncle 3153	8. Capitalize the first word and all important words in titles of books, stories, movies, works of art, musical compositions, etc. a. *Great Expectations* b. *Great expectations* Which title is correctly capitalized? _____ 3154

When? 211	**George drove** *frequently.* Underline the question that the word *frequently* answers: **When? Where? How? How much? How often?** 212
general 479	In grammar, a subordinate word group is one that is *less than a sentence*—one that *does not make sense by itself.* Phrases and clauses are examples of _____ word groups. 480
clause 747	WRONG: **Few people notice** *whom directs a movie.* The object form *whom* is wrong because the clause signal is not the object of the verb **notice** but the subject of the verb _____ within the clause. 748
to spend on entertainment. 1015	**We called a meeting** *so that we could elect officers.* (infinitive phrase) **We called a meeting** _____. 1016
No 1283	RIGHT: **Dad went to Ohio,** *leaving me in charge of the farm.* The present participial phrase should be a part of the sentence containing the noun _____, which it modifies. 1284
a 1551	a. **When I was six years old, my uncle first took me sailing.** b. **When six years old, my uncle first took me sailing.** 1552

a 1819	a. **We beat North High worse than Marshall Tech.** b. **We beat North High worse than we beat Marshall Tech.** 1820
freeze, speak 2086	Even though you may make the mistake of saying **has broke, had spoke,** or **was froze,** you know that the words **broken, spoken,** and **frozen** exist. If there is a form of the verb ending with -*n* or -*en,* use it after any form of **have** or **be.** Underline two verbs that have forms ending with -*n* or -*en:* **rang** **gave** **stole** **went** 2087
	Adjectives can modify only nouns and pronouns—no other class of words. Adverbs modify everything else that can be modified—verbs, adjectives, and other adverbs. A word that modifies any word except a noun or a pronoun is an _____. 2354
b 2620	SHIFT IN PERSON: **Whether** *you* **live in a big city or in the country, nature surrounds** *us.* This sentence is faulty because *you* is in the second person and *us* is in the _____ person. 2621
None 2887	**One should be suspicious of any investment** *which offers an unusually high rate of return.* 2888
a 3154	Do not capitalize the articles *a, an,* and *the* or short prepositions and conjunctions in a title except when they are the first word of the title. a. *Gone with the Wind* b. *Gone With The Wind* Which title is correctly capitalized? _____ 3155

How often? 212	**George drove** *away.* Underline the question that the word *away* answers: **When? Where? How? How much? How often?** 213
subordinate 480	When we put an idea into a clause rather than into a sentence, we say that we *subordinate* it. When we subordinate an idea, we express it in a word group that is (*more, less*) than a sentence. 481
directs 748	Now we shall change the wording of our sentence: **Few people notice** *who the director was.* The direct object of the verb **notice** is not the clause signal *who* but the entire noun _____. 749
o elect officers. 1016	Lesson **27** Other Types of Reduction [Frames 1018–1058]
Dad 1284	a. **Dad went to Ohio, leaving me in charge of the farm.** b. **Dad went to Ohio. He left me in charge of the farm.** c. **Dad went to Ohio. Leaving me in charge of the farm.** Which one of the above three items is incorrect? _____ 1285
a 1552	a. **Written in simple language, any child can enjoy this book.** b. **Written in simple language, this book can be enjoyed by any child.** 1553

b 1820	a. **Brazil has a greater area than any country in South America.** b. **Brazil has a greater area than any other country in South America.** 182
gave, stole 2087	In this and the following frames, supply the correct forms of the two verbs in parentheses. After any form of **have** or **be,** think whether the verb has an *-n* or *-en* form. If it has, use it. It _____ (*cost*) **ninety cents for the distance we had** _____ (*ride*). 2088
adverb 2354	Although a few adjectives end in *-ly* (*homely, manly, lonely*) the *-ly* ending usually signals an adverb. We can make an adverb of almost any adjective by adding *-ly* to it. Write the adverb form of each of the following adjectives: **sad** _____ **prompt** _____ **cheerful** _____ 235
first 2621	a. **Whether** *you* **live in a big city or in the country, nature surrounds** *you.* b. **Whether** *you* **live in a big city or in the country, nature surrounds** *us.* Which sentence is correct? _____ 2622
None 2888	**It turned out that Shirley Smith** *who was chosen Dairy Queen* **is allergic to milk.** 2889
a 3155	Write the following title correctly: *the return of the native* _____ 3156

Where? 213	Words that modify verbs are called **adverbs.** The fact that the word ad*verb* contains the word *verb* will help you to remember that adverbs modify _____. 214
less 481	a. **The rain stopped.** b. **when the rain stopped** Which is a subordinate word group because it is less than a sentence? _____ 482
clause 749	*who the director was* Within the noun clause, the subject of the linking verb *was* is not *who* but _____. 750
	Reduction is the same principle as using a tack—and not a spike—to fasten a calendar to the wall. If either a *clause* or a *phrase* says exactly the same thing, use the _____. 1018
c 1285	WRONG: **I sent for a free booklet.** *Advertised in a magazine.* "*Advertised in a magazine*" is a past participial phrase. Does it have a subject and verb, and does it make sense by itself? (*Yes, No*) 1286
b 1553	a. **Because the man was wearing a blue uniform, Dave mistook him for a policeman.** b. **Wearing a blue uniform, Dave mistook the man for a policeman.** 1554

b 1821	a. **Next year's team will be as good as this year's, if not better.** b. **Next year's team will be as good, if not better, than this year's team.** 1822
cost, ridden 2088	**Stanley was** _____ (*choose*) **because he has always** _____ (*drive*) **carefully.** 2089
sadly promptly cheerfully 2355	There are hundreds of modifiers that have both an adjective and an adverb form. a. **bad rough noisy easy careful** b. **badly roughly noisily easily carefully** Which group of words consists of adverbs? _____ 2356
a 2622	A pronoun should also agree with its antecedent in number. Use a singular pronoun to refer to a singular antecedent. Use a plural pronoun to refer to a _____ antecedent. 2623
Smith, Queen, 2889	**In our living room we don't have a single chair** *that is really comfortable.* 2890
The Return of the Native 3156	Write the following title correctly: *how to choose a vocation* 3157

verbs 214	Many adverbs—especially those that tell *how*—end with **-ly**. In fact, we form many adverbs by adding **-ly** to adjectives: **polite—politely, graceful—gracefully, fearless—fearlessly.** A *careful* **person drives** *carefully.* The adverb in this sentence is _____. 215
b 482	a. **The rain stopped.** b. **when the rain stopped** We subordinated the idea in sentence *a* by adding the clause signal _____. 483
director 750	*who the director was* When we straighten out this clause by putting the subject first, we get: *the director was who* Since *who* completes the linking verb *was*, it is a (*subject complement, direct object*). 751
phrase 1018	If either a *phrase* or an *adverb* says exactly the same thing, use the _____. 1019
No 1286	RIGHT: **I sent for a free booklet** *advertised in a magazine.* The past participial phrase should be a part of the sentence containing the noun _____, which it modifies. 1287
a 1554	Lesson **43** **Repairing Dangling Word Groups** [Frames 1556–1580]

a 1822	a. **The Pacific is the largest of any other ocean in the world** b. **The Pacific is the largest ocean in the world.** 182
chosen, driven 2089	**The suspect had** _____ (*swear*) **that the ca** **was not** _____ (*steal*). 209
b 2356	The adverbs made by adding -*ly* to adjectives usuall answer the question **How?** about the action of the verb. **Dean ate his soup** *noisily*. The adverb *noisily* answers the question **How?** about th action of the verb _____. 235
plural 2623	SHIFT IN NUMBER: **You should train a** *dog* **before** *they* **ge too old to learn.** This sentence is faulty because the plural pronoun *they* i used to refer to the singular noun _____. 262
None (*or* living room,) 2890	**My father** *hearing of this opportunity* **moved our family t Oregon.** 289
How to Choose a Vocation 3157	9. Capitalize the names of historical events, periods, an documents. **World War II**　　**Monroe Doctrine**　　**Bill of Rights** **Colonial Period**　**Battle of Gettysburg**　**Ten Commandment** Copy the words that require capitals: **The crusades took place during the middle ages.**　315

carefully 215	We have seen that adjectives have a *fixed* position in the sentence—usually before the words they modify. Most adverbs, by contrast, are very *movable*. **I finally finished the final chapter.** The word that can be shifted to another position is the (*adjective* **final,** *adverb* **finally**). 216
when 483	**when the rain stopped** Because this type of subordinate word group answers the question **When?**—like an ordinary adverb—it is classified as an _____ clause. 484
subject complement 751	**Few people notice** (*who, whom*) *the director was.* Because the clause signal is a subject complement, we use the subject form (*who, whom*). 752
adverb 1019	1. Sentence 3. Phrase (verbal, appositive, prepositional) 2. Clause 4. Single word (adjective, adverb) As we move down this list from 1 to 4, the sentence elements become (*simpler, more complicated*). 1020
booklet 1287	a. **I sent for a free booklet. It was advertised in a magazine.** b. **I sent for a free booklet. Advertised in a magazine.** c. **I sent for a free booklet advertised in a magazine.** Which one of the above three items is incorrect? _____ 1288
1555	Don't hesitate to start your sentences with word groups that do not tell **whom** or **what** they are about. They add interest to your writing. Just remember that you owe your reader this information (*somewhere in, at the beginning of*) the main statement that follows. (*Turn to the next frame.*) 1556

b 1823	In this and the following frames, cancel or add any words or letters that are necessary to make the comparisons logical: **Our way of life is very similar to Canada.** 1824
sworn, stolen 2090	**Any food that is not** _____ (*eat*) **will be** _____ (*throw*) **out.** 2091
ate 2357	The most common error in the use of adjectives and adverbs is failing to use the adverb (*-ly*) form to describe the action of a verb. The fact that *verb* is part of the word ad*verb* will remind you always to use an adverb to modify a _____ 2358
dog 2624	a. **You should train a** *dog* **before** *they* **get too old to learn.** b. **You should train a** *dog* **before** *it* **gets too old to learn.** Which sentence is correct? _____ 2625
father, opportunity, 2891	**This book will be valuable to anyone** *wanting to take better pictures.* 2892
Crusades, Middle Ages 3158	Copy the words that require capitals: **Twenty years after the american revolution, the louisiana purchase greatly increased the size of the new nation.** 3159

adverb *finally* 216	**Our friends ∧ have ∧ come ∧ for dinner ∧. (often)** Can the adverb **often** be inserted in the sentence at each point indicated by a caret (∧)? (*Yes, No*) 217
adverb 484	**We continued our game** *when the rain stopped.* The adverb clause *when the rain stopped* modifies the verb _____. 485
who 752	WRONG: **Few people notice** *whom the director was.* The object form *whom* is wrong because the clause signal is not the object of the verb **notice.** The object of the verb **notice** is the entire _____ _____. 753
simpler 1020	1. Sentence 3. Phrase (verbal, appositive, prepositional) 2. Clause 4. Single word (adjective, adverb) When we reduce a word group, we move (*up, down*) the above list of sentence elements. 1021
b 1288	WRONG: **Pat showed her bad manners.** *By laughing at my car.* *"By laughing at my car"* is a prepositional phrase with a gerund as the object of the preposition *By.* Can a prepositional phrase be written as a separate sentence? (*Yes, No*) 1289
...e beginning of 1556	When your introductory word group lacks a subject, tell **whom** or **what** it is about at the beginning of your main statement. Failure to supply this information results in an error known as a _____ word group. 1557

Canada's. *or* that of Canada. *or* Canada's way of life. 1824	The double bass is the largest of all the other members of the violin family. 1825
eaten, thrown 2091	I would have _____ (*speak*) to Mr. Price if I had _____ (*see*) him. 2092
verb 2358	The reward was divided (*equal, equally*) between the two boys. To explain *how* the reward **was divided,** use the adverb _____. 2359
b 2625	a. Most things are cheaper when you buy them in large quantities. b. Most things are cheaper when you buy it in large quantities. Which sentence is correct? _____ 2626
None 2892	Lesson **81** Review: Uses of the Comma [Frames 2894–2913]
American Revolution, Louisiana Purchase 3159	10. Capitalize all sacred names: God the Almighty our Father Christ Lord the Holy Ghost Saviour the Virgin Copy the words that require capitals: The stained-glass window pictures the virgin holding the christ child. 3160

Yes 217	Because adverbs are often movable, we frequently find them several words away from the verbs they modify. **Aunt Mary talks about her operation** *continually.* The adverb *continually* modifies the verb _____. <div align="right">218</div>
continued 485	**We continued our game** *when the rain stopped.* Because the clause signal **when** starts a *subordinate* word group and also *connects* this word group with the sentence, we call it a **subordinating conjunction.** The subordinating conjunction in the above sentence is _____. <div align="right">486</div>
noun clause 753	Now we shall put the same idea in a different way: **Few people pay any attention to the** *director.* The noun *director* is the object of the preposition _____. <div align="right">754</div>
down 1021	a. **We play the game** *in a different way.* b. **We play the game** *differently.* When we reduce the prepositional phrase (4 words) in sentence *a* to the adverb *differently* in sentence *b*, do we change the meaning in any way? (*Yes, No*) <div align="right">1022</div>
No 1289	WRONG: **Pat showed her bad manners.** *By laughing at my car.* The prepositional phrase answers the question **How?** about the verb _____ in the main statement. <div align="right">1290</div>
dangling 1557	What is the difference between a *misplaced modifier* and a *dangling word group?* A *misplaced modifier* is not in its proper place with relation to the word it modifies. A *dangling word group,* on the other hand, often has no word at all to modify and therefore appears to modify the (*right, wrong*) word. <div align="right">1558</div>

~~other~~ 1825	**Our gas bill was three dollars more than our neighbor.** 182.
spoken, seen 2092	**The pipe had** _____ (_burst_) **because the water** **had** _____ (_freeze_). 209.
equally 2359	**Noel must have done** (_poor, poorly_) **on his test.** To explain _how_ Noel **must have done** on his test, use the adverb _____. 236.

a
 	
2626
	Don't hesitate to use **he** when a statement applies equally
	to either sex. The expressions **he or she** and **his or her** are
	awkward.
	
	    A person should wash _his_ **hands before** _he_ **eats.**
	
	Does the above sentence apply to women as well as to men?
	(_Yes, No_)
	                                                                   2627

	In this and the following frames, supply the necessary com- mas. If no commas are required, write _None._ **Many years have passed since then and many changes of** **course have taken place.** 2894

Virgin,
Christ Child
 	
3160
	Too many capitals are as serious an error as too few. Do not
	capitalize—
	
	    FOODS: **spaghetti, hamburgers, brownies, angel food**
	
	Copy the words that require capitals:
	
	We ate chop suey at a chinese restaurant on Campus street.
	                                                         3161

talks 218	*Tomorrow* **my cousins will drive back to Springfield.** The adverb *Tomorrow* modifies the verb _____. <div align="right">219</div>
when 486	**We lost our way** *because we made a wrong turn.* ·The subordinating conjunction in the above sentence is _____. <div align="right">487</div>
ˉ to 754	a. **Few people pay any attention to the** *director.* b. **Few people pay any attention to** *who directs a movie.* In sentence *a,* the object of the preposition **to** is the noun *director.* In sentence *b,* the object of the preposition **to** is the noun clause _____. <div align="right">755</div>
No 1022	By reduction we do not mean eliminating words that add to the meaning or interest of a sentence. When we reduce a word group, we make (*no, a slight*) change in the meaning. <div align="right">1023</div>
showed 1290	a. **Pat showed her bad manners. By laughing at my car.** b. **Pat showed her bad manners by laughing at my car.** Which sentence is right because the prepositional phrase is in the same sentence as the verb **showed,** which it modifies? _____ <div align="right">1291</div>
wrong 1558	To avoid a dangling word group, you must tell **who** or **what** either (1) in the introductory word group itself or (2) at the beginning of the main statement that follows it. **When a small baby, a bee stung me on the nose.** Does this sentence tell **who** in either place? (*Yes, No*) <div align="right">1559</div>

neighbor's. *or* that of our neighbor. *or* neighbor's gas bill. 1826	Death Valley, California, is hotter than any region on earth. 182.
burst, frozen 2093	**59** Lesson **Another Group of Three-Part Verbs** [Frames 2095–2131
poorly 2360	WRONG: **Noel must have done *poor* on his test.** This is wrong because the adjective *poor* cannot modify the _____ **must have done.** 236.
Yes 2627	a. **Before a person votes, he or she should inform himself or herself about the candidates.** b. **Before a person votes, he should inform himself about the candidates.** Which sentence is better? _____ 262.
then, changes, course, 2894	**We had to wait for the principal was busy when we arrived at his office.** 289.

Chinese, Street
 	
3161
	Do not capitalize—
	   GAMES: **baseball, hockey, checkers**
	   MUSICAL INSTRUMENTS: **violin, piano, saxophone**
	Copy the words that require capitals:
	My cousin Henry sees every colby football game because he plays the trumpet in the college band.
	
	316.

will drive 219	a. **One of the windows** *occasionally* **sticks.** b. **One of the windows sticks** *occasionally*. c. *Occasionally* **one of the windows sticks.** In which sentence is the adverb farthest away from the verb it modifies? _____ 220
because 487	The grammar term for the clause signals that start adverb clauses is *subordinating* _____. 488
who directs a movie 755	**Few people pay any attention to** *who directs a movie.* Within the noun clause, the subject of the verb *directs* is the clause signal _____. 756
no 1023	In the previous lesson, we reduced clauses to phrases built on present and past participles, gerunds, and infinitives. These word groups are simpler than clauses because they do not contain subjects and _____. 1024
b 1291	a. **Pat showed her bad manners. She laughed at my car.** b. **Pat showed her bad manners by laughing at my car.** c. **Pat showed her bad manners. By laughing at my car.** Which one of the above three items is incorrect? _____ 1292
No 1559	a. **When a small baby, I was stung on the nose by a bee.** b. **When I was a small baby, a bee stung me on the nose.** In which sentence is the question **Who?** answered sensibly in the introductory word group? _____ 1560

other 1827	The rat has been the most destructive of any other animal on this planet. 1828
	There are a number of irregular verbs that follow the pattern of the verb **ring.** PRESENT PAST PAST PARTICIPLE **ring** **rang** **(have) rung** Underline the vowel in each of the above three forms of the verb **ring.** Vowels are *a, e, i, o, u.* 2095
verb 2361	a. **The company is always quite . . . in handling complaints.** b. **The company always handles complaints quite . . . .** In which sentence would you use the adjective **prompt** because it would modify the noun **company?** _____ 2362
b 2628	WRONG: **When a** *student* **plays football,** *you* **must keep in condition.** This sentence is wrong because the pronoun *you* disagrees with its antecedent in (*number, person*). 2629
wait, 2895	Before fireworks were prohibited hundreds of children were maimed blinded and killed every Fourth of July. 2896

Cousin, Colby
 	
3162
	Do not capitalize—
	    OCCUPATIONS: **engineer, artist, lawyer, minister**
	    DISEASES: **measles, mumps, flu, chicken pox, polio**
	Copy the words that require capitals:
	Just before easter our minister got pneumonia and was taken to the Oakfield hospital.
	
	3163

c 220	There are hundreds of adverbs that give information about verbs. In addition, there are some special adverbs that control the "power" of adjectives and other adverbs. *very* **hot** *somewhat* **hot** *rather* **hot** *so* **hot** *quite* **hot** *extremely* **hot** *slightly* **hot** *too* **hot** The italicized adverbs modify the adjective _____. 221
conjunctions 488	You have had much practice in using the conjunctions **and, but,** and **or** to make compound sentences. These conjunctions, **and, but,** and **or,** are sometimes called **coordinating** (co- means *equal*) **conjunctions** because they connect words and word groups that are (*unequal, equal*) in rank. 489
who 756	WRONG: **Few people pay any attention to** *whom directs a movie.* The object form *whom* is wrong because the clause signal is not the object of the preposition **to** but the subject of the verb _____ within the clause. 757
∖ **verbs** *(or predicates)* 1024	Here is an adjective clause that can be reduced to something even simpler—a prepositional phrase. **The apples** *that were in the window* **looked larger.** **The apples** *in the window* **looked larger.** By reducing the adjective clause to a prepositional phrase, we eliminate _____ words. (How many?) 1025
c 1292	WRONG: **The customer soon returned.** *To get his money back.* "*To get his mony back*" is an infinitive phrase. It explains *why* about the verb _____ in the main statement. 1293
b 1560	a. **When a small baby, I was stung on the nose by a bee.** b. **When I was a small baby, a bee stung me on the nose.** In which sentence is the question **Who?** answered in the main statement? _____ 1561

most destructive of all the animals . . . *or* more destructive than any other . . . 1828	Rewrite this sentence correctly: **I study as hard, if not harder, than Phil.** _____ _____ 182⁹
ring, rang, rung 2095	PRESENT PAST PAST PARTICIPLE **ring** **rang** **(have) rung** Does the vowel remain the same in any two forms of this verb? (*Yes, No*) 2096
a 2362	a. **The company is always quite . . . in handling complaints.** b. **The company always handles complaints quite . . . .** In which sentence would you use the adverb **promptly** be- cause it would modify the verb **handles?** _____ 236³
person 2629	WRONG: **Always reread a** *letter* **before you mail** *them.* This sentence is wrong because the pronoun *them* disagrees with its antecedent in (*number, person*). 263⁶
prohibited, maimed, blinded(,) 2896	**A bank will not hire any person who is known to gamble.** 289⁷

Easter, Hospital
 	
 3163
	Do not capitalize—
	      TREES: **elm, maple, willow, pine, birch**
	      FLOWERS: **rose, peony, orchid, dandelion**
	 Copy the words that require capitals:
	 The yellow chrysanthemums with the scarlet oak leaves make the display of the Meyer flower shop very colorful.
	
	 316⁴

hot 221	*very* **awkwardly** *rather* **awkwardly** *so* **awkwardly** *quite* **awkwardly** *somewhat* **awkwardly** *too* **awkwardly** All the italicized adverbs modify the (*adjective, adverb*) **awkwardly**. 222
equal 489	Because the two parts of a compound sentence are equal in rank, they are connected by a (*coordinating, subordinating*) conjunction. 490
directs 757	**Few people pay any attention to** *who directs a movie.* How do we know that the clause signal is not the object of the preposition **to**? If the clause signal *who(m)* were the object of the preposition **to**, the clause would have no (*subject, object*). 758
two 1025	**This is a matter** *which is of great importance.* Reduce the italicized adjective clause to a prepositional phrase: **This is a matter** _____. 1026
returned 1293	a. **The customer returned to get his money back.** b. **The customer returned. To get his money back.** Which sentence is right because the infinitive phrase is in the same sentence as the verb **returned**, which it modifies? ——— 1294
a 1561	If your introductory word group answers the question **Who?** or **What?** do you need to answer this question again at the beginning of your main statement? (*Yes, No*) 1562

I study as hard as Phil, if not harder. 1829	Rewrite this sentence correctly: **This is one of the fastest, if not the fastest, car on the road.** _____ _____ 1830
No 2096	PRESENT PAST PAST PARTICIPLE **ring** **rang** **(have) rung** Notice that the past and past participle are different. The vowel **a** in the past turns to _____ in the past participle. 2097
b 2363	Underline the correct word: **My sunburn hurt** (_bad, badly_) **for several days.** 2364
number 2630	In this and the following frames, circle the _N_ when the pronoun disagrees with its antecedent in _Number,_ the _P_ when it disagrees in _Person._ Then cross out the incorrect pronoun (and sometimes the verb, too), and write your correction above. _N P_ **A person is expected to keep their appointment.** 263
None 2897	**We shall be at the Chippewa Motor Hotel 850 Laurel Street Brainerd Minnesota until Tuesday May 10.** 289

Flower Shop
 	
3164
	Do not capitalize—
	  BIRDS: **robin, blue jay, crow, pheasant**
	  ANIMALS AND FISH: **terrier, spaniel, elephant, catfish**
	Copy the words that require capitals:
	We plan to take our collie with us to Moose lake, but we shall leave our canary with grandma Voss.
	
	316

adverb 222	**Too many people vote without sufficient information.** The adjective **many** modifies the noun **people.** What adverb modifies the adjective **many?** _____ 223
coordinating 490	Conjunctions such as **because, when, if,** and **unless** are called **subordinating conjunctions** because they connect a word group of (*higher, lower*) rank than a sentence. 491
subject 758	Now let us look at another sentence: **The producers must consider** *whom a movie might offend.* The pronoun *whom* cannot be the subject of the verb *might offend* because the verb already has a subject, the noun _____. 759

of great
importance.
 	
1026
	Sometimes you can do even better by reducing the adjective clause to a single adjective.
	
	    The plane carries a raft *that is made of rubber.*
	    The plane carries a *rubber* **raft.**
	
	Does the five-word adjective clause say any more than the one-word adjective *rubber?* (*Yes, No*)
	
	1027

a 1294	a. **The customer returned. He wanted his money back.** b. **The customer returned. To get his money back.** c. **The customer returned to get his money back.** Which one of the above three items is incorrect? _____ 1295
No 1562	If your introductory word group *does not* answer the question **Who?** or **What?** do you need to answer this question at the beginning of your main statement? (*Yes, No*) 1563

This is one of the fastest cars on the road, if not the fastest.

1830

Lesson 51 — Removing Deadwood from Sentences

[Frames 1832–1854]

---

u

Supply the missing forms of the verb **ring:**

PRESENT	PAST	PAST PARTICIPLE
ring	_____	**(have)** _____

2097

2098

---

badly

Underline the correct word:

A family can live more (*economical, economically*) **in a small town.**

2364

2365

---

his
N ~~their~~

N P **When people were in debt, you used to be put in prison.**

2631

2632

Hotel, Street,
Brainerd,
Minnesota,
Tuesday,

The time will come however when nations will settle their differences around the conference table not on the battlefield.

2898

2899

Lake, Grandma

11. Capitalize proper adjectives that modify common nouns.

Dutch apple pie	Swiss cheese	Spanish moss
Chinese checkers	Harvard beets	American elm

Copy the words that require capitals:

Our french poodle and siamese cat get along well together.

3165

3166

Too 223	**Lois speaks French very fluently.** The adverb **fluently** modifies the verb **speaks.** What adverb modifies the adverb **fluently**? _____ 224
lower 491	Because adverb clauses are of lower rank than the sentence to which they are attached, they are connected by (*coordinating, subordinating*) conjunctions. 492
movie 759	*whom a movie might offend* When we straighten out this clause, we get: *a movie might offend whom* The clause signal *whom* is the (*subject, direct object*) of the verb *might offend.* 760
No 1027	**This is not a good book for people** *who are nervous.* Substitute a single adjective for the adjective clause: **This is not a good book for** _____ **people.** 1028
b 1295	Sentence fragments can result from splitting off a clause or a phrase from the beginning of a sentence, as well as from the end. a. **I wandered among the crowd. Looking for a familiar face.** b. **Looking for a familiar face. I wandered among the crowd.** The sentence fragment comes first in (*a, b*). _____ 1296
Yes 1563	*While peeling onions,* **my eyes always smart.** Does either the introductory word group or the main statement tell **who** is *peeling the onions?* (*Yes, No*) 1564

We remove deadwood from a tree because it contributes nothing to the life or productiveness of the tree. By "deadwood" in sentences, we mean empty words and phrases that add nothing to the meaning or to the interest.

Cross out two words that add nothing to the meaning of:

Mr. Lovett was an elderly man in age.

1832

---

rang, (have) rung	The next seven verbs that we study follow the **ring-rang-rung** pattern. One should help you to remember the others. Supply the missing forms:

ring	rang	(have) rung
sing	sang	(have) _____

2098

2099

---

economically

A few adverbs have two forms—one with *-ly* and another without; for example, **slow—slowly, quick—quickly, loud—loudly, fair—fairly, cheap—cheaply.** The shorter form is frequently used in brief commands and on traffic signs.

  a. **Drive ... !**   b. **I always eat my meals ....**

In which sentence is the adverb **slow** acceptable? _____

2365

2366

---

they

P ~~you~~

N P   **When a person gets angry, they should count to ten.**

2632

2633

---

come, however, table,

For the protection of small children matches drugs and sharp objects should be kept out of their reach.

2899

2900

French, Siamese

In this and the following frames, copy only the words in each sentence to which capitals need to be added:

Among the sponsors of the Good Will club are father Cole of Trinity church, mayor Phillips, a judge, a doctor, and my uncle George.

3166

3167

very 224	**The lake was slightly rough.** The adverb **slightly** modifies the _____ **rough.** 225
subordinating 492	Every sentence that contains an adverb clause is a (*complex, compound*) sentence. 493
direct object 760	(*who, whom*) *a movie might offend* Because the clause signal is the direct object of the verb *might offend,* we choose the object form _____. 761
nervous 1028	Often the single adjective to which we reduce an adjective clause is a present or past participle. **Milk is a necessity for any child** *that is growing.* **Milk is a necessity for any** *growing* **child.** In the second sentence the adjective clause has been reduced to a (*present, past*) participle. 1029
b 1296	a. **Though I don't collect them. Stamps interest me.** b. **Stamps interest me. Though I don't collect them.** The sentence fragment comes first in (*a, b*). ____ 1297
No 1564	Sometimes it is difficult or awkward to tell **who** or **what** at the beginning of your main statement. While peeling onions, _____?_____ Since it would be difficult to continue this sentence, it would be best to tell **who** in the (*introductory word group, main statement*). 1565

in age 1832	Some people try to impress others by using pretentious language, by repeating themselves, and by expressing themselves in a roundabout way. a. **Aunt Sara was one who was a determined person.** b. **Aunt Sara was a determined person.** The sentence containing "deadwood" is sentence (a, b). 1833
sung 2099	Supply the missing forms: | PRESENT	PAST	PAST PARTICIPLE
---	---	---
ring	**rang**	**(have) rung**
sink	——	**(have) sunk**
shrink	**shrank**	**(have)** ——	 2100
a 2366	a. **Play ...!** b. **The store treats all customers ....** Although both **fair** and **fairly** are adverbs, in which sentence should **fairly,** rather than **fair,** be used? —— 2367
he N ~~they~~ 2633	N P **Can you really judge a person's character by their handwriting?** 2634
children, matches, drugs(,) 2900	**Mrs. Bilby folds and puts away every bag and every used piece of wrapping paper.** 2901
Club, Father, Church, Mayor, Uncle 3167	**Perhaps grandma Wiles will spend easter with my aunt in the east.** —————————— 3168

adjective (*or* subject complement) 225	**Elsie can type quite rapidly.** The adverb **quite** modifies the _____ **rapidly.** 226
complex 493	In every complex sentence that contains an adverb clause, you can expect to find a (*coordinating, subordinating*) conjunction. 494
whom 761	**The producer must consider** *whom a movie might offend.* We choose the object form *whom* because it is the direct object of the verb (*must consider, might offend*). 762
present 1029	**Nothing disgusts me more than a child** *that has been spoiled.* **Nothing disgusts me more than a** *spoiled* **child.** In the second sentence the adjective clause has been reduced to a (*present, past*) participle. 1030
a 1297	a. **John completely overhauls each motor. Before selling the car.** b. **Before selling the car. John completely overhauls each motor.** The sentence fragment comes first in (*a, b*). _____ 1298
introductory word group 1565	When it is awkward to tell **who** or **what** in the main statement, change the introductory word group to a *complete adverb clause,* leaving the main statement as it is. a. **While peeling onions, my eyes always smart.** b. **While I peel onions, my eyes always smart.** Which sentence is correct? _____ 1566

a 1833	The way to make a theme longer is to develop your thoughts and to add ideas. Don't pack it with empty words that waste your reader's time. ∧ **I think that the plot is weak.** To lengthen your theme, would it be a good idea to add the words **In my opinion** at the point indicated? (*Yes, No*) 1834
sank, (have) shrunk 2100	Supply the missing forms: | PRESENT	PAST	PAST PARTICIPLE
---	---	---
ring	**rang**	**(have) rung**
spring	_____	**(have) sprung**
swim	**swam**	**(have)** _____	 2101

b
 	
2367
	When an adverb has two forms—one with *-ly* and another without—the longer form is preferred in formal usage.
	
	  a. **Please come** *quick!*
	  b. **A good executive can make important decisions** *quick.*
	
	In which sentence would it be advisable to change the adverb *quick* to *quickly?* _____
	
	2368

his N ~~their~~ 2634	*N P* Once a player takes his hand off a checker, you can't take back the move. 2635
None 2901	The newspaper praised Fred Kaslow the driver of the bus for his cool skillful handling of the emergency. 2902
Grandma, Easter, East 3168	My dad often says that he married my mother because she was born on the fourth of July, and he therefore would not run the risk of forgetting her birthday. 3169

adverb 226	You have now seen that besides modifying verbs, adverbs can also modify other modifiers. By "other modifiers" we mean *adjectives* and _____. 227
subordinating 494	a. **when, as, since, where, after, as if, because, unless, so that, although,** *etc.* b. **and, but, or** Which one of the above groups consists of subordinating conjunctions—*a* or *b?* _____ 495
might offend 762	The way in which a noun clause is used in a sentence has nothing to do with your reason for choosing **who** or **whom.** (*True, False*) 763

past
 	
1030
	Any adjective clause that identifies someone or something can be reduced to an appositive phrase very simply.
	
	    Corn, *which was our main crop,* **did poorly that year.**
	    Corn, *our main crop,* **did poorly that year.**
	
	This reduction eliminates two useless words: _____ and _____.
	
	1031

b
 	
1298
	In this and the following frames, one of each pair of word groups is a sentence, and the other is a fragment. Draw a circle around the letter of the complete sentence.
	
	    a. **As soon as I realized my mistake.**
	    b. **I soon realized my mistake.**
	
	1299

b 1566	*Sitting on the step,* **my foot fell asleep.** The introductory word group is dangling because it was not the **foot** that was *sitting on the step,* but a person. It would be easier to correct this faulty sentence by answering the question **Who?** in the (*main statement, introductory word group*). 1567

No 1834	"Deadwood" also results from a lack of careful revision. Keep working at a sentence until you succeed in removing all useless words and roundabout expressions. a. **There is a great deal of value connected with this book.** b. **This book has great value.** Which sentence is better? _____ 1835
sprang, (have) swum 2101	Supply the missing forms, following the **ring-rang-rung** pattern: PRESENT PAST PAST PARTICIPLE **begin** _____ **(have)** _____ **drink** _____ **(have)** _____ 2102
b 2368	Although we frequently hear **sure** (instead of **surely**) used as an adverb in informal conversation, to many people it sounds slangy and slipshod. He *surely* **gave our suggestion his careful consideration.** The adverb *surely* is required because it modifies the verb _____. 2369
he P ~~you~~ 2635	*N P* **It's exciting to hook a sailfish because they put up a big fight.** 2636
Kaslow, bus, cool, 2902	**You know Ralph that any player who breaks the training rules is suspended for the season.** 2903
Fourth 3169	**The president urged full support of the United nations.** _____ 3170

adverbs 227	In this and the following frames, the position of the periods should tell you whether the missing word would be an adjective or an adverb. **Our hotel room was very . . .** The missing word (such as *small, shabby,* or *comfortable*) would be an (*adjective, adverb*). 228
a 495	a. **A serious fire broke out, and the building was empty.** b. **A serious fire broke out while the building was empty.** One sentence merely adds one fact to another. The other sentence explains *how* the two facts are related. Which sentence brings out more clearly the *relationship* between the two ideas—*a* or *b?* _____ 496
True 763	To decide whether to use the pronoun **who** or **whom,** you need to look only (*inside, outside*) the clause. 764
which, was 1031	**The next event,** *which was a tug of war,* **was won by the freshmen.** Write in the appositive phrase to which the italicized clause can be reduced: **The next event,** _____**, was won by the freshmen.** 1032
b 1299	Continue to draw a circle around the letter of each complete sentence: a. **I laughed until my sides ached.** b. **Laughing until my sides ached.** 1300
introductory word group 1567	a. **As I was sitting on the step, my foot fell asleep.** b. **Sitting on the step, my foot fell asleep.** Which sentence is correct? _____ 1568

b 1835	Some sentences remind us of a person who walks around the block to get to the house next door. The best sentence is one that—like an arrow—goes straight to the mark. **Before the realization of what had happened came to me, it was too late.** Could this sentence be improved by revision? (*Yes, No*) 1836
began, (have) begun drank, (have) drunk 2102	a. **rang, sang, sank, shrank, sprang, swam, began, drank** b. **rung, sung, sunk, shrunk, sprung, swum, begun, drunk** Which group consists of simple past verbs that you would use *without* the forms of the helping verb **have** or **be**? ——— 2103
gave 2369	Underline the correct word: **Young people (*sure, surely*) appreciate a parent's interest in their activities and problems.** 2370
it puts N ~~they put~~ 2636	*N P* **The less exercise one takes, the less food you need.** 2637
know, Ralph, 2903	In the remaining frames, put circles around any commas that should be omitted. If all the commas in any sentence are necessary, write *Correct*. **When we finally reached the stadium, we drove around, and looked for a place to park.** 2904
President, Nations 3170	**Our assignment was to write an interpretation of "the Death of the Hired man" by Robert Frost, the new england poet.** ——— 3171

adjective 228	**We . . . find Skippy in a neighbor's yard.** The missing word (such as *often, usually,* or *sometimes*) would be an (*adjective, adverb*). 229
b 496	a. **A serious fire broke out, and the building was empty.** b. **A serious fire broke out while the building was empty.** Which sentence is a complex sentence because it contains a subordinating conjunction? _____ 497
inside 764	If the clause signal is the subject or subject complement, use the subject form (*who, whom*). 765
a tug of war 1032	Do you remember that a gerund is a noun formed by adding *-ing* to a verb and that a gerund can be used in any way that a noun is used? **The ladies raised money** *by selling cakes.* Here the gerund phrase *selling cakes* is the object of the preposition _____. 1033
a 1300	a. **It was woven from discarded scraps of cloth.** b. **Woven from discarded scraps of cloth.** 1301
a 1568	In this and the following frames, correct the dangling word group by changing it to a complete adverb clause. Make no change in the main statement. **Being a rainy day, the outdoor track meet was postponed.** _____, the **outdoor track meet was postponed.** 1569

Yes

1836

a. **Before the realization of what had happened came to me, it was too late.**
b. **Before I realized what had happened, it was too late.**

How many useless words are eliminated by the revision of sentence *a?* _____

1837

---

a

2103

a. **rang, sang, sank, shrank, sprang, swam, began, drank**
b. **rung, sung, sunk, shrunk, sprung, swum, begun, drunk**

Which group consists of past participles that you would use *with* the forms of the helping verb **have** or **be?** _____

2104

---

surely

2370

If using **surely** sounds stiff and unnatural to you, you can use the adverb **certainly** in its place.

Supply an adverb with the same meaning as **surely:**

We _____ saved money by painting the house ourselves.

2371

---

one (he) needs
P   ~~you need~~

2637

N P   **Before you take medicine, a person should always read the label.**

(*Note:* In this frame you need to cross out a noun rather than a pronoun.)

2638

---

around ⊙

2904

Films, slides, and models, make a science course, for example, much more interesting.

2905

"The . . . Man,"
New England

3171

Among the exhibits of the Library of congress are the original declaration of independence and the constitution.

3172

adverb 229	**The fair will last for . . . days.** The missing word would be an (*adjective, adverb*). 230
b 497	a. **A serious fire broke out, and the building was empty.** b. **A serious fire broke out while the building was empty.** The relationship between the two facts is brought out more clearly by the (*complex, compound*) sentence. 498
who 765	If the clause signal is the object of a verb or preposition, use the object form (*who, whom*). 766
by 1033	An adverb clause can often be reduced to a prepositional phrase with a gerund phrase as the object of the preposition (*by, for, on, in, before, after,* etc.). *Because we took a short cut,* **we saved five miles.** *By taking a short cut,* **we saved five miles.** The gerund phrase is the object of the preposition _____. 1034
a 1301	a. **Although the movie finally came to a happy ending.** b. **The movie finally came to a happy ending.** 1302
Because (Since, As) it was a rainy day, 1569	**Struggling through the underbrush, the hunter's clothes were badly torn.** _____, the hunter's clothes were badly torn. 1570

four 1837	a. **It tells how the American people conquered the wilderness.** b. **It tells of the American people and the way in which they conquered the wilderness.** Which sentence is better? _____ 1838
b 2104	Underline three verbs that follow the **ring-rang-rung** pattern: **think sing sink wink spring** 2105
certainly 2371	Use **really,** not **real,** as an adverb meaning **very.** Underline the correct word: **Roberta is** (*real, really*) **serious about her plans.** 2372
you P <s>a person</s> 2638	From here on, supply a pronoun that agrees in number and person with its antecedent: **If a person overparks, the police tow _____ car away.** 2639
models⊙ 2905	**We are supposed to memorize, not read, our parts.** 2906
Congress, Declaration, Independence, Constitution 3172	**At various times we have owned a collie, a police dog, an irish terrier, and a persian cat.** _____ _____ 3173

adjective 230	**We studied the road map . . . carefully.** The missing word would be an (*adjective, adverb*). 231
complex 498	a. **The dog won't eat, and he seems to be hungry.** b. **The dog won't eat although he seems to be hungry.** The relationship between the two facts is brought out more clearly by the (*compound, complex*) sentence. 499
whom 766	When a noun clause begins with **whoever** or **whomever**, we make our choice in exactly the same way as we did with **who** and **whom**. Underline the correct word: **Mrs. Torrey tells** (*whoever, whomever*) *will listen* **about her operation.** 767
by 1034	*When he saw his final grade,* **Ron leaped with joy.** Complete the following sentence by supplying a gerund phrase as the object of the preposition *On:* *On* _____, **Ron leaped with joy.** 1035
b 1302	a. **He gave no signal to the car behind him.** b. **Giving no signal to the car behind him.** 1303
While (As) he struggled through the underbrush, 1570	**Unless thoroughly cooked, a person should not eat pork.** _____ _____, **a person should not eat pork.** 1571

a 1838	Avoid repeating in the same sentence the meaning already stated by another word or group of words. Cross out two repetitious words: **The modern car of today is a complicated machine.** 1839
sing, sink, spring 2105	Underline three verbs that follow the **ring-rang-rung** pattern: **swim fling skin begin drink** 2106
really 2372	a. **The test was** *real* **difficult.** b. **The party was a** *real* **success.** The word *real* should be changed to *really* in sentence (*a, b*). _____ 2373
his 2639	**The poster shows a person how _____ should put on a life preserver.** 2640
Correct 2906	**No, I should not like to meet Mr. Parker, when he is angry.** 2907
Irish, Persian 3173	**The members of our latin class sent Alva an african violet after her operation for appendicitis at the Bennett hospital.** _____ 3174

adverb 231	**The clerk felt very . . . about her mistake.** The missing word would be an (*adjective, adverb*). 232
complex 499	a. **when, as, since, where, after, as if, because, unless, so that, although,** *etc.* b. **and, but, or** Which group of conjunctions shows *more specifically* the relationship between the two facts or ideas they connect—the (*subordinating, coordinating*) conjunctions? 500
whoever 767	**Mrs. Torrey tells** *whoever will listen* **about her operation.** *Whoever* is correct because it is the (*subject, object*) of the verb *will listen* within the clause. 768
seeing his final grade, 1035	**You can often frighten away wild animals** *if you will hit two stones together.* Supply a gerund phrase as the object of the preposition *by:* **You can often frighten away wild animals** *by* _____ _____. 1036
a 1303	a. **Which makes her look much taller than she is.** b. **It makes her look much taller than she is.** 1304
Unless it (the pork) has been roughly cooked, 1571	**Used for only a short time, the Sibleys expect a good price for their car.** _____ _____, **the Sibleys expect a good price for their car.** 1572

of today 1839	Reduce the following wordy sentence to only four words: **John's attitude toward his father was that he had respect for him.** _____ 1840
swim, begin, drink 2106	In this and the following frames, supply the correct forms of the verb in parentheses. All follow the **ring-rang-rung** pattern. **After the bell had _____ three times, it _____ once again.** (*ring*) 2107
a 2373	Although -*ly* is used mainly to change adjectives to adverbs, it is also used to change a few nouns to adjectives; for example, **friend-ly, neighbor-ly, father-ly, order-ly.** **Our new neighbors are unusually** *friendly.* The word *friendly* is an adjective because it modifies the noun _____. 2374
he 2640	**Why don't you boys help _____ to some lunch?** 2641
Mr. Parker⊙ 2907	**Not a thing was broken, or lost, or mislaid as a result of our moving.** 2908
Latin, African, Hospital 3174	**Dr. Carver, the great negro agricultural chemist, refused money for his discoveries because he felt that he was doing god's work.** _____ 3175

adjective 232	**It is . . . hot at the equator.** The missing word would be an (*adjective, adverb*). 233
subordinating 500	We can give a sentence many different meanings merely by changing the subordinating conjunction. **I shall not tell Ruth . . . I see her.** Underline the only subordinating conjunction that does *not* fit into the above sentence: **when until so that if unless although** 501
subject 768	Underline the correct word: (*Whoever, Whomever*) *the country elects* **will face serious problems.** 769
hitting two stones together. 1036	*Before I joined the club,* **I attended several meetings.** Supply a gerund phrase as the object of the preposition *Before:* *Before* _____, **I attended several meetings.** 1037
b 1304	In this and the following frames, write an *S* for each word group that is a *Sentence,* and an *F* for each word group that is a *Fragment*. Write your answers on the two lines in the same order as the word groups. **This article recommends electing our Presidents. By a direct vote of the people.** _____ _____ 1305
Because (Since, As) it (the car) was used for only a short time, 1572	**Seeing a large crowd around the car, our curiosity was aroused.** _____ _____, **our curiosity was aroused.** 1573

John respected his father. 1840	In this and the following frames, improve each sentence by crossing out the number of useless words indicated in the parentheses: **It would do more harm than it would do good to your car. (3)** 1841
rung, rang 2107	**The shirt** _____ **more than it should have** _____. (*shrink*) 2108
neighbors 2374	Since words such as **neighborly, fatherly,** and **orderly** are adjectives, they cannot be used to modify verbs. WRONG: **Mr. Haines discusses literature** *scholarly*. This sentence is wrong because the adjective *scholarly* cannot modify the verb _____. 2375
yourselves 2641	**Some of the customers made it difficult for the clerk by rushing** _____. 2642
broken⊙ lost⊙ 2908	**The alligator has a thick, tough, leathery, hide.** 2909
Negro, God's 3175	**A boys' chorus from the Burbank high school sang "Joy to the world" and several french christmas carols at the december meeting.** 3176

adverb 233	An adjective can modify only two classes of words: nouns and pronouns. An adverb, however, can modify _____ classes of words. (How many?) 234
so that 501	**The boys greeted each other . . .** *nothing had happened.* Underline the clause signal you would use to explain **how** the boys greeted each other: **unless as if although so that** 502
Whomever 769	*Whomever the country elects* **will face serious problems.** *Whomever* is correct because it is the (*subject, object*) of the verb *elects* within the clause. 770
joining the club, 1037	Here is an adjective clause, too, that can be reduced in the same way: *We have a plan* **that would improve the bus service.** Supply a gerund phrase as the object of the preposition *for:* **We have a plan** *for* _____ _____. 1038
S F 1305	Write an *S* (for *Sentence*) or an *F* (for *Fragment*) for each of the two word groups: **Thinking that the gun was empty. He jokingly pointed it at his friend.** _____ _____ 1306
Because (Since, As) we saw a large crowd around the car, 1573	**While writing my summary of** *Macbeth,* **my baby sister kept interrupting me.** _____ _____, **my baby sister kept interrupting me.** 1574

it would do 1841	The dashboard on the inside of the car has also been improved. (3) 1842
shrank, shrunk 2108	All of us _____ more cider than we should have _____. (*drink*) 2109
discusses 2375	neighborly fatherly scholarly lovely Since these adjectives already end in -*ly*, can we make adverbs of them by adding another -*ly*? (*Yes, No*) 2376
him (her) 2642	Don't judge a person entirely by _____ clothes. 2643
leathery⊙ 2909	To tell the truth, I tried to be friendly, but Bob didn't respond. 2910
High School, World, French, Christmas, December 3176	Our pastor told about the four chaplains of the catholic, jewish, and protestant faiths who went down with linked arms when their ship was sunk by the germans in world war II. _____ 3177

three 234	Lesson **7** The Prepositional Phrase as a Modifier [Frames 236–277]
as if 502	**Bob studies at night . . .** *he completes his work in the afternoon.* Underline the clause signal you would use to explain **on what condition** Bob studies at night: **until** **whenever** **because** **unless** 503
object 770	Underline the correct word: **I have great admiration for** (*whoever, whomever*) **wrote this article.** 771
improving the bus service. 1038	**The French class has a new tape recorder** *on which they listen to their pronunciation.* Change the adjective clause to a prepositional phrase with a gerund: **The French class has a new tape recorder** _____ _____ *to their pronunciation.* 1039
F S 1306	Write an *S* (for *Sentence*) or an *F* (for *Fragment*) for each of the two word groups: **Although the dog is friendly to the family. It is very unfriendly to others.** _____ _____ 1307
While (As, When) I was writing my summary of *Macbeth,* 1574	From here on, correct each sentence by answering the question **Who?** or **What?** at the beginning of the main statement. Make no change in the introductory word group. **Having studied hard, my test score disappointed me.** **Having studied hard,** _____ _____. 1575

on the inside 1842	She weighed the meat on a scale in order to see if she had been cheated. (5) 1843
drank, drunk 2109	We _____ where we had never _____ before. (*swim*) 2110
No 2376	lovely neighborly fatherly scholarly To make adverbial modifiers of these -*ly* adjectives, we must put them in prepositional phrases that can modify verbs: for example, **in a fatherly way, in an orderly manner.** **Mr. Haines discusses literature** *in a scholarly manner.* The italicized phrase modifies the verb _____. 2377
his (her) 2643	Once a customer has worn a dress,_____ cannot return it. 2644
Correct 2910	When we hit the wet, and slippery pavement, our car skidded badly. 2911
Catholic, Jewish, Protestant, Germans, World War 3177	The zinnias bloom in august, but the asters do not bloom until fall. 3178

The picture ... the desk is amusing.

Is the **picture** *on, in, near, over,* or *behind* the **desk?** We need a word to show the *relationship* between the noun **desk** and the noun _____ .

236

---

unless

503

Mark applied for the job ... *he read the advertisement in the newspaper.*

Underline the clause signal you would use to explain **when** Mark applied for the job:

because　　**as soon as**　　**although**　　**where**

504

---

whoever

771

Underline the correct word:

Scholars have argued about (*who, whom*) **wrote Shakespeare's plays.**

772

---

for listening

1039

A prepositional phrase can sometimes be replaced by a single adjective or adverb.

The cashier looked at the check *in a suspicious way.*

Substitute an adverb for the italicized prepositional phrase:

The cashier looked at the check_____ .

1040

F S

1307

Thoreau took to the woods. To discover how simply a person could live. _____ _____

1308

I was disappointed in my test score.

1575

When inflated with air, six people can be carried on this raft.

When inflated with air, _____

_____ .

1576

on a scale in order 1843	After the time that our family moved to Argyle, I did not see Uncle John very frequently from then on. (6) 1844
swam, swum 2110	The game had already _____ when it _____ to rain. (*begin*) 2111
discusses 2377	WRONG: **Mr. Dale spoke to Earl** *fatherly.* This sentence is wrong because the adjective *fatherly* cannot modify the verb **spoke**. Supply a prepositional phrase that will include the adjective *fatherly:* **Mr. Dale spoke to Earl** _____. 2378
she 2644	The graduate should choose a college that is outstanding in the field of _____ choice. 2645
wet⊙ 2911	The Springfield Electric Company, which employs many young people, will not hire any boy or girl, who has not completed high school. 2912
August 3178	Lesson **89** Review: The Principles of Graphics [Frames 3180–3208] *page 472*

picture 236	The picture ⏜ on the desk is amusing. The word that now shows the relationship between **desk** and **picture** is _____. 237

as soon as
 	
504
	Our guide tied the canoe to a tree . . . *it would not drift away.*
	Underline the clause signal you would use to explain **why** the guide tied the canoe to a tree:
	
	      as if **where** **since** **so that**
	      505

who 772	Underline the correct word: **The jury could not decide** (*who, whom*) **they could believe.** 773
suspiciously. 1040	**You can buy a film at the store** *on the corner.* Substitute an adjective for the italicized prepositional phrase: **You can buy a film at the** _____ **store.** 1041
S F 1308	**Situated at the southern tip of Florida, Everglades Park is a vast wilderness of plants, birds, and animals.** ____ ____ 1309
this raft can arry six people. 1576	**Reaching for the sugar, the cream pitcher was overturned by my dad.** **Reaching for the sugar,** _____ _____. 1577

the time that, from then on 1844	Shirley had unusual self-confidence in herself when she went shopping to buy something for herself or someone else. (5) 1845
begun, began 2111	The chorus ＿＿＿＿＿＿＿ the same numbers that they had ＿＿＿＿＿＿＿ at their spring concert. (*sing*) 2112
in a fatherly way (manner). 2378	Correct the following sentence: Mr. Cornelius, our grocer, treats all his customers very *neighborly*. Mr. Cornelius, our grocer, treats all his customers ＿＿＿＿＿＿＿ ＿＿＿＿＿＿＿＿＿＿＿＿＿＿＿＿＿＿. 2379
his (her) 2645	Lesson **74** Pronouns That Mean One [Frames 2647–2685]
girl⊙ 2912	Don't yawn, or look at your watch, when you are entertaining guests. 2913
	a. Bert pulled over to the side of the road, and the oil truck passed him. b. Bert pulled over to the side of the road, and let the oil truck pass. Omit the comma in sentence (*a, b*). 3180

on 237	**Jerry strolled . . . the park.** Did Jerry stroll *through, past, around,* or *toward* the park? We need a word to show the *relationship* between the noun **park** and the verb _____. 238
so that 505	**Mr. Hart put in a pinch of grass seed . . .** *he pulled out a weed.* Underline the clause signal you would use to explain **where** Mr. Hart put in grass seed: **after so that if wherever** 506
whom 773	Underline the correct word: **The jury could not decide (***who, whom***) was telling the truth.** 774
corner 1041	In this and the following frames, reduce each italicized word group to the construction indicated in parentheses: **The author** *who wrote this story* **knows a lot about sports.** (prepositional phrase) **The author** _____ **knows a lot about** **sports.** 1042
F S 1309	**I have more than two thousand stamps. All of which are** **different.** _____ _____ 1310
my dad overturned the cream pitcher. 1577	**Rolled very thin, you can make five dozen cookies from this batter.** **Rolled very thin,** _____ _____. 1578

in herself, to buy something 1845	**Of all the hunter's articles of equipment that he uses, his rifle is the most important to him. (7)** 1846
sang, sung 2112	The ship _____ where several other ships had _____ before. (*sink*) 2113
in a very neighborly way (manner). 2379	Do not use **kind of** and **sort of** as adverbial modifiers meaning **rather** or **somewhat** except in relaxed conversation. They are out of place in formal writing or speaking. a. **I felt** *kind of* **embarrassed about my mistake.** b. **The public is** *kind of* **dubious about campaign promises.** In which sentence is *kind of* inappropriate? _____ 2380
	The pronouns **everyone** and **everybody** are peculiar words. They are often singular and plural at the same time. They are singular in form because they are built upon the words **one** and **body,** which are (*singular, plural*). 2647
yawn⊙ watch⊙ 2913	## Lesson 82 How to Use Semicolons, Colons, and Dashes [Frames 2915–2955]
b 3180	You may omit the comma and the conjunction in a compound sentence and replace them with a _____. 3181

Jerry strolled *through* **the park.**

The word that now shows the relationship between **park** and **strolled** is _____.

Fear is good . . . *it leads you to protect yourself.*

Underline the clause signal you would use to explain **under what condition** fear is good:

though   **if**   **because**   **unless**

Underline the correct word:

(*Who, Whom*) **contributed this money is a deep and dark secret.** •

The employee must state the reason *why he was absent.*
(prepositional phrase)

The employee must state the reason _____

_____ .

Many college students help to pay their expenses. By doing odd jobs in their spare time. ____ ____

---

this batter will
can) make five
dozen cookies.

1578

While waiting for a bus, a passing car splashed me.

While waiting for a bus, _____

_____ .

articles of, that he uses, to him 1846	The reporter spent a week in the town of Belding in order to observe the differences that exist between city life and small-town life. (7) 1847
sank, sunk 2113	The five common irregular verbs that follow often cause errors that give the impression of uneducated speech. PRESENT PAST PAST PARTICIPLE **do** **did** (not **done**) **(have) done** Fill in the correct forms of **do**: I _____ what anyone else would have _____. 2114
b 2380	In more formal speech and writing, use the adverb **rather** or **somewhat** instead of **kind of** or **sort of**. Correct the following sentence: **The public is** *kind of* **dubious about campaign promises.** **The public is** _____ **dubious about campaign promises.** 2381
singular 2647	**Everyone** *is* **ready.** **Everybody** *was* **impatient.** Do the pronouns **Everyone** and **Everybody** take singular or plural verbs? _____ 2648
   2915	SEMICOLONS **His car was out of gas, and mine had two flat tires.** This is a compound sentence. Its two main clauses are connected by the conjunction _____. 2915
semicolon 3181	*Fortunately* **the tornado missed our town.** *Occasionally* **Mr. Baxter forgot to give an assignment.** Putting commas after the italicized adverbs would give them (*more, less*) emphasis. 3182

through 239	A word that shows the relationship of the noun or pronoun that follows it to some other word in the sentence is called a **preposition.** A preposition shows _____ship. 240
if 507	See how simple it is to combine two sentences by using an adverb clause. **As** ∧ *The man came closer.* **I noticed a scar on his cheek.** We change the italicized sentence to an adverb clause by adding the subordinating conjunction **As.** Then we change the period after the first sentence to a _____. 508
Who 775	Underline the correct word: **The newspaper would not reveal (***who, whom***) their informant was.** 776
or his absence. 1043	**The article offers many suggestions** *that are practical.* (adjective) **The article offers many** _____ **suggestions.** 1044
S F 1311	**Lesson 36 Other Types of Sentence Fragments** [Frames 1313–1350]
was splashed by a passing car. 1579	**By sitting around and talking, our work will never get done.** **By sitting around and talking,** _____ _____. 1580

the town of, in order, that exist 1847	When he had his examination, it showed that he needed dental work to be done in his mouth by a dentist. (13) 1848
did, done 2114	PRESENT PAST PAST PARTICIPLE go went (have) gone (not *went*) Fill in the correct forms of **go**: Joan _____ to say good-by to Iris, but Iris had already _____. 2115
rather *or* somewhat 2381	a. **It made us *sort of* sad to leave the old farm.** b. **Jefferson was *sort of* fearful of centralized government.** In which sentence is *sort of* inappropriate? _____ 2382
singular 2648	**Everyone *is* ready. Everybody *was* impatient.** Although **everyone** and **everybody** are singular in form and always take singular verbs, we think of them as meaning a number of persons, rather than a single person. Although **everyone** and **everybody** are *singular* in form, they are somewhat _____ in meaning. 2649
and 2915	A semicolon may be used in place of the conjunction **and, but,** or **or** to connect the main clauses in a compound sentence. **His car was out of gas; mine had two flat tires.** The two main clauses of this compound sentence are not connected by a conjunction but by a _____. 2916
more 3182	a. *For the first time in many years* **we won every game of the season.** b. *For the first time* **we won every game of the season.** A comma would more commonly be used in sentence (*a, b*). 3183

relationship 240	Many prepositions show relationships in **position.** POSITION: *in, on, by, under, below, beneath, above, over,* *beside, behind, across, against,* etc. Underline the preposition that shows position: **box of crackers** **man from Mars** **car behind us** 241
comma 508	a. **The man came closer. I noticed a scar on his cheek.** b. *As the man came closer,* **I noticed a scar on his cheek.** We have combined the two sentences by making a (*com-pound, complex*) sentence. 509
who 776	Underline the correct word: **The orchestra extends an invitation to** (*whoever, whomever*) **can play a musical instrument.** 777
practical 1044	**People** *who are irritable* **do not make good clerks.** (adjective) _____ **people do not make good clerks.** 1045
	Don't let an appositive phrase become a fragment. WRONG: **The home run was hit by Kent.** *The first man at* *bat.* *"The first man at bat"* is an appositive phrase. Does the appositive phrase have a subject and a verb? (*Yes, No*) 1313
we will never get our work done. *or* we will never finish our work. 1580	Lesson **44** **Parallel Construction** **for Parallel Ideas** [Frames 1582–1612]

When he had, it, to be done in his mouth by a dentist 1848	**My handicap that I have is in not being able to pronounce the sound of new words that I am not familiar with. (13)** 1849
went, gone 2115	PRESENT PAST PAST PARTICIPLE **run** **ran** **(have) run** Fill in the correct forms of **run:** **Curtis** _____ **for the same office for which his** **father had** _____**.** 2116
b 2382	Correct the following sentence: **Jefferson was** *sort of* **fearful of centralized government.** **Jefferson was** _____ **fearful of centralized government.** 2383
plural 2649	**everyone** **everybody** Shall we use singular pronouns to refer to these words because of their singular form, or shall we use plural pronouns because of their plural meaning? Those who consider form more important than meaning would use (*singular, plural*) pronouns. 2650
semicolon 2916	**I tried to explain; he was too angry to listen.** In this compound sentence the semicolon takes the place of the conjunction (*and, but*). 2917
a 3183	a. **Before we bought our new car, we got prices from several dealers.** b. **We got prices from several dealers, before we bought our new car.** Omit the comma in sentence (*a, b*). 3184

behind 241	Some prepositions show **direction.** DIRECTION: *to, from, toward, down, up, at* **The rock rolled down the mountain.** The preposition **down** shows the _____ in which the rock rolled. 242
complex 509	**The man came closer, and I noticed a scar on his cheek.** *As the man came closer,* **I noticed a scar on his cheek.** The relationship between the two facts is brought out more clearly by the (*compound, complex*) sentence. 510
whoever 777	Underline the correct word: **Lincoln had a kind word for** (*whoever, whomever*) **he met.** 778
Irritable 1045	**These toys were made of materials** *which had been discarded.* (past participle) **These toys were made of** _____ **materials.** 1046
No 1313	**The home run was hit by Kent.** *The first man at bat.* Does the appositive phrase make sense by itself? (*Yes, No*) 1314
	When you dress in the morning, you may select any shoes you please as long as they make a matching pair. Similarly, when you express two or more similar ideas, you may use any type of word group you wish as long as they (*match, differ*). 1582

that I have, in, the sound of, that I am not familiar with 1849	In the remaining frames, rewrite each sentence to express the idea more directly. (If your answer differs from that in the key, count your answer right if you have eliminated useless words.) **The meal that I receive the most enjoyment out of is break-** **fast.** _____ 1850
ran, run 2116	PRESENT PAST PAST PARTICIPLE **come** **came** (not **come**) **(have) come** Fill in the correct forms of **come**: **Earl** _____ **home an hour ago, but Allen hasn't** _____ **home yet.** 2117
rather *or* somewhat 2383	In this and the following frames, underline the correct modifier or, in some cases, the word appropriate for formal usage: **Clarence types fast but not very** (*accurate, accurately*). 2384
singular 2650	**Nearly everyone** *likes* **to see** *his* **name in print.** In this sentence, both the verb and the pronoun that refers to **everyone** are (*singular, plural*). 2651

but
 	
2917
	A semicolon can also take the place of the clause signal **because** in a complex sentence.
	    a. **The bird couldn't fly; its wing was broken.**
	    b. **The streets were icy; traffic moved slowly.**
	In which sentence does the semicolon take the place of the clause signal **because?** ____
	2918

b 3184	a. **While we discuss the teacher sits among the class and listens.** b. **While we eat we often watch television.** To avoid misunderstanding, it would be advisable to use a comma after the short introductory clause in sentence (*a, b*). 3185

direction
 	
242
	A few prepositions show relationships in **time.**
	TIME: *before, during, after, until, till*
	    a. **Brush your teeth . . . meals.**
	    b. **Park your car . . . the corner.**
	Which sentence requires a preposition that will show a *time* relationship? _____
	
	243

complex 510	Combine each pair of sentences by changing the italicized sentence to an adverb clause. Write the full sentence, keeping the ideas in the same order. *Veal is not my favorite meat.* **I sometimes eat it.** _____ _____ 511
whomever 778	Underline the correct word: (*Whoever, Whomever*) **wrote this courageous editorial deserves a lot of admiration.** 779
discarded 1046	**I was kept awake by the faucet** *that was dripping.* (present participle) **I was kept awake by the** _____ **faucet.** 1047
No 1314	**The home run was hit by Kent,** *the first man at bat.* Now the appositive phrase makes sense because it is in the same sentence with the noun _____, which it explains. 1315
match 1582	The principle of expressing similar ideas in a similar or parallel way is known as **parallel construction.** This principle means that if you put one idea into a prepositional phrase, you should also put a parallel idea into (*a prepositional phrase, an adverb clause*). 1583

I enjoy (my) breakfast most. 1850	**Judy started going with another boy, and this boy that she started going with was very popular.** _____ _____ 1851
came, come 2117		PRESENT	PAST	PAST PARTICIPLE
---	---	---
come	**came**	**(have) come**
run	**ran**	**(have) run**	 To avoid a very common error, notice that **come** and **run** are two-part, not one-part, verbs. The form that is different from the other two is the _____ form. 2118
accurately 2384	**Ron** (*sure, surely*) **understood that I needed this money** (*badly, bad*). 2385
singular 2651	When the pronoun that refers to **everyone** or **everybody** is possessive (*his, her*), the singular pronoun sounds sensible and is preferred in formal writing and speaking. Underline the pronoun preferred in formal usage: *Everybody* **has the right to state** (*his, their*) **mind.** 2652
a 2918	A comma by itself cannot connect two main clauses. Only a semicolon has the power to hold main clauses together without the help of the conjunction **and, but,** or **or.** a. **I shook the branches, the apples came tumbling down.** b. **I shook the branches; the apples came tumbling down.** Which sentence is correct? _____ 2919
a 3185	**When people are at home, do they strew papers, tin cans, and bottles, around their yards?** Omit the comma after the word _____. 3186

a
 	
243
	Still other prepositions, such as *of, for, about, with, except,* and *but* (when it means *except*), show many different kinds of relationships between the words they relate.
	
	EXAMPLES: **a pound <u>of</u> tea** **a story <u>about</u> war**
	                a letter <u>for</u> me **a cake <u>with</u> frosting**
	
	Each of the underlined words is a _____.
	
	                                                                      244

Although veal is not my favorite meat, I sometimes eat it.
 	
511
	Follow the directions given in the previous frame:
	
	    Skippy hid under the sofa. *He was afraid of the storm.*
	
	_____
	
	_____
	
	                                                                      512

Whoever 779	In conversational English, **who** and **whoever** are often used in place of the object forms. In formal speech or writing, however, **whom** and **whomever** are the correct object forms. a. INFORMAL: **I wonder ... Peggy will invite.** b. FORMAL: **The public wonders ... the mayor will blame.** The pronoun **who** would be considered an error in (*a, b*). 780
dripping 1047	**Julie Monahan,** *who is the main character,* **is an unusual girl.** (appositive phrase) **Julie Monahan,** _____**, is an unusual girl.** 1048
Kent 1315	a. **The home run was hit by Kent. He was the first man at bat.** b. **The home run was hit by Kent. The first man at bat.** c. **The home run was hit by Kent, the first man at bat.** Which one of the above three arrangements is incorrect— *a, b,* or *c?* _____ 1316
a prepositional phrase 1583	If you put one idea into an infinitive phrase, you should also put a parallel idea into (*a participial, an infinitive*) phrase. 1584

Judy started going with another boy who was very popular. 1851	**The reason that I got up early was that I had work that needed to be done.** _____ _____ 1852

past
 	
2118
	PRESENT PAST PAST PARTICIPLE
	  come **came** **(have) come**
	  run **ran** **(have) run**
	
	The past forms of **come** and **run** are _____ and
	
	_____. 2119

surely, badly 2385	**No teacher could have been more** (_patient, patiently_) **than Mr. Thomas.** 2386
his 2652	Though we hear the plural pronoun _their_ widely used to refer to **everyone** and **everybody** in informal English, it is likely to be criticized in formal writing or speaking. **Has** _everybody_ **turned in** _their_ **paper?** This sentence is acceptable as (_informal, formal_) usage. 2653
b 2919	When there are other commas in a compound sentence, the important comma that breaks the sentence into two parts gets lost among the others. **My Cousin Tom was popular, good-looking, and athletic, and, to tell the truth, I was a little jealous of him.** The _compound sentence_ comma follows the word _____. 2920
bottles 3186	**An old sailor and his dog and his cat lived in this small weather-beaten shack.** One comma is required after the word _____. 3187

<table>
<tr>
<td>

preposition

244
</td>
<td>

The noun or pronoun that follows a preposition is called its **object**.

The man in the next seat was a doctor.

The preposition is **in;** the object of the preposition is the noun _____.

245
</td>
</tr>
<tr>
<td>

Skippy hid under the sofa because (since, as) he was afraid of the storm.

512
</td>
<td>

You are the oldest. **It was your responsibility.**

_____

_____

(_Note:_ Count your sentence right if it makes good sense, even if you did not use the same clause signal given in the answer.)

513
</td>
</tr>
<tr>
<td>

b

780
</td>
<td>

a. **The Senate is likely to approve . . . the President appoints.**
b. **You can vote for . . . you want.**

In which sentence would **whoever** be more acceptable as conversational usage? _____

781
</td>
</tr>
<tr>
<td>

the main character

1048
</td>
<td>

Steve's General Store, _which is the only store in the village,_ **sells everything from lollipops to washing machines.** (appositive phrase)

Steve's General Store, _____

_____, **sells everything from lollipops to washing machines.**

1049
</td>
</tr>
<tr>
<td>

b

1316
</td>
<td>

Now look at another cause of sentence fragments—the sentence with a compound predicate.

We climbed the tower and looked at the scenery.

The above sentence has a compound predicate that makes (_one, two_) statement(s) about the subject **We** in the first word group.

1317
</td>
</tr>
<tr>
<td>

an infinitive

1584
</td>
<td>

Bert's dad promised _to buy a new car._

In the above sentence, what Bert's dad promised is expressed in an (_infinitive phrase, adverb clause_).

1585
</td>
</tr>
</table>

I got up early because I had work to do. 1852	I sent a defective pen to you approximately a month or so ago to have a repair job done on it for me. _____ _____ 1853
came, ran 2119	Notice the similarity between **come** and **become**: PRESENT PAST PAST PARTICIPLE **come** **came** **(have) come** **become** **became** **(have) become** Fill in the correct forms of **become**: **Howard** _____ **a draftsman although he could** **have** _____ **an engineer.** _____ 2120
patient 2386	**In those days people lived** (*simpler, more simply*) **than they do today.** 2387
informal 2653	a. *Everyone* **should wash** *their* **hands before touching food.** b. *Everyone* **should wash** *his* **hands before touching food.** Which sentence would be more acceptable in formal speech or writing? _____ 2654
athletic 2920	When other commas are present, it is a good idea to change the *compound sentence* comma to a semicolon. **My Cousin Tom was popular, good-looking, and athletic; and, to tell the truth, I was a little jealous of him.** Using a semicolon instead of a comma after **athletic** makes the break in the sentence (*more, less*) conspicuous. 2921
small 3187	**Louis Bleriot, a French aviator, flew across the English Channel, on July 25, 1909.** Omit the comma after the word _____. 3188

<table>
<tr>
<td>

seat

245
</td>
<td>

A group of words that begins with a preposition and ends with its object is a **prepositional phrase.**

The cause of this sudden explosion remains a mystery.

The prepositional phrase begins with the preposition **of** and ends with its object _____.

246
</td>
</tr>
<tr>
<td>

Since you are the oldest, it was your responsibility.

513
</td>
<td>

Mr. Doyle decided to buy our car. *We had already sold it.*

_____

_____

514
</td>
</tr>
<tr>
<td>

b

781
</td>
<td>

UNIT 4: OTHER DEVICES OF SUBORDINATION

Lesson **21** **Subordination by Present Participles**

[Frames 783–822]
</td>
</tr>
<tr>
<td>

the only store in the village

1049
</td>
<td>

After he had saved all this money, **Brooks lost it.** (prepositional phrase with gerund)

_____, **Brooks lost it.**

1050
</td>
</tr>
<tr>
<td>

two

1317
</td>
<td>

A careless writer sometimes creates a fragment by cutting off the last part of a compound predicate.

WRONG: **We climbed the tower.** *And looked at the scenery.*

The italicized word group lacks a (*subject, verb*).

1318
</td>
</tr>
<tr>
<td>

infinitive phrase

1585
</td>
<td>

Bert's dad promised *to buy a new car.*

To buy a new car is an infinitive phrase.

If you wanted to state a second promise that Bert's dad made, it would be better, for the sake of parallel construction, to use an (*adverb clause, infinitive phrase*).

1586
</td>
</tr>
</table>

I sent you a pen approximately a month ago for repair. 1853	**The reason for my having been absent is that my chemistry class visited a factory where they make glass.** _____ _____ 1854
became, become 2120	In this and the following frames, supply the correct forms of the verbs in parentheses. Be sure to use the past participle after any form of **have** or **be.** Several verbs following the **ring-rang-rung** pattern. **Miss Doyle had** _____ (_go_) **to the office to see why the bell had been** _____ (_ring_). 2121
more simply 2387	**It was** (_rather, kind of_) **surprising that the public accepted the news so** (_calm, calmly_). 2388
b 2654	So far we have been dealing with the possessive pronoun _his_. The situation is somewhat different when we use the nominative pronoun _he_ or _she_ or the _____ pronoun _him_ or _her_. 2655
more 2921	**The mature reader enjoys a novel for its ideas, its portrayal of character, and its literary style, but the youthful reader, generally speaking, looks for excitement, suspense, and sudden surprises.** To make the sentence break more conspicuous, substitute a semicolon for the comma after the word _____. 2922
Channel 3188	A _restrictive_ clause is essential to the meaning of a sentence. A _nonrestrictive_ clause merely adds a fact that is unessential to the meaning of a sentence. The clause that should be set off with commas from the rest of the sentence is the (_restrictive, nonrestrictive_) clause. 3189

explosion
 	
246
	We need prepositional phrases to express meanings that cannot be expressed by a single adjective or adverb.
	
	    a glass *for water* **a** *water* **glass**
	    a glass *for milk* **a** *milky* **glass**
	
	Which adjective is not the equivalent of the corresponding prepositional phrase—*water* or *milky*? _____ 247

Mr. Doyle decided to buy our car after we had already sold it. 514	*Peaches are plentiful.* **They are very poor.** 515
	In this unit we study other useful devices for subordination that will help us to write more mature sentences. When we subordinate a fact or an idea, we express it in a word group that is (*more, less*) than a sentence. 783
After saving all this money, 1050	*If you will make notes of important facts,* **you will make reviewing easier.** (prepositional phrase with gerund) _____ _____, **you will make reviewing easier.** 1051
subject 1318	**We climbed the tower.** *And looked at the scenery.* "*And looked at the scenery*" is a predicate that makes a statement about the subject _____ of the first word group. 1319
infinitive phrase 1586	a. **My dad promised** *to buy a new car* **and** *that he would let me drive it.* b. **My dad promised** *to buy a new car* **and** *to let me drive it.* In which sentence are the italicized word groups parallel? ——— 1587

I was absent
because my
chemistry class
visited a glass
factory.
1854

Lesson 52

Review: Problems of Sentence Construction

[Frames 1856–1876]

---

gone, rung

Sally quickly _____ (*do*) **the dishes and** _____ (*run*) **up to her room.**

2121

2122

---

rather, calmly

In spite of the customer's bad manners, the salesman conducted himself (*gentlemanly, in a gentlemanly manner*).

2388

2389

---

objective

When the pronoun that refers to **everyone** or **everybody** is nominative (*he, she*) or objective (*him, her*), we are often forced to use the plural pronoun *their* (or *them*) to prevent absurdity.

> *Everybody* **had warned me, but I didn't believe** *him.*

Does the singular pronoun *him* make good sense in this sentence? (*Yes, No*)

2655

2656

---

style

COLONS

A colon says to the reader, "Look ahead. Here it comes." and directs his attention to what follows.

> a. **I am taking five courses.**
> b. **I am taking five courses:**

You expect the courses to be listed after (*a, b*).

2922

2923

---

nonrestrictive

a. **The Presidents** *who accomplished most* **were the most severely criticized.**
b. **My father** *who used to be a track star* **gave me valuable advice.**

The italicized clause should be set off with commas in sentence (*a, b*).

3189

3190

milky 247	**We walked** *with care.* **We walked** *carefully.* **We traveled** *by train.* **We traveled** *trainly.* The adverb *carefully* can be substituted for the prepositional phrase *with care.* Is there a proper adverb that can take the place of the phrase *by train?* (*Yes, No*) 248
Although peaches are plentiful, they are very poor. 515	In this and the following frames, convert each *compound* sentence to a *complex* sentence by changing the italicized statement to an adverb clause: *I opened the cabinet,* **and a jar fell out.** _____ _____ 516
less 783	Prepositional phrases and adverb, adjective, and noun clauses are **subordinate** word groups because they (*do, do not*) make complete sense apart from a sentence. 784
By making notes of important facts, 1051	**There seemed to be no way** *in which we could reduce our expenses.* (prepositional phrase with gerund) **There seemed to be no way** _____ _____. 1052
We 1319	**We climbed the tower and looked at the scenery.** This sentence is right because a predicate belongs in the same sentence with its _____. 1320
b 1587	**The company wants a driver** *who knows the city.* In the above sentence the qualification for the driver is expressed in (*a prepositional phrase, an adjective clause*). 1588

Here is a letter written by a father to his son's camp coun-
selors at Camp Michiwaki. Each sentence contains one of
the errors studied in this unit. At the top of each frame,
circle the letter of the error found in that frame. Then revise
the sentence correctly.   (*Turn to the next frame.*)

1856

---

did, ran

2122

Water _____ (*become*) **a serious problem after**

the well had _____ (*run*) **dry.**

2123

---

in a gentlemanly
manner

2389

Some of the umpire's decisions (*sure, certainly*) **seemed**
(*unfair, unfairly*) **to most of the fans.**

2390

No

2656

a. **We hope** *everyone* **will attend, but** *he* **never does.**
b. **We hope** *everyone* **will bring** *his* **parents to the meeting.**

In both sentences, a singular pronoun is used, according to
rule, to refer to *everyone*.

In which sentence does following the rule result in absurdity?

———   2657

---

b

2923

Use a colon (:) before an item or a series of items introduced
by a statement that is grammatically complete.

      a. **My favorite courses are . . .**
      b. **These are my favorite courses . . .**

After which statement would you use a colon because the
statement is grammatically complete? _____

2924

---

b

3190

**The child feared many things; for example, electrical storms
and the dark.**

Instead of using the semicolon, you could use (*a dash,
a period followed by a capital letter*).

3191

No 248	Most prepositional phrases are used as modifiers—either as an adjective or as an adverb. A prepositional phrase which—like an adjective—modifies a noun or pronoun is called an **adjective phrase.** An adjective phrase does the work of an _____. 249
When I opened the cabinet, a jar fell out. 516	Follow the directions given in the previous frame: **Jim insisted on changing the tire, and** *he had on his best suit.* _____ _____ 517
do not 784	**Verbals** are also useful devices for subordination. A **verbal** is a verb that has crossed the boundary line and become another class of word without completely losing its identity as a verb. A word that functions as both a verb and an adjective would be classified as a _____. 785
of reducing our expenses. 1052	**Unfortunately, the family has never been fully responsible** *in financial matters.* (adverb) **Unfortunately, the family has never been fully responsible** _____. 1053
subject 1320	a. **We climbed the tower. We looked at the scenery.** b. **We climbed the tower and looked at the scenery.** c. **We climbed the tower. And looked at the scenery.** Which one of the above three arrangements is incorrect— *a, b,* or *c?* _____ 1321
an adjective clause 1588	**The company wants a driver** *who knows the city.* *Who knows the city* is an adjective clause. If you want to state a second qualification for the driver, it would be better, for the sake of parallel construction, to use (*an adjective clause, a prepositional phrase*). 1589

a. dangling word group   b. faulty pronoun reference
c. faulty comparison

Never having been away from home before, we hope that you will give our son special attention.

_____,
we hope that you will give him special attention.

1857

---

became, run

2123

When my sweater _____ (_come_) **back from the cleaner, I noticed that it had** _____(_shrink_) **a great deal.**

2124

---

certainly, unfair

2390

Three can sit very (_comfortably, comfortable_) **in the front seat.**

2391

---

a

2657

When following the rule does not lead to absurdity, it is better —especially in formal usage—to refer to **everyone** or **everybody** with a (_singular, plural_) pronoun.

2658

---

b

2924

You would not write—
        My favorite course is: math.
So don't make the same mistake by writing—
        My favorite courses are: math, history, and biology.
Colons should not be used after statements that are grammatically (_complete, incomplete_).

2925

---

a dash

3191

We have many aunts, uncles, and cousins, and all, of course, must be invited to the wedding.

To make the main break in this compound sentence more conspicuous, change the comma after the word **cousins** to

a _____.

3192

adjective 249	**the** *corner* **house** Because *corner* modifies the noun **house,** it is an *adjective.* **the house** *on the corner* Because the phrase *on the corner* also modifies the noun **house,** it is an _____ *phrase.* 250
Jim insisted on changing the tire although he had on his best suit. 517	*You wait long enough,* **and everything comes back into style again.** _____ _____ 518
verbal 785	The three kinds of verbals that we study in this unit are all "double-duty" words that have some of the characteristics of both a verb and another class of words—sometimes a noun, sometimes an adverb or an adjective. Look at the word *verbal.* As its name suggests, every verbal is formed from a _____. 786
financially. 1053	**Some children have unusual talent** *in music.* (adjective) **Some children have unusual** _____ **talent.** 1054

c
 	
1321
	A noun-participle (absolute) phrase consists of a noun followed by a present or past participle that modifies it.
	
	    a. **Dripping with rain**
	    b. **His raincoat dripping**
	
	Which item is a noun-participle phrase? _____ 1322

an adjective clause 1589	a. **The company wants a driver** *who knows the city* **and** *who has a good safety record.* b. **The company wants a driver** *who knows the city* **and** *with a good safety record.* In which sentence are the italicized word groups parallel? _____ 1590

a Since (Because, As) our son has never been away from home before, 1857	a. misplaced modifier b. nonparallel construction c. incorrect omission of words **We will telephone daily to inquire whether he is happy, comfortable, and his health is good.** **We will telephone daily to inquire whether he is** _____ _____ . 1858
came, shrunk 2124	**We had** _____ (*sing*) **only a few songs when the** **lights** _____ (*begin*) **to flicker.** 2125
comfortably 2391	**It was** (*somewhat, sort of*) **surprising that the strike should end as** (*sudden, suddenly*) **as it began.** 2392
singular 2658	Underline the pronoun that would be more appropriate in formal writing and speaking: **Under a democracy, everybody has the right to express** (*his, their*) **opinions.** 2659
incomplete 2925	The statements that require colons often contain the words *following, as follows, these,* or *there are.* a. **The ingredients of waffles are: flour, milk, eggs. . . .** b. **Waffles contain the following ingredients: flour, milk, eggs. . . .** The colon is used correctly in sentence (*a, b*). 2926
semicolon 3192	a. **The three basic rights mentioned in the Declaration of Independence are: life, liberty, and the pursuit of happiness.** b. **The Declaration of Independence mentions three human rights: life, liberty, and the pursuit of happiness.** The colon is correctly used in sentence (*a, b*). 3193

adjective 250	**the** *corner* **house** **the house** *on the corner* The *adjective* comes before the noun it modifies. The *adjective phrase* comes (*before, after*) the noun it modifies. 251
If you wait long enough, everything comes back into style again. 518	**I'll set the alarm, and** *I'll be sure to get up early.* _____ _____ 519
verb 786	**a** *cold* **wind** Because the word *cold* modifies the noun **wind**, it is an _____. 787
musical 1054	**Mr. Hollis listens** *in a patient way* **to all complaints.** (adverb) **Mr. Hollis listens** _____ **to all complaints.** 1055
b 1322	A noun-participle phrase is often mistaken for a complete sentence. a. **His raincoat** dripped. b. **His raincoat** *dripping.* Which item is a complete sentence? _____ 1323
a 1590	a. **It was cruel** *to catch the bird* **and** *keeping it in a cage.* b. **It was cruel** *to catch the bird* **and** *to keep it in a cage.* Which sentence is better? _____ 1591

b
 	
happy,
comfortable,
and healthy.
 	
1858
	a. misplaced modifier b. *is when* or *is where* error
	         c. incorrect omission of words
	Do not force him to eat salad, which he never has and never will eat.
	Do not force him to eat salad, _____
	_____ .
	                                                    1859

sung, began 2125	**The bone had** _____ (*spring*) **back into place** **before the doctor** _____ (*come*). 2126
somewhat, suddenly 2392	**Lesson 67 Choosing Modifiers After *Sense* Verbs** [Frames 2394–2430]
his 2659	anyone anybody each someone somebody each one no one nobody either Can these pronouns mean either a boy or a girl, a man or a woman? (*Yes, No*) 2660
b 2926	a. **These are the primary colors: red, blue, yellow.** b. **The primary colors are as follows: red, blue, yellow.** c. **The primary colors are: red, blue, yellow.** d. **The following are the primary colors: red, blue, yellow.** In which sentence is the colon incorrect because it does not follow a grammatically complete statement? _____ 2927
b 3193	**Many of Bach's relatives,** *brothers, uncles, and cousins,* **were also musicians.** To make it clear that the italicized nouns are used as appositives, change the commas after **relatives** and *cousins* to (*semicolons, colons, dashes*). 3194

<table>
<tr>
<td>after

251</td>
<td>Adjective phrases—just like adjectives—are often used after linking verbs as subject complements.

    a. **The lilacs are beautiful.**
    b. **The lilacs are in full bloom.**

In which sentence is an adjective phrase used as a subject complement? _____

252</td>
</tr>
<tr>
<td>I'll set the alarm so that I'll be sure to get up early.

519</td>
<td>*Sally smells roses,* **and she begins to sneeze.**

_____

_____

520</td>
</tr>
<tr>
<td>adjective

787</td>
<td>**a *stinging* wind**

Because the word *stinging* modifies the noun **wind,** it is also an _____.

788</td>
</tr>
<tr>
<td>patiently

1055</td>
<td>**Remember not to leave things such as mops and pails on the stairs** *to the basement.* (adjective)

Remember not to leave things such as mops and pails on the _____ **stairs.**

1056</td>
</tr>
<tr>
<td>a

1323</td>
<td>   a. **His raincoat** *dripped.*
    b. **His raincoat** *dripping.*

Which item is *not* a sentence because it contains a present participle rather than a verb? _____

1324</td>
</tr>
<tr>
<td>b

1591</td>
<td>   a. **Ammonia is used** *for softening water* **and** *for dissolving grease.*
    b. **Ammonia is used** *for softening water* **and** *to dissolve grease.*

Which sentence is better? _____

1592</td>
</tr>
</table>

c which he never has eaten and never will eat. 1859	a. misplaced modifier b. nonparallel construction c. faulty pronoun reference **Also, if there is any skin on chicken, he will refuse to eat it.** **Also, he will refuse** _____ _____ 1860
sprung, came 2126	**The *Titanic* had** _____ (*run*) **into an iceberg and** **had** _____ (*sink*). 2127

	look smell taste feel hear (sound)
	These verbs that relate to our senses have two different meanings. One requires an adverb, the other an adjective.
	    a. **Joey *looked* at the cake.**
	    b. **The cake *looked* delicious.**
	Looked means an action of the eyes in sentence (*a, b*).
	
	2394

Yes 2660	Although a pronoun such as **anyone, anybody, someone, somebody** can mean either sex, we can use the masculine pronoun *his, he,* or *him* to refer to such pronouns. *Anyone* **who never changes** *his* **mind has stopped learning.** Does this statement, as it is worded, apply to either sex? (*Yes, No*) 2661
c 2927	a. **The rent includes the following items: gas, electricity, and water.** b. **The rent includes: gas, electricity, and water.** In which sentence is the colon used correctly? _____ 2928
dashes 3194	**Dad predicted that I would change my mind, and I did.** To make the end of this sentence more forceful, change the comma to a _____. 3195

b 252	Each of these sentences contains a linking verb: a. **The plane was on time.** c. **The crops were dry.** b. **The piano seems in tune.** d. **The ring is of no value.** In which sentence is the linking verb *not* followed by an adjective phrase used as a subject complement? _____ 253
Whenever (*or* when) Sally smells roses, she begins to sneeze. 520	Lesson **14** Understanding Adjective Clauses [Frames 522–561]
adjective 788	**a** *cold, stinging* **wind** Which adjective was formed from a verb—*cold* or *stinging*? _____. 789
basement 1056	a. *There are curtains in the kitchen.* **They need washing.** b. **The curtains** *that are in the kitchen* **need washing.** c. **The curtains** *hanging in the kitchen* **need washing.** d. **The curtains** *in the kitchen* **need washing.** e. **The** *kitchen* **curtains need washing.** Which sentence states the idea in the fewest words? _____ 1057
b 1324	**His raincoat** *dripping.* Does a present participle by itself have the power to make a complete statement about a subject? (*Yes, No*) 1325
a 1592	When similar ideas are expressed in a similar way, we say that the construction is _____. 1593

c to eat chicken if there is any skin on it. *or* to eat any skin that is . . . 1860	a. misplaced modifier b. *is when* or *is where* error c. faulty comparison **Be especially careful not to serve any food to our child that is spoiled.** **Be especially careful not to serve** _____ _____. 1861
run, sunk 2127	**The police had** _____ (*become*) **suspicious when** **the boy** _____ (*run*) **away from home.** 2128
a 2394	a. **The water** *felt* **cold.** b. **The customer** *felt* **the material.** In which sentence does *felt* mean an action of the hands? _____ 2395
Yes 2661	It is generally better to use the pronoun *his* to refer to both sexes than to use *his or her,* which is clumsy. a. **Somebody has forgotten to put** *his* **name on** *his* **paper.** b. **Somebody has forgotten to put** *his or her* **name on** *his or her* **paper.** Which sentence is preferable? _____ 2662
a 2928	a. **Scandinavia consists of three countries: Norway, Sweden, and Denmark.** b. **Scandinavia consists of: Norway, Sweden, and Denmark.** The colon is used incorrectly in sentence (*a, b*). 2929
dash 3195	a. **The coach said, "This is our last chance to win."** b. **The coach said, "this is our last chance to win."** Which sentence is correct? _____ 3196

c 253	A prepositional phrase can also be used as an adverb. **spoke** *proudly* Because *proudly* modifies the verb **spoke,** it is an *adverb.* **spoke** *with pride* Because the phrase *with pride* also modifies the verb **spoke,** it is an _____ *phrase.* 254
	We have just studied adverb clauses—clauses that are used as adverbs. Now we turn our attention to the **adjective clause.** As its name suggests, an adjective clause is a clause that is used as an _____. 522
stinging 789	**a** *stinging* **wind** The adjective *stinging* was formed by adding _____ to the verb *sting.* 790
e 1057	a. *There are curtains in the kitchen.* **They need washing.** b. **The curtains** *that are in the kitchen* **need washing.** c. **The curtains** *hanging in the kitchen* **need washing.** d. **The curtains** *in the kitchen* **need washing.** e. **The** *kitchen* **curtains need washing.** These sentences illustrate the process of _____. 1058
No 1325	a. **His raincoat** *dripping.* b. **His raincoat** *was dripping.* In sentence *b,* we have made the present participle part of a verb by adding to it the helping verb _____. 1326
parallel 1593	Suppose that we should wish to enumerate the various duties of an office secretary: **The duties of the secretary are** *to receive visitors, opening the mail,* **and** *she types letters.* Is each of the three duties expressed in the same type of word group? (*Yes, No*) 1594

page 508

a (to) our child any food that is spoiled. 1861	a. dangling word group b. nonparallel construction c. incorrect omission of words **While eating his meals, no one should hurry him.** _____ , **no one should hurry him.** 1862
become, ran 2128	**We had** _____ (_swim_) **for only a few minutes** **when it** _____ (_begin_) **to rain.** 2129
b 2395	a. **The cook** _tasted_ **the soup.** b. **The medicine** _tasted_ **bitter.** In which sentence does _tasted_ mean an action of the tongue? _____ 2396
a 2662	Because some people feel uncomfortable in using the masculine pronoun _his_ in statements that refer to both sexes, they fall back on the plural pronoun _their_, which is acceptable as informal usage. **If** _anyone_ **should call, take** _their_ **number.** This sentence is acceptable as (_informal, formal_) usage. 2663
b 2929	A colon may be used before a single item that is introduced by a complete statement. **Only one thing stopped me from going: my lack of money.** a. **Vic had only one ambition: to win an athletic letter.** b. **Vic's only ambition was: to win an athletic letter.** The colon is used correctly in sentence (_a, b_). 2930
a 3196	a. **"Is anybody hurt?" asked the policeman.** b. **"Is anybody hurt," asked the policeman?** Which sentence is correct? _____ 3197

adverb 254	Like the adverbs they resemble, adverb phrases answer the questions *When? Where?* and *How?* about verbs. **The car turned** *at the next intersection.* Underline the question that the adverb phrase answers: **When?**　　**Where?**　　**How?** 255
adjective 522	An adjective modifies a noun or pronoun. **I just read an** *interesting* **article.** The word *interesting* is an adjective because it modifies the noun _____. 523
ing 790	An adjective that is formed by adding *-ing* to a verb is called a **present participle.** We can turn any verb into a present participle by adding *-ing* to it (sometimes making a minor change in the spelling). The present participle form of the verb *lose* is _____. 791
reduction 1058	**UNIT 5: ACHIEVING SENTENCE VARIETY** Lesson **28**　Shifting Word Order in the Sentence [Frames 1060–1093]
was 1326	To serve as a verb, a present participle must be combined with some form of the verb *be.* 　　a. **His raincoat was dripping.** 　　b. **His raincoat dripping.** Which item is a sentence because the present participle is combined with a form of *be?* _____ 1327
No 1594	a. **The duties of the secretary are** *to receive visitors, opening the mail,* **and** *she types letters.* b. **The duties of the secretary are** *to receive visitors, to open the mail,* **and** *to type letters.* Which sentence is correct because the italicized word groups match? _____ 1595

a While he is eating his meals, 1862	a. dangling word group b. nonparallel construction c. faulty comparison **Eating slowly is better for him than not to eat at all.** **Eating slowly is better for him than** _____ _____. <div align="right">1863</div>
swum, began 2129	**When Dick** _____ (*come*) **over, Earl had already** _____ (*go*) **to bed.** <div align="right">2130</div>
a 2396	look smell taste feel hear (sound) When these verbs mean actions of the body, use adverbs to describe these actions—just as you use adverbs to describe any other actions. Underline the correct word: **We smelled gas very** (*distinct, distinctly*) **in the kitchen.** <div align="right">2397</div>
informal 2663	Although you may use in conversation whatever forms seem natural to you, use only singular pronouns to refer to antecedents such as **anyone, anybody, someone,** and **somebody** in all careful speech and formal writing. Underline the proper pronoun for formal usage: **Nobody can escape the consequences of** (*his, their*) **actions.** <div align="right">2664</div>
a 2930	<div align="center">DASHES</div> The dash is not a general punctuation mark that may be used for all purposes. Its uses are just as exact as those of any other punctuation mark. May a dash be used to take the place of any comma or period? (*Yes, No*) <div align="right">2931</div>
a 3197	a. **"Roses are particular," said the gardener, "they need just the right soil."** b. **"Roses are particular," said the gardener. "They need just the right soil."** Which sentence is correct? _____ <div align="right">3198</div>

255

Where?

During *the night* **it snowed.**

Underline the question that the adverb phrase answers:

When?   Where?   How?

---

article

a. **I just read an** *interesting* **article.**
b. **I just read an article** <u>which</u> <u>interested</u> me.

The clause in sentence *b* does the same job as the adjective *interesting* in sentence *a*.

The clause *which interested me* is therefore called an

_____ *clause.*

---

losing

The present participle form of the verb *win* is _____.

Sentences are usually parts of a paragraph—with other sentences before and after them. In a particular position, one sentence pattern might suit your purpose much better than another. Should the pattern of any preceding sentences influence a sentence that you might, at the moment, be writing? (*Yes, No*)

---

a

a. **Frank walked into our living room. His raincoat was dripping.**
b. **Frank walked into our living room. His raincoat dripping.**

The noun-participle phrase which is written as a fragment is found in (*a, b*).

---

b

a. **The duties of the secretary are** *to receive visitors, to open the mail,* **and** *to type letters.*
b. **The duties of the secretary are** *receiving visitors, opening the mail,* **and** *typing letters.*

Are both sentences correct? (*Yes, No*)

b not eating at all. 1863	a. misplaced modifier b. nonparallel construction c. faulty comparison **Do not force him to play childish games, because his interests are just like a grownup.** **Do not force him to play childish games, because his interests are just like** _____. 1864
came, gone 2130	**Walter** _____ **(*drink*) the milk that his little brother should have** _____ **(*drink*).** 2131
distinctly 2397	a. **Our costumes *looked* rather curious.** b. **Everyone *looked* at our costumes curiously.** In which sentence does *looked* mean an action of the eyes? _____ 2398
his 2664	a. **If that is *someone* for me, ask *them* to wait.** b. **If *someone* is falsely accused, *they* have the right to defend *themselves*.** In which sentence would the use of the plural pronoun(s) be acceptable because the situation is informal? _____ 2665
No 2931	To some extent dashes are used like commas, but they are stronger, more forceful marks that interrupt a sentence more abruptly. a. **Tony's hit, a line drive to center field, won the game.** b. **Tony's hit—a line drive to center field—won the game.** Which sentence makes the appositive more forceful? _____ 2932
b 3198	a. **"Where all men think alike," said Walter Lippmann, "no one thinks very much."** b. **"Where all men think alike," said Walter Lippmann, "No one thinks very much."** Which sentence is correct? _____ 3199

page 512

When? 256	**We mended the picture** *with paste.* Underline the question that the adverb phrase answers: **When?** **Where?** **How?** 257
adjective 524	**I just read an article** *which interested me.* Now look at just the adjective clause. Does it have a subject and a verb? (*Yes, No*) 525
winning 792	a. **We have a** *good* **team.** b. **We have a** *winning* **team.** In which sentence does a present participle modify the noun **team?** _____ 793
Yes 1060	You may wish to avoid repeating a word or a sentence pattern. You may consider that one pattern sounds better than another in a particular situation, or that it gives an idea more needed emphasis. Could a sentence be good in itself but poor at a particular point in a paragraph? (*Yes, No*) 1061
b 1328	**His wrist bandaged,** This noun-participle phrase contains a (*present, past*) participle. 1329
Yes 1596	The basic idea of parallel construction is this: If your first item begins with a participle, then all should begin with participles. If your first item is a clause, then all the others should be _____. 1597

c
a grownup's.
or those of a
grownup. *or* a
grownup's
interests.
1864

a. nonparallel construction   b. faulty pronoun reference
c. faulty comparison

He has, by the way, read more books than any boy or girl in his class.

He has, by the way, read more books than _____

_____.

1865

---

drank, drunk

2131

Lesson **60** **Three Tricky Pairs of Verbs:**
Lie–Lay, Sit–Set, Rise–Raise

[Frames 2133–2175]

---

b

2398

Everyone *looked* **at our costumes (curious, curiously).**

In this sentence, *looked* means an action of the eyes. To describe this action, we should choose the adverb (*curious, curiously*).

2399

---

a

2665

Underline the proper pronoun for formal usage:

Anyone **who fails to report a crime is shirking** (*his, their*) **moral duty.**

2666

---

b

2932

a. **This horse—high-spirited and nervous—was hard to control.**
b. **This horse, high-spirited and nervous, was hard to control.**

Which sentence makes the adjectives more forceful? _____

2933

---

a

3199

Insert any necessary apostrophes:

Myra hurts peoples feelings and then wonders why she isnt popular.

3200

How?
 	
257
	An adverb phrase can also answer the question *Why?* about a verb.
	
	    a. **I often read science fiction** *for a change.*
	    b. **I often read science fiction** *for a few days.*
	
	In which sentence does the adverb phrase explain *Why?* in regard to the verb? _____
	
	258

Yes 525	**I just read an article** *which interested me.* Although the adjective clause has a subject and a verb, does it make sense by itself apart from the sentence? (*Yes, No*) 526
b 793	Besides being formed from a verb, a present participle resembles a verb in still another way: It may take a direct object or a subject complement, as no ordinary adjective can do. **I found Roy** *reading a magazine.* (Roy read a magazine.) The present participle *reading* is completed by the direct object _____. 794
Yes 1061	In furnishing a room, you can't say whether a particular chair is good or bad without considering the other furnishings with which it must fit in. Can the same be said of a particular sentence pattern? (*Yes, No*) 1062
past 1329	a. **His wrist bandaged.** b. **His wrist was bandaged.** Which item is *not* a sentence because it contains a past participle rather than a verb? _____ 1330
clauses 1597	If your first item is an adjective, then all the others should be _____. 1598

c any other boy or girl in his class. 1865	a. *is when* or *is where* error b. faulty pronoun reference c. faulty comparison **Our son plans to become a scientist because it is his greatest interest.** **Our son plans to become a scientist because** _____ _____ . 1866
	To lie means "to rest in a flat position" or "to be in place." **To lay** means "to put (down) or to place something." Underline the correct word or words: **You ought** (*to lie, to lay*) **down and rest for a while.** 2133
curiously 2399	a. I *felt* **my pocket . . . to see if my wallet was there.** b. I *felt* **very . . . about my test score.** In which sentence would you use the adverb **anxiously** because *felt* means an action and the adverb **anxiously** would describe this action? _____ 2400
his 2666	The same problem arises when you use the words **a person** or **any person** to make a statement that applies to either sex. INFORMAL: **Can** *any person* **park** *their* **car here?** FORMAL: *Any person* **can improve** *his* **speech if** *he* **tries.** Formal usage requires a (*singular, plural*) pronoun. 2667
a 2933	A dash gives more force to an added idea than a comma. a. **Only one person knew the combination to the safe, and he was out of town.** b. **Only one person knew the combination to the safe—and he was out of town.** Which sentence is more forceful? _____ 2934
people's, isn't 3200	Insert any necessary apostrophes: **Freds injuries were slight, but hers were more serious.** 3201

a 258	An adverb phrase—just like an adverb—can often be moved from one position to another in the sentence. **My father takes a nap** *after dinner.* *After dinner* **my father takes a nap.** The fact that a prepositional phrase can be moved shows that it is an _____ *phrase.* 259
No 526	a. **A tree surgeon removed the** *dead* **branches.** b. **A tree surgeon removed the branches** *that were dead.* Both the adjective *dead* in sentence *a* and the adjective clause *that were dead* in sentence *b* modify the noun _____. 527
magazine 794	**I found Roy** *feeling lonesome.* (Roy felt lonesome.) The present participle *feeling* is completed by the subject complement _____. 795
Yes 1062	Because English is a subject-first language, we naturally begin most of our sentences with the subject. a. **The whole pile of dishes went down.** b. **Down went the whole pile of dishes.** In which sentence does the subject come first? _____ 1063
a 1330	a. **His wrist bandaged.** b. **His wrist was bandaged.** In sentence *b,* we have made the past participle part of the verb by adding it to the helping verb _____. 1331
adjectives 1598	In expressing parallel ideas, it doesn't matter which pattern you use at the beginning so long as you follow through with (*the same, a different*) pattern. 1599

b science is his greatest interest. 1866	a. misplaced modifier b. *is when* or *is where* error c. faulty comparison **Do not let him watch violent television shows before he goes to bed, which are likely to give him nightmares.** _____ _____ 1867
to lie 2133	Of the two verbs **lie** and **lay, lie** causes most of the trouble. PRESENT PAST PAST PARTICIPLE **lie** (to rest) **lay** **(have) lain** Notice especially that the past form of **lie** is _____. 2134
a 2400	**look smell taste feel hear (sound)** Much more commonly, these same verbs are used as *linking* verbs that express no action at all. They link an adjective in the predicate with the subject it describes. **The cake looked** *delicious.* The adjective *delicious* modifies the subject _____. 2401
singular 2667	Underline the proper pronoun for formal usage: *Any person* **can train** (*himself, themselves*) **to concentrate.** 2668
b 2934	Supply a missing punctuation mark that will give more force to the added idea: **Joe said that nothing could stop him from going to college and he meant it.** 2935
Fred's 3201	Insert any necessary apostrophes: **This girls job is to check the mens and ladies wraps.** 3202

a. **They have improved the design** *of the car.*
b. **A crowd was standing** *around the car.*

adverb

In one sentence the phrase can be moved; in the other it can't.

Which sentence contains an adverb phrase? _____

260

---

branches

527

a. **A tree surgeon removed the** *dead* **branches.**
b. **A tree surgeon removed the branches** *that were dead.*

The adjective *dead* in sentence *a* comes *before* the noun it modifies.

The adjective clause *that were dead* comes (*before, after*) the noun it modifies.

528

---

lonesome

795

Like the verb from which it is made, a present participle may be modified by an adverb.

The lawyer defended his client, *believing firmly in his innocence.*

The present participle *believing* is modified by the adverb

_____.

796

---

a

1063

Another way of achieving sentence variety is to begin a sentence, now and then, with an adverbial modifier—an adverb, an adverb phrase, or an adverb clause.

Underline the adverb phrase that can be put ahead of the subject:

I never trusted ladders after that experience.

1064

---

was

1331

a. **Carl returned to the game, his wrist bandaged.**
b. **Carl returned to the game. His wrist bandaged.**

Which arrangement is correct? _____

1332

---

the same

1599

In the following exercise, each sentence contains three parallel ideas arranged in columns to make comparison easier. You will find that one of the ideas does not match the other two. Your job is to rewrite this "misfit" so as to bring it in line with the other two ideas, thus making the construction

_____.

1600

a Before he goes to bed, do not . . . shows, which are likely to give him nightmares. 1867	a. dangling word group b. nonparallel construction c. incorrect omission of words **Please look in, now and then, during the night to keep him covered and seeing that he doesn't fall out of bed.** **Please look in, now and then, during the night to keep him covered and** _____ _____. 1868
lay 2134	PRESENT PAST PAST PARTICIPLE **lie** (to rest) **lay** **(have) lain** Use these rhymes to remember the forms of this verb: **"Yes-ter-day** "In pain** **In bed he lay."** **He has lain."** The past participle of **lie** is _____. 2135
cake 2401	When used as linking verbs, "sense" verbs serve much the same purpose as the linking verb **be** (*is, am, are—was, were, been*). **The water** *felt* (= *was*) **cold.** The verb *felt* serves as a linking verb—like *was*—to show that the adjective **cold** modifies the subject _____. 2402
himself 2668	Underline the proper pronoun for formal usage: *A person* **should have the courage of** (*their, his*) **convictions.** 2669
college—and 2935	**His three sons, Elwood, Tom, and Stanley, are in the oil business together.** Can you be sure whether this means three or six people? (*Yes, No*) 2936
girl's, men's, ladies' 3202	Copy the correct words: (*They're, Their*) **testing** (*it's, its*) **engines before taking off.** 3203

b 260	**A pot** *of stew* **was simmering** *on the stove.* This sentence contains both an adjective phrase and an adverb phrase. The adverb phrase comes (*before, after*) the adjective phrase. 261
after 528	It is easy to see why an adjective clause must come *after* the word it modifies. **A tree surgeon removed the branches** *that were dead.* If we put the adjective clause before the noun *branches*, which it modifies, the sentence would be very (*smooth, clumsy*). 529
firmly 796	Participles—with their related words—form useful phrases known as **participial phrases.** These phrases are used as adjectives to modify nouns and pronouns. **The dog,** *shivering with cold,* **came into the house.** The participial phrase modifies the noun _____. 797
after that experience 1064	a. **I never trusted ladders after that experience.** b. **After that experience, I never trusted ladders.** Which sentence would it be better to use after you had written a number of subject-first sentences? _____ 1065
a 1332	a. **Our engine was repaired. We continued on our way.** b. **Our engine repaired, we continued on our way.** c. **Our engine repaired. We continued on our way.** Which one of the above three arrangements is incorrect? _____ 1333
parallel 1600	Rewrite only the "misfit" on the corresponding line at the side to make it parallel with the other two: **The new cars are tested for** a. **speed,** _____ b. **comfort, and** _____ c. **if they are safe.** _____ 1601

a. misplaced modifier   b. dangling word group
c. incorrect omission of words

b
to see that he
doesn't fall out
of bed.

1868

If he coughs, sneezes, or any other symptom of a cold, wire us at once.

If he coughs, sneezes, _____

_____, wire us at once.

1869

(have) lain

2135

Complete these memory rhymes:

     "Yes-ter-day   **"In pain**

       In bed he _____."   **He has _____."**

2136

---

water

2402

Whenever a "sense" verb is used as a linking verb, you can generally put a form of **be** in its place.

       a. **The sky** *looks* **cloudy.**
       b. **The sailor** *looks* **at the sky.**

In which sentence is *looks* used as a linking verb because you can put *is* in its place? _____

2403

---

his

2669

anyone	anybody	each
someone	somebody	each one
no one	nobody	either

In formal writing or speaking, refer to these words by using (*singular, plural*) pronouns.

2670

No

2936

Use dashes to set off a series of appositives that might be confused with the nouns they explain.

His three sons—Elwood, Tom, and Stanley—are in the oil business together.

The dashes make it clear that you are talking about (*three, six*) people.

2937

They're, its

3203

Copy the correct words:

     (*Your, You're*) **the only one** (*who's, whose*) **not going.**

3204

after 261	**We saw** *through the telescope* **the outline** *of a ship.* The adverb phrase comes (*before, after*) the adjective phrase. 262
clumsy 529	In a previous lesson, you saw that an *adverb clause* can often be shifted from one position to another. **I watched television** *after I studied.* Can the adverb clause *after I studied* be moved to another position? (*Yes, No*) 530

dog
 	
 797
	A participial phrase can often be shifted about.
	
	     Shivering with cold, **the dog came into the house.**
	     The dog, *shivering with cold,* **came into the house.**
	     The dog came into the house, *shivering with cold.*
	
	 Can a participial phrase be some distance away from the noun it modifies? (*Yes, No*)
	      798

b 1065	Underline the adverb clause that you could put ahead of the subject: **Our sales increased as soon as we lowered our price.** 1066
c 1333	a. **Tuesday being Election Day. The banks will be closed.** b. **Tuesday is Election Day. The banks will be closed.** c. **Tuesday being Election Day, the banks will be closed.** Which one of the above three arrangements is incorrect? ——— 1334
c. safety. 1601	**Rick's theme was not accepted because** a. **of its lateness,** ————————— b. it was too short, and ————————— c. **it was written in pencil.** ————————— 1602

c or shows (has, develops) any other symptom of a cold 1869	a. dangling word group b. faulty pronoun reference c. *is when* or *is where* error **In your camp bulletin, it says that parents may not visit during the first two weeks.** _____ **that** **parents may not visit during the first two weeks.** 1870
lay, lain 2136	PRESENT: *Lie* **down. Don't** *lie* **in the sun. The rug** *lies* **on the floor. Your letter is** *lying* **on the desk.** Fill in the correct words: **I asked Mother to** _____ **down, but she was already** _____ **down.** 2137
a 2403	**look smell taste feel sound** When these verbs show no action but are used as linking verbs, they are followed by adjectives that describe the subject. Underline the correct word: **Our garden looks** (*beautiful, beautifully*) **in the spring.** 2404
singular 2670	In this and the following frames, underline the pronoun (and sometimes the verb, too) that is appropriate for formal writing or speaking. Watch out for one sentence in which the sense makes the use of a plural pronoun necessary to refer to *everyone* or *everybody*. **A person cannot select** (*their, his*) **own ancestors.** 2671
three 2937	Supply the missing punctuation: **Several pieces of equipment a file, a typewriter, and a duplicator were contributed by the Men's Club.** 2938
You're, who's 3204	In each of the remaining frames, you will find four phrases, one of which is incorrect with respect to capitalization. Copy this *one* phrase only, making the necessary corrections. a. **her new spring outfit** c. **read "the thing in the pond"** b. **in a Buick car** d. **at the Overton High School** 3205

before 262	When we have two (or more) prepositional phrases in a row, each phrase can modify a different word. **We put a drop of water under the microscope.** The phrase **of water** modifies the noun **drop.** Which word does the adverb phrase **under the microscope** modify? _____ 263
Yes 530	**The teacher scolded the little girl** *who wandered away from the group.* Can the adjective clause *who wandered away from the group* be moved to another position? *(Yes, No)* 531
Yes 798	**The train roared past,** *leaving a trail of smoke.* The participial phrase is separated by several words from the word it modifies, the noun _____. 799
as soon as we lowered our price 1066	a. **The fish jumped the hook** *as I pulled in my line.* b. *As I pulled in my line,* **the fish jumped the hook.** Which sentence arouses more suspense by keeping you guessing until the end? _____ 1067
a 1334	If both word groups are sentences, add a period and a capital, or a semicolon. If one word group is a fragment, make no change except to add a comma if needed. Write only the word before and after the space between the word groups. **The lake was choppy no small boats ventured out.** _____ 1335
a. it was late, 1602	**In cooking class, we learned** a. **to prepare meat,** _____ b. **baking cakes, and** _____ c. **to make salads.** _____ 1603

b Your camp bulletin says 1870	a. nonparallel construction b. faulty pronoun reference c. faulty comparison **Therefore, if he gets homesick or any special food is wanted, tell him to telephone us immediately.** **Therefore,** _____ _____, **tell him to telephone us immediately.** 1871
lie, lying 2137	PAST: **Yesterday I** _lay_ **in bed until noon. Dad** _lay_ **back in his chair and took a nap. The food** _lay_ **on the table all day.** _Lay_ is the past form of the verb _____. 2138
beautiful 2404	**A field of sweet clover** _smells_ **very pleasant.** In this sentence, the "sense" verb _smells_ is used as (_an action, a linking_) verb. 2405
his 2671	**I believe that everyone should set a reasonable goal for** (_themselves, himself_). 2672

equipment—
duplicator—
 	
2938
	Use a dash to indicate hesitation in speech or a broken-off sentence.
	    a. **"She—she broke my dolly," sobbed little Linda.**
	    b. **"If he ever asks to borrow my car again—"**
	In which sentence does the dash indicate hesitation in speech? _____
	
	2939

c. read "The Thing in the Pond" 3205	a. **a great author** c. **my father's uncle** b. **a shot for the Flu** d. **at Niagara Falls** _____ 3206

put 263	Two (or more) prepositional phrases can also modify the same word. **Dad flew to Houston on Friday.** The phrase **to Houston** modifies the verb **flew.** Which word does the phrase **on Friday** modify? _____ 264
No 531	An adjective clause must always follow the noun or pronoun it modifies. Can an adjective clause ever come at the very beginning of a sentence? (*Yes, No*) 532
train 799	We have now become acquainted with three kinds of word groups that are used like adjectives to modify nouns. ADJECTIVE PHRASE: **a girl** *with a dog* ADJECTIVE CLAUSE: **a girl** *who was walking her dog* PARTICIPIAL PHRASE: **a girl** *walking her dog* All three word groups modify the noun _____. 800
b 1067	Putting an adverbial modifier, now and then, ahead of the subject adds variety to your writing. It also creates a greater feeling of (*suspense, confusion*). 1068
choppy. No *or* choppy; no 1335	Continue to follow the directions for the previous frame: **The lake was choppy no small boats venturing out.** _____ 1336
b. to bake cakes, 1603	**All our neighbors are** a. **kind,** _____ b. **friendly, and** _____ c. **give help.** _____ 1604

a if he gets homesick or wants any special food 1871	a. misplaced modifier b. faulty comparison c. faulty pronoun reference **Be sure that they don't tease him, for he often develops temper tantrums.** ——————————————————————— **for he often develops temper tantrums.** 1872
lie 2138	PAST PARTICIPLE: **She** *has lain* **in bed most of the day. The dog must** *have lain* **down in the mud. This rug** *has lain* **there for years.** The past participle of **lie** that should be used after any form of **have** or **be** is ——————. 2139
a linking 2405	**A field of sweet clover** *smells* **very pleasant.** Because *smells* is used as a linking verb, it is followed by the (*adjective, adverb*) **pleasant.** 2406
himself 2672	**No one must be made to feel that** (*he is, they are*) **forced to contribute.** 2673

a
 	
2939
	Use a dash to indicate a sudden turn in the thought before an idea is completed.
	
	    "We stopped at—what was the name of that town?"
	
	Supply the missing punctuation:
	
	    "That car well, I just can't describe it."
	
	2940

b. a shot for the flu 3206	a. **for Mother's Day** c. **south of the park** b. **a college football star** d. **a school in the south** ——————————————————————— 3207

flew 264	A prepositional phrase can modify the object of the preceding prepositional phrase. **The family lived on the edge of a great forest.** The phrase **on the edge** modifies the verb **lived.** Which word does the phrase **of a great forest** modify? _____ 265
No 532	a. **The chair collapsed** *when I sat down.* b. **I sat on a chair** *which was broken.* In which sentence can the clause *not* be moved to another position? _____ 533
girl 800	To change a sentence to a participial phrase is simple. *(We)* *heard a loud crash.* **We rushed to the window.** ↓ *Hearing a loud crash,* **we rushed to the window.** To change the italicized sentence to a participial phrase, drop the subject *We* and change the verb *heard* to the present participle _____. 801
suspense 1068	Another reason for departing from the usual subject-first word order is to give emphasis to a particular idea. On entering your room, you would be more likely to notice a piece of furniture if it *(were, were not)* in its usual position. 1069
choppy, no 1336	**Our job was to watch for forest fires** **and report any sign of smoke.** _____ 1337
c. helpful. 1604	**Iris spent the afternoon** a. **lying on the sofa,** _____ b. **reading a novel, and** _____ c. **she ate chocolates.** _____ 1605

c
 	
Be sure that the boys (children, etc.) don't tease him,
 	
1872
	a. nonparallel construction b. *is when* or *is where* error
	           c. faulty comparison
	A temper tantrum, as you know, is when a child holds his breath and turns blue from anger.
	
	In a temper tantrum, as you know, _____
	
	_____.
	
	                                     1873

lain 2139	Fill in the missing forms of **lie:** PRESENT PAST PAST PARTICIPLE **lie** (to rest) _____ **(have)** _____ 2140

adjective
 	
2406
	Underline the correct word:
	
	       The old house smells (*musty, mustily*).
	
	                                       2407

he is 2673	**Each girl is encouraged to join a club of** (*their, her*) **own choice.** 2674
car—well 2940	Use dashes to set off a sharp interruption in the thought of a sentence. **Once—and once was enough—I investigated a hornet's nest.** Insert the sentence **that's our dog** on the blank line, and punctuate it: **Patty** _____ **first noticed the flames.** 2941
d. a school in the South 3207	a. **the Hale drug company** c. **a French horn** b. **next Tuesday night** d. **his idea of God** _____ 3208

edge 265	Remember— A prepositional phrase that modifies a noun or a pronoun is called an *adjective phrase.* A prepositional phrase that modifies a verb is called an _____ *phrase.* 266
b 533	a. **The chair collapsed** *when I sat down.* b. **I sat on a chair** *which was broken.* Which sentence contains an adjective clause? _____ 534
hearing 801	**I picked up the hot pan.** (*I*) *thought it was cold.* ↓ **I picked up the hot pan,** *thinking it was cold.* To change the italicized sentence to a participial phrase, drop the subject *I* and change the verb *thought* to the present participle _____. 802
were not 1069	In the very same way, a word that has been moved from its usual position attracts more attention. The normal word order of an English sentence is— **Subject—Verb—Complement** If we put the complement first, it would attract (*more, less*) attention. 1070
fires and 1337	**The circus is a national institution a part of our national tradition.** _____ 1338
c. eating chocolates. 1605	**We traded in our car because** a. **the engine burned oil,** _____ b. **the smooth tires, and** _____ c. **the body was rusty.** _____ 1606

b a child holds his breath and turns blue from anger. 1873	a. dangling word group b. nonparallel construction c. faulty pronoun reference **Please remind him to write us every day and that he should brush his teeth after every meal.** **Please remind him to write us every day and** _____ _____. 1874
lay, (have) lain 2140	**To lay** means "to put down or to place something." PRESENT PAST PAST PARTICIPLE **lay** (to put) **laid** **(have) laid** The past and past participle forms are (*alike, different*). 2141
musty 2407	**The old house smells *musty*.** The adjective *musty* is correct because it modifies the noun _____. 2408
her 2674	**We should elect someone who can give all** (*his, their*) **time to the organization.** 2675
—that's our dog— 2941	Use either a dash or a semicolon before the words **for example** when they follow a complete statement. **Many words imitate sounds—for example,** *crash, bang, splash.* Would a semicolon serve equally as well as a dash in this sentence? (*Yes, No*) 2942
a. the Hale Drug Company 3208	

adverb 266	In this and the following frames, each sentence contains two phrases, one marked (a) and the other marked (b). **The prize (a) for the best essay is a trip (b) to New York.** After each letter, indicate whether the corresponding phrase is an *adjective* or an *adverb* phrase: (a) _____ *phrase;* (b) _____ *phrase* <div align="right">267</div>
b 534	a. **The bank discharged the employee** *who gambled.* b. **The bank discharged the employee** *because he gambled.* In one sentence the clause can be shifted; in the other, it can't. Which sentence contains the adjective clause? _____ <div align="right">535</div>
thinking 802	*(Bob) needed a haircut.* **He looked for a barber shop.** <div align="center">↓</div>*Needing a haircut,* **he looked for a barber shop.** In changing the italicized sentence to a participial phrase, we lost the subject _____. <div align="right">803</div>
more 1070	**Terry would not accept this money.** The noun **money** is the (*subject complement, direct object*) of the verb **would accept.** <div align="right">1071</div>
institution, a 1338	**You can't change your face you can change your expression.** _____ <div align="right">1339</div>
b. the tires re smooth, and 1606	**Fish jump out of the water** a. **to shake off parasites,** _____ b. **to catch flies, and** _____ c. **escaping enemies.** _____ <div align="right">1607</div>

CONTINUED ON PAGE 2

b (to) brush his teeth after every meal. 1874	a. dangling word group b. *is when* or *is where* error c. incorrect omission of words **We would appreciate your keeping a watchful eye on the companions whom he associates.** **We would appreciate your keeping a watchful eye on** _____ _____ . CONTINUED ON PAGE 2 1875
alike 2141	PRESENT PAST PAST PARTICIPLE **lay** (to put) **laid** **(have) laid** Use the verb **lay** only when the sentence tells *what* was **laid** (put) somewhere. **George** *had laid* **his cards on the table.** What *was laid* on the table? _____ . CONTINUED ON PAGE 2 2142
house 2408	When a sentence states that something has a certain *look, taste, smell, feel,* or *sound,* the "sense" verb is then used as (*an action, a linking*) verb. CONTINUED ON PAGE 2 2409
his 2675	**Any girls interested in this job should see Miss Lane as soon as (***they, she***) can.** CONTINUED ON PAGE 2 2676
Yes 2942	a. **Our dog has several bad habits for example, chasing cars.** b. **Our dog has several bad habits for example, chasing cars.** In each sentence, insert a different punctuation mark before **for example.** CONTINUED ON PAGE 2 2943

page 534

We built the wall (a) with stones (b) from our farm.

(a) adjective
(b) adjective

After each letter, indicate whether the corresponding phrase is an *adjective* or an *adverb* phrase:

(a) _____ *phrase;* (b) _____ *phrase*

267

CONTINUED ON PAGE 1 268

There are only a small number of *clause signals* that start adjective clauses:

a

who (whose, whom), which, that

These adjective clause signals are (*the same as, different from*) those that start adverb clauses.

535

CONTINUED ON PAGE 1 536

(Bob) needed a haircut. **He looked for a barber shop.**
Bob
Needing a haircut, ~~he~~ **looked for a barber shop.**

Bob

To let the reader know the name of the person you're writing

about, you must substitute **Bob** for the pronoun _____

803

in the main statement. CONTINUED ON PAGE 1 804

---

a. **Terry would not accept this money.**
b. **This money Terry would not accept.**

direct object

Which sentence gives greater emphasis to the direct object

money? _____

1071

CONTINUED ON PAGE 1 1072

---

face. You
or
face; you

Suspected of being a spy   the man was shadowed day and night.

_____

1339

CONTINUED ON PAGE 1 1340

Rosemary does her work

c. to escape
enemies.

a. **with willingness,**   _____

b. **quickly, and**   _____

c. **accurately.**   _____

1607

CONTINUED ON PAGE 2 1608